Barth in Conversation

Barth in Conversation

Volume 1, 1959–1962

Edited by Eberhard Busch

Translated by
The Translation Fellows of the Center for Barth Studies
Princeton Theological Seminary

Karlfried Froehlich, German Editor
Darrell L. Guder, English Editor
David C. Chao, Project Manager

WESTMINSTER
JOHN KNOX PRESS
LOUISVILLE • KENTUCKY

© 2017 The Center for Barth Studies

Original German-language edition, *Gespräche, 1959–1962*,
copyright © 1995 Theologischer Verlag Zürich.

First English-language edition
Published by Westminster John Knox Press
Louisville, Kentucky

17 18 19 20 21 22 23 24 25 26—10 9 8 7 6 5 4 3 2 1

Book design by Drew Stevens
Cover design by Marc Whitaker / MTWdesign.net
Cover illustration courtesy of the Center for Barth Studies,
Princeton Theological Seminary, on behalf of the
Karl Barth Stiftung of Basel, Switzerland.

Scripture quotations are from the New Revised Standard Version of the Bible, copyright © 1989 by the Division of Christian Education of the National Council of the Churches of Christ in the U.S.A., and are used by permission.

Library of Congress Cataloging-in-Publication Data

Names: Barth, Karl, 1886–1968, interviewee. | Busch, Eberhard, 1937–
Title: Barth in conversation / Karl Barth ; edited by Eberhard Busch ;
  translated by The Translation Fellows of the Center for Barth Studies,
  Princeton Theological Seminary ; Karlfried Froehlich, German Editor ;
  Darrell Guder, English Editor ; David Chao, Project Manager.
Other titles: Interviews. English
Description: First edition. | Louisville, KY : Westminster John Knox Press,
  2017– | Translated from 3 volumes included in Barth's Gesamtausgabe
  entitled Gespräche. | Includes index. |
Identifiers: LCCN 2017041386 (print) | LCCN 2017041876 (ebook) | ISBN
  9781611648423 (ebk.) | ISBN 9780664264000 (hbk. : alk. paper)
Subjects: LCSH: Barth, Karl, 1886–1968—Interviews. | Theologians—
  Switzerland—Interviews. | Theology—History—20th century.
Classification: LCC BX4827.B3 (ebook) | LCC BX4827.B3 A5 2017b (print) |
  DDC 230/.044092—dc23
LC record available at https://lccn.loc.gov/2017041386

Contents

Foreword to the German Edition

The "Conversations" (and interviews) form a special genre within Barth's work. The texts gathered here were not written at a desk in order then to be delivered as lectures in an auditorium or to make them available to a readership. Even when Barth had in some instances prepared a few notes, the conversations emerged in *spontaneous discourse*, in immediate reaction to a challenge, in response to questions posed to him, in engaging the concerns of participants that were articulated directly to him either by individuals or from among a group. Thus his remarks are never the only text here but are always part of verbal exchanges, of talking back and forth—even though they constitute the bulk of the reported content. As a rule, his remarks are not the result of long and thoughtful preparation, nor are they as elegantly formulated as his written thought. Their advantage is obviously the spontaneous, lively speaking that takes place in dialogue with others. The "conversations" document the theologian Karl Barth as one capable of such speech and one willing to do it—the theologian about whom Dietrich Bonhoeffer said in 1931 that he stands both in and "beyond his books." "I find here an openness, a readiness for the objection—which of course should focus on the same goal—and at the same time such a concentration and impetuous insistence upon the matter at hand, in the service of which one may speak proudly or modestly, assertively or without any certainty at all—that it is clearly lacking any intention to have the process primarily serve his own theology."

What is described here as his "Conversations" is what Barth generally called "Answering Questions." The term is apt because it points toward the imbalance between the contributions of the conversation partners and his own remarks. Those conversation partners often formulated not only questions but also objections, theses, and countertheses. But however phrased, their contributions aimed at receiving "answers" from him, information, positions, and explanations. It is only in this sense that one can describe these documents as "conversations." Still, to a great extent, they are more than mere responses to questions, though newspaper, radio, or television interviews represent this type in its purest form (and only those pieces that in a formal sense are close to them are called here "Question and Answer Sessions" rather than "conversations"). All the texts, however, even with their character of question answering show more or less expressly a tendency toward authentic *discussions*. One could say that, unlike Barth's occasional lectures and essays, with their natural relationship and proximity to his academic activity in his *university lectures* (which he wrote out word for word), the conversations are more readily comparable to his *seminars*, in which texts by other authors were read and discussed, and even more to his *Sozietäten* (Graduate Colloquia), in which he engaged in intensive discussion of texts and aspects of his own work.

It is thus understandable that he pursued the genre of such "conversations" in almost all of the periods of his theological journey, and not only toward the end. But it is also the case that considerably more of this kind of material is available from the last decade of his life (three volumes are projected to cover this period). One reason for this may be the fact that the taking of precise notes appears to have received more attention only at that late time in his life; another is that one could now make use of the technical option of electronic recording. An objective reason probably was Barth's own impression that in his last years, especially after his retirement as emeritus professor, he increasingly and deliberately chose to express himself in the form of such "conversations." He could even say, "I believe that the day of grand lectures, where one person talks on for hours while the others are condemned to listen to . . . whatever might pop into that person's mind, that day is perhaps—not only for me but perhaps in general—over and gone. Instead, what we need in theology and in the church are—oh my!, I really don't like having to use that stupid term—'conversations.' What I mean by that is simply that people talk with each other and together try to press forward to answers."

The publication of the "Conversations" poses particular challenges in the context of the edition of Barth's collected works. One of the reasons for that is that the documents, in contrast to the texts authored by Barth, are only partially collected and electronically preserved in the archives. It was at times an extremely arduous task, comparable to a detective's investigation, to locate the original texts—and this applies to the remaining two volumes as well. There were times when our searches remained fruitless. This foreword provides an opportunity to invite readers who have in their possession documents that I could not find to make them available to us. For that reason I will list here the "conversations" and their participants from 1959 to 1962 for which, after long and intensive searches, I have not been able to find any documentation:

January 24, 1959	Students from the Ecumenical Institute at Bossey, in Basel
April 14, 1959	Reformed Preachers Seminary Wuppertal, in Bern
April 21, 1959	Interview with an American
April 28, 1959	Interview with a London newspaper
June 20, 1959	Parish Members from La Chaux-de-Fonds, in Basel
November 21–22, 1959	Two conversations in Strasbourg (see No. 6 below)
January 9, 1960	Students of the Ecumenical Institute at Bossey, in Basel
January 18, 1960	Broadcast of a Graduate Colloquium session by the Basel studio of Swiss Radio
May 8, 1960	Conversation in the Radio Program "Was maine Si, Herr Profässer?"
October 19, 1960	Pastors from the Tübingen *Dekanat* (church district), in Basel

January 21, 1961   Students of the Ecumenical Institute at Bossey,
                      in Basel
June 23, 1961   Pastors from Kurhessen (Germany), in Basel
July 2, 1961   Conversation in the Radio Program "Was maine Si,
                      Herr Profässer?"
August 29, 1961   Parish Members from the Bruderholz Parish,
                      in Basel
November 27, 1961   Basel Pastors
January 20, 1962   Students of the Ecumenical Institute at Bossey,
                      in Basel
May 22, 1962   Students in Swift Hall, Chicago
May 24, 1962   Students at Union Theological Seminary, New York

Some of the "conversations" printed below have less than complete documentation.

Even the extant documents of the "conversations" present us with significant problems. The basic problem was precisely defined, mutatis mutandis, as early as 1741 by the editor of Zinzendorf's spontaneously delivered "Pennsylvania Speeches." "Although otherwise the live delivery of such extemporaneous speakers leaves a strong impression, their original statements begin to lose that impact more and more as they are copied. Whereas the oral presentation pierces through the ears and eyes of the hearer into the heart, it tends to be diluted when the speech is reduced to print and then read. The breath that enlivened and moved the dead letters is now lacking. One's experience is comparable to that of a lovely statue that one wishes could speak. . . . One assesses a printed document with entirely different standards compared to an oral presentation."

The difficulty just described can be especially observed in the case of documents conserved by *tape recording*. Sentences that sound entirely understandable and sensible because of the voice's modulation and accenting, even if they are grammatically incorrect or incomplete, often lose their clarity and focus the moment they are put into writing. By comparing the two versions one can learn about the infinitely greater richness of the *viva vox*, of spoken versus written language, and understand their difference. This situation necessitates a subtle editorial processing even of conversations conserved on tape, in spite of their "authentic" content, so that the written text can appropriately capture the oral original. Special attention must be given to the way in which Barth's exploratory discourse would at times include his correcting in subsequent sentences what he had just said so that he could then attempt a new start. It should also be mentioned that some of the tape recordings were faulty, done by unskilled amateurs, with the result that what was said can only be partially understood. This has made hypothetical reconstructions necessary when preparing for print.

In other ways, the *transcripts* written by listeners during the sessions or reproduced afterward based on jottings taken down during the conversation—the bulk of the conversations in this volume fall into these categories—require editing as well. It is clear that these transcripts written during or after the events reflect only the note-takers' sense of what was important, and they preserve this content with the authors' own diction and style. It is also clear that these texts have a somewhat diminished level of authenticity. The editor cannot change this. As a result of the way in which these documents by their very nature present only *segments* or even *fragments* of what was heard, we often encounter leaps, breaks, sometimes mere lists of terms and themes that are relatively unrelated, not to speak of listening errors. The intervention of the editor was needed to reconstruct what was manifestly omitted or to appropriately improve what was unclear or misunderstood. The method followed was, without visible notation, to correct the grammatical mistakes or other kinds of straightforward verbal errors (including those in the taped conversations). Emendations relating to the content for the purpose of improving the understandability of the texts are placed in square brackets. Obviously this procedure has been necessary to a much greater degree than in texts written by Barth himself.

The reader will notice that this volume already contains a significant number of "conversations" conducted by Barth in either English or French. In the original German edition, these texts are translated into German. [In the present volume, the English essays are printed in the original language with the annotations of the German text provided by the English editor.] It should be remembered that these texts were not written by Barth himself nor were they authorized by him. Furthermore, the translation into German seemed to me to be allowable in view of the large amount of such texts in these foreign languages that many of the readers might not master. In some instances, German translations of texts have already been published. [In the German edition,] the original English and French texts can be checked in an appendix to the volume.

Every conversation is preceded by an introduction in which I have provided, as far as possible and necessary, remarks about the origin and conduct of the conversation as well as about its preservation. Since on occasion there are references to earlier publication of some of the segments, there is no separate index of such publications at the end of the book.

It is obvious that the preparation of a volume like this one is possible only with the help of many benevolent colleagues. As first among them I mention Dr. Hinrich and [Ms.] Elisabeth Stoevesandt in the Karl Barth Archive in Basel; particularly the former has graciously accompanied this project with careful and helpful engagement. I also need to thank those who were especially helpful with the collation and editing of the foreign language segments: G. Lippitz, F. Fritze, J.-M. Tétaz, M. Dorn, and finally for their assistance in the editorial process with the texts: T. Kingreen, W. Schutt, M. Albe, A. Donker, and J. Persch. Chr. Dahling-Sander made major contributions as proofreader and in the production of the indices.

Eberhard Busch
Göttingen
February 1995

Translators' Foreword

The three volumes of Barth's "Conversations" in the German Gesamtausgabe [Collected Works] provide an unusual and enriching encounter with the person and thinking of Karl Barth. These edited collections of diverse encounters with Barth were the work of Professor Dr. Eberhard Busch, already well known as Barth's biographer. They were one of the outcomes of years of work at the University of Göttingen, where Busch was Professor of Reformed Theology (the chair that Barth inaugurated in 1921). With the assistance of his students, he painstakingly assembled, edited, and annotated these accounts. The result is a highly readable experience of Barth in retirement. He was sought by a great diversity of groups and individuals and often joined them at the Restaurant Bruderholz not far from his home in the Basel neighborhood of that name. In these discussions, we see how Barth's vast theological project actually works, how it translates into concrete contexts, and how it remains a living, dynamic process, with profoundly important trajectories for the thought and practice of the Christian church.

The translation of the *Conversations* is a project of the Center for Barth Studies at Princeton Theological Seminary. From its inception in the mid-1990s, under the leadership of then Director of the Princeton Seminary Library, Dr. Stephen Crocco, the faculty affiliated with the Center had discussed the challenges of expanding the English translations of Barth's works. Linked to the daunting challenge of such expansion of the English Barth library was the issue of reliable translations. Without in any way diluting our gratitude for the English edition of the *Church Dogmatics*, there were growing concerns about some aspects of that massive project. It was becoming clear that challenging issues were to be confronted with regard to terminology, consistency, accuracy, and stylistic appropriateness. More and more scholars found themselves revising citations from the English edition in order to make points that were congruent with the German text. To foster a higher standard of translation and to encourage expanded translation efforts, the Center for Barth Studies decided to invite a small group of Barth scholars interested in translation issues to meet and work on texts together. The first group gathered in June of 2007, immediately after the annual Barth Studies Conference on campus.

The experience of working together on translation issues proved to be stimulating and rewarding. This small group of avid Barth readers had a solid interest in meeting annually to explore ways to improve the general quality of Barth translation as well as to do actual translation projects as a group. To carry out the first objective, the group began to develop a "glossary" for Barth translations, in which we noted, among other things, our agreement on how certain distinctive terms in Barth's vocabulary might be translated. The group was mentored by Karlfried Froehlich, emeritus professor of church history at Princeton, who is not only a native German speaker but also studied under Barth in Basel. His role has been to interpret the nuances and often complex allusions of the German text so that a resulting English rendition reliably captures the syntax, content, and mood of the German original.

At its first gathering, the group experimented with the translation of Barth's "conversations" in the first of three volumes in the Collected Works with that title: *Gespräche*. The advantage of this volume was that the various documents or chapters could be assigned to different translators. The annual meeting in June was then used as an opportunity for each translator to present challenges and questions that emerged from the actual task of translating texts. For discussion in the meeting, each participant prepared a segment of a current assignment. The sessions proved to be extraordinarily productive, not only in terms of the quality of each translated "conversation," but also as a training process focused on the improvement of translation skills. In 2013 a doctoral student at Princeton, David Chao, joined the project as its program manager. He brought with him not only expertise as an academic theologian and great skill with the computer technology needed to carry out the project. He also had several years of experience in academic publishing as an acquisitions editor. Chao has organized the project, set up systems for tracking the process of translating and editing each segment, and brought the project to a place where publication has become a real possibility. He has facilitated the formulation of policies and practices for "fellows" of the Center for Barth Studies, working out procedures for submission of assigned texts and their editing process. Also beginning in 2013, Kait Dugan, Curator of the Center for Barth Studies, has been instrumental in developing the fellows program through providing institutional support and funding.

The production of this volume has thus gone through several steps: Initial translation by a fellow, review of representative excerpts from the translated text at the annual meeting, critical review of all translations by Professor Froehlich as a multilingual native German speaker, with attention to the faithfulness and accuracy in rendering the German into English, and final editing by Professor Darrell Guder as a bilingual native English speaker, with attention to the quality of the English-language version.

The texts reproduce conversations, not carefully drafted and formulated lectures. The speech is idiomatic and not literary. There are sentence fragments and interjections as a normal part of conversations. In some instances, the German editors have reconstructed the text from cursory notes prepared for a conversation or taken down in the course of a conversation. Square brackets are used by the German editors to indicate such editorial emendations. In most cases we have integrated these clarifications into the translation but have continued the use of square brackets to indicate material that the translator has added to enhance understandability. The annotations of the German original have all been translated, making this volume a valuable resource for study of a great range of themes in Barth's theological project. There are several conversations or presentations that took place originally in English or French. In the German edition, these were translated into German and then annotated. In this volume, the original English text is provided, the French is translated into English, and the annotations have been incorporated. The English originals were also conversational and not carefully written-out lecture texts. Thus at times the English is quite idiomatic and evidences the typical problems of spoken English. Citations from the *Church Dogmatics* (*CD*) are given first in the English edition, followed by the reference (*KD*) to the German original, *Kirchliche Dogmatik*. Where possible, English editions of cited German resources are provided in the footnotes.

Our appreciation for the work done by the original German editors, Professor Busch and his students, has grown as we have engaged these documents. They have created a wealth of scholarship that is a great enrichment of the Barth legacy. It is the hope of the fellows of the Center for Barth Studies that the availability of this resource in English will enhance the serious engagement of Karl Barth's theological legacy, building on the excellent work of our German and Swiss colleagues.

Karlfried Froehlich
Darrell Guder
Princeton Theological Seminary
August 2016

Translators and Assignments

Clifford Anderson, Associate University Librarian for Research and Learning and Professor of Religious Studies, Vanderbilt University: chapters 1, 6, 18, 21

Matthew J. Aragon Bruce, Visiting Associate Lecturer in Theology, Wheaton College: chapters 19, 20

John P. Burgess, Professor of Systematic Theology, Pittsburgh Theological Seminary: chapters 2, 34 (part)

Terry L. Cross, Professor of Systematic Theology and Dean, School of Religion, Lee University: chapters 12, 14, 15, 38

Sven Ensminger, PhD (University of Bristol): chapter 39

John Flett, Associate Professor of Missiology and Intercultural Theology, Pilgrim Theological College, Melbourne, Australia: chapter 16 (part)

David A. Gilland, Lecturer in Systematic Theology, Leuphana Universität, Lüneburg, Germany: chapters 11 (part), 37

Darrell L. Guder, Emeritus Professor of Missional and Ecumenical Theology, Princeton Theological Seminary: foreword, chapters 4 (part), 17 (part)

Judith J. Guder, Retired musician and translator, Princeton, NJ: chapters 4 (part), 17 (part)

Christopher R. J. Holmes, Associate Professor of Systematic Theology, Department of Theology and Religion, University of Otago, Dunedin, New Zealand: chapters 5 (part), 36 (part)

David MacLachlan, Associate Professor of New Testament, Atlantic School of Theology: chapter 16 (part)

Amy Marga, Associate Professor of Systematic Theology, Luther Seminary: chapters 5 (part), 36 (part)

Arnold Neufeldt-Fast, Associate Professor of Theology, Tyndale Seminary: chapters 3, 9

Paul T. Nimmo, King's Chair of Systematic Theology, University of Aberdeen: chapters 11 (part), 35

Mark Reasoner, Professor of Biblical Theology, Marian University: chapters 7, 8

Patricia L. Rich, Translator: chapter 34 (part)

Abbreviated Works

AAS	*Acta Apostolicae Sedis.* http://www.vatican.va/archive/aas /index_it.htm
AGK	Arbeiten zur Geschichte des Kirchenkampfes. Series. Göttingen: Vandenhoeck & Ruprecht, 1959–
Biography	E. Busch. *Karl Barth: His Life from Letters and Autobiographical Texts.* Translated from the German, *Lebenslauf*, by J. Bowden. London: SCM, 1976.
BSLK	*Die Bekenntnisschriften der evangelisch-lutherischen Kirche.* Edited by Deutschen evangelischen Kirchenausschuß. Göttingen: Vandenhoeck & Ruprecht, 1986
Bw.Th. 1	K. Barth. *Briefwechsel.* Vol. 1, *1913–1921.* Edited by E. Thurneysen. Gesamtausgabe 5. Zurich: TVZ, 1973
CCSL	Corpus Christianorum: Series Latina
CD	K. Barth. *Church Dogmatics.* Edinburgh: T&T Clark, 1956–75
CR	Corpus Reformatorum. Halle et al. 1834–
DS	*Enchiridion symbolorum, definitionum et declarationum de rebus fidei et morum.* Edited by H. Denzinger and A. Schönmetzer. 35th ed. Freiburg et al., 1973
EG	*Evangelisches Gesangbuch.* 1993–
EKG	*Evangelisches Kirchengesangbuch.* 1950–
EvTh	*Evangelische Theologie.* Journal
GCS	Die griechischen christlichen Schriftsteller der ersten drei Jahrhunderte. Berlin, 1897–
GERS	*Gesangbuch der evangelisch-reformierten Kirchen der deutschsprachigen Schweiz.* 1952–
Gespräche 1963	K. Barth. *Gespräche: 1963.* Zurich: TVZ, 2005
HpB	H. Heppe. *Die Dogmatik der evangelisch-reformierten Kirche.* Exhibited and verified from the sources, newly revised and edited by E. Bizer. 2nd ed. Neukirchen: Neukirchener Verlag, 1958
Inst.	J. Calvin. *Institutio christianae religionis.* 1559.
JK	*Junge Kirche: Unterwegs für Gerechtigkeit, Frieden und Bewahrung der Schöpfung.* Protestant monthly. 1933–
KBRS	*Kirchenblatt für die reformierte Schweiz.* Basel, 1844–1986
KD	K. Barth. *Die kirchliche Dogmatik.* Munich: Kaiser; et al., 1932–67

KuD	*Kerygma und Dogma: Zeitschrift für theologische Forschung und kirchliche Lehre.* Göttingen: Vandenhoeck & Ruprecht
KV	Köchel-Verzeichnis. Works of Mozart
Lebenslauf	E. Busch. *Karl Barths Lebenslauf: Nach seinen Briefen und Autobiographischen Texten.* Munich, 1975. 5th ed., Gütersloh, 1994
LTK	*Lexikon für Theologie und Kirche*
LW	*Luther's Works* (St. Louis: Concordia Publishing House, 1955–)
MPTh	*Monatsschrift für Pastoraltheologie*
O.Br. 1945–1968	K. Barth. *Offene Briefe: 1945–1968.* Edited by D. Koch. Gesamtausgabe 5. Zurich: TVZ, 1984
PL	Patrologia Latina [= Patrologiae Cursus Completus: Series Latina]. Edited by J.-P. Migne. 217 vols. Paris, 1844–1864
Pr. 1954–1967	K. Barth. *Predigten: 1954–1967.* Edited by H. Stoevesandt. Gesamtausgabe 1. Zurich: TVZ, 1979. 2nd ed., 1981
RD	H. Heppe. *Reformed Dogmatics.* Edited by E. Bizer, translated by G. T. Thomson. London: Allen Unwin, 1950.
rde	Rowohlts deutsche Enzyklopädie. Series. Hamburg: Rowohlt, 1955–
RGG³	*Religion in Geschichte und Gegenwart.* Edited by K. Galling. 3rd ed. Tübingen: Mohr Siebeck. 1956–65. 4th ed., edited by H. D. Betz. 1998–2007
RKZ	*Reformierte Kirchenzeitung*
SC	Sources chrétiennes. Series. Paris: Cerf, 1941–
SchmHJ	H. Schmid. *The Doctrinal Theology of the Evangelical Lutheran Church.* Translated by Charles A. Hay and Henry E. Jacobs. Minneapolis: Augsburg Publishing House, 1961.
SchmP	H. Schmid. *Die Dogmatik der evangelisch-lutherischen Kirche.* Exhibited and verified from the sources, newly edited and revised by H. G. Pöhlmann. Gütersloh: Gütersloher Verlagshaus Mohn, 1979
ThB	Theologische Bücherei. Series. Munich: Kaiser
ThExh	Theologische Existenz heute. Series (or journal). Munich: Kaiser
ThExh NS	Theologische Existenz heute. New series. Munich: Kaiser
ThSt	Theologische Studien. Series. Zollikon-Zurich
TRE	*Theologische Realenzyklopädie.* Edited by G. Krause and G. Müller. Berlin: de Gruyter, 1977–
TZ	*Theologische Zeitschrift*
TzF	*Texte zur Forschung.* Journal. Darmstadt, 1971–
WA	M. Luther. Werke. Kritische Gesamtausgabe [= Weimarer Ausgabe]. Weimar, 1883–
WA.TR	Tischreden. In WA
W.G.Th.	K. Barth. *Das Wort Gottes und die Theologie.* Gesammelte Vorträge 1. Munich, 1924
ZST	*Zeitschrift für systematische Theologie*
ZTK	*Zeitschrift für Theologie und Kirche*

1. Conversation with the Editors of *Kolibri* *1959*

Barth's letter of January 7, 1959, to the London meeting of the European Congress against Nuclear Weapons[1] caused a stir in the Swiss media.[2] In particular, the question he broached in that letter—"whether this opposition [against nuclear weapons] . . . should not be intensified into active resistance (perhaps in the form of an open summons to conscientious objection)"—triggered a lively discussion among the student body at the University of Basel. In an open letter (published in Kolibri, *edited by the Studentenschaft Basel [Basel Student Association], no. 7, January 1, 1959), Peter Lenz accused Barth of "summoning his fellow citizens to an act of treason." Members of the staff of* Kolibri *visited Barth after that and reported about their visit in the subsequent issue[3] under the headline: "Professor Barth and [the Acquisition of] Nuclear Weapons." The passage below reprints only the comments by Barth reported in the article.*

Prof. Barth emphasized that [Swiss acquisition of] nuclear weapons is not his primary concern at present. He did not attend the congress, but only challenged the participants to make an end to lengthy speechifying and finally to walk the talk with action. The call to conscientious objection is an example of an action that might be undertaken. In conversation, however, Barth stated more precisely that he had in mind a partial conscientious objection in connection with the manufacturing and use of nuclear weapons and that he should have said so more clearly in his letter. In view of the pronouncements of biologists and physicists about the consequences of nuclear warfare, it seems to us that this way of thinking is at least defensible. We are glad to learn that, though it should go without saying, Professor Barth does allow that his opponents are proceeding in good faith, if they are thinking independently. We credit him greatly with having given us the opportunity by means of this conversation to become personally acquainted.

---

1. In *O.Br. 1945–1968*, 456–68.
2. Cf. ibid., 459n9.
3. *Kolibri*, no. 8, February 13, 1959.

2. Conversation in the Zofingia I
1959

In 1959 Karl Barth attended two evening conversations on the question of "The Christian and Politics" in the Basel chapter of the student association Zofingia, a member of which he himself was as a student.[1] The first conversation took place on the evening of June 3, 1959, in the association house, and the second (no. 5 below) on November 18, 1959. Records of the conversations from these evenings are kept in the minutes of the association, which are now found in the Basel Staatsarchiv (Zofingerarchiv, 412 EJ 10 xx S. Basel, Protokolle 1959–61). The following is a replication of these minutes in full, including the designation of the speaker by his "Cerevis," his student association nickname. Peter Holderman notes in his introduction to the minutes to the first evening: "Record turnout; headcount almost impossible; hall completely full; happily a large number of association alumni."

Questions

1. What are the role and duties of the Christian as a political citizen? Does Christianity commit the citizen to a certain political stance?
2. Which of the church's rights should a Christian "illegally" defend? (Prohibition of confirmation, worship services)
3. Is a secularized society just as strong an argument against the state as the anti-Christian state? (Western materialism—Eastern materialism)
4. Does the church have a justification or a task to call for refusal of military service? Does the form of government play a role in that case?
5. Is there a difference between the church's position toward the Nazis and toward Communism? If so, why?

Barth: Replying above all to the first question (the tasks of the Christian as a political citizen): A political discussion should be avoided (recalling the previous meeting, sometime around 1942),[2] not because Professor Barth does not want to take a position, but because he would first like to make clear the Christian's tasks. Reply to the first question by means of ten theses:

---

1. Cf. *Lebenslauf*, 47–50, 52–53, 59; *Biography*, 35–38, 41–42, 47.
2. Under January 21, 1942, Barth noted in his calendar, "Discussion in the 'Zofingia' on Church and State." According to the minutes of the meeting (in the Staatsarchiv Basel, Privatarchiv 412, E7, 10 pages), 296–98, Barth experienced opposition at the time because of his critical attitude toward National-Socialist Germany.

1. *The Christian is witness to the kingdom of God (= basileia) that has come in Jesus Christ and is still to be revealed in him.*

The kingdom of God is the reconciliation of the world to God. This has to do with the realization of the unity of divine and human law. Instead of the kingdom of God, one could simply say, Jesus Christ. For the time being, this is a hidden reality [, but nevertheless a reality! Therefore]: the kingdom of God is not an ideal. It is an accomplished fact. The Christian, as a member of the human community, is a witness of the kingdom of God. He is a witness, because it is revealed to him. Because he knows about it, he must point to it.

2. *As a witness of the kingdom of God, the Christian is first and foremost a citizen of this kingdom.*

He is a citizen who definitively resides in this homeland and is obligated to it, although there are yet other citizenships (family, human society). He exists originally and primarily as a citizen of the kingdom of God, and in all other institutions only secondarily, [and his place there is] determined by his first citizenship. This makes the Christian a peculiar person. He is always a lonely bird on the housetop [Ps. 102:7].

3. *The Christian lives in each particular time and situation also as a citizen of a state in one of its different and changing forms.*

There is no Christianity outside of time and space. The Christian's life has a concrete determination. However, he cannot be reduced to his political existence. He lives, also here, as a citizen of and a witness to the existence of the kingdom of God. One should not speak so abstractly of the state. The Christian lives always in one of the different forms of the state, and always in relation to his own state.

4. *The Christian acknowledges the kingdom of God in the provisional order of God for the establishment and preservation of relative justice, relative freedom, and relative peace in his state.*

It [the state he faces] is a manifestation of God, intended for the present in-between time, a transitional time before the establishment of the kingdom of God. This [life in the in-between time] is not a vacuum, because there is [from God] the church and the state. [The state] is an interim solution also, because all state order is only concerned to provide external security, freedom, quiet, and external peace. Let us however be glad for this external security! Wherever coercive force must be used, we are in an in-between stage. Every state provides a relative justice, [which is positively expressed as] a justice in relation to something else—[that is to say, justice in] relation to the kingdom of God.

5. *The Christian does not mistake the state, in any of its many forms, for the kingdom of God.*

The kingdom of God is "absolutely" superior to every occurrence of the state. No state is identical to the kingdom of God. There is no *Divus Caesar*[3] and no *Civitas Dei* (Augustine).[4] There is also no Christian state. No state can [demand] unconditional allegiance and unconditional obedience, otherwise it would be the kingdom of God. The kingdom of God is only real in its

---

3. Title given a posthumously deified Roman emperor.
4. According to Augustine, the *civitas Dei* and the *civitas diaboli* are in conflict with each other in world history, whereby the church is related to the former and the state to the latter, without either ever being identical to its corresponding entity. *The City of God* 21.1, in CCSL 48:758–59.

fulfillment and in Jesus Christ. *Question:* Is there any other safeguard against political totalitarianism?

6. *The Christian does not fear or deny the state in any of its many forms, because each state contains something divine.*

Ancient Christianity existed even in Nero's empire. There is no anti-Christian state, and there is no *civitas diaboli.*[5] The Christian is therefore protected against political skepticism or political despair. A Christian will affirm the state in each form. He distinguishes [certainly between better and worse forms of the state, but he does so] while never pronouncing an absolute yes or no. Therefore [since "each state contains something divine,"] he [the Christian] is not forced [or justified] to take a stance of neutrality [toward the state]. [Rather] he distinguishes between states of lesser or greater justice.

7. *In view of the kingdom of God, the Christian distinguishes between forms of the state insofar as they more or less correspond to the divine appointment.*

He therefore undertakes this differentiation of righteousness [i.e., the examination of whether more or less righteousness prevails in the state] always in view of the kingdom of God.

8. *The Christian, as a citizen of the state, bears witness to the kingdom of God, insofar as he decides in each case for the more appropriate form of the state, meaning the more righteous form.*

Furthermore, he gives his support politically to this chosen form of state.

9. *The Christian decides about the preferable form of the state as well as about the form of his support for it, with a new, free orientation toward the kingdom of God in each particular time and situation.*

The Christian is not bound to any particular ideas (traditional, historical) or to principles of natural law, and so forth. He can, however, have them. "New and free" means independent—for example, even from a democratic majority (which may also be wrong). But he can also go along with the majority. "New" means "not bound to prior decisions."

[In the end, even the forms of the state are themselves in flux.] Even within just one type of the known forms of state, there are considerable nuances. Among the democracies there are so-called people's democracies, managed democracies, and our democracy, and so on. [There are] also different forms of dictatorships: for example, Franco-Spain in the middle of the so-called Free World, contemporary France[6]—even the War Authorization Powers of the Swiss Federal Council [Bundesrat] led temporarily to a small dictatorship.[7]

It is not dictated from heaven to the Christian that he may support only this or that form of the state. It is also possible for him to work actively within a dictatorship: for example, by enduring, by waiting in the quiet hope that the trees will not grow sky-high, or even by cooperating (more or less). It is also possible to work actively against the state for the renewal of the form of the state when

---

5. Cf. ibid.

6. In 1959 Charles de Gaulle became president of France in accord with a constitution he formulated, which Barth understood at the time to restrict the democracy that had previously existed. Cf. *Lebenslauf*, 456; *Biography*, 440.

7. On August 30, 1939, the Swiss Parliament gave the Federal Council (i.e., the federal government) special authorizations to restrict civil liberties (e.g., censorship of the press).

things can no longer go on in this way. [Yet] in every circumstance the Christian will pray for the persons with responsibility for the state.

10. *The Christian is always obligated to assume the particular political stance and action that correspond to his reflection on the kingdom of God.*

It is never a matter of something indeterminate, or of some kind of general good intention. In each concrete case, the Christian has in this sense no choice, but rather only one possibility: the stance that he has been commanded to take. He must stand up for this attitude resolutely.

President: The presidium expresses gratitude for the very interesting talk and is very happy that theology is actually much simpler and more understandable than we would have imagined.

Discussion

Heiner: would like to know if there isn't a contradiction between the fifth and the seventh thesis.[8] [On the one hand, Barth makes the] assumption that every state is still somehow oriented toward the kingdom of God. There is therefore no *civitas diaboli*. And [on the other hand he emphasizes] that no state may require unconditional obedience. "There are, however, certain states that [do] require absolute obedience."

Barth: cannot imagine that there are absolutes; that is not possible on earth. "The objection to the idea that a *civitas diaboli* is possible is derived ultimately on Christian grounds. The devil cannot found a state for himself. The devil has been overcome."

Dr. Krayer: Barth has not made it easy for us, given his extensive theological conceptual framework. The kingdom of God is hidden and yet a reality through Jesus Christ. How is this possible? How is an awareness of that possible, and consequently obedience?

Barth: What will it be now: complicated or simple? Let's have a referendum [among those present]! (*To Dr. Krayer:*) The Christian believes despite all outward reality that God in Jesus Christ has brought about the reconciliation between himself and the world, although [it is] not [yet] visible. One should set aside the various opinions of pastors and professors and read, first of all, the New Testament.

Dr. A. Moppert: understood nine theses. However in one, the sixth, he sees a conflict with the rest: A Christian should not deny the state, and yet he may only act with an eye to the kingdom of God. [He sees] a contradiction [in that]. In relation to the thesis that the Christian takes a particular political stance only with an eye to the kingdom of God, Dr. Moppert cites examples from his work as a judge presiding over criminal court, where he often cannot proceed in a way that is Christian in this sense, since he must continually sentence people to prison.

Barth: In regard to thesis 6: Even the revolutionary does not deny the state. He affirms it, but in a different form. Any decision in Christian terms stands

8. More likely thesis 6 is meant.

under the final criterion of the Bible. As for prison sentences, these are necessary and must be carried out. But even these decisions are only to be made insofar as one reflects on them as a Christian. [In the process] it is important to keep reading the Word.

Reimar: Concerning the duties of the Christian in the state: the Christian does not confuse any state for the kingdom of God. However, Communism is guilty of just such a confusion. Therefore it is the duty of the Christian to reject such absolutism.

Barth: Reaction against Communism [is] only necessary when the Russians are at Lake Constance. We have not yet passed the test [that would then have to be passed]. What we have done up to now is stupid chatter and has not freed anyone from Russian subjugation. To join in, sounding the same note and writing condemning articles, is not necessary since virtually everyone is agreed about Communism. It was different at the time of National Socialism. An acute danger was manifest. Whether out of fascination or fear of attack, numerous people all over Europe began to yield and proposed accommodations.

M. Sim: One never denies the state as such, but rather only its present form. Even a fighter on the barricades affirms the state.

Dr. Gerwig: Communism is a great danger for Christianity. We must fight *before* it reaches Lake Constance.

Barth: A Christianity that is in danger from Communism deserves to perish. The best and surest weapon against Communism is that one become a good Christian.

Heiner: Professor Barth says it is easy to write articles against Communism. However, the people in the East want a decision: *yes* or *no*.

Dr. Moppert: Reimar's question was theoretical, and Professor Barth answered politically. The conflict of conscience that people experience in a Communist state is so awful that such a state has to be rejected. As to the answer that [discussion of] the battle far from the shooting is idle chatter—that is not so in the case of many states. Austria, for example, which at one time was very vulnerable to Communism, now has a very small Communist Party, thanks to the enormous work of the Social Democrats. Dr. Moppert can understand that Communism can be a judgment of God, but then, why not reject Communism the same way as National Socialism?

Barth: One hears [that] question too often.

Rob. Devely: The Christian is a witness to the kingdom of God. Doesn't this lead to self-glorification and therefore to passivity?

Barth: cannot imagine why the one should lead to the other. [He] denies this question vigorously.

Krayer: would like to know whether Professor Barth has changed his views, since he does not have the same immediate reaction to Communism as he did to National Socialism.

Dr. H. Staehlin: Why no rejection of what has happened in Hungary and Tibet?[9] Just because the Russians are still far away?

---

9. On February 2, 1956, China's Premier Chou En-lai announced that Tibet had become a region of China. On October 10, 1956, the Hungarian uprising began.

Barth: has different views concerning Hungary and Tibet and see other factors at work than do the familiar Swiss newspapers such as *Nationalzeitung, Neue Zürcher Zeitung,* and *Basler Nachrichten.* As to Dr. Krayer's question, [Barth's] views have not changed but have developed further along the same lines. One should not make too much, he said, of the mellowing that comes with age. Dr. Krayer is looking for it in [Barth] but has not found it. Barth too has nothing good to say about Communism. But one never finds identical situations in history (National Socialism—Communism).

In closing, Professor Barth assures us that he would, in the event of actual danger from Communism, react just as he did to National Socialism.

3. Dialogue with Representatives of the [Evangelical] Community Movement
1959

This dialogue took place in the morning and afternoon of October 6, 1959, in the Bruderholz Restaurant in Basel, with approximately twenty-five representatives of the Pietist or Community Movement [Gemeinschaftsbewegung] in Germany and Switzerland, specifically with friends of the working group Pietism and Theology, founded by Otto Schmitz in 1957. The dialogue was inspired by the content of volume IV/2 of the Church Dogmatics *(published in German in 1955) and by Barth's avowal in the preface of that volume to attempt to satisfy "the concern of the Pietists and 'Evangelical groups' [Gemeinschaftsleute]" (CD IV/2, p. x [KD, vii]). In 1958, on the initiative of Max Fischer—at the time chair of the Bahnau Brotherhood [Bahnauer Bruderschaft] in Unterweißach (Baden-Württemberg)—a dialogue between Pietists and Barth was agreed upon and prepared through three regional working groups. With respect to the preparations and to the development of the discussion itself, M. Fischer wrote an article titled "Eine erfreuliche Aussprache" [A Gratifying Dialogue], in the* Freundesbrief der [Bahnauer] Bruderschaft *21 (October 1959): 16. Another summary of the encounter comes from an article by H. Schönweiß, who writes: "This encounter between Pietism and K. Barth resulted in significant agreements, above all with respect to what was of fundamental concern. Repeatedly it became apparent in the discussion that revisions and adjustments were necessary in but a few places and that only some concepts and ideas required clarification or interpretation. It was an authentic discussion, that is, undertaken by both with the intent to listen to each other and learn from each other—or better, to learn from the Lord, in whose name we had gathered together" ("Gespräch des Pietismus mit Karl Barth," in* Deutsches Pfarrerblatt *60, no. 15/16 [August 1, 1960]: 351–54).*

A verbatim account of the discussion is preserved in the form of recorded notes. The following text is based on the transcript prepared by Klaus Richter and Hans-Ulrich Weißenstein. The typewritten account was duplicated, and the grammar has been corrected here. This text was also published in a somewhat condensed version under the title "Karl Barth und die Pietisten: Bericht über ein Gespräch [Karl Barth and the Pietists: Report on a Conversation]," in Monatsschrift für Pastoraltheologie *49 (1960): 342–54. This transcript, cited in abbreviated form as "RW," is frequently supplemented by another, typewritten transcript by Johannes Busch in a twofold manner: missing sentences from the first text are added, and differing formulations are noted in the footnotes. All insertions from this second transcript are designated with the initials "JB." According to the first transcript, the following speakers from among the Pietists contributed to the discussion: Dr. Hans Bürki, Ascona-Moscia; Rev. Max Fischer, Unterweißach; Rev. Dietrich Fischinger, Stuttgart-Feuerbach; Architect Otto Knobloch, Göttingen; Rev. Friedrich Kommoß, Stuttgart; Superintendent A. Korthals,*

Kiel; Rev. Müller, Stuttgart; Pastor Fritz Schindelin, Duisburg; Rev. Dr. Hans Schön-weiß, Cannstatt; Rev. Eberhard Weißenstein, Allmersbach im Tal.

1. The Significance of the Christ-Event for Humanity

Weißenstein: The significance of that which Christ has accomplished is expressed in 2 Corinthians 5:17–19; John 3:16; and 1 Corinthians 1:30. In the person of Jesus Christ, humanity is reconciled with God as humanity is loved by God; humanity has its justification and sanctification in Jesus Christ. Karl Barth expresses this in the *Church Dogmatics* in the following manner: all of this is "pregiven" for all in Jesus Christ, and as such all are at least [already] "virtually" and "prospectively," even if not all "actively," what they are in Jesus Christ[1] (*CD* IV/2:275; etc.). Although certain formulations in the *Church Dogmatics* may be overstated, we on the other hand must not overlook the danger that, in these matters and with the excessively sharp point, we surrender the whole style, the biblical accent.

The proof whether or not the New Testament has its own say fully will be found in how anything concerning sin is taught, in the overall tone given to changing one's ways, to the new life, and to the anticipation of the end (final judgment). In other words, how are we to understand the relationship between that which is pregiven and that which must be appropriated by us? Even in these matters Karl Barth finds powerful tones that we evangelicals experience as very congenial. Yet I would like to ask him if, in his writing, there is not a pronounced inclination toward the *positive* statements of being. Throughout the biblical witness there is a tension [between realities]: here indicative, there imperative; already achieved, not yet; the lordship of Christ, the power of sin; the world loved by God, the small flock. These truths stand opposite each other like the corner pillars that support the wide arch of a suspension bridge. We must be cautious that in obedient reflection we avoid the danger of making one corner pillar strong at the cost of the other!

Schönweiß: Is Karl Barth departing from the New Testament's manner of speaking when he says of *all* people that they are *en Christō* [in Christ]—not only loved, but also reconciled, born again, converted, justified, sanctified?[2] Yet the New Testament only speaks in this way of believers. With Barth's wording it can sometimes sound as if personal faith is factored out. What[3] is actually meant by *en Christō*? Who is *en Christō*? All people? Or is it not the case that one must say, Only believers are *en Christō*? We think that we understand his [Barth's] concern: what is decisive has occurred for us. But in some instances we miss the emphasis that calls people to make a decision. Are not some of the formulations as they are found in the *Church Dogmatics* dangerous? That it also depends upon my personal response is a tone that can also be heard in the *Church Dogmatics* here and there. But should not the biblical truth[4] be fully

---

1. In RW: "what Jesus Christ is"; see introduction to chap. 3.
2. Cf. *CD* IV/2:511–21, esp. 511 [*KD* 578–89, esp. 578]: "What has come to it [i.e., the people awakened to faith] *de facto* [as a matter of fact] has come to all men *de iure* [as a matter of right]."
3. The following questions according to JB; see introduction to chap. 3.
4. JB: "the whole biblical truth."

discernable in all places so that understanding is not made difficult by exaggerated formulations?

Barth: *"Tempora mutantur et nos [mutamur] in illis* [The times change, and we change with them]"![5] Forty years ago I could not have dreamed that I could speak in this way with representatives of the Community Movement. At that time I was a "wild man"[6] with respect to Pietism.[7] But I believe the Pietists were different then too.[8] It is fortunate that all of us together are being led forward. After the previous three verdicts,[9] we can approach the questions with confidence. In essentials we seem to be in agreement with each other. I really have come in order to listen. Please speak frankly and feel free to impale me! Despite my age, I don't believe that I have forgotten how to listen.

[To Weißenstein:] There[10] is hardly anything else to say: that is all very positive. Indeed, indicative and imperative, or, as the older dogmaticians said:[11] the achievement and the appropriation of salvation are two corner pillars;[12] both must be seen together. You suggest that in my work one can detect an emphasis on the objective side? Well, that may be the case, and it was perhaps also necessary as a reaction to the overemphasis on the subjective side. I agree with you completely that the two pillars must not be allowed to be merged (into one).

[At the same time to Schönweiß:] Can you say both in one? Indeed, we[13] can never say everything with one word. And we may not and cannot express both of these together either. That is, unless we utter the name of Jesus Christ! Only in Jesus Christ is it impossible to distinguish between objective and subjective, between law and gospel, between indicative and imperative. Both[14] must be said, the one not without the other. But in him both are one. "For in him every one of God's promises is a 'Yes' [and] . . . 'Amen'" [2 Cor. 1:20]. Indeed, at this point I have a "passion": the emphasis is on the Yes. And this Yes should receive the greater emphasis; in face of it the No of God recedes into the background. (It is strange that forty years ago the Pietists charged that one only hears the No

---

5. A saying coined by Emperor Lothair I (795–855). [Actually the sentence is an early modern adage expanding a phrase from Ovid's *Metamorphoses* 15.165: *omnia mutantur, nihil interit.* The attribution to "Emperor Lothair I" is due to a misinterpretation of Georg Büchmann, *Geflügelte Worte: Der Citatenschatz des deutschen Volkes,* ed. K. Weidling, 19th ed. (Berlin: Haude & Spener, 1898), 506, who cites the verse as contained in a poem in praise of Emperor Lothair by the late Latin poet Matthias Borbonius (1566–1629); trans. note.]

6. JB: "a somewhat wild man."

7. Cf. K. Barth, *Der Römerbrief* (Bern: Bäschlin, 1919); rev. ed., ed. H. Schmidt (Zurich: Theologischer Verlag, 1985), esp. in chap. 7 the section "Das Gesetz und der Pietismus," 204–17, as well as 276–94. With respect to Barth's considerably sharper critique of Pietism here than in the second edition of the book in 1922 [ET: *The Epistle to the Romans,* trans. E. C. Hoskyns (London: Oxford University Press, 1968)]; cf. Eberhard Busch, *Karl Barth und die Pietisten: Die Pietistenkritik des jungen Karl Barth und ihre Erwiderung* (Munich: Kaiser, 1978), esp. 129–34 [ET: *Karl Barth and the Pietists: The Young Karl Barth's Critique of Pietism and Its Response,* trans. Daniel W. Bloesch (Downers Grove, IL: InterVarsity Press, 2004), esp. 117–22].

8. E. Busch, *Karl Barth und die Pietisten,* 145–53 [ET: *Karl Barth and the Pietists,* 133–40].

9. [In addition to Weißenstein and Schönweiß,] Max Fischer had also presented an introductory verdict that is mentioned only briefly in indirect speech in the text RW, "the representatives of the community movement present had learned from Karl Barth; but there are still open questions."

10. This sentence according to JB.

11. See HpB 404; ET: Cf. Heinrich Heppe, *Reformed Dogmatics,* ed. E. Bizer, trans. G. T. Thomson (London: Wakeman Trust, 2002), 510; H. E. Weber, *Reformation, Orthodoxie und Rationalismus,* vol. 2, *Der Geist der Orthodoxie* (Gütersloh: Bertelsmann, 1951), 65.

12. The last four words according to JB.

13. The next two sentences according to JB.

14. This sentence according to JB.

in my work.[15] Today apparently the opposite is the case!) The No [of God] is swallowed up into the Yes [of God]. Luther said that the Yes [of God] was still concealed in the No.[16] Passing this on is the task of Christian proclamation. It can also be expressed in the reference to the *seriousness* of the human situation. It can also[17] be witnessed to in the form[18] of the proclamation of judgment. But never may an abstract No be said, such that the No becomes the actual subject matter. The point is that we do not depart from the one reality: Jesus Christ.

[*To Schönweiß:*] You speak of "dangerous formulations." But there are dangerous statements in the Bible as well. Indeed you say that you have understood the matter that is of concern to me; and yet . . . the conclusion of the Second Letter of Peter comes to mind, where it is stated [3:15–16] that "some things" written by "brother Paul" are "hard to understand." No Christian is protected from being misunderstood. It is in fact impossible to say everything in one sentence. Christian truth is not like a chained parrot at the zoo, always sitting at the same place. It is a "bird in flight."[19] It is moving, and you need to constantly turn your head and see where this "bird in flight" might now be. The truth can only be grasped in the continuing movement. Therefore I must urge my readers to be patient when they do not find everything in one place and to continue reading. It is your impression that at times it seems as though I am saying that human decision is no longer possible or necessary. Can you show me a larger or smaller section of the *Church Dogmatics* in which a discussion of human decision is absent? Of course human decision can only ever *follow* the decision of God. And that is why the *Church Dogmatics* is so thick. For this reason I have been accused of always speaking in "spirals."[20] In fact one must always speak of the one and the other. I would not like, for example, to pursue a dogmatics that would not at every point also be ethics.

Nevertheless, I feel uneasy if one constantly speaks about "decision." For Bultmann everything is reduced to the "decision."[21] And in his book *The Nature of Faith*, Ebeling speaks of "faith" where he should say "Jesus Christ."[22] Hence, caution with the word "decision"! What is crucial is the preceding decision of God, which human beings are to *appropriate*.

Who are the *en Christō*? Are they the Christians or all human beings? In 2 Corinthians 5:17–[21] Paul speaks of people who have their being "in Christ."

15. Documented in E. Busch, *Karl Barth und die Pietisten*, 163–66 [ET: *Karl Barth and the Pietists*, esp. 151–54].

16. M. Luther, *Fastenpostille* (1522), WA 17/2:203, 227–28, Sermon on Matt. 15:21–28: "Yes is in there, but deeply and secretly and seems to be a No."

17. JB: "perhaps once so."

18. JB: ". . . form of a threat, or the form . . ."

19. This metaphor is found frequently in the writing of the young Barth: *Der Römerbrief* (1919), 384, 391; Karl Barth, *W.G.Th.*, 40 [ET: "The Christian's Place in Society," in *The Word of God and the Word of Man*, trans. Douglas Horton (New York: Harper Torchbooks, 1957), 282]; Karl Barth, *The Epistle to the Romans*, trans. Edwyn C. Hoskyns (London: Oxford University Press, 1968), 198.

20. No reference found. [Cf. G. W. Bromiley and T. F. Torrance, "Editor's Preface (1956)," *CD* I/2:vii; trans.]

21. Cf., e.g., R. Bultmann, *Geschichte und Eschatologie* (Tübingen: Mohr, 1958), 50–51, 180–82.) [ET: *History and Eschatology: The Presence of Eternity* (New York: Harper & Row, 1957), 44–45, 150–53].

22. G. Ebeling, *Das Wesen des christlichen Glaubens* (Tübingen: Mohr, 1959) [ET: *The Nature of Faith*, trans. Ronald G. Smith (Philadelphia: Fortress, 1961)]. For Barth's judgment of this book, cf. Karl Barth, *KD* IV/4, *Das christliche Leben: Fragmente aus dem Nachlass; Vorlesungen, 1959–1961*, ed. H.-A. Drewes and E. Jüngel (Zurich: Theologischer Verlag, 1976; 2nd ed., 1979), 59–61 [ET: *CD* IV/4, *The Christian Life: Lecture Fragments*, trans. G. W. Bromiley (Grand Rapids: Eerdmans, 1981), 38–39].

Who are those who have their being "in Christ"?[23] With *hēmeis* in verse 21 Paul refers to himself[24]—something he does on occasion; it is then almost identical with *egō*. For Paul, the situation of the human being before God is concentrated initially in the person of Paul: the apostle is *en Christō*. Yet in the same context the door of his being "in Christ" opens toward the outside, toward the community, because an "office," a *diakonia*, has been given to him [v. 18]. Thus the community is included with the statement "We entreat you on behalf of Christ" (indicative), as well as with the challenge "Be reconciled to God" (imperative) [v. 20]. Thus what initially holds true for Paul holds true for the *community* as well.

And then it[25] goes one step further: "God was reconciling the *world* to himself" [2 Cor. 5:19]. In the act of proclamation Paul also takes this third step and proclaims that the "cosmos" is reconciled as well.[26] Paul extends the word of reconciliation further—imperatively *and* indicatively: "God *has* reconciled"! This holds true for himself and then for the community and then also for the world. Faith is not an end in itself: the community believes as *witness*! It proclaims a fulfilled reality "in Christ," not simply a chance[27] (John 3:16). Thus in view of the *en Christō*, we cannot speak of an either-or—either the believers or the world [are reconciled]—not even on the basis of John 3:16. Rather we must speak of a *movement* toward the world. *En Christō*—that holds true initially for the apostle, through him it holds true for the community, [and] through the community it holds true for the world.

This stands everywhere behind the individual statements of the New Testament that apply initially to individual persons only. In John 1:3 the noteworthy statement is made: there is "nothing that was not made through Christ." Compare also Colossians 1:15; Hebrews 1:3. These verses[28] show that the world, *ta panta*, was created through Christ; thus even the *pantes* are his. Precisely as "believers" we know that insofar as we deal with Christ, we deal with the cause of the whole creation. Everything comes from him. From here we must look upon the *pantes*; the *pantes* are of course included in *ta panta* or *pan*! Thus the *pantes* are not simply "outside." They would not exist if Christ were not. Galatians 2:20 holds true first for Paul. But we may repeat it after him. The one in whom we live is before all things. The separation between believers and world is merely preliminary. Of course,[29] there is such a—preliminary—separation: there are indeed those to whom the Word has not yet been said. But the "bird" continues its flight. It is in motion toward the world. Paul runs across the world in order to announce to the world its being in Christ. Shouldn't we be confidently happy that we are allowed to see[30] this motion?

We can say this in summary: We believers (I actually do not like to use the word "believers") must always anew become that which we are—in Christ.

---

23. This question according to JB.
24. Cf. E. von Dobschütz, "Wir und Ich bei Paulus," *ZST* 10 (1933): 251–77.
25. This statement according to JB.
26. Ibid.
27. JB records the statement as follows: "This is said not merely as a possibility or chance, but rather reconciliation is—also for the world—a fulfilled reality in Christ."
28. This sentence according to JB.
29. Ibid.
30. JB: "to know."

The others are already in Christ [and thus] that which they shall still become. In this manner we are bound with the world in solidarity. The beginning and the goal, the Alpha and the Omega, are the same for all: Christ is "the Alpha and the Omega" [Rev. 1:8; 22:13].

Schindelin: We Pietists are indebted to you for your vigorous call away from experience to the Word, to that which is objective. Our question to you is this: Is not the "Again it is written" [Matt. 4:7] also valid? You cited only the first part of John 3:16. The text, however, also reckons with the possibility of being lost. Being lost is viewed as a human work. Indeed, Jesus does not say "You simply did not know it," but rather "You were not willing" [Matt. 23:37]. There is a human response to the salvation available in Christ that deprives humans of salvation. This has great importance for proclamation. Your sermon on the two criminals crucified with Christ[31] does not indicate that in relation to Christ a separation also occurs. Is the unrepentant criminal also saved? Faith is an effect of the Holy Spirit. Nevertheless, unbelief comes under the wrath of God. Compare Romans 2! This must also be made clear in a sermon. There is no excuse for unbelief in the judgment. For this reason I hardly ever conclude an evangelization without also saying this: one can also be *lost!* Compare John 3:36.

Müller: What you have shared regarding the revival movement is certainly a concern for us Pietists as well. For example, [in responding] to a person who came to speak to him, Blumhardt announced the forgiveness of his sins in advance. But do the *Church Dogmatics* not speak too objectivistically in some places? Certainly the opposing movement of human beings against the movement of God's salvation must not be overlooked. The possibility of rebellion is not simply an "impossible possibility," as you describe sin (e.g., *CD* IV/3:192). Whoever resists Christ under the word of grace is lost. We may add nothing, but also not omit anything. It is nice if one can include the others in such a triumphalistic manner. But there are also places in the New Testament that speak decisively of those who "are outside." This question is important to us, precisely in view of our proclamation.

Schönweiß: Does the New Testament say anywhere that "unbelievers already are what they shall still become"? It certainly says that "God so loved the world," "reconciling the world to himself" . . . , but not "He has made them all *believers!*"

Barth: No, not believers!

Schönweiß: In the New Testament, however, the one who is *en Christō* is the *believer.*

Barth: "In Christ" *all* are what believers may already believe they are. This is what we are told [in the New Testament]. In[32] Christ all are justified, sanctified, and born again [1 Cor. 1:30]—in other words, that in which believers already believe. Of course not everyone believes. Indeed we can also respond with unbelief. Faith is an event between me and the Word[33] . . . Even the community

---

31. Sermon on Luke 23:33 [in the Basel prison] on Good Friday, April 19, 1957. Karl Barth, *Den Gefangenen Befreiung! Predigten aus den Jahren 1954–1959* (Zollikon: Evangelischer Verlag, 1959), 80–91 [ET: "The Criminals with Him," in K. Barth, *Deliverance to the Captives,* trans. M. Weiser (New York: Harper & Row, 1961), 75–84].

32. The following two sentences according to JB.

33. Here it is conceivable that between the preceding and the subsequent sentences something like the following sentence was uttered: "Even the 'believing' church has no control over this event."

must still let itself be reconciled with God. It too should take to heart that which is told to the world.

Schönweiß: The community has already actualized it. It is always again called back to the beginning. That world, however, has not yet even begun.

Müller: Is sin[34] really the "impossible possibility"? At some point it could be too late [for repentance]. The final emphasis [on this point] is missing in the *Church Dogmatics.*

Fischer: Human beings can in fact reject grace. What are the consequences for our proclamation? Proclamation confronts the person with the decision and transmits the gift of salvation (cf. the meaning of the Word preached in volume I [of *CD*]!).[35] Our preaching is given its weight with the possibility of rejecting [this gift]. "Today, if you hear his voice, do not harden your hearts" [Heb. 3:7–8].

Barth: Thus, what appears to be missing in my work is "You were not willing!" [Matt. 23:37]. As much as you do not wish to defend Pietism, I also do not wish to defend the *Church Dogmatics.* Nevertheless,[36] which modern dogmatics speaks as often about sin as the *Church Dogmatics*? Who has dealt with sin at such length and under so many different aspects as I? I think that I did indeed take sin seriously.

I must admit that I am not very comfortable when you say that the possibility of being lost must be mentioned, for instance, at the conclusion of an evangelization address. What then is proclamation all about? It is about tirelessly calling sinners to repentance—[and] to do so in the manner that Jesus did it. He made himself common with the sinners. Certainly the danger of being lost lurks behind sin,[37] behind unbelief. Indeed, that is how it is presented in the Bible—more strongly in the New Testament than in the Old! But[38] does it appear there as an independent statement? Nowhere does it have the dignity of an independent theme. Not even in Romans 2! [Indeed, there in] verse 16 [it is stated], ". . . on the day when, *according to my gospel*, God, through Jesus Christ, will judge that which is hidden"! What is important is the call to human beings to take the step toward the place where they already belong. Is it not the case (in Scripture) that evil is indeed sighted, but that the proclamation [nonetheless always] continues onward? That in *paraclēsis* and paraenesis human beings are [always only] called back to where they already belong?

All of this has its[39] significance especially *within* the Christian community. The task of the believer is to call the nonbeliever to repentance. [But] where actually is the nonbeliever? In me of course! I myself am first and foremost the one who does not believe. In Romans 7 Paul finds the sin in himself. Then, however, Romans 8:1 continues with the victory of Christ. That the possibility of unbelief exists is something we know, we Christians above all others, and above all about ourselves! But we also know what is stronger and greater [than all sin]. If we console ourselves for the "sin that dwells within us" [Rom 7:17]

34. According to JB: "really only."
35. *CD* I/1:88–99, in the paragraph "The Word of God in Its Threefold Form," in the section "The Word of God Preached" [*KD* 89–101].
36. The following two questions according to JB.
37. "[B]ehind sin" according to JB.
38. This sentence and the next according to JB.
39. As in JB, rather than "some" in RW.

with the *einai en Christō*, must we then not also grant it to the poor rogues, to "those standing outside"? The first word of the sermon, the gospel of the Yes of God, must also be its last.

[*To Schindelin:*] It did not please me to hear that, at the end of a sermon, people are dismissed with a threat. We know about the possibility of being lost. Indeed, we state it, as does the Bible. But there is something more important[40] than the statement "You were not willing!" [Matt. 23:37]. Indeed, we also know what is still better. After the word about being lost in John 3:16, there immediately follows in verse 17: "Indeed, God did not send the Son into the world to condemn the world, but in order that the world might be saved through him." The negative is expressed—[but only] in the context of the gospel. [One should take heed of] Romans 2:[16,] "according to my gospel"! [In] Revelation 14 [v. 6, it is precisely] the angel of judgment that appears with the "eternal gospel"! Indeed, even the judgment of God is in reality salvation. God is, first of all, creating order. Sin is neither "the first" nor "the last." Let us speak earnestly about sin, but within *this* context [of the gospel of the one who in truth is "the first and the last"]! It is better to risk the danger of proclaiming too much gospel than risking the other danger [of speaking too little about sin]! We will [still] speak about the kind of wretch the human being is, in their lostness and stupidity, but we will speak about it—with the risk of it hurting—[always only] in the context of the Alpha and Omega [who is Christ] (Rev. 1:8; 1:17; 21:6; 22:13).

Schindelin: On[41] the objective level we accept everything you are saying. But we also see another level. I hope that the book of Acts has not yet been run down here, as one New Testament professor has recently tried to do in front of his students, deliberately . . .

Barth: Who is this scoundrel?

Schindelin: . . . but in our circles it can still be cited. The tenor of Acts is not "Now you *know* it; earlier you did *not know* it . . ."

Interjection: Of course it is! Acts 14:16; 17:30.

Schindelin: Instead, it is always about a movement of the will, not of knowledge. I would like to compare it with marriage: either I am married, or I am not married. And similarly, either I am a believer, or I am an unbeliever. Thus, is there not a decision of faith according to which humanity is divided into two groups, [whereby] the one group [is created] on the basis of a onetime Yes [of the person to Christ]?

Barth: You always speak of "two groups." [Yet] I am [always still] bound in a twofold manner. I, who speak in the name of the first group—of the "married" or of the "believers"—also have the spirit of the other group, of the "unbelievers," within me. Should this really be our cause: to discern[42] a little heap[43] of believers here and a little heap of[44] [un]believers there? Yet according to Ephesians 2 the dividing wall has been broken down [2:14]. The gentiles are now "citizens" and also "members of the household" [Eph. 2:19]. That is the "sure and worthy" truth [1 Tim. 1:15].

40. JB: "some really more important."
41. In RW: "in . . ."
42. JB reads "to gather."
43. JB: "a little house full . . ."
44. As in n. 42 above.

Fischinger: Certainly we do not wish to fall out of the Yes into the No. When I preach I announce the Yes of God. But in the course of my preaching the anti-Christian [element] gathers strength until it shows itself as "nothingness"! [See] 2 Corinthians 2:15–16: "For we are the aroma of Christ to God among those who are being saved and among those who are perishing; to the one a fragrance from death to death, to the other a fragrance from life to life." In fact it is through our preaching that this separation takes place.

Barth: It does *in fact* occur in this manner. But the concern cannot be to spread "the aroma of death to death." Along with [our real concern] we painfully observe that the No also exists; [but] it is the unfortunate event [that should not happen].

Fischinger: Jesus speaks of the *dei* [it must be]; the community takes this on. "You will be hated by all nations because of my name" [Matt. 24:9].

Barth: [But] that does not mean that *we* must *make* ourselves hateful, so that the world can and must hate us!

Schönweiß: But is there not a difference between someone who has fundamentally said Yes and someone who has fundamentally rejected it—even if we agree that a Christian must continually repent?

Barth: Of course that does make a difference. *Metanoeite* is no longer [the word] addressed to the Christian. Instead [nonetheless], "Put on Christ!" [Rom. 13:14]. Is this not the same? Yes, indeed,[45] both groups remain, but the dividing wall between them is removed. One cannot convert to the Savior and then rejoice that one [now] no longer belongs to the other group [of sinners and children of the world]!

Schindelin: This type of "joy" is not what concerns us.

Barth: The [two] groups are there. But it is in the shade that they exist as [separate] groups, and the light is that the "dividing wall" between them has fallen.

Schindelin: [No,] the light is to step from one group into the other.

Kommoß: We tremble [fearing] that we have not told the other person of the offer of God with sufficient clarity, and that perhaps for this reason he is still in the other group. We are concerned that we truly deliver the whole gospel. I would like to share the judgment of a man who heard Billy Graham in Berlin.[46] "I constantly heard: 'You must make a decision,' but too seldom: 'You have been given a gift.'"

Schönweiß: We wish to say to him [the unbeliever]: In Christ the door is open; walk through!

Fischer: One even lets the sun shine onto the other. People should realize: You have been given a gift; you *may* make a decision.

Barth: That too is my concern. If that is the opinion of everyone [here], then the controversy is settled.

Kommoß: The neuter statements made by students and vicars of our established church always strike me. We do not proclaim a "subject matter"; rather what is important is that human beings are placed into a relationship with a

---

45. This sentence as in JB.
46. The American evangelist Billy Graham came to Berlin on June 26–27, 1954, for an evangelistic crusade. On June 26, he spoke at the City Mission Church in Südstern Square, and on June 27 to 80,000 people in the Olympic Stadium.

person, with the Lord Christ, that we come under the charge of a Lord. And then it also means "Woe is me if I am *not* in this relationship with Christ!"

Barth: Formulated in this way, I can accept this.

Fischer: Can one also add that a decision against faith today need not be taken as final, that God can also be merciful later?

Barth: Where would we be if God didn't always deal with us in this way?

Müller: Turning to God always has a flip side, that I also turn away from an anti-person, from "nothingness." If with the first statement we testify, "God has turned toward us," then we must also testify to the second, "Turn away from . . . !" The sermon also has an exorcistic effect. This too is a concern of Pietism.

Barth: I do not really like to hear that there are two statements. The first message is always the person of Jesus Christ, in whom a decision about you is made. If we decide otherwise, then it doesn't work. That is really an "impossible possibility." The second statement, "Turn away from . . . !," is implied in the first.

With regard to my sermon on the two criminals:[47] It is a daring sermon, first, insofar as it was delivered in prison, that is, among those who are obviously sinners and criminals.[48] It really jumped out at me then: "They were crucified *with him*" [Luke 23:33; cf. Matt. 27:38, 44], and I drew upon Paul's "crucified with Christ" [cf. Rom. 6:6]. From there the following two thoughts [occurred to me]: What is noteworthy about the crucifixion is finding Jesus in such bad company and to find the criminals in such good company—to find *us* in such good company. In light of[49] the danger of "dangerous" statements, I do not wish to flee to the law. The real danger is falling back into the law. My concern about Pietism is that in it the law is always reignited from the embers.

When I reached the end of the "Prolegomena" of the *Church Dogmatics* twenty-five years ago,[50] I breathed freely. Until that point I had to fight. I had to fight my way free, as it were, from all kinds of worldviews and ideas,[51] theologies, and false teachings. Now, with the polemics behind me, I could simply move on to the doctrine of God [and] present positively what God is. Since then I fight only in a very indirect way. I no longer have the need to lampoon Pietism directly. [For me] Pietism is a front only insofar as it stands together with rationalism; and as subjectivism—and this context, historically, is undoubtedly present![52]—Pietism is a copartner behind the rise of rationalism and its consequences. Perhaps you have also noticed that over the course of my work I have continued to move closer to a figure who is also numbered among the Pietists: Count Zinzendorf.[53] There is also much that is terrible in his work ("Brother Lamb");[54] but in essence I am probably in agreement with him. My respect for

---

47. "The Criminals with Him," *Deliverance to the Captives*, trans. M. Weiser (New York: Harper & Row, 1961), 75–84; see also n. 31 above.

48. Here "and criminals" follows JB.

49. In RW: "from."

50. *CD* I/1 (German, 1932) and I/2 (German, 1938).

51. The last three words according to JB.

52. The parenthesis according to JB.

53. Cf. *CD* IV/1:275, 522, 628, 683, 756 [*KD* 302, 582, 701, 763, 845].

54. A song about the Trinity by N. L. Count von Zinzendorf: "Daddy, Mommy, and their little flame, Brother Lamb with his little dove: Bless us tiny blood-filled particles of dust." Cited by J. A. Bengel, *Abriß der so genannten Brüdergemeine* (1751; reprint, Berlin: G. Schlawitz, 1858), 54 (listed there as song no. 1942).

him continues to grow. He is becoming increasingly respectable to me. But, let us remember, in his own day Zinzendorf too was an opponent of the prevalent Pietism.[55]

2. On Conversion

Bürki: I would like to formulate our common concern as two questions directed to ourselves.[56] First, why is there so much *legalism* and arrogance among us who speak of conversion? Second, why are we so *self-assured*? Legalism arises when people think they have achieved something themselves in relation to their conversion. Certainty comes about when repentance is seen as a single and completed event of the past. We[57] Pietists not only *see* the danger of legalism and self-certainty, but we also *fight* tenaciously against it. Thus the question that arises for us is this: how should we speak of conversion so that these two dangers are avoided?

To the first: God "commands all people everywhere to repent" (Acts 17:30). To obey a command is not merit, but purely doing one's duty. Not to obey is disobedience, sin. Practically, this command of God occurs in every proclamation: as[58] luring, enticing, admonishing, threatening, and so forth. We wanted to keep the whole range of variations on these forms[59] in mind.

What then must the one who is addressed do? He must allow something to occur to him. In this context,[60] the Bible often uses the passive imperative: "Be reconciled to God!" (2 Cor. 5:20); "Let yourselves be saved from this corrupt generation" (Acts 2:40). The course of this process [in which one "lets" oneself be saved] is, according to Romans 10:14–[15] (there in reversed order): to be sent, proclaim, hear, believe, call on God. It is important[61] that calling on the name of God is part of it, for "everyone who calls on the name of the Lord shall be saved" (Acts 2:21). Compare, for example, the resurrection of Lazarus (John 11:1–45). Of himself, Lazarus can really do nothing. He is dead. But then he is encountered by God's command in Jesus Christ: "Lazarus, come out!" (John 11:43). Now he *can* come out, and now he *must* as well, that is, he himself.[62] He has no excuse if he does not come; he will then have forfeited his life, his salvation.

To the second: Christian existence began at a specific point in the past and continues on, constantly renewing itself. It is like a birth. Because of it there is life, and life grows. The singular act of the beginning does not exclude but rather includes continual, constant growth.[63] Colossians 2:5–8 holds both together: "You have received, . . . so live in him"! Similarly Colossians 1:22–[23]. Here the phrase "provided that" is important for Pietism, which does not sufficiently

---

55. For supporting evidence, cf. S. Eberhard, *Kreuzes-Theologie: Das reformatorische Anliegen in Zinzendorfs Verkündigung* (Munich: Kaiser, 1937), 74–123, 156, 213, and often.
56. The following is from the discussion in the afternoon session.
57. Following JB up to the next colon.
58. The remainder of the sentence follows JB.
59. The last two words in JB.
60. The last three words as in JB.
61. This sentence follows JB.
62. The final phrase according to JB.
63. Ibid.

recognize the ongoing struggle. It destroys false security. [For] example: Peter on the water (Matt. 14:22–33). On account of the command of Jesus, he can walk on the water; but alone he cannot keep himself up, even for a second. He is continually dependent on Christ. As soon as he is no longer in the constant connection of faith [with Christ], he must sink.[64]

Third, what occurs in conversion? The question of the *assurance of salvation* arises here. What is decisive for us Pietists as well is not the "experience" of conversion, but rather the fact of conversion. [Thus] 2 Corinthians 5:17: *ei tis* [if anyone] . . . ! That human beings become a *kainē ktisis* [new creation] is anything but self-evident; rather it depends on the assumption "*If anyone* is in Christ . . ." Thus [it is] a clear condition. God is the one who implements the condition. *He* relocates me "in Christ." This act of God creates assurance of salvation, not certainty of salvation. Assurance of salvation happens, because and to the extent that my salvation is grounded in Christ, because and to the extent that I am "in Christ." Assurance of salvation should not be confused with the certainty of salvation; this too is a concern for us. It is not at our disposal. There is no assurance of salvation without the Holy Spirit, who is bestowed on us in conversion. That brings us to a condition of "already now" and simultaneously "not yet." The human person receives the Holy Spirit in conversion as a "first installment." The first installment is, however, "not yet" everything, not that which is final.[65]

Conversion is part of the *offer* of God: you may repent. Therefore no shotgun conversion! The preacher should not just preach at the hearers, but lead [them] to Jesus, where the person can say, "Finally, I know in whom I can place my trust." Without assurance of salvation, no congregation can be built up, no growth can occur. [For] example, Andrew leads Peter to Jesus: "We have found the Messiah" (John 1:41).

Korthals: It appears that Professor Barth understands conversion somewhat differently than we do. According to his view, in the Bible one finds only people who are *in the process* of being converted, who at best can say of themselves: "I awake."[66] In our view, what is treated in the *Church Dogmatics* under the topic of "awakening"[67] belongs to the topic "sanctification, new life." Certainly conversion is not an end point, but it is the point at which something new begins, the first step out of lostness. Does the story of the Prodigal Son end with the decision "I will get up and go" (Luke 15:18)? No, further steps necessarily follow. But the first step, conversion, is qualitatively superior to the ones that follow (sanctification). Consequently, Barth's critique of the old *Ordo salutis* [order of salvation][68] does not appear to us to be completely justified.

How is the person to be addressed? As the one "converted at Golgotha,"[69] or as one who is lost? It is my view[70] that the person is not to be addressed as

---

64. This entire sentence as in JB.
65. JB writes here: "'Already now' we have the first installment, the Holy Spirit. 'Not yet': we only have a deposit."
66. Cf. *CD* IV/2:554 [*KD* 627], 560–61 [*KD* 634].
67. *CD* IV/2, with the title "Awakening to Conversion," 553–84 [*KD* 626–60].
68. *CD* IV/2:502–4 [*KD* 568–69].
69. *CD* IV/2:583 [*KD* 660]: "Who of us then, in relation to our own conversion or that of others, can seriously know any other terminus for this event than the day of Golgotha, in which He accomplished in our place and for us all the turning and transforming of the human situation . . . ?"
70. Up to the end of the sentence as in JB.

someone who is already saved. The address "You are saved" does not connect as long as the person does not know "I am lost, I must first be saved." What is the reason for the reluctance to speak of the "converted"? Is this reluctance not rooted in the miserable state of the converted? Barth says that we may not claim the great categories of the New Testament for ourselves.[71] Accordingly, conversion appears to be a kind of carousel ride:[72] one doesn't really get any further. However, according to the New Testament, believers are people who are no longer in the constant process of being converted, but those for whom conversion is *behind* them. With respect to themselves, not only can they say "I awake" but rather "I *am* awake," "I *am* converted." For Pietism, conversion is like the obtaining of a new axis around which the one converted now moves; earlier, the individual moved around his own axis. Repentance cannot mean that one does not advance but remains treading evermore on the same spot. The converted in Corinth are certainly disappointing, but they *are* the converted.

Kommoß: What concretely do we mean when we speak of conversion? The New Testament distinguishes between the singular, basic occurrence and the turning around that happens time and again, using the distinct concepts of *epistrephein* [to turn around] and *metanoein* [to repent]. What concerns us presently is the basic conversion. In [that latter] conversion I realize that I cannot convert myself. God has turned toward me. But this conversion is indispensible. We cannot tell the person that with baptism and confirmation one has already become a disciple.

Barth [to Bürki]: I[73] have listened favorably. I do not know where I would contradict you. All[74] of that is fine. All of that can be found in my language in the *Church Dogmatics.* . . .

Bürki: I still have to express my concern more precisely. Despite the correct theology, I see among dialectical theologians endless[75] discombobulation when[76] someone asks [them], "What must I do?" The Bible answers this question clearly: "Repent, and be baptized every one of you . . ."—again a passive imperative—"and you will receive the gift of the Holy Spirit" (Acts 2:38). Clear separations and decisions resulted from such a directive: in the one case, hearers of the Word were cut to the heart, and they obeyed (Acts 2:37, 41). In another case, the Word also cut them to the heart, but they did not obey (Acts 7:54; or Acts 17:32, 34). Paul's proclamation of conversion had a threefold effect: ridicule, interest, faith. Our predicament is that this separation no longer takes place with the sermon. In Switzerland, all people head home from church confidently, just as they came:[77] unchallenged, unchanged.

Barth: All right,[78] there is this separation. You have now emphasized what we had called the "flip side" this morning. The[79] "decision" for Christ also has

---

71. *CD* IV/2:583 [*KD* 659]: "How feeble is the relationship, even in the best of cases, between the great categories in which the conversion of man is described in the New Testament and the corresponding event in our own inner and outer life!"
72. Barth rejects this in *CD* IV/2:572–74 [*KD* 647–49].
73. This sentence in accordance with JB.
74. Ibid.
75. This is JB's term.
76. Following JB up to the end of the sentence.
77. The parenthetical phrase following JB.
78. This sentence in accordance with JB.
79. Ibid.

a back side. Indeed, this back side exists: there are people who do not let themselves be moved by the Word. [But] should this back side become a second topic beside the first? This did not appear to be the case in your first verdict.

Bürki: The second topic is included in the first.

Barth: [But how both belong together is the question.] It is a matter of superordination and subordination. You should stand by your first verdict. The other side was there, namely, the divine decision for humanity as superordinated to the human decision. But now I am getting nervous again.

[To Korthals:] Here,[80] I think, I actually need to raise an objection. I must object to the opinion that the proclamation of Christ does not "connect" unless the lostness of humanity is proclaimed. How can I inform people of their lostness without proclaiming Christ to them? Lostness as an independent theme, without Christ, in empty space? The cross of Christ is sufficient! If one starts from this point, there is no need to fear and think that one is not "connecting." What you are saying is the old mug's game: first make people feel really bad, and then comes the gospel. Precisely the other way around is correct: first the gospel, then everything else will have its say.

You want to emphasize, "I *am* awakened," "I *am* converted." A sentence that begins with "I" is seldom good—even if the best and most beautiful statement should follow (i.e., "awakened," "converted," etc.).[81] If, for a moment, you were to set aside the address of *hagioi* directed to the Corinthians, you would likely think, with everything else that he says of them, of unconverted [people]. *You* think it is important to say, "I am awakened!," and none other than *Paul* writes to the [believing] Ephesians: "Sleeper, *awake*! Rise from the dead!" (Eph. 5:14). Of course humans live in time, and that means, even in terms of one's conversion, that at some point there is a beginning. "Becoming a believer" is an event in real life, even if it cannot be precisely dated. It begins at some point, whether in a shorter or longer stretch of time, or in an instant.

[To Kommoß:] You refer to the fact that not everything is completed with infant baptism and confirmation. But to whom do you tell this? You are aware of my statement on infant baptism.[82] I am in agreement: infant baptism and confirmation are not identical with being born again.

3. Conversion as Calling and Sending into Service

Barth: To[83] all of this something further must still be said. With this I would like to give the discussion a new twist. The stories of conversion in the Bible are always *stories about calling*. What is primarily at issue there is not that this [or that] individual becomes a new being and is converted[84]—that is also implied!

---

80. Ibid.
81. The content in parentheses according to JB.
82. Cf. K. Barth, *Die kirchliche Lehre von der Taufe* (Zollikon: Evangelischer Verlag, 1943). In the Winter Semester 1959–60 following this dialogue, Barth began with the lecture course on his doctrine of baptism for the *Church Dogmatics*, which was published in 1967 as *KD* IV/4 (*Fragment*) [ET: *The Christian Life (Fragment): Baptism as the Foundation of the Christian Life*, trans. G. W. Bromiley (Edinburgh: T&T Clark, 1969)].
83. This sentence in accordance with JB.
84. The preceding three words following JB.

But what is crucial is that such a person is called: "Come, I need you!" At[85] issue is that one is called into service. None of those who are being called are towering figures. But they are not first told, "You are a bad person." In the case of Paul, Christ does not say, "Turn away from Judaism!" but rather, "I need you." Everything else is included within this call. What makes Christians Christian is that they are given something to do. Look again at Paul. He is not said to have lived in a particular darkness [and that he should now be something else]; rather he is *immediately* called from being a persecutor to being a *witness* (Acts 9:15; 26:15–18). That is the rebirth, that is his renewal. *Charis* [grace] and *apostolē* [apostleship] are one (Rom 1:5).

The trouble I have with regard to Pietism is not the two dangers that were cited by you, Dr. Bürki, namely, legalism and arrogance. What concerns me is whether all Pietists know [that] what is of vital importance is not that *I* will be saved, but rather what will *become* of my salvation. The ultimate issue is not my personal salvation, but rather that through Christ I am taken into the *hēmeis* [we], taken into service. Can conversion be an end in itself? *Kainē ktisis* [new creation] (2 Cor. 5:17)! We are to share in the new creation of God. If that is so, one begins to lose some of one's self-importance as a converted individual. It[86] is no longer important that *I* am awakened, converted, a believer. Rather, what is important is What will be next? What will happen now? Where am I needed and taken into service?—Please allow a gentle question by a friend of Pietism: What now is the future of the "communion with the Lord and with the brethren"? What posture follows from the conversion? Does the presence of the converted have significance in the *world*[87] and *for* the *world*? What[88] stance do the converted take, for example, with regard to mammon? The *new*—that should be demonstrated in the posture toward mammon.

I must still go one step further. You know that I have always been very involved in German affairs. Where are the converted when it matters in the world? Where were the Community Movement Christians when Hitler came?[89] Where were they after the war when the politics of Adenauer came, when the new rearmament came? Where are they in the saga of the atomic bomb? Shouldn't their presence be noticeable in these areas? According to my observation one could not count on the Pietists in these burning questions. Where were they? In their chapels?[90] Or did they run with the large herd? The new in them should have been recognizable by the fact that they did *not* run with the world. Conversion is the conversion of the *whole* person. There is no conversion where a person becomes apolitical. Please do not take offense at what I said! But on this point I am perturbed and would have gladly had more help from the converted.[91]

Schindelin: We do not want to defend ourselves. But in spite of that, I would like to try to answer the last reproaches. True, the Pietists were not among the

85. This sentence in accordance with JB.
86. Up to the next dash in accordance with JB.
87. The last three words in accordance with JB.
88. This sentence following JB.
89. On this see E. G. Rüppel, *Die Gemeinschaftsbewegung im Dritten Reich: Ein Beitrag zur Geschichte des Kirchenkampfes* (Göttingen: Vandenhoeck & Ruprecht, 1969).
90. "Chapel" is also the Swiss expression for the gathering places of such Christian fellowships.
91. As in JB; RW instead uses "Christians."

staffers of the High Command of the Church Struggle, but nonetheless, Immer and Humburg, for example—both Pietists—were significantly involved.[92] And even the small flock that opted for the Confessing Church at that time consisted to a large extent of Pietists or came from Pietist homes. Inadequate theological clarity was primarily to blame for the weakness of Pietism at the beginning.

Regarding [the concept] of conversion as sending: Even so, as Jesus sent out his disciples, he said: "Rejoice that your names are written in heaven!" (Luke 10:20). Perhaps this joy is not simply egotism. Also, we should not overlook the fact that—when one looks at history,[93]—there is an abundance of initiatives [*Werke*] (foreign missions, inner mission)[94] that were established by the Revival Movement. Thus the Pietists understood what sending is. . . .

Barth: I respect that, and I have also recognized it in writing recently. . . .[95]

Schindelin: On the question How do conversion and new life emerge?, in the Bible we constantly encounter the human question "What do you wish that I should do?" (Acts 22:10; cf. 9:6). This question precedes conversion itself; only then does the appeal to repentance and conversion follow. For many people, a demand of God is God's inbreaking into their lives. The one called upon can withhold the answer, the obedience. This aspect must exist and be proclaimed, even if it does not constitute the whole. It seems to me that the pivotal point of our conversation is to be found here.

Fischer: Today we suffer from increasing godlessness, and in this situation we ask how and what we must proclaim. Schniewind has impressed upon us the notion that "repentance is joy."[96] The recognition of lostness comes with joy in Jesus Christ. Do not therefore look long for points of contact, but rather begin with the cross! It does not depend on the vocabulary, but rather that the gospel is delivered. Even the word about Christ is the word about the lostness of humanity. It has been our struggle for years to make the cross of the Lord the starting point. Conversion is about the whole issue of guilt; God grant that our word of forgiveness connects there!—We Pietists do[97] know that to be converted means to be sent. When we hold evangelizations, it is not only about saving souls, but rather about the realization that love extends into many areas.

Fischinger: We need to consider your word to us about conversion as an "end in itself." But I ask myself if I could say what you said in your verdict on the German question in the same way. Two questions arise for me. First, would

---

92. Karl Immer (1888–1944) was the director of the Erziehungsverein Neukirchen [Educational Society of Neukirchen] in 1925–27, and pastor of the Reformed Congregation of Barmen-Gemarke in 1927–44. In the latter role he was a driving force in the Confessing Church. Paul Humburg (1878–1945) was the general secretary of the Deutsche Christliche Studentenvereinigung [German Christian Student Union] in 1919–21, Bundeswart [Regional Warden] of the Westdeutscher Jungmännerbund [West German Young Men's Association], and in 1929–43 pastor of the Reformed Congregation of Barmen-Gemarke. Since 1934 he was president of the Confessional Synod in the Rhineland. From 1934 to 1936 he was also a member of the Erste Vorläufige Leitung der deutschen Evangelischen Kirche [First Preliminary Governing Body of the German Evangelical Church].

93. The text between dashes as in JB.

94. The text in parentheses as in JB.

95. Cf. *CD* IV/3:18–38 [*KD* 18–40]. In RW: "Barth acknowledges that and refers to an appreciative passage in IV/3."

96. J. Schniewind, *Das biblische Wort von der Bekehrung* (Göttingen: Vandenhoeck & Ruprecht, 1948), 3: "The return to God is joy." See also J. Schniewind, *Die Freude der Buße: Zur Grundfrage der Bibel* (Göttingen: Kleine Vandenhoeck-Reihe, 1956), 3.

97. JB has: "for some time."

the No that we must say to nuclear weapons today not mean that we must say No to war as such? From this follows, second, a question of principle: Should we always preach first and primarily the indicative? Can[98] we never say to the world just the imperative in our proclamation? As a test of the correctness of the proclaimed indicative, could one not say the same also as an imperative? Today the call is important in discipleship.

Barth: It could indeed be the case that the Christian witness in the world is often an *imperative*. Perhaps one would have to say to the drinker very clearly, "Stop binging," or to the state, "Away with the atomic bomb!" But *how* should that be said? By all means on the basis of the indicative!

And to your first question with regard to war: With the atomic bomb we are actually at a turning point in relation to our position on war. We must remind ourselves again about the original stance of Christianity toward war. In the first three centuries it was impossible for a Christian to become a soldier. Today we are not yet that far again, but we are underway toward this goal. It must start with the fight against the atomic bomb.

Schönweiß: The Pietism that is concerned about itself is waning. The call to repentance goes forth so that the repentant one can serve and glorify his Lord.

Barth: [Again,] there is no *charis* [grace] that is not also *apostolē* [sending].

Kommoß: I have a practical difficulty when we talk about conversion. In the Old Testament repentance, frequently proclaimed, was unsuccessful time and again. It is the new in the New Testament that the *Lord* must do something in order for it to succeed. In dealing with younger theologians,[99] the following difficulty became clear to me: In sermons today the acts of God are, by and large, described with great accuracy. But how this should look practically in everyday life, what should now follow, is not explained. And even then, if one would ask a pastor about it in the vestry after the sermon, "What must I do in order that . . . ?," a shrug would probably be the answer, or he would speak once more exclusively of the acts of God. It is not so much you, professor, but in our opinion it still is the Barthians who are responsible for this development in our context.

We confess that in view of the proclamation of conversion, we ourselves face a huge practical difficulty. We really don't know how to answer the question "*Where* is repentance necessary for me?" "*What form* must my repentance take?" How can we give people help, so that God becomes God *to them*? It would be easier if I could always say *who* God actually is. What does God require *now*? Woe to the church that cannot provide an answer to this concrete question. If it cannot do it, then everything remains [stuck] in systematics. We must constantly ask that God show us this concrete point.

Barth: Indeed,[100] that is an absolutely decisive question. I am glad that you make a certain distinction between me and my students. I see two types of people among my students: those who have nothing to say in this regard, and those who know it much too well.

98. This sentence follows JB.
99. JB: "with many younger theologians."
100. This sentence follows JB.

Kommoß: And in eschatology too, it is not a matter of "things" [*Neutra*], but rather of the person of the judge of the world. Even for Paul it was not entirely certain whether he would achieve *sotēria* [salvation].

Barth: The only thing of which he was certain was that he expected Christ as the Lord.

Fischer: [Again,] regarding the political stance of Christians: one[101] must also consider what many Germans, especially refugees, went through during and after the war. The political stance of many Germans can be understood from their experiences during the Russian invasion in 1945. A panic fear of those demonic powers that became visible in Communism is still alive among many. In addition, we have an aversion to extracting clear political directives from the New Testament. Too much abuse has already occurred by this practice, be it under the flag of *deutsch-national* or National-Socialism, and so forth.

Schindelin: I am completely on the side of those who oppose nuclear weapons. I have signed a petition opposing the atomic bomb. I would also be prepared to carry a poster through the streets and[102] to protest against it. But that is a question of understanding. I recognize that people who are truly brothers draw different conclusions. You cannot judge other Christians on their position regarding the atomic bomb, let alone condemn them, as long as it is on the basis of Scripture that they feel bound to a certain position—different from my own. Number one must be that the person comes into a right relationship with God. Does that become clear in his attitude to Christ, or in his attitude to the atomic bomb?

Barth: Yes, yes, the others are indeed "brothers"! Even Paul recognizes such people as brothers[103]—but precisely as "false brothers" [Gal 2:4]. Of course we cannot condemn anyone, but on our part we must give witness to the will of God as we have come to know it. Naturally[104] no concrete directives for our contemporary political situation can be simply read in the Bible. At issue is not primarily our relation to the Bible, but our relationship to a *person*. (In fact, here it really depends on the personal relationship between Jesus Christ and us, of which Pastor Kommoß spoke.)[105] And when false brothers arise within a community and factions develop,[106] then the opponent must be asked, Can you account for your Yes to this matter before Jesus Christ? Or do you have some kind of morality or a Christ who is not the whole Christ (as was the case with a "heroic" Christ, or at another time a "social-ethical" Christ)? Ever new questions arise. And then in a concrete case it can occur that I suddenly find someone whom I had regarded as my brother to be on the other side. New hours of obedience and of hope emerge. And then it will be necessary, here and now, to *awaken* anew.

---

101. This sentence follows JB.
102. Follows JB to the end of the sentence.
103. The sentence to this point according to JB.
104. As in JB; RW says "obviously."
105. This sentence according to JB.
106. RW: "There will always be false brothers arising from the church; separations emerge. Then the other must. . . ."

4. Concluding Reflections

Bürki: Our discussion has shown that we are one in many matters of Scripture. We, who are active in practical work as evangelists, are in great distress[107] on the question of authority. As mentioned, to a great extent this is because of the influence of your school. Your former position against Pietism still has a hold on many minds. The fronts are still entrenched. For example, look how the Swiss hymnal was purged of Pietist hymns![108] Those who have followed the *Church Dogmatics* would recognize a convergence [with Pietism] on your part. Your students who have not, however, are only familiar with your (superseded) original position. Therefore we ask, could you perhaps provide in a minipublication a detailed statement of your assessment of Pietism today?

Barth: When you are on the road between the seventy-third and seventy-fourth year of life, you don't count on too much more time. My task is to continue with the *Church Dogmatics* as far as possible. This project is the contribution that I can make. Besides, "it will be better in heaven, when I sing in the choir of saints."[109] I will hardly be able to find time for such secondary tasks. It is much more important that you yourselves articulate your contribution in such a manner that you take the wind from the sails of those false criticisms of Pietism.[110]

I give you the following piece of advice: put aside the name "Pietism"! All words that end with "ism" are terrible. "Calvin-ism"! I, for example, do not wish to be called a "Calvinist"! Or something really horrible is "Lutheran-ism"! We should never advocate any "-isms." You should seek to simply support a Christianity that is in conformity with the gospel! It is not the point to become servants of some particular "Fathers." The only thing that matters is the one

---

107. JB: "dire straits."

108. The proportion of songs of Pietist origin is significantly less in the 1952 German-language hymnal of the Swiss Reformed Church (*GERS: Gesangbuch der evangelisch-reformierten Kirche der deutschsprachigen Schweiz*) than in the preceding hymnal of 1891 (*Gesangbuch für die evangelisch-reformierte Kirche der deutschen Schweiz*). The new 1952 hymnal has a long prehistory, which dates back to 1919. It reached an important milestone with the publication of a sampler volume [*Probeband*] in 1941. Cf. F. L. Christ, "Wie es zu dem neuen Gesangbuch gekommen ist [How the new hymnal came about]," *KBRS* 98 (1942): 242–46. This was preceded by passionate discussions including many participants in, among other places, the *Kirchenblatt für die reformierte Schweiz*, particularly dense in vol. 91 (1935), in which no less than thirty-six contributions on this theme are found. In the issues of that year, the following authors pleaded specifically for the re-inclusion of Pietist hymns: Heinrich Gelzer (122–23), Wilhelm Rütimeyer (140–41), Paul Balmer (146–47), Karl Stückelberger (171–72), Fanny Alioth (172), Hans Anstein (182–83), Heinrich Hoffmann (183–85), Hans Brenner-Eglinger (202–3), Lukas Stückelberger (217–19), Robert Ehret (265–66; on 265: "Is it really the case that we should only be allowed to sing what is dialectically flawless?"), and Ernst Hauri (346–47; on 347: "Dialectical theology is far from what the people can grasp and understand. . . . If a hymnal is created from this faith perspective, it will never be able to truly take root in congregations and for many will once again clear the path into the [Evangelical] Community Movement as the best option"). Cf. also E. Schick, *Die Botschaft des Pietismus in den theologischen Kämpfen der Gegenwart* (Basel: Heinrich Maier, 1938), 6: "Vast areas of our church and wide circles of our congregations are being torn asunder . . . : it is the tear between theology and piety. The context for this tearing is the widely conducted fight against Pietism today. . . . A large portion of the Protestant Church's treasury of hymns is deemed to be suspect, to name just one example, in order to justify the theological fight against a portion of our congregations. One fights the 'pious individual' in order to hit saintly witnesses of the past as well."

109. From the hymn, "O daß ich tausend Zungen hätte [O that I had a thousand tongues]," by Johann Mentzer (1704).

110. RW adds here in brackets: "Barth asks about movements in the church and in Pietism as well as outside of the church in Germany: New Apostolic Church—fundamentalists—'moral re-armament': 'Are they still there with their odd four absolutes?'"

person: Christ. And if I might add, we should not always speak about "our concern [*Anliegen*]." *An-liegen*—what does that even mean? To lean against something? No, to *stand*! To stand like a man!

Kommoß: We spoke about "being in Christ" and about "conversion," about matters of content. Actually, we made an effort to learn from the Lord. We did this together in the name of Jesus, and for this we can be thankful.

Fischer: All participants extend their heartfelt thanks that you, Herr Professor, have made this conversation possible.

4. Interview by Georg Wolff and Hermann Renner
1959

In the Christmas number of the news magazine Der Spiegel *13, number 52 (December 23, 1959): 69–81, there appeared a story titled "Karl Barth: News of an Unknown God." Beneath the title photo was a headline: "God's Happy Partisan." Along with the sketch of his vita and the illumination of his theological work, the central point of the article was the portrayal of Barth's political engagement. The basis of this article, among others, was an interview that the* Spiegel *editors, Georg Wolff and Hermann Renner, held with Barth at his home on November 13, 1959. Statements made by him in this interview were apparently transferred directly to this article. Of the passages quoted verbatim, the following probably come from the interview.*

If up until the appearance of the *Römerbrief*[1] Barth had interpreted the God-human relationship exclusively with a focus upon God, after that a turning toward man slowly began. "First, in the *Römerbrief*, I wrote on the God-ness of God. But as a professor in Göttingen,[2] I couldn't just continually say to my students 'God, God, God!' I noticed that in the end humanness itself is not something to be taken lightly, and I began to reflect more and more on the humanness of God."

"How would all knowledge of God's forgiveness help the Christian . . . if God somehow lacked this humanness?"

At this point Barth realized that in Christ that contradiction was resolved, historically as well as symbolically, between God the unapproachable, the "God who is God"—and God the knowable, the "human God." Christ is the narrow space where God and the human are separated and bound together at the same time. The God whom Barth worships today has granted the human person a "soul by nature Christian," by virtue of which even the sinful person, independent of God the Father, can bring about relatively valuable "small realizations of the kingdom of God."

According to his theology, there exists no churchly authority in ethical questions, and certainly not in political matters. Therefore with a certain nonchalance Barth is able to handle matters which [. . .] in worldly thinking are of great importance. Church admonitions or simple brotherly admonitions from person to person shall then, according to Barth, "only remind the one addressed that as a human being belonging to God, each person is confronted by the God of all humanity."

---

1. What is meant is the revision, Munich: Kaiser, 1922 (15th printing, Zurich: Theologischer Verlag, 1989).
2. In 1921–25.

Once in the 1920s when Barth was a professor in Germany, in a Berlin theological society he was accused of understanding nothing about Prussia. Barth answered with the request of any of those present to document their Prussian credentials by telling the story of the Battle of Königgrätz. Today Barth says, "None could do it, but I would have been able to do it!" (The remark of the visitor that the father of the then German chancellor Adenauer accomplished wonders of bravery in that battle, however, appears to lessen the graying Basel theologian's enjoyment of Prussia's glory).

5. Conversation in the Zofingia II
1959

On November 18, 1959, Barth resumed his discussion of the "Christian and politics" with the Basel student association Zofingia, which he had begun on June 3, 1959 (see chap. 2 above). On this occasion the topic of the discussion was "the Christian and the Swiss State." The minutes drawn up by Christian Thalmann are found in the place mentioned in the introduction to chapter 2. Concerning Barth's opinion on the Hungarian uprising of 1956 expressed at the close of this conversation, the minutes remark: "During this discussion, a member of Zofingia deserted the hall, slamming the door. Another complained afterward that because of Barth's remarks, he became physically ill. The others appear to have escaped without further injuries."

Schniggel: Welcome to the speaker, Professor Dr. Karl Barth. The points of view can move considerably closer together at this time. The ten theses[1] shall be the starting point for the discussion. We are presumably included in the "fleshpots" of Adenauer.[2] But what kind of reproaches can be raised against our state and our society? In addition to this, the association would like to turn to a discussion of the question of Hungary.

Barth: is happy to hear that the commission does not expect a new speech from him, but rather intends to take up and continue the discussion from the summer semester. But whether this can become more concrete depends upon us. Barth himself is not a politician; therefore, he would like to be instructed by our thinking. Regarding Hungary, he would rather not speak. If it absolutely must be done, then perhaps at the close of the evening. More important is the question of our homeland.

Four Theses

1. The Swiss Commonwealth is neither *civitas Dei* nor *civitas diaboli*,[3] but rather a community tolerated and willed by God.

---

1. See above, chap. 2.
2. Cf. Karl Barth, *Brief an einen Pfarrer in der DDR* (Zollikon: Evangelischer Verlag, 1958), reprinted in *O.Br. 1945–1968*, 401–39; ET: K. Barth and J. Hamel, *How to Serve God in a Marxist Land* (New York: Association Press, 1959). There Barth quotes favorably (46) from the letter of the sender: "You fear in your own words, 'nothing more than a liberation according to Adenauer's ideas, which would lead us back to the fleshpots of Egypt.'"
3. In chap. 2 above, see n. 4.

2. The Christian is primarily a citizen of the kingdom of God, and secondarily a citizen of our state. As such, he must also witness to the kingdom of God.
3. [We must time and again] weigh the question [which form of the state is appropriate in relation to the kingdom of God] (see theses 7 and 8 of the last lecture [chap. 2 above]).
4. Decision for the more appropriate form of the state. In what does this decision consist for us Swiss citizens?

In greater detail:

1. Since the *individual person* as such is the being loved by God, a more just form of Switzerland would better respect the rights and dignity of the individual. Everyone for each one (mountain farmers, indentured children).[4] Today, however, the individual is run over, not so much by the state as much as by other interest groups, to which the state has surrendered the field. Here the state fails to act as an advocate for the individual person. In this respect, the Christian elects the more just form of the state. Pastoral care (care for the individual) must not be separated from politics.

2. Moreover, *the community* should have a greater profile. In the Christian view, the human does not exist alone; he can never be thought of without the "You." One for all! But genuine community! No abstractions! Cantons,[5] the people, the authorities, and so forth should be more genuine communities, not merely abstract subjects of politics, who muddle along with mutual compromises and do politics in this way.

3. The human exists just as little without co-humans as without the God who stands over him and to whom he is responsible. A more just state would not only care for a freedom that exists on paper. It would [also] make sure that the individual could use this freedom in responsibility before God [as freedom *for* . . .]. Today, however, the individual is at the mercy of such a variety of influences that he can no longer make responsible use of this freedom. At the least, the average person has no possibility of staying freed from these influences. Is equality ensured under such circumstances? Should the possibility not be offered to every person of fulfilling the duties entrusted to oneself? Even to the weak person of weak character, to the one less intellectually developed, even of a duty that is, quantitatively speaking, of no special consequence! Concretely: advertising, radio, the press, and so forth, should be reined in correspondingly. And in regard to equality: women must have equal rights.[6]

4. The *particularity* of the Swiss character must be accepted by us. But God guides not only Switzerland. God's goal is, in general terms, freedom, general

4. Children, e.g., orphans who were—until the recent past—given up as foster children to families who received money from the communal fund for the poor. These children were used mostly for hard work.
5. *Stände*, which in Swiss German is a synonym for cantons. The *Ständerat* is the smaller chamber of the Swiss Parliament in which every full canton is represented by two deputies; the half-cantons by one.
6. The right to vote and to stand as a candidate for election was first introduced for women on the cantonal level in Basel-Stadt in 1966, and on the level of the Swiss Confederation in 1971. In February 1959 its introduction had been declined by a vote of the people. An opinion of Barth's in advance of this vote is found in *O.Br. 1945–1968*, 459.

participation in duties and rights. An integration of Europe, to be sure, cannot come at the cost of our particularity! For the latter is given to us as a duty.

On several problems of Swiss politics:
Federalism: Indeed, we do exist in this form of the state in an exemplary fashion.
Democracy: As direct as possible—not as in the USA, Germany, England.
Parties: Politics should not essentially be done through parties.
Neutrality: We do not need to be ashamed. Mediation is also a historical task.
Aid: Especially aid to non-European peoples. Note Wahlen's proposal![7] [Helping] without egoism, despite the fact that we also deem it politically necessary to help others.

Discussion

Schniggel: How should we formulate the "freedom for"? (see responsibility before God [above]).

Dian: Every ideal must be expressed in normative form by the state. How can the demand for equality (cf. protection of the mentally or psychologically challenged from negative influences) and the demand for democracy be expressed as a norm?

Barth: All norms need to be applied. The norm must therefore be drawn up in such a way that individual cases can be handled according to it. Example: the English legal system. Moreover, the task of the state must be understood as far as possible to be merely educational: education for responsibility—only secondarily can there be a restriction of freedom.

[To Schniggel:] One day there might be an outbreak of revulsion in reaction to advertising. From this insight, a demand for laws to curb these excesses could arise. But they would have to be concrete!

Sim: Such curtailing of freedom will conjure up the danger of state interference.

Barth: [That] is possible. The danger of interference can come from the state and from all sides. In any case, [one must] watch out here.

Jobs: Is there any possibility of determining in principle (in our country) how far a civil right may be restricted without its actual content getting lost (e.g., freedom of the press)?

Barth: The question of the worker has not *in principle* been resolved (in our case) but through the gradual curtailment of the freedom of business and trade.[8] Although at that time everyone predicted the decline of freedom, this calamity did not occur.

---

7. *Bundesrat* [i.e., member of the Swiss national government, the Federal Council] Friedrich Traugott Wahlen (1899–1985; in office, 1959–65) on various occasions advocated the elimination of trade barriers in Europe and international cooperation for the prosperity of the nations.

8. Cf. the article "Right to Carry On a Trade [Gewerbefreiheit]" in *Schweizer Lexikon in sechs Bänden* (Lucerne: Verlag Schweizer Lexikon, 1992), 3:76: "It was the federal constitution of 1874 that first expressly guaranteed the freedom of trade and commerce. In 1894 industrial circles failed in their attempt to grant to the government the competence to enact unified regulations concerning the nature of trades. In the aftermath, the call for protectionist measures of all kinds led to an ever-wider granting

Jobs: [What you are saying about "freedom for" and the necessary curtailing of "freedom" for its own sake, that] does not seem to be a principled solution but rather a compromise.

Barth: In spite of that, it is not a compromise.

Dres: This "freedom for" is misused by non-Christians. [There must also be] spontaneous freedom.

Barth: What is that?

Dres: What should one say as a non-Christian [as one who does not recognize the presuppositions by which you speak of "freedom for"]? You have obviously not thought of such people!

Barth: If what we Christians regard as freedom is true, we take responsibility for it, even if others cry bloody murder!

Luzi: Is the ban of Communism in the Federal Republic of Germany[9] an instance of [Christian] "freedom for" [, according to which not everything is permitted)?

Barth: There is no [special] Communist anti-Christianity. In the East today, what is taking place is only what we in the West have already prepared long since. The antichrist is first of all among us. Our task is to do better!

Luzi: But what if I as a Christian come to the conclusion that Communism is not, according to your way of thinking, appropriate?

Barth: We have to struggle against Communism—but by becoming Christians.

Luzi (impatiently): Just the same, do we not have the right to forbid Communism?

Barth: No! Let us nonetheless be happy that there is no need for us to ban them.

Dian: And the ban of Communist teachers?[10]

Barth: That would have the consequence that Communist teachers would not come out. As clandestine Communists, they would cause even greater harm.

Dian: The harm is already great enough. Does the state not have the right to hold in check an enemy of its institutions, even if it concerns [institutions] that are irrelevant from the Christian point of view?

---

of competence to the government to enact economic policy measures. The high point of this development was reached in the economic crisis of the 1930s, when by means of urgent federal resolutions directly protective governmental measures in favor of specific branches were introduced. Following foreign precedent, cooperative models were developed, which shortly before the outbreak of World War II led to the draft of a constitutional article concerning the declaration of the generally binding nature of agreements within particular trade groups. Because of the outbreak of war, the bill never came to a vote. As part of the revision of the Federal Constitution's economic articles that barely passed in 1947, article 31bis stipulates that the Federal Government, if the collective interest justifies it, can enact regulations in order to preserve important branches of the economy whose existence is endangered or in order to foster the professional efficiency of the self-employed—if need be in deviation from the [principle of] freedom of trade and commerce."

9. Ban of the Communist Party of Germany by the Federal Constitutional Court [*Bundesverfassungsgericht*] on August 8, 1956.

10. The question of the tolerability of Communist teachers was a cantonal affair and may have been discussed against the backdrop of the Hungarian uprising of 1956. On the federal level, the directive to exclude "untrustworthy" civil servants, employees, and workers, and to scrutinize individuals' political trustworthiness existed as early as 1950. Cf. *Staatsschutz in der Schweiz*, ed. G. Kreis (Bern: Haupt, 1993), 304–33.

Barth: [I] don't know [of any institutions that would be irrelevant to Christians].

Saladin: Does the Christian not have to go to battle against the state within a totalitarian state?

Barth: Within the order in which he is located, he should of course take the necessary steps that correspond to his faith.

Schniggel: What does it mean to "collaborate" in a totalitarian state?

Barth: One [should] do one's best even there.

Saladin: Would the church not face any problems there?

Barth: Christians in the GDR have a wonderful opportunity to prove themselves. They are in the minority (and therefore free of false considerations). Students from East Germany who studied with Barth gladly returned there. Even with respect to Communism, Christianity has more staying power.

Saladin: Must we not [then] long for the circumstances of the GDR in our country?

Barth: No! [What is to be desired]—at best—[is that we look there] in order to see what Christianity looks like.

Schniggel: Let us return to Switzerland! Where do we find the right formulation [of what the state is to do]? Liberalism has certainly failed. What then?

Barth: It failed because it had a formal concept of freedom. With *that* freedom one could not have met the Communist danger, had it come in 1860 already. Let us be glad that we are better off [today at this point]. [We must] carry on from here!

Jobs: [Is there a] Christian politics?

Barth: No.

Schniggel: Is it [i.e., politics which calls itself Christian] not better than something different?

Barth: Where would that better thing be? No, [there are only Christians in politics. What the Christian must do in politics, how he has to vote or pick a party is,] in each case, [a] free and new decision, made in the context of parties but without a binding commitment to a party ideology. [A] state is [something and must always be something which is] living. No state-orthodoxy, please!

Fünfshilling: [What is the] place of the theologian in the army? Should he be a chaplain or not?

Barth: That depends upon the circumstances.

Schniggel: Please, Professor Barth, now talk about your opinion concerning Hungary.[11] (He agrees to [do so] after some murmuring.)

Barth: What is needed is an *understanding* of the political situation. At that time people in the West as well as in Switzerland did not want this. Instead, they organized "minutes of silence" and practiced with Molotov cocktails. It was a psychosis. What was the situation really like? The Western powers in Yalta agreed to a zone of influence for the Soviets.[12] Now they were suddenly crying for help, when the Soviets—partly also on the basis of Western radio broadcasts—must have feared losing their sphere of influence and thus

---

11. Schniggel is referring to the situation of the Hungarian uprising of October 1956.

12. A meeting of the USA, Great Britain, and the USSR (Roosevelt, Churchill, Stalin) in Yalta (Crimea) from February 4 to February 12, 1945. The documents of the conference were first published on February 17, 1956.

intervened with armed force. The atrocities [which were then taking place in Hungary] must be blamed on the Western powers, which first handed the Hungarians over to the Soviets [at Yalta], and then called on them to resist in [1956], without the intention of genuinely standing with the Hungarians.

The [former] Hungarian democracy must not be subsequently glorified.[13] Even in 1948, houses of worship were used for national demonstrations. The instigators (in the case of the uprising of 1956) were for the most part young people who gave spontaneous expression to their outrage [over blatant abuses]. They were not necessarily supporters of the West. In part they were even Horthy reactionaries.[14]

The worst thing is that we regularly protest when it costs nothing, when we don't have to help. In the [Second World] War the scene looked different. One treaded lightly [in our country] in order not to provoke the Germans. The same was true in the Abyssinian conflict:[15] [Had one protested,] one would have had to accept economic repercussions. Karl Barth will open his mouth when the Soviets are standing at Lake Constance. He will then [perhaps] be the only Swiss [who does so].

Schniggel: thanks the speaker for his words, especially for having disappointed us, should we have hoped that we would receive from him a prescription for all cases.

13. After the deposition of the Hungarian King Charles IV in 1921, the Regent (*Reichverweser*) Horthy (see n. 14) impeded the development of democracy. In the Hungarian republic, proclaimed on January 2, 1946, a politics of nationalization was inaugurated under President Zoltan Tildy, which switched to Communist rule in 1947–48.

14. From 1920 to 1944, Miklós Horthy (1868–1957), supreme commander of the Hungarian troops in World War I, led as Regent a dictatorial regime of nationalistic character in Hungary. In 1941 he joined Hitler's attack on the USSR. Arrested as a war criminal by the Western powers after the end of World War II, he was not handed over to the Hungarian government but was able to emigrate to Portugal in 1948. From there he offered his services to the uprising of 1956 in Hungary.

15. The annexation of Abyssinia (Ethiopia) by Italy in May 1936.

6. Conversations in Strasbourg
1959

Karl Barth was awarded an honorary doctorate from the University of Strasbourg on November 22, 1959. During his visit on that occasion, he took part in two discussions. On the prior evening, he discussed the announcement of the subsequent Second Vatican Council by Pope John XXIII and its attendant problems with a small circle of theologians, including A. Dumas, G. Casalis, and Y. Congar (cf. Lebenslauf, *456;* Biography, *440). On the next evening, a three-hour question-and-answer session took place with a circle of young people interested in theology, mentored by G. Casalis (cf. the letter of Ch. von Kirschbaum to G. Barczay, June 12, 1959, unpublished, in the Karl Barth Archives). Fifteen questions—eleven theological and four political in nature, on four sheets of ISO A4 [letter-size] paper—were directed beforehand for this purpose to Barth. The typewritten originals are preserved in the Karl Barth Archives. Otherwise, there are no known transcriptions of these discussions.*

7. Conversation with Prison Chaplains
1960

On his 74th birthday, May 10, 1960, Barth found himself traveling (from Frankfurt in the car of Basel prison chaplain Martin Schwarz), "this time on a hurried drive to Fulda—not as a pilgrim to the grave of St. Boniface . . . , but rather to a convention of German prison chaplains and social workers, who had invited me there for a discussion on the theological problems of this distinct line of work. . . . More than a short jaunt— although we allowed ourselves [on the return trip] to be seriously delayed in Würzburg by Tilman Riemenschneider—this trip, undertaken in the middle of a semester in full steam, could and should not have been."[1] Barth was invited there because since 1954 he served as a guest preacher and counselor in the Basel prison.[2] At the Fulda convention in the Protestant Center [named] Haus Oranien, Barth responded on the morning of May 11 to questions that had been presented beforehand to him by Pastor Dr. H. Kühler, Director of the Evangelische Konferenz für Straffälligenpflege [Evangelical Conference for the Care of Offenders]. Barth's response to the questions, which occurred with about two hundred participants present, constituted the conclusion of the annual meeting of that Conference for the Care of Offenders and simultaneously the opening of the annual meeting of the Conference of Evangelical Prison Chaplains.[3] The following documents are preserved from the conversation:

1. The aforementioned questions, typewritten, proposed by H. Kühler [Text 1].
2. The same questions, typewritten and duplicated, but (at Barth's request) in another sequence.
3. Six octavo leaves in typescript with theses of Barth in catchword form in response to the questions.
4. A typed and duplicated report put together from his notes by the secretary of the conference, Pastor G. Poelchau, at that time of Berlin-Moabit (cited in the following as Text 4).
5. Personal notes of the event by Pastor R. Pfisterer, published under the title, "Recht für den Menschen [Justice for Human Beings]" in Junge Kirche 21 (1960): 404–8.

---

1. From a duplicated circular letter of Barth dated May 15, 1960, to those who congratulated him on his 74th birthday (in the Karl Barth Archive).
2. On this topic, cf. M. Schwarz, *Karl Barth in der Strafanstalt: Bericht des evangelischen Strafanstaltspfarrers 1968* (Basel: Strafanstaltsdruckerei, 1968), 3–10; published again in *KBRS* 125 (1969): 210–13; idem, "Nachbemerkungen," in Karl Barth, *Den Gefangenen Befreiung! Predigten aus den Jahren 1954–59* (Zollikon: Evangelischer Verlag, 1959), 189–90; ET: *Deliverance to the Captives*, trans. M. Wieser (New York: Harper, 1961); published again in Karl Barth, *Predigten 1954–1967*, ed. Hinrich Stoevesandt (Zurich: Theologischer Verlag, 1979), 306.
3. Cf. G. Bartning, "'Es gibt keine hoffnungslosen Fälle—auch nicht unter Straffälligen!': Ein Tagungsbericht," in *Monatsschrift für Pastoraltheologie* 49 (1960): 355–60.

6. *Personal notes of the event, possibly prepared by Pastor G. Staewen, published under the title "Karl Barth und die Straffälligenpflege [Karl Barth and the Care of Prisoners]" in* Stimme der Gemeinde *12 (1960): 569–73[4] (cited in the following as Text 6).*

7. *A rendering by G. Deimling, at that time head teacher at the Wuppertal prison: "Gott hat jeden Menschen gerechtfertigt [God Has Justified Everyone]," in* Der Weg: Evangelisches Sonntagsblatt für das Rheinland, *1960, no. 25.*

8. *Two different audio recordings of the conversation have not been found as yet. However, a transcription put together in Berlin by an unknown hand from one of these recordings is extant. According to a communication from G. Poelchau to the editor, this recording was of very low quality, not only due to the rather poor recording technology, but also to adverse acoustical conditions in the auditorium. The transcription records occasional interjections such as "One doesn't understand a single word. This is really dreadful." In any case, this transcription—cited in the following as Text 8—is incomplete and of no use for the response to questions 4–7.*

In what follows, the theses and catchwords that Barth himself had noted down in preparation for the conversation are printed first (Text 3). Thereupon follows the transcription of the audio recording (Text 8) for the response to questions 1–3 and the questions from the closing discussion, and finally the minutes by G. Poelchau (Text 4) for the response to questions 4–7. Specifically in the rendering of these minutes, reference is made to noteworthy deviations and additions from the other documents mentioned.

A. Barth's Preparation for Question and Answers

I

1. It is possible, according to human knowledge and judgment, that there are ineradicable (i.e., conditioned by heredity, social milieu, constitution) pathological *dispositions* to certain *"crimes."*[5]

2. *Noncriminal* (less dangerous?) ineradicable dispositions (drive for power, egotism, theatricality, restlessness,[6] slothfulness)—everyone a "most unrepentant" one!—are suffered by *all*, even the "healthy humans," by us. . . .

3. *There* we have the crude, the obvious, *here* the creeping, latent manifestation and consequence of the *falling away* (from God, from one's fellow human being, from one's self) in which *every* human being, *all* of humanity, exists.

4. As participants in this falling away, *all human beings* would have to be *lost* "in all eternity."

5. *There is no divine predestination to falling away* and for its criminal or noncriminal manifestations and consequences.

6. But there is a divine predestination (= *Gnadenwahl* [election of grace]) *for deliverance* of all those most unrepentant beings who are lost in all eternity—

---

4. Reprinted under the title "Grundsatzfragen der Gefangenenseelsorge," in M. Schwarz, *Karl Barth in der Strafanstalt: Bericht des evangelischen Strafanstaltspfarrers 1968*, 11–18; and in *Zeitschrift für Strafvollzug* 18 (1969): 5–11, as well as under the title "Antworten auf Grundsatzfragen der Gefangenenseelsorge," in *Strafvollzug: Analysen und Alternativen*, ed. Ulfrid Kleinert (Munich and Mainz: Kaiser, 1972), 46–52.

5. The questions to which Barth's notes correspond are reprinted below in Part B, at the head of each of the corresponding conversation segments.

6. Barth uses the Bavarian expression *Gschaftelhuberei* here for "restlessness" or "hyperactivity."

resolved, realized, and revealed in J[esus] C[hrist], in whom God loved the fallen world, that is, reconciled it with himself—by siding with it in person—justified, sanctified, called it.

7. *Pastoral Care* (in general and for the "incorrigible") is the proclamation of *this* presupposition.

8. Its *presupposition*: [the] pastoral caregiver thinks and speaks as a *sinner*, lost without JC, in unconditional solidarity with *all* who are like him, [and] equally unconditionally from [the vantage point] of the divine *election of grace*, resolved, realized, and revealed in JC.

II

1. *Punishment* = a coercive measure taken by the civil community, required and ordered by its law, against one of its members found guilty of transgressing its law.

2. The *right* for taking such a measure is based on, delimited by, and determined by the task of *care* for the temporal life of all its members, allotted through the grace of God to the civil community: to be exercised by placing all of them under its law's protection, but also under its control.

3. The civil community is not a society of gods but of *humans*. The law governing its care is human law—human also in the form in which it requires and orders the coercive measure against its transgressors. Human is also the judgment of finding someone guilty of a transgression of its law. Finally, human also is the coercive measure to be taken against the transgressor, the punishment as such. Its *humanness* is at the same time its *limit* and its *destination*.

4. Taken and carried out as a humanly limited, but also destined *measure of care*—without any claim to be divine—even the *punishment* is fulfillment of the *task* assigned to the civil community through the *grace* of God.

5. As a *human* (not a divine!) measure of *care*, the punishment *cannot* be understood and carried out as *atonement*, that is, as reparation for the transgression that occurred by means of an *evil* to be inflicted on the transgressor.

6. The *purpose* and *goal* of the punishment as a human measure of care is at the same time the *proclamation* of the dignity of the law governing the civil community and the protection of its *other members* from the transgressor and his likes, *and* the protection of the transgressor from his own self, the prevention of further transgressions by him, his education toward understanding and respecting the law that protects and controls him also.

7. The task of *pastoral care* toward the punished: to make clear to him the meaning of his punishment not as a deserved evil but as a necessary measure *of care*, actually in his favor, and thus—here in this form!—as an expression of divine *grace* even for him.

8. Its *presupposition*: that the care provider acts as the advocate of this meaning of the punishment and its practical consequences perceptibly, unequivocally, and bindingly even in addressing the organs of the justice system who pronounce and carry out punishment, and [in dealing with] the general public.[7]

---

7. The four words "perceptibly, unequivocally, and bindingly" are a handwritten addition by Barth in the typescript.

III

1. [The] atoning death of J[esus] C[hrist] = the perfect reparation accomplished by God himself of the human transgression of *his* command—and therefore even more so of all human laws. "[The] b[lood] of J[esus] C[hrist] . . . makes us . . ." [1 John 1:7b]: Offering of h[is] life for suffering *the totality* of *all the evil* following *any* transgression.

2. Therefore all human transgression is transgression *forgiven* in JC (not transgression threatened by a corresponding evil). All reparations through compensation—possible anyway only for God—[are] obsolete in JC [and] forbidden as problematizing the action of God.

3. Understanding of punishment as *atonement [is] excluded.* To all transgressors of divine and human laws, only the *forgiveness* obtained in JC—to be grasped in *faith*—can be preached. Human *punishment* can be understood and carried out only as a measure of *care*, not as a compensational infliction of evil.

4. The *death penalty* [is] excluded because killing the transgressor may perhaps (?) be justified as proclamation of the dignity of the law, perhaps (?) as protection of the other members of society, but *not* as measure of *care* for the transgressor himself.

5. Death penalty for *high treason in case of war?* Supported in *CD* III/4[8] as

(a) a measure of combat (not punishment!) by the state in the abnormal situation of being at war: the traitor has acted as "enemy" [and] must bear the consequences.

(b) his death [is] better even for him, because his continued life in the midst of those betrayed by him [is] impossible ("care"?). Is war as such [still] justifiable? If not, then [this] argument is pointless.

IV

(Question [re] Law Go[s]p[el]—here posed as practical question of the pastoral care of the imprisoned, thus on the psy[chological]-pedag[ogical] level. Answer on the same level in the form of *counterquestions*.)

1. Assuming that [the] *CD*[9] is wrong—with *which law* does one try to awaken knowledge of sin? [the] Ten Commandments? natural law? categ[orical] imperative? *Volksnomos* [peoples' law]? a mixture? or indeed law of Christ?

2. How does one try to *give clout* to the law? *Which God* is called upon as its giver and guarantor: angry *Deus absc[onditus]* [hidden God]? or loving *Deus revel[atus]* [revealed God]?[10] or both alternating? or indeed unequivocally the God revealed in JC? Which *consequence* was announced for denying the acknowledgment of sin? Damnation and hell? or indeed the grace turned even toward the ungrateful, the grace that waits even for him?

3. Did this attempt succeed in leading a person *further* than into contrition and *past* the temptation of self-justification—as in *Luke 15*?[11]

---

8. *CD* III/4:448, §55.2 [*KD* 512–13].

9. Cf. esp. *CD* II/2:511–12, §36.1; and *CD* IV/1:363–67, §60.1 [*KD* II/2:566–67 and IV/1:401–2].

10. Martin Luther, *De servo arbitrio* (1525), WA 18.685–86; ET: *Bondage of the Will*, trans. E. G. Rupp, P. S. Watson, A. N. Marlow, and B. Drewery, *LW* 33 (Philadelphia: Fortress, 1972), 140, against Erasmus emphasized the necessity of distinguishing between the *Deus quatenus est praedicatus (revelatus)* [God as he is preached (revealed)] and the *Deus absconditus in maiestate* [God hidden in majesty].

11. The last three words are a handwritten addition in the typescript, entered by Barth.

4. Through the competent preaching of the gospel, of the cross of Christ, of the justifying, sanctifying, calling grace of God,
(a) are depressed people really made more depressed ("terrible" grace), and
(b) are frivolous people made yet more frivolous? ("cheap" grace)?[12]
5. If so, could the reason not be that the pastoral caregiver himself did not yet really understand and competently pursue the road from the gospel to the law, from the knowledge of Christ to the knowledge of sin?
6. Should it really be dangerous to address the inhabitants of the "penitentiary" (prisoners and personnel!) without reservation and hopefully as a *community of J[esus] C[hrist]* (of sinners, really lost but delivered and pardoned in him) and therefore with the *whole* gospel (inc[lusive] of its law)? Do we ourselves *believe* in the *gospel for us* when we withhold it from the "criminals"? "With you is forgiveness, that you may be feared" [Ps. 130:4]. Rhein[land] Catechism.[13]

V

1. In antiquity, were there actually prisons in our sense of penal institutions? Was there not just investigative imprisonment ending in death or release? or protective custody for unsentenced suspects, disgraced, dangerous persons?
2. If we should encounter "a prisoner for the faith": Why are you free to visit me as a pastoral caregiver? Why [are you] not my fellow prisoner?
3. [The] "reason for being in prison" [is] certainly important at the beginning, but scarcely for the duration of the (individual) pastoral care to the prisoner![14]

VI

[1.] The practical goal of the proclamation of the gospel in prison: the *punishment* as the given fact outwardly uniting all occupants of the house may and should be understood, administered, received (endured!) by all of them as a *measure of care*, not as atonement.
2. [That] means for the pastoral caregiver in relation to the *prisoners*: that he himself consistently sees, addresses, and deals with them as people punished *in this sense* (not as atoning!)—for whom JC has died and risen not in vain.
3. In relation to the *penal authorities and the prison staff*: that [the caregiver] has to promote among them fundamentally and practically the understanding and administration of punishment *in this sense*—that in any given case he has to intervene (if necessary against them) as caregiver (advocate!) for the prisoners.
4. "Tiresome 'miniwars' over individual issues"? For the prisoner, probably always a "great war"! In prison, the credibility of the proclamation of the gospel among authorities, staff, and [prisoners] (they are the main characters!)

---

12. The expression *schreckliche Gnade* [terrible grace] may have been coined by Barth in analogy to the term *billige Gnade* [cheap grace] used in question 4 (see below under "'Gospel and Law' in the Pastoral Care of Prisoners"), which goes back to Dietrich Bonhoeffer, *The Cost of Discipleship*, trans. R. H. Fuller and I. Booth (New York: Simon & Schuster, 1995). The book begins with the sentence "Cheap grace is the deadly enemy of our Church" (43).

13. Barth has added the psalm verse and the reference to the Rhenish Catechism by hand on the fourth of his preparatory leaves. On this catechism, see below, n. 35.

14. Handwritten addition of Barth at this place on the fifth leaf: "3. *Not* on account of faith? Then as the representative of a humanity that, according to [the word of] God, rejected JC [Jesus Christ] as a rebel and for which he died."

completely depends on the caregiver not avoiding this pleading for, or battle with, authorities and personnel—thus on his *fighting* the "miniwars."

B. Barth's Response to Questions in Fulda

Kühler:[15] It gives me special pleasure to be able to welcome Professor Barth of Basel. No words need to be wasted regarding his significance. It is all the more significant for us that recently a book of sermons that he preached in the Basel prison has been published.[16] That makes clear how much he has taken the prison work to his heart. I may therefore confidently welcome Professor Barth as one of us. In the church here and there the standpoint is encountered that certain persons, who are not suitable for radio sermons and as spa preachers, are still good enough for the prison, where there is nothing more to ruin anyway. On the contrary, it must be maintained that here is a calling worthy of the sweat of the noblest.[17]

Barth: Highly respected gathering, my dear brothers and sisters, I am grateful first of all for the friendly reception that you have accorded me here. I am happy to consider myself as one of you—but not in the sense as though I were an expert in the questions that occupy you here. The fact that I have delivered some sermons in the Basel prison and allowed them to be printed in no way entitles me to step up here as one who understands this matter better than you or even understands it equally well. Rather, what I can add to you here is actually only a little theology relative to the issue that concerns all of us here. And now, if I may, I will proceed immediately to answering those questions posed to me. You have them before you. It is probably not . . . well, it is perhaps good if I read the questions once more beforehand, so that, while listening, you can once more consider them. And then I will attempt to give an answer, point for point. So, the first question reads:

1. Predestination and "Ineradicable Dispositions"

Question 1: Is there a divine predetermination to a person becoming an incorrigible criminal, that is, a single human being who is lost in all eternity? And in this case, what is the meaning of the election of grace [Gnadenwahl] for the message addressed to the most unrepentant? What form should pastoral care then take? Where are its limits?

Barth: Let me try to answer by saying the following. If you would allow me, I'll take up the matter point for point, in a somewhat schoolmasterly fashion.

First: It is possible—we have to say, according to human knowledge and judgment—that there are ineradicable dispositions, pathological dispositions conditioned by heredity or the social milieu or the individual physical-psychological

---

15. The greeting by H. Kühler is reproduced from the minutes by G. Poelchau (Text 4). [Trans.: see introduction to chap. 7.]
16. K. Barth, *Den Gefangenen Befreiung!*, now contained in *Predigten 1954–1967* [ET: *Deliverance to the Captives*].
17. The expression "worthy of the sweat of the noblest" comes from the ode, "Der Zürchersee [Lake Zurich]," written in 1750 by Friedrich Gottlieb Klopstock.

constitution of a human being, toward specific crimes, that is, to actions or ways of acting that bring the affected person into more or less serious conflict with the law. I say, it is possible. One would probably have to be a physician, sociologist, and psychologist to give a definitive answer here [that] there is something like this. I do not presume to say [that] there is—and also not [that] there is not, but I only say, it is possible.

One thing is certain (*second* point): We all suffer from "ineradicable" dispositions—not directly toward a crime but to ways of conduct and action that at first sight may seem rather harmless but are perhaps of an even more dangerous kind. In one person it may be an ineradicable drive for power, in another an ineradicable egotism, in a third an ineradicable theatricality, in the fourth an ineradicable restlessness,[18] and in the fifth an ineradicable slothfulness. . . . I will not continue. But who of us does not carry some such ineradicable disposition in himself? And who of us would then not have to say, in my own way I am also a "most unrepentant" one—I!? Even the healthy humans, even we church functionaries, theologians, counselors, social workers! If someone could see, not only as we see each other here, but rather through and into us people, how many strange dispositions would perhaps become visible? And—I come back to the first point—what now is really more dangerous and worse: that pathological disposition that we know in our friends in prison also, or our own? That is an open question.

Third point: All right, now, how do these things relate one to the other? There we are probably dealing with the pathological dispositions and here with the healthy ones—both in quotation marks, so to speak; we are probably dealing there with the crude, the obvious [manifestations], the ones that then become a concern for society and definitely dangerous, and here, among the rest of us and in ourselves, with the creeping, the latent, and secretly perhaps all the more effective (I must now move into theology) consequences of the falling away in which we humans all exist: the falling away from God, which is always at the same time also a falling away from our fellow human being and at the same time, for us all, a falling away also from ourselves. All of us humans, the whole of humanity, exists in this falling away.

And therefore, *fourth:* "Lost in all eternity" (as it was formulated in the question), in all eternity all humans would have to be lost, [because] we all are participants in this falling away, even though we say, the one more seriously and the other not so seriously.

Point *five:* There is no divine predestination to falling away. One should never confuse such dispositions as have been mentioned above with divine predestination nor [confuse] the latter with the former. There is no divine predestination to falling away and for these criminal or noncriminal manifestations and consequences.

But there is, point *six*, a divine predestination: it is the predestination of the "election of grace" [*Gnadenwahl*], the word is mentioned in the question, the election of grace for the redemption of all who "are lost in all eternity." [This includes] the entirety of "all the most unrepentant," who we are, all of us, [experiencing] a divine predestination of the life of humans and of humanity,

18. See n. 6 above. Barth uses the same word here.

which is resolved, realized, and revealed in Jesus Christ, in whom God has loved not a pleasant world, but a very unpleasant one, not a good but an evil [world], [with] not one loving and praising [God], but he has loved a world that has indeed fallen away from him—which in this case means he has given himself for it [cf. Rom. 4:25; 8:32], has reconciled it with himself [cf. 2 Cor. 5:19], and in Jesus Christ has justified it before him, has sanctified and called to himself the world and every human being (really every human being!). All for the sake of his great love! Not because the world, not because any human being deserves it, but because this was and is God's kind, good will, and it will remain so!

Point *seven:* Task and limit of pastoral care—pastoral care, which is really a task that concerns all people, but now, that which is our special interest here, [concerns] those people more or less destined to be pathologically disposed and thus destined to walk on the road to crime. Pastoral care to them—what can that mean? I can generally—and I am being asked in general—only say: Pastoral care to all and especially to those people must under all circumstances be—speaking in old or new tongues to win ever anew, to recover, to bring ever anew before people (but [as] a truth that before all else we have to sow and receive *ourselves* ever anew!): the proclamation of this predestination, the proclamation of this divine grace itself. Therefore the limit of pastoral care, [the line] that one may not cross, where one must never arrive, will always be where we would cease to proclaim this election of God's grace in all its depth, in its whole power. Every step aside from this way would be false, and we would condemn ourselves thereby, if we would take such a step here.

Point *eight*, for a conclusion: The presupposition of such pastoral care, which consists under all circumstances in this proclamation, must be the unconditional solidarity of the pastoral caregiver with those to whom he is sent, for whom he is permitted to be there. His unconditional solidarity with them—namely, in two dimensions, I would say. First, it must [be clear]—this is the presupposition of any possible pastoral care—that I stand with my fellow human being unreservedly as a sinner who would be simply lost without Jesus Christ. And then second, that I stand with my fellow human being equally unreservedly, equally unconditionally, as with a human, concerning whom God in Jesus Christ did resolve, for whom God in Jesus Christ did accomplish and reveal what this word "election of grace" signifies: God's *free* choice. God chose grace, and God chose grace for all of us. These are, in general terms, the presuppositions; this is the one presupposition of possible pastoral care in the prison or in any noncriminal civil community.

This is what I wanted to say in relation to the first question. And now I may perhaps inquire whether the questioner is satisfied with this answer, whether what I have said can reassure and please him, or whether there is still something that should be explained. [. . .] We come to the second question. The first had its difficulty, but the second is perhaps even more difficult.

2. Care as the Purpose of Punishment

Question 2: What is the meaning and purpose of the punishment imposed by the secular judge, according to an evangelical understanding? A purely secular matter or also a divine one? Can the pastoral care of the imprisoned not take into account the respective sentence, and does it have to aim at the internal and faith-based acceptance of the measures of the secular penal system? But is not the divine forgiveness of sin rendered unbelievable if human penal practice is being sanctioned? That is, can nonforgiveness here on earth also be divine forgiveness? Is secular punishment also divine grace?

Barth: In order to understand each other here, we probably have to agree on what we mean when we speak of "punishment" in the sense that interests us here. May I propose the following definition[?] We understand punishment to be a coercive measure taken by the civil community, required and ordered by its laws, against one of its members found guilty of violating its laws. Let us see whether we get by with this. Once more I will highlight the individual parts of the definition.

Punishment is *[first]* a compulsory measure that is taken by the civil community or its representatives against one of the members of this society: against a member who is guilty of violating its law. The measure, the coercive measure taken by the civil community, however, is not taken arbitrarily, but it is required, and it is also ordered—namely, by the law of the civil community. That would be the first point on this matter: the definition.

On the *second* point: What right does the civil community have to take such a coercive measure (which we want to designate as punishment) against one of its members? The Christian-theological answer would have to be: the right for taking such a measure is based on, but also limited by and in its substance must be determined by the task allotted to the civil community by the special grace of God. The civil community has from God the task of *care*—may I for once define it in this way?—namely, the care for the daily life of all its members. It exercises this care by placing all of its members under the protection, which also means, however, under the control of its laws.

Third point: We have to consider that the civil community is not a community of gods but of *humans*. And that means: the law governing its care is a human law. It is human also in the form in which it requires and orders the coercive measure, that is, the punishment against its offender. Further: human is also the judgment that finds a particular person guilty of having violated the law. And finally: human also is the coercive measure, the punishment as such. And now I would say: yes, human . . . humanness is the limit, but humanness is also the destination of the punishment, of the coercive measure. [. . .]

Fourth point: As a humanly limited, which means not a divine but a human, all too human, yet also humanly determined and thus "human" measure of care—all without pretension to being divine, but also taken and carried out without any sinking down below the level of humanness—even the punishment is fulfillment: a fulfillment of the task assigned to the civil community by the grace of God. Even the punishment! Even this use of a coercive measure!

Fifth point: As a human and nondivine measure and now therefore as a measure of care, the punishment *cannot* under any circumstances be understood and carried out as *atonement*. Not as atonement, that is, not as restitution of the transgression that occurred by means of an evil now inflicted on the so-called criminal, the transgressor.

Rather—*sixth* point: The purpose and goal of the punishment as a human measure of care, which has nothing to do with atonement, is now at the same time (a) the stern proclamation of the dignity of the law that is in force in the civil community (that the dignity of the law is proclaimed when necessary is also a measure of care); further, (b) the punishment is a measure of care also in the sense that through it the other members of society who have not broken the law are protected, "secured," from the transgressors and people like them who may be in existence already or will be in the future. But now further, (c) the measure of care, as the coercive measure of the punishment, applies of course also and especially to the transgressor as such. The transgressor is first of all quite simply protected from himself, from further transgressions or at least some further transgressions. That belongs to this care for the transgressor. It does not begin first when he is released from prison; rather, by going to prison he comes into this care. [To this care also belongs] naturally his or her education—let me say at the outset: his education toward understanding and respecting the law that protects him (he too is under the protection of the law!) but controls him as well. In regard to the transgressor, education will have to mean, generally speaking, that he is being called to order through the punishment. And that is a beneficial thing. [However,] that has nothing to do with atonement and also nothing with restitution; rather, in it the punishment becomes visible to other people as well as to the criminal as an element of God's grace, which is directed to all.

Seventh point: I see the task of pastoral care toward the one being punished to be to make his punishment understandable to him, not as an evil inflicted on him, deserved by him, and therefore to be patiently endured, but rather as the necessary measure of care precisely for his own sake and then as a certainly very strange manifestation, yet [indeed] as a manifestation of the divine grace, which reaches out even to him, even in this form.

Eighth point: Once again the presupposition of pastoral care, now under this aspect! For the basic presupposition in this regard consists in this, that for his own person, but not only for himself, but also and decisively vis-à-vis the organs of the penal system, judicial and executive (down to the simple guards, the sergeants, and the overseers), and not only in addressing them, but also in addressing the general public, the pastoral caregiver acts as the unconditional advocate for this meaning of punishment as a measure of care and then, of course, for all practical consequences of this understanding of punishment, and that he does this perceptibly, unequivocally, and bindingly. A pastoral caregiver will never become credible, at least vis-à-vis the prisoner, if he does not insist on this cleanly and exactly and has completely ceased to work with the idea of atonement. This is my answer to question 2. May I ask, whether the questioner feels he has received some kind of answer or whether there is something I should add?

Jürgensmeyer: I believe we now still need to speak about whether the idea of atonement, which you have so categorically rejected, must really drop out completely. Is this something to reject, and does it come under your verdict that punishment is retribution? God is an avenger. He repays.

Barth: "Mine is the vengeance, I will repay" [Deut. 32:35; Rom. 12:19]. Yes, God!

Jürgensmeyer: Yes, he repays. And he delegates it also to the state [. . .]. The state [is] authorized [. . . so] that it can inflict an evil on the transgressor of the law. For punishment is simply an evil that relates in as just a balance as possible to the violation of the law. Only when we have clarified this, when we have made it clear, not only theoretically, but also to the prisoner, that he must humbly bow down under this [inflicted evil]—I would not call it atonement; for me the term atonement has a different content—only then can we come to all [the conclusions] to which you lead us, Herr Professor. And I go there with you. However, I would not let myself to be talked out of this presupposition so easily that punishment is a retribution, and that on account of God.

Barth: Is there someone in the gathering who wants to help me?

Participant I: [I must concur with Karl Barth in this], the judge in a criminal court is undoubtedly forbidden to execute inappropriate vengeance. That is off-limits for the judge. However, when he judges, he should certainly pose the question of justice. Whether one puts that under the concept of atonement is yet another question: whether what happens for the sake of justice would then have to be understood under the concept of atonement. But I find, [. . .] the following would be the central question, which I would have to pose: what is the relation of this [pastoral] care to the question of justice as the measure of any form of punishment to be imposed?

Barth: My answer will be: the just[19] punishment is the one that is a measure of care in the most inclusive sense of the term. I have [actually] not only said, care for the prisoner or the criminal; I rather said, care for all members of the community. Let us be clear: the law must be upheld. The community must be protected. However, now even the criminal himself should be protected from himself. And a punishment is therefore at the same time just punishment to the extent that it fulfills these postulates. I did not to want to introduce the concept of justice here because it was not mentioned in the question. But in this sense, I am happy to take it up.

Participant II: May I offer a little help from the perspective of anthropology, also in support of Herr Professor Karl Barth? The difference between the criminal and the citizen is not so great, really. For what we call criminal, what the jurist defines sometimes as the criminal propensity, is indeed no peculiar, special productivity of a human being but its very contrary: a defective condition, a weakness, nothing more than that.

Participant III: [. . .] I believe, one presupposition [of the fact] that there is resistance to the notion of punishment as a measure of care is this, that most people have a strong preconception of the relation of care to justice, punishment, and atonement. In discussions by jurists, it has often been said that criminal law should not sink down to become a law of care. This term "sink down" already shows quite clearly that one applies a certain value system and believes punishment to be more than care. Of course, if one starts from this presupposition, one can certainly come to the conclusion that what has been said is a "sinking down." But I believe that, especially [if one argues] from theology, one must arrive at the [point] that care is more than punishment and that the higher justice lies not in the atonement, but in the care.

Barth: I hope you have understood that I am really not interested in allowing the concept of punishment to sink down but on the contrary to lift it up.

---

19. Text 4 reads: "most just."

Namely, if one grasps the fundamental point: as an action of the state in executing its divine mandate, even punishment is a proof [and] a manifestation of divine grace, then I arrive at the concept of care and must put what the justice of punishment is as well as, of course, everything that has to do with its execution under the standard: is it care, understood in the most comprehensive sense of the term? Care is a *human* task in the best sense. We humans can do it, and we also should do it. On the other hand, atonement, retribution—that cannot be our thing. That is God's work. And we have the task to do the other. We will come back to this when we take up question 4.

Participant IV: I cannot agree with what was just being said: atonement is a divine measure, a divine action. Once Augustine said, one should let criminals leave prison, so that they can atone in freedom.[20] I do not believe that we today can project that into our present. But the idea is still correct that atonement is a personal and free power of the human who owns up to his guilt. Atonement is something the human can and should do by himself—in the free moral decision—saying yes to his own guilt.

Barth: But, excuse me, we still must understand: atonement is a reparation; atonement is not only the recognition of sin: it is more than that. And there I do fear that Father Augustine was just catholic. Tell me, sir, in which evangelically possible sense can one say that the human person can atone!?

Participant V: Aren't you now carrying our confessional differences into the fourth century? Today they are not the same as then.[21]

Barth: Yes, I have already heard talk on this. All right, then, I don't want to emphasize the word "catholic." I only want to say, when Augustine said the human himself should atone in freedom, he was thinking along the line that the human—of course, empowered by God's grace—is himself in the position to repair what he has done wrong. And now, I do not think that that is an idea which is tenable before the gospel.—Perhaps we want to move on to the third question, because this whole issue of the atonement comes up once more there—in fact, the theological argument for what I have now first presupposed negatively: absolutely not atonement! For the moment I must stick to it: Absolutely not! Under no circumstances! Let us totally get rid of that concept of atonement and replace it with the concept of care!

3. Meaning and Problem of Atonement

Question 3: What significance does the atoning death of Jesus Christ have for secular penal law or for the secular forms of punishment? Does this death exclude the death penalty once and for all? And why this and not all other punishments as well? Why the exception in the case of high treason?

Barth: All right, here we have a long way ahead of us. I must or I may begin with what is decisive. *First:* The atoning death of Christ . . . is the one reparation

---

20. Cf. F. A. K. Strauss, *Im Kerker vor und nach Christus: Schatten und Licht aus dem profanen und kirchlichen Cultur- und Rechtsleben vergangener Zeiten; in drei Büchern* (Leipzig: Mohr, 1895), 120. Cf. Augustine, *Ep. 153.6 ad Macedonium*, in PL 33, col. 655: "Once we have freed certain condemned criminals from the hands of your punishing [secular] justice, we still separate them from the fellowship of the altar so that by undergoing [ecclesiastical] penance they make expiation to him whom through their sin they had scorned, punishing themselves" [ET in *Augustine: Political Writings*, ed. E. M. Atkins and R. J. Dodaro (Cambridge: Cambridge University Press, 2001), 74.

21. This comment is inserted from Text 4.

of all human transgressions that is only possible for God, yet accomplished by God himself, perfect, sufficient for all times and for all people—[reparation] of the human transgression of his command and, one should think, this inference from greater to lesser is valid [and] therefore even more so of the transgression also of all *human* law. "The blood of Jesus Christ makes us pure from all sin" [1 John 1:7b]—that is, in the offering of his life a removal occurred, an annulment of evil entirely, of all evils that could and should correspond to the human transgression. He has actually given satisfaction for all of us so that nothing is left for us to do in terms of satisfying once again and making reparation. Rather, what is to be repaired in the restitution and renewal of human life, which has been destroyed by the falling away of the human, has happened in him.

Inasmuch as this is so, one now has to say—*second*—in Jesus Christ all human transgression is *forgiven* transgression. And "forgiven" means not still threatened again by corresponding evils, not again placed under the law: Can reparation be made? Shouldn't there be compensation?[22] The whole idea of a reparation—I still believe this is what one must understand atonement to be!—because it is something only possible for God, yet God has accomplished it—must be regarded as a possibility that is superseded in every regard by Jesus Christ. And if we—and that is the reason why one has to be a little harsh here—now again would want to come and say, well yes, atoning still must be done, then this is actually an insult to the honor of God. In this way we problematize what God has made well. We doubt [it] for we are in fact suggesting, This is not sufficient, and now a little atoning is still necessary. We should keep our hands off this!

Third point: Thus the understanding of punishment as atonement is excluded. What is to be proclaimed to all transgressors of divine law and human laws is only the sin *forgiven* in Jesus Christ. We will still come back to the problem that has already been mentioned here this morning. "With you is *forgiveness*, that you may be *feared*" [Ps. 130:4]. But *forgiven* sins and *not* unforgiven sins! And anything that then is to be said about "fear" and new life and new obedience can positively be said only from there. To all transgressors forgiveness is to be proclaimed, a forgiveness that they may and should grasp in faith. Whereas that which now happens as human punishment, what the community takes upon itself by daring to subject a person to this coercive measure, that can—I always mean it in a Christian sense, from [the vantage point of] the gospel!—only be understood as a measure of care, not as a compensating infliction of evils, and it can also only be carried out accordingly. Keeping it in-house—we are now speaking here with each other as Christians, aren't we?—we would like to understand what the situation is as seen from the [vantage point of the] gospel. How the authorities [see it], who [. . .] think about this from the perspective of the state, is first of all up to them. But when they ask us, What have you as Christians to say to this?, then, I think, we must unequivocally give *the* answer, and then watch what they do with it and whether they want to listen to us. But our trumpet must give a clear sound here [cf. 1 Cor. 14:8]. And I believe that even the jurists and the politicians will prefer it when they hear from the church a clear response—and then precisely *this* clear response: not atonement, but care!

22. "Compensation" according to Text 4.

I come to the *fourth* point: now the problem of the death penalty is being strongly set before us. All right, on the basis of our presuppositions, inasmuch as I might be able to say [that] we have established presuppositions here, the death penalty is simply excluded because the killing of the criminal might perhaps—but even this just perhaps; many question marks would have to be added—be a proclamation of the dignity of the law. I don't believe it, but—perhaps, who knows. And second, perhaps the death penalty might make sense as protection of the other members of society. Perhaps!—I don't trust that story, whether this is a secure protection even just of society. But one thing is absolutely certain: . . . the death penalty cannot be understood as a measure of care for the punished, the transgressor. And now, since everything depends on *this*, I would say: Fundamentally, one can only say No to the death penalty because it is shipwrecked on this matter of the concept of care.

Now I come to a difficult point; I must not evade it, and still it frightens me a little. To name it: I am being asked now about the situation concerning the death penalty for high treason in the case of war. I am in a quandary there because in my *Church Dogmatics*, volume III/4, I myself made an exception at this point.[23] The questioner has probably raised this issue here not without cunning. Now, I must on the one hand attempt to explain myself briefly, and then on the other hand also say that today I perhaps would no longer write what I have written there. But let me explain to you first how I meant it at that time. It was written rather soon after the end of the Second World War,[24] under the impression of a string of some twenty serious cases of high treason that occurred among us in Switzerland; in most cases they resulted in the death penalty.[25] It is never good for a theologian to allow himself to be impressed by historical circumstances. And I got myself a little bit into a trap there in that I thought I could write dogmatics or ethics on the basis of the present time. One should never do that.

But now, watch out! I want to tell you—for those who are not aware of it— how I justified it there. In reality, it was not at all my intention to qualify the death penalty for high treason in time of war as punishment, not as that which we here have called punishment, but rather as a fighting measure of the state in dire straits, in a wholly abnormal situation, namely, the abnormal situation of war. With what he did, the traitor has placed himself on the side of the enemy and has taken the risk: as one shoots at the enemy, so one now also shoots at him. He knew that this was coming. He must bear the consequences. He is now being fought by his own state. Punishment? Strictly speaking, this is not really punishment. In war one does not punish the foe but treats him as a foe. Think about it—does this make sense to you? Well, *to me* it does not make full sense anymore![26]

23. See n. 8 above.

24. The volume appeared in 1951; its material was delivered in lectures from the winter semester 1949/50 to the winter semester 1950/51.

25. The death penalty for high treason was for the most part carried out in the case of practically unimportant collaborators. Incidentally, K. Barth regarded the official politics of the Swiss Federal Council during the time of Hitler, "its position notoriously reached under foreign pressure . . . together with certain revolting injustices in the treatment of foreign refugees and internees, as the real dishonor inflicted upon the Swiss name at that time" (K. Barth, *Eine Schweizer Stimme: 1938–1945* (Zollikon: Evangelischer Verlag, 1945; Zurich: Theologischer Verlag, 1985), 10.

26. Possibly Barth's criticism of this argument belongs also in the context of his criticism of a deficiency in his comments in *CD* III/4 that he identified in his conversation with the *Kirchliche Bruderschaft*

My second argument was then that one perhaps may say that for the traitor in wartime—where he has acted in a way that he put thousands, perhaps tens of thousands of his compatriots, into danger of losing their lives, perhaps out of totally base motives—it is indeed a good thing when he is being destroyed. For his existence among his people really has become an inherent impossibility. And this is also the way one can justify it vis-à-vis the traitor himself, the death penalty, let us say his shooting. That was my second argument. You can ponder yourselves whether it convinces you. To *me* it is no longer completely convincing.[27]

And why not? Indeed, because meanwhile war itself and as such has become so problematic through that which we have witnessed since then, through the light into which war has moved: through the problem of the atomic bomb, so that the presupposition of the whole thing is falling down or appears to be falling down. Everything one still may have been able to say in favor of war up till now—and in an almost suffocated voice I still said some things in that volume [CD] III/4[28] that could perhaps still be said for the necessity of war, that one cannot totally reject it, but when it comes to atomic war, then that's the end. Then each argument in favor of war is meaningless. For atomic warfare cancels the presuppositions of war, namely, that the intention is to protect one's homeland. With every such action one destroys not only the enemy, but also oneself. Atomic war is universal suicide. If that is true, then there really cannot be war any longer. There must be no war anymore. And then there is no longer a death penalty for high treason. The whole thing collapses in itself. Perhaps, if I had reflected more thoroughly at that time already, not only on the situation of Switzerland in case of war—that is where I came from—but rather on Hiroshima,[29] then I would not have written those pages or would have written them in a completely different way. You see, even as a theologian one can come into a situation where under specific circumstances one must confess a frank "*Pater, peccavi* [Father, I have sinned]."[30] Let this be done herewith. Now, that is what I have to say concerning the third question.

All right, do we want now to take up once again that whole matter of atonement? I do not see it as [legitimated] from [the vantage point] of the death of Christ. Has it become clear to you that one cannot grab again for oneself what Christ has done for us and do it over, as if he had not died for all humans and one could play atonement tricks once again?

Question: That would mean, wouldn't it, that punishment as atonement is altogether impossible and that punishment is only valid as a measure of care?

Barth: Yes, absolutely.

[Church Brotherhood] *in Württemberg* (= *Gespräche 1963*, no. 11). In section 4 of this conversation ("The Problem of the Just War") he finds fault with [the fact] that, in the respective passage in CD III/4 concerning the question of the "just war," he did not treat the problem of the *way* of conducting a war: "such and such a thing must not happen even in war, e.g. to kill prisoners."

27. Yet Barth had already in CD III/4:441, §55.2 [KD 505] remarked in regard to the argument that the death penalty could be an act of compassionate kindness: "But what are we really doing when we commend a man to God and yet abandon him as hopeless from the human standpoint? The goodness of God is still addressed to him, but the fact that others cannot cut him off from it surely does not excuse the unfaithfulness of which they are guilty in relation to him."

28. CD III/4:461–65, §55.2 [KD 528–34].

29. The American drop of an atomic bomb on Hiroshima on August 6, 1945.

30. Luke 15:18, 21 Vulgate.

Rohlfs: Still on the question of reparations. It is clear that from [the vantage point of] the gospel I cannot say, I want to make reparation through my punishment. But as Zacchaeus says after forgiveness was declared to him, "To those whom I have defrauded I want to restore something" [cf. Luke 19:8], should we not in the same way rejoice if one of our inmates says, To the woman whom I have robbed of so and so much, I want to give this back now afterward through honest work? Would this not show that he has taken God's forgiveness really seriously? And shouldn't it be the goal of our pastoral care to help the person to the point that he comes forward with this echo of forgiveness himself if possible? We speak all the time [merely] of reparation. Perhaps it would be more appropriate if we had two concepts: reparation—I mean, seen theologically— reparation over there as atonement, but here as echo. Would that we had two different words for that!

Barth: Good! I have no problem saying "Yes" to this. But this then has nothing more to do with punishment, right? Zacchaeus offered it of his own, and Jesus did not say "Yes" and "No," [but] let it happen. That is certainly fine. And if a criminal now does something similar, so much the better. However, it cannot be the meaning of punishment that he should be expected to deliver some reparation. And when he acts this way, he himself will be the last one to think: well then, by this I now have atoned! *That* is not atonement. You said "echo" . . . ! I could agree with that. It means [that] he does not want to duplicate the original voice but wants to [do something] just as a rock sends back a small sound. That is nice. But it is not atonement. In this case we are quite in agreement.

Comment (of a judge): I would not say anything if I did not have the impression that the question which found expression here is a common one. Our conversation is preburdened by the use of certain concepts that indeed in themselves are as problematic as the concept of "atonement." I attempt to address the issue that is at stake. You mention, Herr Professor, for instance in the doctrine of God, the opposition between righteousness and mercy.[31] The judge, who in no way claims to carry out the judgment of God in the Fulda District Court, experiences in his concrete action the contradiction between justice and compassion as an antinomy that cannot be balanced so easily, but in which the proper weight of justice, which also leads to an evil, must have its say together with the dignity and in the form of the law. And for this inner weight it is necessary that the problematic concept of atonement, be it adequate or inadequate, [. . . not be relinquished]. In its essential content it is meant to express that the evil we impose has indeed a certain weight of its own, which must be received and must be assumed by us, [and] we may expect an acceptance of that by the sentenced person. This side of the issue . . . is not the only one, and the standard of justice that is required of us as judges has in a definite sense its contour and its significance and dissolves [in your argument] into a certain one-sided expediency. Thus the antinomy of justice and compassion, it seems to me, is not maintained in your conception.

Barth: Well, I believe I am still being misunderstood if it is said that the severity, so to speak, the justice, receives short shrift; that it is dissolved, so to speak, in a great stream of love. I must repeat time and again: when I want the

---

31. *CD* II/1:368–406, §30.2, esp. 375–77 [*KD* 413–57, esp. 422–23].

whole issue placed under the concept of "care," it is also a matter of the dignity of the law. And what is at stake is also, of course, the protection of society. Now surely it is a foregone conclusion that these two first elements remain in force as well, that this care for the person concerned, the punished transgressor, is at the same time an evil. There is no question that nobody likes going to jail. And he will certainly have to suffer. What I wish to see avoided is only that this infliction of an evil is, so to speak, incorporated into the concept of the meaning of punishment. I do not quite see why even the judge could not readily embrace this concept of punishment. And as to what concerns the theological background, the relation between justice and compassion, it seems to me that in the relevant volume there [in the *CD*][32] I do not retreat a single inch. In the doctrine of God my attempt was to show that the justice of God is a compassionate justice. Nothing is softened here and nothing is blurred, so to speak. When it comes to these two concepts, "justice" and "compassion"—instead of saying, There is a "tension" (that is the popular term, isn't it?); they are opposed!, one of them should interpret the other.

Kühler: I believe it would give Professor Barth no greater joy than that the conversation continue in this way. He likes nothing better than that people speak with one another in this way. But now first a pause of ten minutes!

Barth: That is good.

4. *"Gospel and Law" in the Pastoral Care of Prisoners*

Question 4: The CD rejects the possibility of the knowledge of sin through the law. But is not the proclamation of the gospel precisely before prison inmates easily misunderstood as cheap grace? Does the interweaving and the simultaneity of the knowledge of Christ and the knowledge of sin in the proclamation not make the depressed still more depressed and the preaching of the gospel that all guilt is forgiven the frivolous still more frivolous?

Barth:[33] The question of "gospel and law" has indeed played a very large role for me in my theological work.[34] Here, however, this question is posed as a practical question of pastoral care for the imprisoned, therefore so to speak on the psychological-pedagogical level. I want to answer it on the same level. Admittedly, much must remain unsaid. What is meant in the *Church Dogmatics*? My concern was to be in step with the truth of which Psalm 130:4 speaks: "With you is *forgiveness*, that you may be *feared*." Here I can point to something recent: the Evangelische Kirche im Rheinland [Protestant church in the Rhineland] intends to publish a new catechism. In it one reads: "God wills that we be obedient to him and that we praise him with our whole life. . . ."[35] I can

32. See ibid.
33. The text in the following sections is taken from the less literal and detailed minutes of G. Poelchau (Text 4).
34. K. Barth, *Evangelium und Gesetz*, ThExh 32 (Munich: Kaiser, 1935). Cf. also n. 9 above. In addition, H. Gollwitzer, "Zur Einheit von Gesetz und Evangelium," in *Antwort: Festschrift zum 70. Geburtstag von Karl Barth* (Zollikon: Evangelischer Verlag, 1956), 287–309; G. Wingren, "Evangelium und Gesetz," in ibid., 310–22; E. Schlink, "Gesetz und Paraklese," in ibid., 323–35. Further, H. J. Iwand, *Gesetz und Evangelium*, ed. W. Kreck, Nachgelassene Werke 4 (Munich: Kaiser, 1964).
35. *Evangelischer Katechismus: Entwurf des Katechismusausschusses der Evangelischen Kirche im Rheinland* (Düsseldorf: Katechismusausschuss der Evangelischen Kirche im Rheinland, 1960), 11: "In this Word, God proclaims to us his command. God wills that we be obedient to him and praise his goodness with our whole life."

underline every sentence here. What this booklet contains is also the teaching of the *Church Dogmatics*. To the person who posed to me the question on the relationship of "gospel and law," I would like to answer in the form of some *counterquestions*.

First: Suppose the *Church Dogmatics*, and also Psalm 130 and this new catechism of the Rhineland church are in the wrong: with which law then do you want to attempt to awaken knowledge of sin? Which law could do that? the "Ten Commandments" [Exod. 20:2–17]? "natural law"?[36] Immanuel Kant's categorical imperative[37] or Fichte's "Instruction for a Blessed Life"[38] or the "*Volksnomos* [people's law]" of 1933[39] (which now has suddenly disappeared again from German territory!) or a mixture of all of them? Or perhaps yet indeed the "law of Christ" [1 Cor. 9:21; Gal. 6:2]? Then we would be in agreement. This is what awakens knowledge of sin [cf. Rom. 3:20].

Second: On the basis of your concept of law, how do you give clout to the demands of the law? Which God is addressed as the giver and guarantor of the law? Is it the angry *Deus absconditus* [hidden God]? Or is it the loving *Deus revelatus* [God revealed] in Jesus Christ?[40] Or is it alternately the one and the other? And further, what consequences do you set before the eyes of people and suggest to them if they refuse the knowledge of sin? Damnation and hell—or yet indeed the grace turned even toward the ungrateful, the grace that waits for him also? Will you display an ugly face when someone resists? Or will you lead the resister who does not want to acknowledge the law and whom you want to guide to the knowledge of sin, to the divine grace?

Third: How did you fare when you tried it with a law different from the law of Christ? Did you succeed to lead a person *further* than into contrition, *past* the temptation of self-justification? The type of the imprisoned Pharisee is certainly not only present in the Basel prison. Did you succeed to lead a person to that of which Luke 15 is speaking?

Fourth: Has it ever happened that through a competent proclamation of the gospel based on Scripture, through a genuine proclamation of the cross of Christ, through the proclamation of the justifying, sanctifying, and calling grace of God present and effective in Jesus Christ, the depressed have become more depressed? In that case, grace would be "terrible grace"! Or that the frivolous have become yet more frivolous? In that event the grace of God would

---

36. Old Protestant Orthodoxy developed the doctrine of a *lex naturalis* [natural law] or *naturae* [of nature] according to which the divine law was implanted in man before the fall in his nature and according to which that law continued to be preserved for him in some (more or less) limited measure even after the fall. Cf. HpB 233 [ET: RD 292]; SchmP 327 [ET: SchmHJ 512–13].

37. I. Kant, *Kritik der reinen Vernunft* (1788), §7 [ET: *Critique of Practical Reason*, trans. and ed. M. Gregor (Cambridge: Cambridge University Press, 1997), §7: "Fundamental Law of Pure Practical Reason: So act that the maxim of your will could always hold at the same time as a principle in a giving of universal law" (28); I. Kant, *Grundlegung der Metaphysik der Sitten* (1785) [ET: *Groundwork of the Metaphysic of Morals*, trans. H. J. Paton (New York: Harper & Row, 1964), §52]: "There is therefore only a single categorical imperative and it is this: 'Act only on that maxim through which you can at the same time will that it should become a universal law.'"

38. J. G. Fichte, *Die Anweisung zum seligen Leben* (1806; reprint, Leipzig: Eckhardt, 1910) [ET: *Characteristics of the Present Age: The Way towards the Blessed Life, or, The Doctrine of Religion*, trans. W. Smith, 4th ed. (London: Trübner, 1889; reprint, Washington, DC: University Publications of America, 1977).

39. Cf. W. Tilgner, *Volksnomostheologie und Schöpfungsglaube: Ein Beitrag zur Geschichte des Kirchenkampfes*, AGK 16 (Göttingen: Vandenhoeck & Ruprecht, 1966). For critical remarks on this topic, see *CD* III/4:307–9, §54.3 [*KD* 348–49].

40. See n. 10 above.

indeed be "cheap grace"![41] But has a genuine proclamation actually ever had this result?

Fifth: If this should really have happened, could the reason not be that the pastoral caregiver himself did not yet understand the road and the slope from forgiveness to fear, from gospel to law, from the proclamation of Christ to the knowledge of sin? Perhaps he has also traveled too heavily on the Lutheran track so that the poor prisoner could not grasp the call to repentance? Perhaps it could also be a consequence of spiritual sloth or a result of [the fact] that he has received the gospel only with [the] head, but not into the heart. It must go through the heart, otherwise it does not go at all. Otherwise it doesn't surprise me if the depressed become yet more depressed, the frivolous yet more frivolous.[42]

Sixth: To all who are afraid of the sequence gospel–law and want to reverse it: Should it really be dangerous to regard and understand the inhabitants of the penitentiary unconditionally and hopefully as the community of Jesus Christ? Prisoners as well as the prison staff! The prison community is a community of Jesus Christ to whom we have to preach. The congregation is [always] an assembly of people who are lost and condemned but in Jesus Christ are pardoned and redeemed.[43] Something has called the prisoners to the church service, and it is not "dangerous" to address them as a community and to speak to them with the whole gospel—including the healing, ordering, caring law of God. If we consider that to be dangerous, how does our own faith in the gospel fare? Don't we live by entrusting ourselves to this gospel? Are we allowed to deny or withhold from the "criminals" that which we live by ourselves?

5. On the Praxis of Pastoral Care to the Imprisoned

Question 5: Does the church's contemporary pastoral and social care for prisoners, which mainly has to do with criminals, occur in situations essentially different from what is presupposed in the majority of the biblical texts that talk about being in prison for the sake of faith and about martyrdom? Does the specific reason for imprisonment make no difference for the mode of proclamation to inmates?

Barth: To this question I can only speak briefly. Up until now I have not given myself much of an account of what the prison situation was in antiquity and how prisons at that time relate to prisons in our modern time. In antiquity, were there actually prisons in our sense of penal institutions already? Apparently not. Presumably there was at that time only some kind of investigative imprisonment, in which one would be held until execution or release occurred. Presumably there was also a sort of protective detention of unsentenced suspects, disgraced, dangerous persons.[44] When we compare our contemporary

---

41. See n. 12 above for background of "terrible grace" and "cheap grace."

42. The last sentence is here introduced from Text 6.

43. Here Text 6 has the following sentence: "Is then the community of Jesus Christ something other than such a community in the prison, 'lost, condemned, but through Jesus Christ redeemed and pardoned'?"

44. Cf. P. Pollitz, *Strafe und Verbrechen: Geschichte und Organisation des Gefängniswesens* (Leipzig: Teubner, 1910), 4: "The penal legislation of ancient times knew only physical and financial punishments; the former was at times executed as the death penalty, at times as mutilation, the latter as compensation for past wrongdoing. . . . He who could not pay the compensation would be sold into servitude

prisons with the "prisons" of antiquity, we are likely dealing with a different, changed institution.

But if today there should be "prisoners for the sake of the faith" once again, what would be the situation for us prison chaplains when one such prisoner meets us in prison? Wouldn't we then be asked: why do you run around free and aren't also locked up?[45] Why aren't you my fellow prisoner?

If the ones with whom we today usually have to do in prisons are not there for the sake of faith and also not martyrs, at any rate they are representatives of a humanity that rejects the word of God. In their case, this rejection has manifested itself in this particular form; among us it has not.[46] They have done something that has marked them as sharing the state of enemies of God. At the same time, it must not be forgotten that they are simultaneously also representatives of the humanity for whom God intervened in Jesus Christ. We must address them on the basis of their lostness as well as their deliverance.

Certainly one also has to speak with the prisoners about the particular, concrete reason for their imprisonment—but probably only at the start of their detention. However, it is hardly important in the long run for the pastoral care of the prisoner. Rather, he has to be distracted [from this topic] soon. And in any case, one must always accept him as a *whole* human being. The prisoner is not only a criminal but also a human being. The best start for the pastoral care conversation is from the level of being human (family, domestic relations, etc.).[47]

Question 6: Does the task and responsibility of the pastor and caregiver extend into the affairs inside the penal system, including relations to the prison staff and the higher authorities in law enforcement? Does our professional status commit us to silence for reasons of our cohumanity, or shall we make an effort to attend to the redress of grievances, to influence humane resocialization efforts of the modern instruments of jurisdiction, to collaborate in matters of legal pardons, in short, to fight a tiresome miniwar over individual issues?

Barth: We already spoke of a practical goal for proclaiming the gospel in the prison. For one of its practical goals is to make the punishment clear as the experience that unites all inhabitants of the prison house outwardly and now may be and should be understood by all as that which it is: a measure of care. It should be carried out, received, experienced, and endured as such a care. That is also one (not the only!) goal of the pastoral care of prisoners.

That this is also a practical goal means, for the pastoral caregiver in his relationship to the prisoners, that he is with them not only as caring for them "pastorally," using a number of techniques, professional tools, and tricks, but that he rather fundamentally and consistently sees, addresses, and treats them as

---

or slavery or employed in public works (this among the Romans and the Germanic tribes). . . . The dungeon, however, is not unknown even in the older penal system, but in principle it served only for the detention of the defendant until his sentencing."

45. Perhaps Barth here alludes to an anecdote, which is passed down from M. Niemöller's pretrial custody in 1937: A prison chaplain asked him, "But Brother! What brings *you* here? Why are you in prison?" To which Niemöller replied, visibly angered by the thought of the large number of pastors imprisoned like him: "And Brother, why are you *not* in prison?" See Dietmar Schmidt, *Martin Niemöller* (Hamburg: Rowohlt, 1959), 135 [ET: *Pastor Niemöller*, trans. L. Wilson (Garden City, NY: Doubleday, 1959), 106–7].

46. Instead of this sentence, Text 6 has "In our case it has not been noticed, for we also have rejected him."

47. The two last sentences are inserted here from Text 6.

human beings who are being punished in this sense. The pastoral caregiver must absolutely not slip back into a stage where he views the sentenced lawbreakers as people who have to atone. He has rather to view, to address, and to treat them as people for whom at any rate Jesus Christ has not died and is risen in vain. That will often be difficult for him. He must therefore pray about it time and again.[48]

The staff and the authorities belong also to the surroundings of the prison chaplain. Fundamentally he has to advocate among them—theoretically and practically—an understanding and administration of punishment once again in this sense of a measure of care. That is also his responsibility. His pleading for a right understanding of punishment may [then] at times turn into conflict and struggle. Even against the prison staff and the authorities, if necessary the pastoral caregiver must in any given case be found on the side of the prisoner and not on the side of the penal authority, which misunderstands punishment. Here manly pride before the thrones of the authorities is needed![49] He must be the caregiver and the advocate for the prisoners, the advocate of a punishment rightly understood.

Yes, indeed, "a tiresome miniwar over individual issues"! For the prisoner, the individual issues are probably always a "big war." For in it decisions are often made that are important for his entire existence. The credibility of the gospel proclamation in the prison, among the authorities, the staff, and not least among the "main characters" themselves, depends on the pastoral caregiver not avoiding this pleading for an implementation of the punishment in the sense of its being care and eventually [not avoiding] the fight with the authorities and staff. The "miniwar" must not *tire out* the caregiver. It must be *fought*—from week to week, from year to year. This faithfulness in little things[50] is important and imperative.

Question 7: Is the pastor adequate as the single representative of the local congregation within the penal system? And what must happen, that the forgiveness of the community not only be recited, but also practiced? Can it be done, for example, in the form that church elders, as delegates of the home congregations, participate in the worship service and the celebration of the Lord's Supper?

Barth: I am pleased to hear this question. It sounds so well Reformed. There should be a contact established between the home congregation and the prisoners; I assume that is what the questioner wanted to say. I can only say "Yes" to this. When elders or council members or others from the home congregation participate in the worship service and the Lord's Supper in prison, this is a significant expression of solidarity.

Let me still add something here. The gospel exists only in the congregation,[51] the congregation only in the gospel. The prison congregation admittedly is not

---

48. The last two sentences are inserted here from Text 6.
49. "Manly pride before the thrones of the authorities" according to Text 6, instead of "A man's courage before the thrones of bureaucrats" in Text 4. The Text 6 version is closer to the lines of Friedrich von Schiller's "Ode To Joy," lines 89–92, to which Barth alludes here: "Männerstolz vor Königsthronen— / Brüder, gält es Gut und Blut— / Dem Verdienste seine Kronen, / Untergang der Lügenbrut!" [Manly pride 'fore kingly power— / Brothers, cost it life and blood— / Honor to whom merits honor, / Ruin to the lying brood!]
50. Cf. Matt. 25:21; Luke 16:10.
51. The following passage up to "a congregation takes form within the prison?" is inserted from Text 6.

the home congregation. But is it completely impossible that a congregation takes form within the prison? Is it impossible that inmates act as organists and sextons and that a church choir is formed in the prison? We should search for methods and ways to let a congregation form itself and function within the prison. At the time the prisoner is not in his home congregation, but now his congregation is here. For this reason one cannot shy back from the question in what way the prisoners can share responsibility for the proclamation and thus make the worship service and the pastoral care their own concern. For they must on no account remain just the object of care but should [also] be acting subjects. We should therefore invite them to share responsibility in the proclamation. This will certainly have to be done cautiously and prudently,[52] but not too timidly. A certain confidence is appropriate here.

6. Inquiries

Comment: To return once more to your criticism of the concept of atonement: I think that the equation atonement equals reparation is insufficient. God's atonement is the restitution of his holiness. One cannot explain punishment as a measure of care to the person who does not believe in Christ.

Barth: We *ourselves* must first of all believe firmly in Christ. If we do that, then we must not withhold the gospel from the others either: we must also call them to faith. And can we do that without remembering that not only they but also we ourselves must always say regarding our own faith, "I believe, dear Lord, help my unbelief!" [Mark 9:24]? I did not say: In your pastoral care leave aside faith in Christ and proceed only with the care! In this faith in Christ not only is it made clear that punishment must be understood and administered as care, but first and foremost the holiness of God is recognized. And it is certainly at the cross of Golgotha that we come to know the ["holy"] God of the Old Testament best.

Question: I want to ask in reference to [your argument on the issue of the death penalty in the case of] high treason: whether it is not also "care" when one executes the violent criminal?

Barth: Formerly, that was my position too. But today I consider this a very doubtful argumentation.

Question: In your response to the question about the relation of "gospel and law" you posed some counterquestions.[53] I would like to add a remark here: Of course, for us the law can only be the law of Sinai. But doesn't the knowledge of sin still come through the law? Compare Romans 7:7, "I did not know sin except through the law"! A missionary also preaches first the law, doesn't he?

Barth: How did it actually work in Paul's case? The law did not conquer him but the "Damascus experience" [cf. Acts 9:1–9]. Was the path of Paul a path from law to gospel or the reverse? At Damascus he first came to know the real law: the "law *of Christ*" [cf. 1 Cor. 9:21]. Now[54] he is placed under the real law, under the law of which he says, it is just and good [cf. Rom. 7:12], and where he

---

52. The part "have to be done cautiously and prudently" is taken from Text 6.
53. See section 4 above.
54. From "Now . . ." our textual reproduction again follows the transcript of the audio recording of the conversation (Text 8). The transcript for this section, however, has significant lacunae.

protests against the notion that the law is overthrown but rather [says that it] is to be established [cf. Rom. 3:31]: the law of Christ. Moreover, I believe that the general discussion on this question leads us too far astray. I am sorry that my counterquestions did not make more of an impression on you.

Indeed, what is the law of Sinai? You mean the Ten Commandments? Fine. But still, Luther said, when asked, How about the Ten Commandments?, that they are the *Sachsenspiegel* [Mirror of Saxony] for the Jews.[55] And what does that mean, that the Jews have their *Sachsenspiegel* as the other peoples also do? All right, [one then concluded,] there is a natural law. And the Ten Commandments are the interpretation of the natural law[56]—and then we are right in the middle of the *lex-naturalis*-theology,[57] aren't we?, where you apparently are headed. Fine. But if you want to choose the Ten Commandments in Luther's interpretation,[58] that is something different [from understanding them as *Sachsenspiegel* or—God forbid!—natural law]. Indeed, then we are already in the middle of the New Testament. The Ten Commandments in Luther's interpretation, "You should fear and love God . . ."[59]—well now, that is more [than] the "Sinai law," that is the law of Christ.

Question: But Jesus did come back to the Sinai law in the Sermon on the Mount, did he not?[60]

Barth:[61] Oh, come on! You can't say, can you?, that the law of Christ [. . . as it is proclaimed in the Sermon on the Mount . . .], the law that leads to baptism and [can] lead people to the knowledge of sin [. . . might be understood as such a *Sachsenspiegel*]. Rather it is the *proclamation of the kingdom of heaven*—that is what the Sermon on the Mount is. [The issue here is] whether the self-proclamation

---

55. M. Luther, WA 18:18.14–17 [ET: *Against the Heavenly Prophets in the Matter of Images and Sacraments*, trans. B. Erling and C. Bergendoff, *LW* 40 (Philadelphia: Muhlenberg Press, 1958), 98]: "Therefore one is to let Moses be the *Sachsenspiegel* of the Jews and not to confuse us gentiles with it, just as the *Sachsenspiegel* is not observed in France, though the natural law there is in agreement with it." [–Trans.: The *Sachsenspiegel*, or *Mirror of Saxony*, was a compilation of medieval legal texts that enjoyed considerable influence in Europe.]

56. Thus Luther himself already could say, e.g., in *Exegesis of the Ten Commandments from the 19th and 20th Chapters of the Second Book of Moses, preached at Wittenberg (1528)*, WA 16:431.26–28: "God, however, has given to the Jews . . . the Ten Commandments . . . , which are nothing else but the law of nature, which is naturally inscribed in our heart."

57. What is meant is a theology—as advocated in the eighteenth century—that in consequence of the teaching mentioned in n. 36 understood the law of God as knowledge innate to the human being and made this knowledge a constitutive element of theology. For Barth's interpretation of this theology, cf. *CD* IV/1:368–87, §60.1 [*KD* 407–27]; further, K. Barth, *Die protestantische Theologie im 19. Jahrhundert: Ihr Vorgeschichte und ihre Geschichte* (Zollikon: Evangelischer Verlag, 1947; Zurich: Theologischer Verlag, 1994), 85–92 [ET: *Protestant Theology in the Nineteenth Century: Its Background and History*, introduced by C. E. Gunton, trans. B. Cozens and J. Bowden (Grand Rapids: Eerdmans, 2002), 105–13].

58. M. Luther, *Der kleine Katechismus* (1529), in *BSLK* 507–10 [ET: *A Short Explanation of Dr. Martin Luther's Small Catechism*, no trans. (St. Louis: Concordia, 1965), 5–8]; and *Der große Katechismus* (1529), in *BSLK* 560–645 [ET: *The Large Catechism of Martin Luther*, trans. Robert H. Fischer (Philadelphia: Fortress, 1959), 9–55].

59. M. Luther, *Der kleine Katechismus*, *BSLK* 507.42–43 [ET: *A Short Explanation of Dr. Martin Luther's Small Catechism*, 5]. The explanation for the First Commandment: "We should fear, love, and trust in God above all things." The explanation of all other commandments begins consistently with the words: "We should fear and love God so that . . ."

60. The reference is to the citations from the Decalogue (Exod. 20) in Jesus' Sermon on the Mount: Matt. 5:21, 27.

61. In Text 8, the following section is especially sketchy. Therefore, it must be specially emphasized here that the provision of missing text elements in square brackets is purely an attempt at reconstruction. On Barth's understanding of the Sermon on the Mount, cf. *CD* II/2:686–700, §38, no. 2 [*KD* 766–82].

of Jesus Christ, the revelation [of himself as Lord and Savior comes true. Mere recitation of some general law—] nothing of this sort is found in the Sermon on the Mount. "Therefore I say unto you now, so that you [believe in me!"⁶²—that is what is special here . . .].

Kühler [?]: Many questions still remain open, I believe. I think therefore that we [should] provide the opportunity that we, especially the interested questioners, meet here in a smaller group after lunch. Assuming, however, that we can impose on you [, Herr Professor].

Barth: Yes, on me you certainly can. But as I know from experience, in Germany there is a holy law of the afternoon nap.⁶³

Question: I still would have a question about the care by the state. Namely, I would agree with you—with your remarks inasmuch as they envision a constitutional state. But, I think, it needs to be said in this context, that we have at our borders a criminal state, where, for instance, the procedure is that his farm is taken away from a farmer, and when he resists he may be locked up. For me, it would be difficult as a pastoral caregiver to convince that person of the care of the state. I would still like to perhaps see this discussed a tiny bit more.

Barth: Well, the issue that there are people who are unjustly punished was not at all part of the discussion here. Is that the case which you have in mind? "Unjust punishment"—of course, [. . .] we do perceive the [. . . difficulty of this concrete question of arbitrary human court sentences], but that still does not alter our problem, namely, that punishment can only have meaning as a welfare action.⁶⁴ That is something different.

Comment: It is a concern for me that even the believer who is released does not abandon the flight from Christ.

Barth: Yes, I also don't abandon it and you perhaps not either. It is not a special problem of the released prisoners. Precisely at this point we are in solidarity with them.

Question: On your answer to the first question: According to the teaching of the Bible and the Reformers, isn't there also a condemnation?

Barth: Well, you see now, how one moves around in a circle. I think I spoke there quite clearly of God's election of grace. Of course, it is correct: we are all under the condemnation; no doubt about it. We are all, all of us, falling away and therefore condemned. And now this our condemnation does not remain on us. Now Jesus Christ becomes the condemned one. On Golgotha, was it not he who was the condemned one? "My God, my God, why have you forsaken me" [Matt. 27:46]. Therefore, [as the hymn puts it,] "all sin You have borne, or we should have to despair."⁶⁵ There is the condemnation—there! And now we want to view it there where God himself has planted⁶⁶ it, and want then to say to ourselves: "Okay, this one there, who as the bearer of our condemnation suffers and dies, is elected by God to do that, to bear our condemnation. And

62. Cf. the antitheses of the Sermon on the Mount: "But I say to you . . ." (Matt. 5:22, 28, [32,] 34, 39, 44).
63. The comment, Barth's answer, and the following question are missing in Text 8 and are here reproduced from Text 4.
64. The subordinate clause "that punishment can . . . welfare action" is inserted here from Text 4.
65. From the first stanza of the song "O Lamm Gottes unschuldig," by Nicolaus Decius (circa 1522). *GERS* 139; *EKG* 55; *EG* 190/191.
66. The spoken word was probably "placed" or "rolled."

in him we are now not condemned, but in him we are now God's dear children, we are now elected. And now we may and should think from this [start]. Then condemnation is something that is behind us. Not that *we* have put it behind us, not that we have overcome it in some upswing of faith. But Christ has done it for us. And now we are allowed to accept it. And I must repeat it time and again: it would be an insult to the honor of God if we did not want to do this and were to continue groaning over condemnation and so forth, and then perhaps even look for condemnation only among others and secretly think to ourselves: I am on the good side; I am elected. No, no, not so! We all, all of us really belong on the bad side, to the condemned—and are transferred without our own merit, purely through grace, to the good side and may rejoice in our election and say, "If God be for us, who can be against us?" [Rom. 8:31]. And we must and may now say that to all people. I have to ask ever again, How would you believe it for yourself? You do want to believe it for yourself, don't you? But how can you believe it for yourself when you withhold it from anyone else, to believe the same also for him? We Christians must believe it for the others as well, [and] how [much so!], or we may.

A woman: Professor Barth, as a very simple laywoman here in this group [. . .] I would like to thank you for this wonderful and uplifting hour. You have shown us all the way into humility—according to the word of Jesus: "Whoever is without sin, let him cast the first stone" [John 8:7] [. . .]. During my annual trips to the Bernese Alps in Switzerland, where I seek recovery for myself, I am looking forward every year to finding a particular small calendar. In it I found this little leaf [with an exposition by you] which I have been carrying around with me for many years. With these your own words I would like to give you a parting greeting: "But who sits in the judgment seat? . . . The gracious and merciful One who even when he is angry and punishes, and especially then, does not desire that anyone be lost, but that all, Christians and non-Christians, be saved and come to the knowledge of the truth. He judges only where, because, and when he is about to love and to bless."[67]

Barth: I thank you.

---

67. K. Barth, *Brief an einen Pfarrer in der Deutschen Demokratischen Republik* (Zollikon: Evangelischer Verlag, 1959), 16–17 [ET: "Letter to a Pastor in the German Democratic Republic," in K. Barth and J. Hamel, *How to Serve God in a Marxist Land* (New York: Association Press, 1959), 55]: "But who sits in judgment? Not the instrument, but the One who uses it and holds it in his hand, the gracious and merciful One. . . ."

8. Conversation with Kurt Marti
1960

A conversation, which Kurt Marti conducted with Karl Barth on May 20, 1960, served apparently as the preparation of his essay "Karl Barth" in Du: Kulturelle Monatschrift *[Cultural monthly] 20 (September 1960): 25–30. The article conveys little of the content and course of the conversation. For this reason, we do not offer a transcription in the framework of this publication. Following the biographical thread from the "Aargau village pastor" all the way to the "St. Jerome in his study, 'if only in a Swiss version,' as Barth, sitting at his desk, once commented with a smile," Marti sketches the flow of Barth's theological thought.*

9. Interview by Alexander J. Seiler
1960

Between June 29 and July 2, 1960, the University of Basel celebrated its five hundredth anniversary. Barth chose not to participate in the celebrations as a protest against the politically motivated decision of the University Cabinet [Regenz] not to invite representatives of universities from Eastern Bloc countries.[1] Nevertheless Barth provided two shorter contributions to publications for the anniversary and granted an interview on June 3, 1960, to Dr. Alexander J. Seiler, a journalist with the Basel National-Zeitung, on questions of the mission of the university present and future. Together with similar interviews with Max Imboden (Law), Gerhard Wolf-Heidegger (Medicine), Karl Jaspers (Philosophy), and Tadeus Reichstein (Chemistry), this interview appeared under the caption "Theologie in der entgötterten Welt [Theology in the De-Divinized World]" on June 26, 1960, in the Sunday supplement of the National-Zeitung, vol. 116, no. 290, June 26, 1960.

Seiler: Herr Professor, when the University of Basel was founded,[2] theology was still the queen of sciences. Today the layperson might have the impression that theology is a distinctly professional course of studies, largely isolated not only from the other sciences but also from modern reality, which is shaped and dominated especially in the Christian West by an almost pseudo-religious "faith in science." How do you evaluate the situation of theology in this respect?

Barth: Indeed, the current situation of theology cannot be compared to that of five hundred years ago. At that time, the university was one member within an all-encompassing *corpus christianum*[3] and as such had a spiritual character in its entirety. Nevertheless, I am not convinced that one can speak today of an actual remoteness of theology either in relation to the other sciences or in relation to modern reality. On the contrary, within the last fifty years theology has experienced a certain ascendency—and with it the church as a social reality. Fifty years ago theology did indeed stand in the corner. Today theology—when it is done properly—finds an echo not only in the realm of the church, but also in the scientific and public realm, which would have been almost unthinkable then. Indeed, since the Enlightenment the church has, by and large, been able

1. Cf. K. Barth, "Würdige und unwürdige Teilnehmer? [Worthy and Unworthy Participants?]," *National-Zeitung* (Basel) 117, no. 457 (October 4, 1959) (= *O.Br. 1945–1968*, 477–81).
2. The charter for the university was granted by Pope Pius II (Enea Silvio Piccolomini) on November 12, 1459; the opening ceremonies were held in the choir of the Basel Münster on April 4, 1460.
3. This term describes medieval society as a legal unit at once spiritual and secular in character. It was introduced into modern discussion by Karl Eugen Rieker (1857–1927). See J. Heckel, "Corpus Christianum," in *RGG*[3], vol. 1, cols. 1871–73.

to assert itself time and again with a remarkable tenacity and to stay alive in the face of the antireligious and nonreligious currents.

Seiler: But precisely by means of such self-assertion, has the church, and with it theology, not been pressured into assuming the role of a conservative power, as Carl Friedrich von Weizsäcker formulated it recently in his Basel lecture on Galileo?[4] And in playing this role, must it not fail to live up to its actual Christian calling precisely in these times of radical revaluation and upheaval? Christianity was once the religion of confession. Today, has it not become essentially a religion of silence, a type of societal *sous-entendus* [assumption] that commits to nothing?

Barth: Yes, of course, I know only too well what you mean. Christianity, the church—meaning infant baptism, confirmation, burial, perhaps also the Federal Day of Prayer in Switzerland[5]—that is Christianity for a great number of people who pay their church taxes today. We should not harbor any illusions about it. Of course, this has nothing to do with Christianity. Of course, a Christianity that does not confess is not Christianity at all. But let us make no mistake: if it does wish to confess, then matters can easily become risky. Authentic Christianity is a dangerous thing, even in the pious city of Basel. And it is precisely here that one finds the specifically modern task of theology, as I have attempted to integrate it into my life's work: to present anew in every dimension what Christianity actually is, with all its consequences and all of its dangers. And, at least from my experience, I can say that to the extent to which theology does that, it always finds a hearing and is respected. In contrast, theology as bridge-building, as mediation, evasion, cover-up—that fades away today more than ever before. Thus wherever one finds that chasm between theology and reality of which you spoke at the outset, theology itself is most to blame. And this is not because it is essentially "out of touch with the world," but rather because it has misunderstood its own task.

Seiler: In other words, you believe that theology, if it understands itself correctly, can give modern people fresh impulses that are suitable to show them a way out of their existential distress, their neuroses and psychoses, their "loneliness in the crowd,"[6] their blind compulsion towards self-annihilation?

Barth: That is indeed what I believe; otherwise I would have given up on theology long ago. But theology can only do this if it does not secularize itself. Theology, as teaching and as the "care of souls," begins at the precise point where psychology and psychiatry end: at the question of the meaning of existence, the meaning of the whole. It is precisely this question—from which modern life systematically attempts to distract human attention—that theology

4. For the occasion of the upcoming anniversary of the university, the Protestant and Roman Catholic student pastors organized a lecture series during Advent 1959 titled "The University and the Christian." In this series the lecture delivered by C. F. von Weizsäcker on Galileo in the Peterskirche, to which Seiler refers, was extemporaneous and thus was not published in this form. Nonetheless von Weizsäcker did contribute a similar text with the same title "Galileo Galilei" in *Universität und Christ: Evangelische und katholische Besinnung zum 500jährigen Bestehen der Universität Basel*, ed. Robert Leuenberger et al. (Zurich: Evangelischer Verlag, 1960), 43–62.

5. The Eidgenössische Dank-, Buss- und Bettag [Swiss Federal Day of Thanksgiving, Prayer, and Repentance] was established in 1832 by the state as a religious-patriotic holiday and is celebrated on the third Sunday in September.

6. An allusion to the title of David Riesman's *The Lonely Crowd: A Study of the Changing American Character* (New Haven: Yale University Press, 1950).

must relentlessly pose and seek to answer today. Only then will it find an echo. Here too it is crucial that theology does not simply limp more or less grudgingly behind reality, as it has essentially done since the seventeenth century, but rather that it openly confronts Christian doctrine with reality.

Seiler: Would then the atomic bomb—that terrible emblem and "writing on the wall" of our time—not provide a marvelous opportunity for Christian renewal, even without sharing the view of Martin Niemöller that it is the perfect materialization of the Christian commandment to love the enemy?[7] Can Christianity "live with the bomb"[8] without critically engaging the bomb?

Barth: Christianity can only "live with the bomb" by living *against* the bomb. The tepidity with which the church in Switzerland has grappled with the question of nuclear armament is abominable—I have no other word to describe it.[9] It is that type of approach to the burning questions of the times that drives even the best of Christians into a type of "inner Diaspora"—we need to be clear about that. But it is always the same old problem: if the church attempts to live with the world, to accommodate, then it is despised. If the church protests, it will be pushed into the corner but on the whole perhaps more respected.

Seiler: Pushed into the corner—that leads us back to the starting point of our conversation. Is it not the case in our "accommodated," "worldly" Christianity today, that knowledge and technology—which in their omnipresence rule everyday life—have pushed faith into a corner, where it fortifies itself against the former, but outside, in everyday life, it leaves behind a vacuum for the (again I cite C. F. Weizsäcker)[10] "pseudoreligion" of faith in the equally palpable and—for the majority—impenetrable technical results of the natural sciences? Precisely those things that you mentioned as the basis of a "silent" Christianity—birth, marriage, death—have now become thoroughly rationalized, "natural," and banal events that have lost all their earlier transcendent, "supernatural," or "numinous" shine. Thus the following question imposes itself: Where is the true place of faith in a world that presents itself to human beings from childhood on as manageable, tractable, rationally controllable by them?

Barth: The human is in the world, in its midst. We should take notice: today there are far fewer atheists, at least of the militant variety, than even fifty years ago. Especially among the natural scientists, who at that time formed the

---

7. Seiler is perhaps thinking of Martin Niemöller, "Totale Abrüstung heute—Tor zum Weltfrieden morgen" (Lecture given on January 27, 1960), in M. Niemöller, *Reden: 1958–1961* (Frankfurt a. M.: Stimme-Verlag, 1961), 206–14, 214: "The atomic bomb . . . can be a blessing and a gracious gift of God for us if we allow our eyes to be opened to see that our generation is being challenged today to listen to the voice of its Creator and Redeemer, who does not wish the sinner, the rebellious human, to die and be lost but repent and live. Open the gate! —For behind it the charge and the gift of God are waiting: peace on earth!"

8. An allusion to Carl Friedrich von Weizsäcker's *Mit der Bombe leben: Die gegenwärtigen Aussichten einer Begrenzung der Gefahr eines Atomkrieges* (Hamburg: Die Zeit, 1958).

9. Here Barth is referring to the conflict in the Theological Commission of the Federation of Swiss Protestant Churches to the question of the nuclear armament of the Swiss Army in the year 1958. The conflict resulted in a majority opinion signed by Ph. Daulte, K. Guggisberg, V. Maag, Ph. Menoud, E. Schweizer, and E. Staehelin, and a minority opinion signed by K. Barth, J. Courvoisier, E. Grin, and J. J. Stamm. The latter expressed a clear No to the nuclear armament of the Swiss Army. Both were published under the same title: "Thesen der Theologischen Kommission zur Frage der nuklearen Ausrüstung der Schweizerischen Armee," in *RKZ* 99 (1958), cols. 525–26 and 529–30.

10. Cf. C. F. von Weizsäcker, "Galileo Galilei," 62: "In terms of the definition of heresy—the absolutizing of a partial truth—modern secularism seems to me to deserve the name of a Christian heresy."

avant-garde of atheism, one today finds remarkably many religiously oriented people. Especially with scientific advancements into infinite dimensions, those limits of humanity have become visible, about which our engineered everyday life deludes us. The "neuroses" and "psychoses," of which you spoke, are no doubt in the end nothing other than a flight from these limits in fear of the indefiniteness—a flight, perhaps more accurately, from precisely this fear in which human beings might find their being and with it the relation to God unlocked. However, as far as the disappearance of the "numinous" from everyday life is concerned, this can only be welcomed by Christianity. The numinous is the space for false gods. Christianity, however—and this is its innermost nature—knows neither something supernatural nor natural as such, but only the connection of the two, the unity of both. It is not a matter of satisfying a "religious need"—that is, one need among many. To this extent there is the possibility, precisely in a de-deified world, that the message of God will become audible. Certainly I would not go as far in this regard as that archimandrite from Moscow[11] who explained to me a while ago during a visit to Basel that there is absolutely no reason why his church should not say yes to the atheist state. For precisely the atheist state as a completely and thoroughly rationalized, purely earthly organization, allows the church to concentrate completely on its own realm of worship. Even if I would never wish this extreme case for our context, I do believe that today a more honest relation exists between the "de-numinized" state and the "de-numinized" church than previously, and that on this basis an authentic encounter of church and world would certainly be conceivable.

Seiler: Thus on the whole your view of the contemporary situation of theology is rather optimistic. Nevertheless, is there not a certain discrepancy between the upswing of theoretical theology, to which you personally have contributed so significantly, and the situation of practical theology, that is, of pastoral care? In a recent essay a Swiss theologian wrote of the "churches' alarming recruitment difficulties," conditioned not least by the "clear devaluation of the pastoral profession."[12] What possibilities do you think the theological faculties have to counteract this devaluation?

Barth: I am not convinced that the problem is primarily a result of inadequate education. The preparatory training of young pastors today, especially in the practical realm, is better than earlier, and considerably more is being done to make the transition from the classroom to the practice of ministry easier for them. Moreover, I believe that a rigorous and comprehensive theoretical education is still the best that the university can contribute to the practical life. Best practice is always the result of the best theory. I even have a mild apprehension with regard to certain tendencies toward the "technicizing" of theology; for in the vocation of the pastor, everything depends on *what* one has to say; the correct What will result in the correct How.

Seiler: Would you also apply this observation to the situation of the university in general, which in this technocratic era, of course, is characterized by

---

11. No further information can be found in Barth's records about the visit of an archimandrite from Moscow.

12. Seiler is perhaps referring to K. Guggisberg, "Nachwuchsprobleme der theologischen Fakultäten," *Schweizer Monatshefte* 40 (1960): 327–35.

the old humanistic ideal of education having to give way increasingly to the demands of professional and vocational training?

Barth: That the university prepares for vocations will not change; nor will the fact that the requirement for specialized training grows constantly. But it is precisely in this situation that it is critical for each student to be educated to be an independent thinker in their situation. With respect to institutional reforms, only the idea of a general curriculum [*Studium generale*] appears promising to me. I personally would be supportive of the university requiring one or two years of such general, higher preparatory education—which the *Gymnasium* [academic high school track] can apparently no longer deliver. It is good and right to point to the significance of the individual personality of the instructor. In the last analysis, it is the case that the mystery of instruction and of research lies in the person. But the point is, in the last analysis. Therefore one should not hedge around when talking about institutional reforms that the university should undergo in order to fulfill, beside its professional training tasks, also the formational task that is implied in its name.

Seiler: If you describe the university's most important task as educating for independent thought, then what is your assessment of the future of free research? It appears to be threatened by the technocracy on both sides of the Iron Curtain as state and industry tend toward setting purpose-driven, immediately translatable technological goals for research.

Barth: I am glad you are asking this question, for without a doubt it points to a major problem of modern science, in the West as much as in the East. Everything depends on whether we in the West will also recognize, admit, and debate it early enough. If we do this instead of flattering ourselves[13] with beautiful speeches celebrating the glories of free research at Western universities, then the largest part is done. From the diagnosis of the danger shall arise the only possible therapy: namely, the uncompromising self-assertion of the university in service of the truth.

13. Cf. the introduction to this interview.

10. Questions and Answers at the Conference of the World Student Christian Federation in Strasbourg 1960

For years the World Student Christian Federation had been working on a project titled "The Life and Mission of the Church." The project was supposed to conclude with a "Teaching Conference" in Strasbourg in 1960. On July 19, 1960, Barth was a guest at the conference for a question-and-answer session. The text of the conversation is published under the title "Theologians Answer Student Questions: Karl Barth," in The Student World *53 (1961): 151–67. In* Die Welt war meine Gemeinde: Autobiographie *[The world was my church: Autobiography] (Munich: [Piper,] 1972), 442, W. A. Visser 't Hooft wrote, "This conference proceeded in a way very different from what the leadership of the Federation had hoped and expected. The presentations made by D. T. Niles, Lesslie Newbigin, Karl Barth, and me appeared not to be what the students wanted. What had happened? David Edwards expressed it this way: 'There was, it appears, too much talk about the life of the church; what interested the students was what would stand up in the world. And there was too much talk about mission; what the students wanted to hear was the affirmation of this world.'" As the source of the citation, Visser 't Hooft referred to* The Ecumenical Advance, [vol. 2 of] A History of the Ecumenical Movement, 1948–1968 *[Geneva: World Council of Churches, 1968], 406.*

1. The Kingdom of God and the Church

Question: What is the relation between the mission of the church and the movement of the kingdom of God?

Barth: What is meant by this term "kingdom of God"? There is no kingdom of God that is not in itself movement. The kingdom of God is an actual dynamic reality. The kingdom of God means God's sovereignty, God's claim, and God's action. Instead of speaking of the kingdom of God, we may also safely say "the living Christ": the living Christ himself is the kingdom of God, the living Christ striving toward the ultimate revelation of what he did, toward the ultimate revelation of his victory over sin and death accomplished in his earthly life. We speak about the kingdom of God when we speak of the outpouring and the effects of the Holy Spirit. There is no difference between God's sovereignty, the action of Christ, and the reality and effects of the Holy Spirit.

Now when we speak of the mission of the church, we also mean something that happens, a movement, something of dynamic character. But now we are in the realm of humanity, together with Christ, yet of humanity. The mission of the church means the movement of man dependent on the kingdom of God, and related to it an action of men who are chosen and who are called to the knowledge and obedience of the kingdom of God, to faith, to love, to hope. They are not called to replace the kingdom of God or to establish it. They are not called to fulfill the purpose of the kingdom. They are but men. They *are* called to an act of obedience in complete subordination, in an unrestrained humility over against the kingdom of God. Do not confuse the kingdom of God and the mission of the church. The two are related to each other, but they will never be identical. First the kingdom and then the mission of the church. The kingdom is the work of God from above, and the mission of the church is the answer to it.

But what does the mission of the church mean? The mission of the church is the task of reflecting, like a mirror, the kingdom of God, the work of Christ and of the Holy Spirit. To *reflect* it, not to *do* it! We can also say that the task of the church, its mission, is to proclaim the kingdom, or, to use the biblical term, "to witness to it." A witness is a man who has seen and heard something that happened; he himself cannot do what happened, but because he saw and heard it, he can witness to it. In his person the fact itself is proclaimed. That is the situation of the church, because the church is God's [people], is Christ's people, and the reason for the existence of the church is simply and totally its mission. The church does not have [the task] to govern, but to serve God's own work; not to do the work of God, but to serve his work.

And the work of God that the church has to serve is to create in the world interest in it [God's kingdom], so that there are, both inside and outside Christianity, always new people who become eager listeners of the kingdom. The church has to make signposts in the world. The way is there and the goal is there, but the signposts are lacking. Signposts point in two directions, backward to the work of Christ in history, and to the cross on which the reconciliation of the world with God has been accomplished once for all, and forward to the ultimate revelation of that which was completely fulfilled, Jesus Christ, and of which we are allowed to be witnesses and signpost builders.

Debater: It seems to me that in the world we are called to be obedient to the word [of God], and that if we are to manifest the reign of God in the world, or if we are to be obedient, we must seek to manifest God's word in the world, to be obedient to him, not simply to point to the kingdom but actually to allow God's word to reign in our lives to the extent that the Spirit gives us the courage to be faithful to the word. I have some questions about our simply building signs to point to the kingdom, and I feel that we are really called to risk ourselves in the world, manifesting God's love among men.

Barth: I must stick to what I have said. Our task is to point, and it would be a great and admirable thing if each one of us would point to the kingdom. We are pointing in many other directions than the kingdom. If a man becomes obedient to the word, if he does his best, his very existence is a work of pointing to God. It cannot be our task to become a second or a third or a fourth word of God. We can be only human words, but human words who answer to God's word. Don't ask too much; it will be enough if a servant is faithful. He remains only a servant; he doesn't become a master. He doesn't become like God, but he remains what he is, a poor, sinful man, but a man who is in charge of this wonderful task: to indicate that there is such a thing as the kingdom of God.

Don't reach too high! Don't try to have a bird in your hands that is high up on the wall, but hold what you have and what you shall have [cf. Rev. 3:11].

Question: You speak of not doing the works of God but simply serve them, or serve God's purposes. I think we have a tendency to identify these two things, to think that when we are serving the Lord we are doing his work. What is the importance of the distinction between doing the work of God and serving God?

Barth: The work which has to be done is certainly the work of the Lord. The Lord commands, and he has servants, and they must do what he wills, but they remain servants. They cannot do it of themselves, but out of the spirit of their Lord. They are only serving the Lord without being lords themselves. That must be differentiated. He commands, we have to obey.

2. The Christian and Politics

Question: Is there a Christian basis for political action in the problems of today?

Barth: What is meant by the term "political action"? As I understand it, political action means responsible cooperation within the realm of the administration[1] of human (*human*, not divine) freedom, human justice, human order, human peace. A man who is politically active cannot be indifferent to this dispensation, this administration, but he feels himself responsible for seeking, even in the human sphere, freedom, justice, order, and peace.

Now is there a Christian basis for such political action? My answer runs thus: today as always God is Lord, not only within the realm, not to say the walls, of the church, but also outside the so-called religious sphere of life. God is a Lord of the whole world, and so what we call political administration is something that cannot be carried on independently of his will and intention. Participation in political administration and action can and must be a form of what we have called Christian service in the world.

Now, what is the meaning of God's logic[2] in this political administration? In what sense are politics not outside the kingdom of God? On this I say, political administration that is seeking to discover and apply human freedom and justice is an opportunity given to the world. The relation between God's logic and the existence of status[3] and order may be found in the idea of God's patience. God is patient. It seems not yet to be the will of God to make an end of things. We have repented,[4] and we shall have an opportunity to live and to repent, an opportunity to believe, an opportunity for everybody to go forward, aware or

---

1. In *Inst.* 4.20, J. Calvin titles his doctrine of the state "De politica administratione" [ET: "Civil Government"]. This "government" or "administration" stands in a certain relationship to the "ministry of the Word of God," which is the general theme of book 4. For his designation of the political realm, Barth quite deliberately uses this term. The German term *Verwaltung*, which would be translated with the English word "administration," lacks the intended and implied tone and sense of the Latin concept. We shall not translate it here but will use the terms "administration" and "administer."
2. The term "logic," which appears here in the English-language text, makes no sense. The translation here is based on the assumption that the word actually used was "lordship."
3. The word "status" in the English text could be the result of hearing or transcribing incorrectly. Here we will read the more probable term "state."
4. In the original English text, this phrase "we have repented" is inserted, which makes little sense in this context. Probably Barth corrected this sentence with the sentence that follows.

unaware that we come from the cross of Christ and are going toward his ultimate revelation. We could not do so if there were not order in the world, and a certain freedom and peace; not the peace of the kingdom, not the justice of God, but a human thing: the freedom, justice, and peace guaranteeing that men may live together, not disturbing one another, giving mutual help for life in this world, always looking backward to the cross and forward to God's revelation.

Our human political administration may be called a kind of preparation *for* God's way of salvation—but only a preparation! There is no possibility that by political means we may be saved, or the world reconciled, or divine peace attained. But there is a possibility that the realm in which we live, this earthly realm, may be a room in which the gospel can be preached, in which repentance is possible, in which also hope is possible for the end. Perhaps the famous word "civilization" is a good way to describe this preparation. Civilization means that we may be a little civil, not very, but civil enough.[5] Civil means citizen, so as citizens we can be Christians and the world can be addressed in the name of Jesus Christ. Take the word "civilization," a very humble word, but it is the goal of political administration. I wouldn't speak too loudly of culture: that is too much. Let us be modest, let us be humble, and accept this Christian basis for political action.

Perhaps now you would ask me to say more concretely, more practically, what political action on such a Christian basis can mean? Let me make two points. First of all, a Christian serving his Master, not being himself a master, but a servant, cannot be indifferent to political administration. There is no possibility for a Christian to retreat from the political aspects of life. He is responsible not only for the weakness of the church, but also for the possibility of this weakness, and this possibility means that we must take seriously the question of politics, peace, and justice in the world. We are involved; we are not at liberty to do what we like or to let others busy themselves about it. No, a Christian is asked to take full responsibility for what happens in this world.

Second, if there can be no negation of political administration and political action, neither can there be any deification. It is possible to overestimate political action, and this will happen when people believe that by political action they can force upon humanity the kingdom of God. It is just not possible. The kingdom on earth will never be made by human beings. We are too bad a lot to build the kingdom of God. That is not our task; God will do it himself. Wherever people believe in one system or ism or another—democratism, Communism, autocratism—you have an overestimation of politics, a deification of this sort of work, which must be done. All kinds of political danger arise out of such deification.

What should be the positive goal of Christian political action? Maybe I am putting it too simply, but it seems to me that the goal of all political action must be to give every man the opportunity to live, not because his life as such is important, but because life has its destination in the kingdom of God. And in order to give man the opportunity to live, there must be order and peace. That, I think, is the criterion of good and bad politics. Bad politics will always be those where the human being is overlooked, overrun, where certain ideas or interests or self-centered purposes are held in the name of politics, without regard to human existence. And all good politics will be actions in which man, in his prime, in his weakness, and in his tasks, man as child and as adult, is allowed to exist. A state that guarantees the existence of man is a good state. In reality there will always be a mix-up between good and bad politics. There is no ideal state and no divine state. We shouldn't speak too quickly of a kind of angelic politics, nor of demonic politics. The reality is always something in between, something very relative. We have to take our stand forcefully and decisively, but at the same time with modesty and humility.

Question: Many of us here live in countries that are undergoing severe political crises. I think it is only normal that we should discuss them in the church for our mutual enlightenment. My question is this: should such dialogue take place in the church as a whole, at the level of the universal church? We do not like to interfere in the affairs of other countries, and we often object to people of other nationalities telling us what we ought to do in our country. But do such interference and such nationalistic reactions have meaning when we seriously consider what is Christ's community of servants in the universal church?

Barth: If one member suffers, then the whole body suffers. If the church in one part of the world finds itself in a crisis because of the political situation there, then inevitably all the other churches that together form the universal church are concerned with this situation, and there is dialogue. But what kind of dialogue? I can imagine that a dialogue would be possible between, say, a French Christian and a Swiss Christian like me. Do you think it would be good for a Christian in our country to say publicly what he thinks about the crisis in which the former is involved? I think that, at the moment, the greater the crisis and the greater the difference of opinion about it, then the greater the possibility for other parts of the church or their members to give advice, if necessary, and the greater the responsibility to give it for all to hear. Christian dialogue is something special.

How do I know to whom I am speaking? Without wanting to reject what the questioner proposed just now, I would, from a practical point of view, prefer to speak with him in private about the problems with which he is concerned, because he has not actually asked a precise question, and I cannot therefore give a precise answer. In any case, the precise question and answer should not, perhaps, be made public in an assembly such as this.

Question: You have spoken about the good quality that allows an individual to be free, that is concerned for every individual. How far is it true to say that this freedom of which you speak is too much tied to the idea of liberal democracy of the West, which itself finds expression in what people speak of as "freedom" in the Christian sense? What would you say to someone who does not seek freedom in the sense of liberal democracy, and how can a Christian in a nonliberal democratic setup realize this freedom of which you speak? It appears to me, as a non-European, that you speak of freedom in the sense of liberal democracy.

Barth: Maybe there is a little misunderstanding of what I have said. I did not emphasize especially the idea of freedom. Freedom is also important, but what I said is that good politics must be politics that are concerned with the existence of the human being as such. This may also imply his freedom, but the existence of man does not imply only freedom; it means also peace, the opportunity to live together with his neighbor; it means also community. But it always means man, man and not principles, man and not interests, man and not money, for example. And I think this is not a special idea of Western liberal democracy. Think of Karl Marx: he spoke of the liberation of man, and he was right to say it. Now the question is whether this liberation of man has continued in the Communist era. Communist politics, and politics of other kinds, if they are good politics, are concerned about man. When I speak of freedom, I do not mean freedom to do what I like, but freedom to live a responsible life in which I myself can answer and can be obedient, and can understand my situation as over against that of my neighbor. Such a state of life is freedom. It implies justice and peace. But I am certainly not defending a special liberal democratic notion of politics. What I have tried to say is to be applied to every form of government.

Question: Your criterion for good and bad politics is concern for man's existence. Is there no place in Christianity, therefore, for violent political action that inevitably involves the loss of life, but that in many instances seems to be the only alternative, the only way out of a particular political situation?

Barth: I do not think that violent action can be absolutely excluded from politics. If there is to be such a thing as public order, and there are people who will not live in order, there must be a police force. That is violent action, perhaps not with guns and cannons, not to speak of atom bombs, but every police action is a violent action, and it cannot be excluded. Certainly every violent action can only be an ultimate resort, because where violent action takes place, there will always be the danger that the goal of political action is endangered. It cannot be excluded, but it *should* be excluded. Force can be an argument only in the last instance. But I would not permit myself to forbid the state, in principle, to use power and so also violence. The question is not that of violence and power as such, but rather of the realm in which they must be used, and here we come to the question of war and atomic war. But I think the question was not on war but whether in principle violence is absolutely forbidden, and I should say, no, it is not forbidden, but avoid it if possible.

Debater: We had a lecture this morning by an Orthodox which seemed to indicate that God was present in history, living at the center of the church in the Eucharist. I should like you to indicate how you think God is present in history, because you seem to put him outside history, to say that God has control only when all history is at an end, and that God is not acting in history, which seems to be a dispensation for repentance. This seems to me to be inaccurate.

Barth: First, I must oppose the notion of a God who lives only in the Eucharist and within the walls of the church, a God who is imprisoned, so to speak. Christianity would then be the prison of God. This is not so. God rules the whole world, the whole of our existence, not only when we go to church and partake of the Eucharist. Always we are being asked what is the will of God. We have to listen to the Word of God, which we hear in the Scriptures and in the church, but we have to listen to the same Word when we live outside the walls of the church, if we are to live not only in an act of piety, but also in our daily work and in politics. The Bible tells us that what I have called the political dispensation is not a human invention, but it is willed by the grace and the patience of God, that there may be outward peace and justice. To seek out this peace, to find out what it means and to serve it—that is listening to the voice of God, in the world, in history, where he is present. He would be a very poor God who was only present here among Christians!

Question: We are living in a world in which there are political revolutions all around us. What attitude should a Christian take toward such political revolutions, and what part should he play in them?

Barth: It depends on the kind of revolution. I have taken some small part in what could be called the revolution against Nazism in Germany. There were good Christians who were even more involved in this revolution. But this was Nazism, and it depends on what you mean by revolution. Just as not every political order is good, so not every revolution, as such, is a good thing. I am not speaking in general terms or giving a general answer to the question of whether a Christian can take part. Perhaps he can. Maybe he is even asked to do it. Think of Bonhoeffer. He was asked to do it and he did it. It is impossible to set general limits.

3. On the Reality of Evil and Hell

Question: Can the image of God in man be destroyed? What is the meaning of hell? Should teaching about hell be part of the proclamation of the gospel?

Barth: Notwithstanding the fact that we are now to busy ourselves with hell, I am glad that we can shift from the dangerous question of politics to a theological question! The term "image of God" is related to the creation of man. Let me say, first of all, that following Scripture and knowing that the world is created by the same God who is acting and revealing himself in Jesus Christ, we must say that creation as such is God's good work, in which there is no fault. Maybe that creation is soiled, is endangered, is threatened; maybe in creation there is suffering, a great deal of suffering; maybe the human creature can and does sin and can as sinner be damned and loathsome. But creation and creature as such cannot be destroyed, annihilated. The most terrible things may happen, and they do happen, but not destruction, not dissolution, not negation. God is and remains faithful to his work, and even where it seems that only the wrath of God can hang over the creature, the creature remains in the hands of his Creator. The creature, as such, cannot fall into oblivion. That would mean destruction. And now concerning especially man. Yes, it is true, man is created in the image of God. What is meant by this? Man is created as God's partner, God's vis-à-vis. Man is created as the counterpart of God, as a companion of God. God in creating man has expressed his will not to be alone, to have a vis-à-vis who is able to respond to him, to answer him, and this aspect of man as a respondent, a partner of God, I think that is the image of God. Man is created as a being who in a kind of mirror reflects the glory of God's love. God loves his creatures, and knows that among the other creatures there is man who is able to be this mirror, to answer, or to give an echo to the voice of God. To what extent is man such a partner, such a companion, such a mirror of God and of his love? Insofar as God has created man destined for himself. Man, as such, is not isolated from or against God. Whether he is a believer or an unbeliever, man as such is destined for God. And this destination of man for God cannot be destroyed. It remains, even in the worst sinner, even in the murderer, even in Hitler or Mussolini. If this real and enduring disposition and destination of man is violated by man, then he is an unhappy man indeed, but it remains.

Another side of this image of God is that man is never alone. He is not alone because God is always with him, and he is created together with the other: man and woman [Gen. 1:27]. And perhaps this togetherness of man and wife is the most intimate form of the image of God. Two of them, even on earth, not only man here and God in heaven, but also on earth two of them, and the togetherness of man and wife is, so to speak, the original of all togetherness on earth between human beings. Humanity as such means cohumanity. Man alone, or wife alone, is no man. You cannot be man except together with other men. That will never be lost. Even if we fight one another, even if we hate one another, even if we are indifferent to one another, we remain together: there is a relation from man to man; we belong together.

And then, maybe, the image of God means also this indestructible togetherness of what we call soul and body. Man is an inseparable unity of soul and body, a governing soul and a serving body, but always together. You cannot be only soul, only spirit. Spiritualism is nothing! Materialism is even worse! But you are always spirit and matter, soul and body, together. There is an order, and this order, as such, is also a part of the image of God, which cannot be destroyed.

The last point is the existence of man as a historical being, living in time, beginning here and ending there. Man is not eternal and without time, but limited between birth and death, and that means history: our way from birth to death, living from year to year and knowing that we must live it out. Now we are young, and we become older and older, and then it all ends. This is what it means to be a historical being. This is also a form of our existence, which corresponds to the existence of God, because God is a living God, doing something in his time, he obviously eternally and we temporally. This image of God cannot be lost, cannot be destroyed. So, I can answer the first part of the question only in the negative. There can be no destruction—many disturbances, many disasters, and many terrible things, but not destruction.

Now we come to hell.[6] You shouldn't laugh! There is nothing to laugh at! What does hell mean? I think hell means to be in the place where you are once for all damned and lost without ceasing to exist, without losing the image of God, being what you are but being damned and lost, separated from God, whose creature you are, separated also from your neighbor, from the cohuman being, and separated in yourself—because there is such a thing as separation, a division, an opposition in our own existence. I think that what we are told about the fire of hell means this dissolution, this separation of man. That is hell: an existence in contradiction to the purpose of our Creator and in contradiction to our existence in itself; not a dissolution of our existence, but a contradiction of our not-to-be-destroyed existence.

Should teaching about hell be part of the proclamation of the gospel? No! No! No! The proclamation of the gospel means the proclamation that Christ has overcome hell, that Christ has suffered hell in our place, and that we are allowed to live with him and so to have hell behind us. There it is, but behind us! Teaching of hell can only mean belief in God, and then you have no reason

---

6. The English text here refers to the laughter of the audience in response to this sentence.

to fear hell. Don't fear hell, believe in God! Believe in Christ! Hell can only be where there is no faith. But you are invited to believe, and then hell can only be, so to speak, the limit of a life in faith, not something to be looked at but something to be left behind you. We are invited, if I may say it, to show our backsides to hell! It has been told of Luther that once he believed he was being plagued by the devil, and he did what I said in the literal sense of the word![7] That is a great thing to do! First, we must be Luther, and then we can do that! So please understand me. I would not take a light view of hell: it is a very serious thing, so serious that it needed the Son of God to overcome it. So there is nothing to laugh about, but there is nothing to fear, and there is nothing to preach. What we have to preach is fearlessness and joy in God, and then hell remains aside.

Question: You say there is no destruction of the creature, and in connection with the problem of hell, I should like to ask what you think about the resurrection of all flesh, *apokatastasis* [Trans: restoration], to use the technical term?

Barth: The resurrection of the dead and the restoration of all things are not quite the same, are they? They are not interchangeable terms. There can be resurrection of the dead without restoration of all things. But I'll accept the question. What do we mean by *apokatastasis*? It is the theory that finally and ultimately all men, and possibly the devil too, will be saved, whether they wish it or not. It is a theory first propounded by Origen[8] and then by many others. It is a very agreeable theory: it is very pleasant to imagine that everything turns out right in the end. I have never upheld this theory and never shall. On the other hand I should certainly not uphold the converse: I should not say that the end will be as we see it portrayed in the early paintings: some people in heaven and the rest in hell. But what we *can* do is realize that complete reconciliation and salvation are prepared for all men in Jesus Christ, that all men are invited to believe in Jesus Christ, that all men will one day have to appear before Jesus Christ as their judge, and the judge will be free to pass judgment. We should not presuppose that the judge will put these people, these awful people, on one side, and on the other the good, who will then march white-clad into heaven, while the yawning mouth of hell swallows up the others. We cannot say that because we know that he has overcome hell, but he has the liberty to decide to whom he will give the benefit of this victory over hell. Neither can we say, according to the *apokatastasis* theory, that all will be saved. We shouldn't try to solve this problem of the future automatically, but can only say: there is full salvation for all men in Christ; we are invited to believe in him, we want to do the best we can, and it shall be revealed to us before his judgment throne (cf. 2 Cor. 5:10) what we have done in our mortal life, good or bad.

Question: We have been told that the devil plays an important part in history. I should like to ask you if you think that, our own sin and disobedience apart,

---

7. Johannes Aurifaber reports of Martin Luther (WA.TR 5:211.7–27 [no. 6817]) that he told about such an occasion with the wife of a Wittenberg innkeeper, who is supposed to have reacted to the devil in the way just described. See also WA.TR 3:50.17ff. (no. 2884); and WA.TR 1:31.22ff. (no. 83).

8. See Origenes, *De principes*, ed. von H. Görgemanns and H. Karpp, TzF 24 (Darmstadt 1976), I,6.2; II,1.3; III,5.6 [ET: Origen, *On First Principles*, ed. G. W. Butterworth (London: SPCK, 1939), I.6.2: 53; II.1.3: 78; III.5.6: 242]; Origenes, *In Evangelium Ioannis Commentariorum*, hrsg. E. H. Lommatsch (Berlin 1831), v. 1, 16, 91–93.

there can be another power that separates us from God and that we can identify with the devil?

Barth: I must confess that I know so little of the devil that I cannot give a definition of him. I know of the effects of his existence, but I have never met him in person as Luther did. So I find it is asking too much to give some kind of a definition. Perhaps the devil is even the being who cannot be defined because of his nature, because he is the devil. He is certainly not a creature of God. He can only be, perhaps, the reason of the unreasonableness of sin. The devil is, as I like to say, the impossible possibility that cannot be defined. What is the relation between him and our sin? I am sure that I am responsible for my sin, but I also know that my sin is greater than myself, stronger than myself, and maybe this reason of sin and this force of sin may be called the devil. *But,* as with hell, we are not invited to make reflections on the devil! Please don't! It isn't necessary, it doesn't help, to make a picture of the devil. We can't deny him, but don't busy yourself with him. Live with God in Christ, obedient to his Holy Spirit, and then the devil will fly away like an evil beast who can't live with you. Chase him out, as Luther did. Perhaps even with the help of a little ink![9] Writing dogmatics, for example!

Question: You have just stated that hell is where there is no faith. I should very much like to know how I can relate this statement to the non-Christian religions. Would you describe non-Christians as already living in hell?

Barth: With the question so phrased, it is difficult to give an answer. I didn't mean to say that. Faith in Christ is not a religion: it has nothing to do with religion. Faith can only be where the gospel is and where man has heard the gospel. If man has heard the gospel and thus may believe a little, then he knows that without faith he will be lost. I cannot live without faith. And so long as we just *think* we believe (perhaps we *can't*—that's not the important point, is it?), we do not yet believe; we believe only when we know that we would be lost without faith and shall be saved through faith. But I cannot speak for others. That is not a judgment on people of other religions or convictions—that is not the way. But if I believe, then I believe not for myself alone but also for others; I believe also for those people who have another religion. It is certainly very sad that they have these other religions, and I am here to be a witness to them. But my witness does not imply judging them; I must not judge them, but I may give them a witness of faith. And then, if they come to believe, it doesn't mean that they pass from one religion to another—a completely false concept of Christianity—but that they may come to God, because God has come to them: that is far more than a religion. And if one has this freedom to come to God, one becomes wholly tolerant toward those who follow these peculiar religions such as Islam and Buddhism and Communism, which is also a kind of religion. Yet I believe that Christ died for all these too, and I no longer say that every religion brings salvation, not at all, but witness to them of my faith. Then we will see what happens.

---

9. According to a historically unreliable account, Luther threw an inkwell at the devil while he was staying at the Wartburg in 1521–1522. See J. Köstlin, *Martin Luther: Sein Leben und sein Schaffen* (Elberfeld 1875), vol. 1, 471–72.

4. The Christian Service of Witness

Question: What is the distinction between a witness, an evangelist, and a missionary?

Barth: I don't know whether I am right in thinking that this question comes from our friend Niles![10]

Chairman: You are correct!

Barth: Let me begin with the following statement: Every Christian in his existence as such, and the church or a church in its existence as such, is not a goal in itself, an end in itself. But a Christian and the church or a church exist in order to be a witness, putting up signposts, as we have said, an evangelist, a missionary in the world. Being a Christian, being a church, means being in the world in order to announce the kingdom. We can *only* announce it, but we *must* announce it. Where there is Christianity or a church institution, piety, inner life, going to heaven, which is an end in itself, that is no Christianity, even if it appears in a very strong form. Piety as such is nothing. Christian piety is a life in action in which man serves the purpose of God. Certainly there is such a thing as Christian spiritual life and the life of the Christian in communities, but all pointing to the task of the church.

Now I am asked the *distinction* between witness, evangelist, and missionary. I think these three terms must be understood as simultaneously the individual and social destination and the task of Christianity. They are one thing: they can't be separated. But maybe without separating them, they can be distinguished. If I am right, a *witness*—without excluding his existence as evangelist and missionary—is every Christian in his existence, in his behavior, in his inner and outer life; a witness is the church, in its reality, in its appearance within society, within the world. The Christian and the church as such, without really doing anything, are witnesses: they are signposts. Even if they do nothing—but they must *do* something—their mere existence is a witness. Even if we are not called to tell people such and such a thing, even if we are simply here, eating, drinking, smoking, laughing, even sleeping, being together or being alone, let us be Christian, let us be church, and our existence as such will be a witness.

But this existence as witness includes the second thing: *evangelist*. The Christian, the church as evangelist and, if I am right, evangelist means the unavoidable, necessary act of the continued reformation and renovation of the church itself, and of Christians themselves, because there is never a *perfected* Christian, a *perfected* church, a *perfected* Christianity. The Christian and Christianity and the church as such *need* to be perfected. In this sense, we are all not reformed Christians, but Christians who are to be reformed! We must be renewed, because the church exists only as *ecclesia reformata* [a church reformed], as *ecclesia semper renovanda* [a church always being renewed]. A reformed church means a church that always must be renewed anew.

---

10. D. T. Niles, born 1908 in Sri Lanka, pastor in the Methodist Church there, and director of the office for evangelism of the World Council of Churches in Geneva; General Secretary of the East Asian Christian Conference and President of the World Student Christian Federation. See J. R. Fleming, "D. T. Niles," in *Tendenzen der Theologie im 20. Jahrhundert*, ed. H. J. Schulz (Stuttgart 1966 1967), 543–48. He also spoke at the Strasbourg conference.

And now evangelism.[11] What a word! I wonder if anyone among you could tell me where this word evangelism comes from! In my youth I never heard of it, and now everybody is speaking about evangelism. Is it an invention of my friend Niles? In a good sense, evangelism means the renovation, the reformation of the church, and reformation means coming *back* to the gospel. We believe we have begun with the gospel, we *are* Christians, we *are* church. We need to go back to the gospel, to learn completely anew about Christ, about reconciliation, about his work: that must be repeated every day, every week, every year. Every Christian has to cooperate in the evangelization of himself and of Christianity as such. That is the second stage, so to speak.

And now the third [term]: the church, the Christian, as a *missionary*. If there is a Christian world, and if in the midst of society such a thing as the church, it must have not a static but a dynamic existence. A Christian *cannot* be willing to remain alone. The Christian existence must be an inviting existence, inviting to others. And the church must be a building with many, many windows and doors on all sides, in order that people may go out and that people may come in, in order that we can look out and also that people can look into the church. And that means mission: openness to the world. Not an idle openness, but an active openness. Mission means looking for, and going to, those men who—I shouldn't say who are outside the church; that's not the important thing, but who do not yet know the reality of the kingdom of Christ, of the Holy Spirit. Christ has died also for them. Reconciliation has been made on the cross for them all. But they don't know it: they live without realizing what has been done for them. We as Christians, we as church, we are in charge of telling them. Look at Paul after he had met the living Christ on the road to Damascus [Acts 9:3–19]. He wasn't invited to become a good Christian, to repent, and to live the life of faith, but at the very instant when he was, so to speak, converted, he was called to be an apostle, and an apostle means a missionary. Immediately! And that is our situation. After meeting the living Christ, Paul couldn't stay where he was. He was thrilled, and the whole course of his life was driven by the Holy Spirit. But the Holy Spirit is the kingdom of God, and being driven by the kingdom of God, by the living Christ, by the Holy Spirit, meant going into the world and spending his life in order to show and to tell and to witness to what he was allowed to know. And then he became a missionary. But he couldn't be a missionary without being a witness and an evangelist. He did many things for the reformation of the church of his time, and he was always being reformed himself, and so he was an evangelist. Thus I should unite and distinguish witness, evangelist, and missionary.

---

11. On the use of this concept in the ecumenical discussion since the Amsterdam Conference of the World Council in 1948, see H. J. Margull, *Theologie der missionarischen Verkündigung: Evangelisation als ökumenisches Problem* (Stuttgart 1939), 20–23, 96–97, 116–18.

11. Interview with Hans Weidmann
1960

On September 26, 1960, Pastor Hans Weidmann of Thun visited Barth at his home in Basel to interview him for the Laupen (Canton Bern) Protestant weekly magazine Leben und Glauben *[Life and Faith]. After Walter Mannweiler (1901–60), who in his final years had been a pastor in Solothurn with responsibility on the editorial committee of the magazine for the regular column "Blick auf die Kirchen [A Look at the Churches]," had suddenly died on September 16, Weidmann and a colleague had taken on responsibility for the column at the instigation of Pastor Dr. Walter Lüthi, who had belonged to the editorial committee for fifty years. Having evidently made prior arrangements by telephone, Weidmann wrote to Barth on September 23, 1960: "It is embarrassing for me to steal some of your valuable time. However, it seemed to me to be not a bad idea to begin the new era of* Leben und Glauben *after the distressingly early death of Walter Mannweiler with a clear break. Thus, I would like to bother you for a small interview."*

On October 1, 1960, Weidmann sent Barth the manuscript of the interview he had worked through in the meantime, writing: "You will forgive me if I have filled out some things a little—I hope that it stays true to the views you hold."

The interview was published in Leben und Glauben *35, number 45 (November 5, 1960): 3, under the title "Die Kirche im Wandel der Zeit: Ein Gespräch mit Professor Karl Barth [The Church in the Flux of Time: A Conversation with Professor Karl Barth]" and signed with the pseudonym "Lukas." At the beginning Weidmann describes his visit with Barth. His introductory remarks conclude with the lines: "I set my questions before him. He hesitated a little. . . ." Then Barth's responses follow.*

Barth: I can answer them for you, but only with certain qualifications. My view of the church has never come through the eye of a historian. What *is* has moved me less at any one time than what may *become* through the Word of God in the power of the Spirit. So do not expect too much from me! But let us turn to your *first question!*

Weidmann: Professor Barth, you have devoted your work as a teacher of theology in a lifelong effort to the service of the church, and in closest proximity you have experienced the course of events in Germany as in Switzerland. The church has experienced a great deal of alteration and change during the past fifty years. How do you assess this change in things and the contemporary state of the life of the church in Germany and in Switzerland?

Barth: When I think back on my youth, then I can certainly detect a change. Unquestionably the church today appears outwardly more impressive. Back then, it looked to be on the point of dying out. Sometimes it appeared as if it had been abandoned even by its own people. Today, even in newspapers, which are fundamentally removed from the church, it is treated with a certain respect. To this corresponds also a completely different kind of activity of today's pastors in the church. How many things a pastor has to do! Men's work, women's meetings, youth groups, Sunday school, retreats, camps, films—and even more home visitations than before. In this way the church actually steps more into the field of vision.

The other phenomenon, the spiritual, may well be connected with this: Christian theology today acts as something distinct, something independent. We no longer dwell hidden in a corner as we once did. On that point, things have strangely changed: previously, we theologians had a mighty respect for the worldly wisdom of the poets and intellectuals. Even among us, Goethe's *Faust* enjoyed a reputation almost as a worldly bible, and the same could be said of the philosophers, of Kant and Hegel. For their part, the philosophers hardly noticed us in those days. Now things are completely different. This was especially obvious to me during the "Rencontres [Meetings]" in Geneva.[1] Today the philosophers register every word of ours with concern; they are nervous in the face of theology. I cannot but think of that amusing scene in *The Magic Flute* where the two characters give each other a fright: "Ha! That is the devil for sure!"[2] And there have also been political altercations already, where such a fear of the church on the part of the world has become apparent. . . .

This phenomenon is universal. It even extends to the Catholic Church. Perhaps it is connected to the catastrophes of war. How lonely was our stand as young pastors in 1910 with what we had received from Kutter and Ragaz![3] But today quite generally the Bible has been moved more to the center. Consider this: Around 1917 the adherents of the "positive" position struck the Apostles' Creed from the statutes of the "Protestant Church Association [Evangelisch-kirchlicher Verein]."[4] . . . Today we have the reverse occurrence: liberals in orthodox clothing![5] Everything aims at a middle line, with a quite diligent use of the Bible; that applies even to many of my own students. If I have always done theology in the sense that I took the Bible seriously, then I am of the same opinion even today that one really has to take it seriously. Much more seriously than that great crowd of pastors who have settled down comfortably on the middle line! Today the old polarities[6] have faded to a large extent. One cannot

1. The Rencontres Internationales de Genève [International Meetings in Geneva] are meetings of European intellectuals of very different persuasions for conversation and discussion. Barth took part in the fourth meeting under the theme "Pour un nouvel humanisme [For a New Humanism]" at the beginning of September 1949. The lecture he gave there as well as his report on the conference can be found in K. Barth, *Humanismus*, ThSt 28 (Zollikon: Evangelischer Verlag, 1950).

2. W. A. Mozart's opera *The Magic Flute*, act 1, scene 8.

3. Hermann Kutter (1869–1931) and Leonhard Ragaz (1868–1945) count among the most significant advocates of the religious-socialist movement.

4. Cf. A. Zimmerman, *Fünfzig Jahre Arbeit im Dienste des Evangeliums für das reformierte Schweizervolk: Geschichte des Schweizerischen evangelisch-kirchlichen Vereins, 1871–1921* (Zurich: Kirchenfreund, 1921), 31, 34; cf. also W. Hadorn, "Jahresversammlung des Schweizerischen Evangelisch-kirchlichen Vereins in Baden," in *Der Kirchenfreund* 47 (1913): 334–35. The "positive" position in the Swiss Church, gathered in this association, gave up its adherence to the Apostles' Creed on September 29/30, 1913.

5. Cf. also K. Barth, "Möglichkeiten liberaler Theologie heute," in *Schweizerische Theologische Umschau* 30 (1960): 96. Barth especially saw his Basel colleague Fritz Buri (1907–95) as an example of this form of "liberalism."

6. Since the 1830s there had arisen a strong polarization in the church life of Reformed Switzerland, which continued to have an effect long into the twentieth century, through the appearance of the

make much sense of it: there is much agreement and little opposition. However, one can say that there is certainly much better preaching than before, generally speaking. There is now a biblical depth that was missing in those days.

It seems to me characteristic of the current situation that a general cultural newspaper such as *Du* [*you*], after a varied mixture of articles, can feature an article about toads and frogs and then one about—the theologian Karl Barth.[7] . . . Along with the hooligans, the toads, and the frogs, we are therefore arousing a certain interest!

Weidmann: Professor Barth, the current circumstances are moving so quickly, and new things are making way with such speed and intensity, that the church cannot possibly remain unmoved by it. How do you assess the task of our Swiss church in particular in the face of this global upheaval?

Barth: It is awkward that the question has to be asked in this way. Something is happening in the world, something very radical and profound—and the pastors together with their communities have overslept and are rubbing their eyes, wondering whether they might have something to say about it. . . .*

[* *Weidmann* here inserts the following report into his interview:] At this moment, the telephone rang; the discussion was interrupted, and in his frank way Professor Barth let me in on what the call was about: in Hamburg, a socialist politician had saddled himself with a blasphemy trial, because he had publicly declared that the Christian Democrats were carrying on "Adenauer politics" on workdays and "going to chew the Host on Sundays." This expression was perceived to be blasphemous; a report from the Faculty of Protestant Theology in Hamburg concurred. The politician appealed to Professor Barth; the latter responded that the expression "chewing with the mouth" had played a role in the theology of the sixteenth century,[8] that the term "chewing" was used in John 6[:56], and that he could not consider the expression blasphemous. The socialist presented Professor Barth's written communication and was acquitted. Now the Catholic newspaper *Rheinischer Merkur* was directing an attack against Barth.[9] [Now we return to our discussion.]

"Reformers" [*die Reformer*] (liberals), to whom were opposed the advocates of a "positive" position [*die Positiven*] ("Bible-believing" orthodox). In 1871 the latter formed the "Swiss Protestant Church Association" [Schweizerischer Evangelisch-kirchlicher Verein] (cf. n. 4 above). Both had corresponding branches in many local congregations. In addition, there were "Mediators" [*Vermittler*], who organized themselves as the "Swiss Church Society" [Schweizerische kirchliche Gesellschaft].

7. *Du: Kulturelle Monatsschrift* 20, no. 235 (September 1960): 25–30, by K. Marti, "Karl Barth" (see above, chap. 8, re Marti); and 52–57, by J. Fester and W. Goetz, "Frösche, Kröten, Unken [Frogs, Toads, Fire-bellied Toads]."

8. For instance, the Formula of Concord (1579/80) teaches the "oralis manducatio [chewing with the mouth] benedicti panis et vini, item corporis et sanguinis Christi perfectio" (Solid Declaration VII, 86: *BSLK* 1001.23–25). Such chewing happens "non tamen Capernaitice [in such a way that Christ is *quasi* broken with the teeth], sed supernaturali et coelesti modo [in a supernatural and heavenly way]" (Epitome VII, 15: *BSLK* 799.20–21). There such chewing is maintained both against the spiritualist teaching of a purely spiritual partaking and also against the Catholic teaching of asserting a possible renunciation of partaking in the Eucharist altogether.

9. Cf. H. B., "Karl Barth und die Oblaten," in *Rheinischer Merkur* 15 (February 12, 1960). The article comments sarcastically ("a theological dodge"; "What can a judge accomplish against Karl Barth?") on a postcard from Barth, with which he had intervened by way of a short opinion in a trial against the writer Heinrich Christian Meier. The latter had observed in an ironical comment, "Nachwort zum Katholikentag," in *Die Andere Zeitung*, August 28, 1959: "How then should older people—according to Pius—be an example for younger people, when today even eleven-year-olds recognize that their fathers and mothers indeed chew the host, but do nothing against the atomic bomb?" The words "chew the host" were the grounds for two Catholics to charge Meier with blasphemy. While the

Barth: There is always something wrong with the church when it is the world that first has to call to its attention that it should say and do something. A hundred years ago, it was socialism's turn. How long did it take until people in the church such as Wichern, Stoecker, Naumann, Kutter, and Ragaz stood up and had something to say on the social question! The church is always too late and then no longer makes any real impression. Many a social democrat could not even be lured from his comfort zone by someone like Ragaz. It was similar in Germany with the national movement: the church stood [with mouth] agape and decided that something must be going on here, and—participated. . . . But the prophetic does not consist of subsequently repeating what individuals in the world have already said. It concerns things that the church should simply have known, if it had read its Bible more attentively. Our task is to experience upheaval ourselves. Judgment is supposed to begin at the house of God [cf. 1 Pet. 4:17]. Yesterday as today, we can only allow ourselves to be called to repentance. If only we would do that, before the world is in complete disarray [cf. 1 John 5:19]!

Weidmann: How do you assess, Professor Barth, the current student of theology, who is supposed to grow tomorrow into the responsible position of a "servant of the Word of God"?

Barth: I assess this student optimistically. Since 1921 I have had contact with the young student generation,[10] and I look back on that thankfully. I cannot complain even now. They do participate. My concern is this: What will become of them, when they go out into the church? Will they then also make compromises, swing over to the middle line?

Weidmann: Is the student youth of today not more precocious, less defiant, and less rebellious than before?

Barth: Yes, rebellion and the youth movement: they were around earlier—with a penchant for later becoming Nazi. The student of today is more staid. But in a decidedly positive manner I assess the student's enthusiasm for conscientious exegetical work on the Old and New Testaments. That is something full of promise for the church.

Hamburg theologian K. D. Schmidt thought that the words fitted the legal definition of religious slander, the Catholic theologian Uhde and Karl Barth considered the words to be unobjectionably orthodox. After the defendant had been acquitted, not least on account of Barth's postcard, various polemic responses to his text, both public and private, resulted. Cf. also "Die Theologen waren sich nicht einig: Wurde die Kirche beschimpft? [The Theologians Did Not Agree: Was the Church Insulted?]," in *Die Zeit*, February 5, 1960.

10. After ten years of serving as a pastor, Barth became professor in Göttingen in October 1921.

12. Conversation with Representatives of the Moravian Church (Herrnhuter Brüdergemeine) 1960

On October 12, 1960, Barth met with representatives of the Brüdergemeine (the Moravian Church) from the Federal Republic of Germany (West Germany), from the DDR (German Democratic Republic—East Germany), from Holland and Switzerland, for a discussion in the Zinzendorf House on Leimenstraße, which is the headquarters of the Basel Society of Brethren. The invitation to this occasion was very welcome for him since in his later years he, overcoming a long-lasting mistrust, had learned to value the theology of Zinzendorf to a surprisingly high degree (cf. especially the Church Dogmatics *IV/1:683 =* KD *IV/1:763, but even already in* CD *II/2:568 =* KD *II/2:631). In reference to the points where the lines between them connect, Friedrich Gärtner had already provided a clue: "Karl Barth und Zinzendorf,"* Theologische Existenz, Neue Folge *40 (Munich, 1953). Gärtner was also the one who gave the impetus for the discussion at Basel.*

The gathering had been prepared carefully on the part of the organizers. Different participants had collated Zinzendorf quotations for the four subject areas to be discussed in what follows and had formulated theses as well as questions for Barth. Apparently the tasks related to this had been distributed beforehand. As Hellmut Reichel—the former pastor of the Brüdergemeine in Basel, who served as the discussion leader and sent the preparatory papers to Barth—described it in his accompanying letter of October 6, 1960, these "draft notes" had been mimeographed and were available to all the participants. Besides this, a series of further questions that were directed to Barth in writing came from individual members of the circle. For his part, Barth prepared himself for the meeting by writing down catchwords for each of the four themes. (All these materials are at the Karl Barth Archives.)

Several students of the Brüdergemeine have collated an official report from their collective notes, which then Barth proofread. It was published under the title "Official Report of the Discussion between Prof. Dr. K. Barth and Representatives of the Brüdergemeine," as number 13 (special edition) of Civitas praesens *(Königsfeld/Schwarzwald) in May 1961. This official report is printed in what follows in a slightly emended version.*

Besides Barth and Reichel, the following contributed to the discussion: Pastor Helmut Bintz, Zeist (Holland); Pastor Dr. Hellmuth Erbe, Niesky; Pastor Friedrich Gärtner, Pforzheim; Pastor Dr. Heinrich Gelzer, Emeritus Director at the Mission House in Basel; Pastor Dr. Walther Günther, Königsfeld; Attorney and Notary Dr. Marcus Löw, Basel; Pastor Erich Marx, Bad Boll; Pastor Dr. Heinz Motel, Director of the Brüderunität, Bad Boll; Pastor Hans Preiswerk, Bern; Pastor Heinz Schmidt, Königsfeld; Pastor Paul Theile, Menziken (Aargau Canton, Switzerland); in addition, two doctoral students of Barth: Gyula Bárczay, in whose dissertation Ecclesia semper reformanda: Eine Untersuchung zum Kirchenbegriff des 19. Jahrhunderts [*Ecclesia semper reformanda: An Examination concerning the Concept of the Church in the 19th Century] (Zurich: Evangelischer Verlag, 1961), a chapter (on 38–51) is named* "The Brüdergemeinde concerning the Renewal of the Church"; *and Hans Ruh, whose dissertation carries the title* Die christologische Begründung des ersten Artikels bei Zinzendorf [*The Christological Foundation of the First Article for Zinzendorf], in the series Basler Studien zur historischen und systematischen Theologie (Zurich: Evangelischer Verlag, 1967).*

1. Introduction

Reichel: In the following, what should be at issue for us is not a historical seminar, but rather an interrogation of Zinzendorf in and for our situation here. From such a questioning we hope to gain a benefit for ourselves in our *Brüdergemeine.*

Barth: Honorable Sirs and Brothers! Let me begin with a macarism: Be glad and thankful that you have your *Brüdergemeine!* With Zinzendorf you have a church father who is important and fruitful for the entire church. I would like to resolutely reject the question of abandoning the *Brüdergemeine.* Remain what you are! For me, it was not coincidence or caprice but necessity that over the course of the years I have worked myself closer to Zinzendorf. Earlier I said a few nasty things about Zinzendorf.[1]

If Zinzendorf was right in the most important thing—[yet] not always in the form [of expression], in referring to his center as Jesus Christ, he alone and completely, regarding the relationship of creation and redemption, regarding the view about God's already completed reconciliation with the world, regarding the relationship of gospel and law, regarding the view of the church as the community of the Lamb, the living Christ—if he was right, then I am allowed to say in all modesty that I am also right. My entire theological thinking revolves around this center, and in it I am challenged also. If at all, then Zinzendorf and I stand and fall with each other.

Yesterday, another question from my friend Gelzer[2] was delivered to me. He was asking about the difference between Zinzendorf as the "evangelist" [*euangelistēs*] and me as the "teacher" [*didaskalos*] and "prophet" [*prophētēs*]

---

1. K. Barth, *Der Römerbrief*, 2nd ed. (Munich: Kaiser, 1922), 129; later ed., 127; 15th ed. (Zurich: Theologischer Verlag, 1989), 138. There Barth protests against "that [love] which obscures the distance between God and [humans] and which is not grounded upon the fear of the Lord—as for example, the 'intimacy' of a Zinzendorfian, romantic, or Indian mysticism—it is, in the end, directed towards a 'No-God,' the God of this world," with which we "place ourselves in the line of his enemies." [Cf. K. Barth, *The Epistle to the Romans*, trans. E. C. Hoskyns (Oxford: Oxford University Press, 1933), 151.] Cf. K. Barth, *Die christliche Dogmatik im Entwurf*, vol. 1, *Die Lehre vom Worte Gottes: Prolegomena zur christlichen Dogmatik* (Munich: Kaiser, 1927), 267; ed. G. Sauter, new ed. (Zurich: Theologischer Verlag, 1982), 358: against Zinzendorf's "Jesuolatry"; K. Barth, *Die protestantische Theologie im 19. Jahrhundert: Ihre Vorgeschichte und ihre Geschichte (1932/33)* (Zollikon: Theologischer Verlag, 1947); 6th ed. (1994), 94–98, 101, 112; [K. Barth, *Protestant Theology in the Nineteenth Century: Its Background and History*, trans. B. Cozens and J. Bowden (Grand Rapids: Eerdmans, 2002), 99–105, 107–8, 118–19;] and K. Barth, *CD* I/2:137 [*KD* 150–51].

2. For the relationship of Barth to Pastor Heinrich Gelzer, cf. Bw.Th. 1:534 (List of Names); further, K. Barth, *Briefe: 1961–1968*, ed. J. Fangmeier and H. Stoevesandt (Zurich: Theologischer Verlag, 1975), 2nd ed. (1979), 204–5.

(cf. Eph. 4:11). Why would this question be asked? Perhaps out of the apprehension that a meeting between an elephant and a whale could occur?[3] This is not a good differentiation. Zinzendorf was *also* wise. Whoever speaks like a strong flowing stream as he did is also a teacher. There is a theology of Zinzendorf! And I would also not like to be defined solely as a teacher who is raising his index finger. For me in my own way, it is also an issue of "winning souls for the Lamb."[4] There, no differentiation needs to be made.

2. My Creator, My Savior

Barth: The first subject for our discussion (Theme I), should stand at the beginning since it is the central theme of Zinzendorf: "My Creator, my Savior."[5] It can also be read as "The Savior has created the world."[6] The first formulation is a confession, so to speak, the original confessional sentence, whereas the reverse arises from theoretical reflection. What does this confessional sentence mean? The entire reality of the world, how it is; the entire reality of human individuals, how they are in their existence—all have their basis, origin, meaning, law, and goal nowhere else except in Jesus the Christ, true human being and true God. Thus the Creator is not only generally the Logos, but also concretely the Savior. He is the basis, origin, meaning, law, and goal of everything that is. (Compare Zinzendorf's poem "Allgegenwart [Omnipresence] . . .").[7]

Could Zinzendorf appeal to the Scriptures? In view of the following places—John 1:3, 10 (*panta di' autou*); 1 Corinthians 8:6 (*di' hou ta panta*); Colossians 1:15–[16] (*prōtotokos pasēs ktiseōs*); Hebrews 1:2 (*di' hou kai epoiēsen tous aiōnas*)—I would say, this statement, "My creator is my Savior," spoken broadly, is justified in terms of the New Testament.

However, my question to Zinzendorf would be with respect to the distinction between Father and Son. For it says in 1 Corinthians 8:6: "God, the Father, from whom [*ex hou*] are all things and for whom we exist, and one Lord, Jesus

3. The metaphor of elephant and whale, "which are unable to come to each other," Barth probably took over from Fr. Overbeck, *Christentum und Kultur: Gedanken und Anmerkungen zur modernen Theologie*, ed. C. A. Bernouli (Basel: Schwabe, 1919); reprint (Darmstadt: Wissenschaftliche Buchgesellschaft, 1963), 215–16. Barth applied this metaphor frequently: to his relationship with R. Bultmann as to that with E. Brunner: K. Barth and R. Bultmann, *Briefwechsel: 1922–1966*, ed. B. Jaspert (Zurich: Theologischer Verlag, 1971), 196; 2nd ed. as *Briefwechsel: 1911–1966* (Zurich: Theologischer Verlag, 1994), 192; and correspondingly, three days after this conversation, in his television interview with V. Sproxton below.
4. Cf. stanza 2 of the hymn "Mein Zeugniß in der Welt [My Witness in the World]," in *Gesangbuch zum Gebrauch der evangelischen Brüdergemeinen* (Gnadau: Brüdergemeinen, 1819), no. 1402: "Gott thu mir meine Bitt, über dem Geschäft zu sterben, Seelen für das Lamm zu werben! [God, answer my prayer, to die engaged in the occupation of winning souls for the Lamb!]." Similarly, stanza 2 of the hymn "Seit uns Gottes Geist den Zug," by M. G. Hehl (1705–87), a close coworker with Zinzendorf, in *Gesangbuch der evangelischen Brüdergemeine* (Gnadau: Verlag der Unitätsbuchhandlung, 1927), no. 362.
5. Cf. N. L. von Zinzendorf, *Vier und dreyßig HOMILIAE über die Wunden-Litaney der Brüder, Gehalten auf dem Herrnhaag in den Sommer-Monathen 1747* (n.p.): Zu finden in den Brüder-Gemeinen, 1747), 23: "That is a mystery: all humans have a part in it, . . . *that their Creator is their Savior.*"
6. *Spangenbergs Apologetische Schlußschrift: Worin über tausend Beschuldigungen gegen die Brüdergemeinen und ihren zeitherigen Ordinarium nach der Wahrheit beantwortet werden* (Leipzig and Görlitz, 1752 [reprint, Hildesheim: Olms, 1964]), 570: "In brief, the Savior has created the world."
7. This poem of Zinzendorf titled "O Ens Entium Miserere [O Fount of Founts, Have Mercy]," turns from the worship of the incomprehensible God toward his "enveloped majesty" in the child Jesus. It perhaps comes from the year 1722. The text is found in N. L. Zinzendorf, *Über Glauben und Leben*, selected by O. Herpel (Berlin: Hochweg-Verlag, 1925), 116–18.

Christ, through whom [*di' hou*] are all things . . ." There is a clear difference between Father and Son. Also, Colossians 1:15–[16], where the Son is designated as *eikōn*, the image of God. The New Testament therefore shows that the Savior *also* created the world. Not exclusively, anyway not the Son alone! When Zinzendorf says the Savior is the "actual creator,"[8] he goes too far. And when he characterizes the Father and the Spirit as his "helpers,"[9] then too much is said. Also, the statement "Christ is the Father"[10] goes too far. Indeed, Jesus taught his disciples to pray to the Father, and he himself is the one worshiping the Father.[11] He is the Son of the Father, the one who is obedient to the Father. That Father and Son are one (cf. John 10:30) does not mean that the Son is the Father. Admittedly, a perfect agreement of essence exists. The Son is to be seen as image and mirror of the Father. They act together. The Son is involved in the creation, but precisely as the Son. Most Distinguished Lord Count [von Zinzendorf], not so rashly emotional! The speculation of the old doctrine of the Trinity was certainly speculation, but it was a speculation that was healthier than Zinzendorf's.

The covenant is the internal basis of creation; the creation is the external basis of the covenant.[12] This is the way I would restate what Zinzendorf means here. The creation by itself is not yet the covenant; creation is rather the covenant's presupposition and therefore the external basis of the covenant. Jesus Christ is truly and essentially God as the Son of the Father and as such participates in the creation. He is truly and essentially God *also* in the work and word of God, *also* as the Creator. Think for a moment about Marcion, the grand old christocentric! He fell into the other extreme in that he radically separated the Creator God from redemption. But Zinzendorf is also not right with his blending of Father and Son. If only he had merely said, "*also* the Creator!"

Jesus Christ is recognizable in his death on the cross, that is, in his obedience toward the Father, which he shows in the "Our Father," in Gethsemane, and on the cross. By doing this, he proves himself as the Son, who with the Father is one, but not identical. In view of the Trinitarian unity, one should not merely say "actually the Son," but also "actually" the Father and the Holy Spirit are the subject of the divine action toward the world.

The conclusions that Zinzendorf drew are correct in that he sees anthropology, law, and ethics from the angle of Christology. We want to uphold the thesis "My Creator, my Savior," not only in the eighteenth century, but also today. However, the overflow of feeling we leave to the eighteenth century; we do not need to join in. Thus it remains established: My Creator is my Savior!

Marx: How did Zinzendorf get his emphasis on the humanness of Jesus? Didn't he want to demonstrate clearly the connecting line of thought, that the true God became the true human being in Christ?

---

8. N. L. Zinzendorf, *Eine Sammlung Offentlicher Reden, Von Dem HErrn der unsere Seligkeit ist / und über die Materie von seiner Marter: In dem Jahre 1742*, Pennsylvanische Reden 1–2 (Büdingen: Stöhr, 1746), 1:220: "Who is the actual Creator? . . . None other than Jesus Christ, the true God alone."
9. Ibid.: "God the Father and the Spirit are with him as the *Heylands Gehülffen* [Savior's helpers]: they serve thereby the Lamb."
10. Ibid., 181. "Indeed, in a way it is the case that the Lord Jesus is the actual Father, . . . and that, when it is taken precisely, the 'Our Father' belongs addressed to the Lord Jesus."
11. Cf. Matt. 6:9; 26:39.
12. Cf. *CD* III/1:94, 228 [*KD* 103, 258].

Barth: Yes, indeed! Zinzendorf's formula contains both the emphasis on Jesus' humanity as well as his deity.[13] From the perspective of early church's Christology, there are no problems here.

Gärtner: One will probably have to say that Zinzendorf did not come to terms with the Corinthians passage according to which the Son will become subject to the Father (1 Cor. 15:24, 28).[14]

Barth: One should not place oneself in such situations; one should not sit down on such branches where one then gets in a quarrel with the apostle Paul. —The "Our Father," which has its definite place in the liturgy of the *Brüdergemeine* . . .

Schmidt: At the beginning!

Barth: . . . must surely be taken seriously. There the notion is indeed clear about coming to the Father and consequently about a difference between Father and Son. There can be no disorder in the Trinity. God cannot be characterized as grandfather and the Holy Spirit as mother (as Zinzendorf did occasionally).[15]

Reichel: Here one probably will have to take into account the historical background. Zinzendorf stood in the front lines against deistic speculation, over against which he emphasizes that God is *now* only recognizable in Christ. He once said that one must make religion easy.[16] Is not the individual in the missionary situation overburdened with the doctrine of the Trinity? The sole emphasis on Jesus Christ might be explicable then from the mission situation.

Barth: Yes, yes. It simply always is dangerous in the world of faith and the church if one reacts all too severely to opponents. Even Christology is not to be made into a principle. If one singles out a great truth unprotected, then heresy springs up. The truth is also not to be taken as a possession through "Christocentricity"—in the same way as when a child runs away quickly with a Christmas gift. Christocentricity as a principle by which the Trinity is destroyed is off the mark. We give honor to God when we let him be as he has given himself to be—as Father, Son, and Holy Spirit.

Gelzer: In the 1740s, the exaggeration becomes particularly evident in Zinzendorf; but I remember that in the hymns of 1757 more room was given again to

---

13. Cf. N. L. von Zinzendorf, *Ein und zwanzig Discurse über die Augspurgische Confession: Gehalten vom 15 Dec. 1747 bis zum 3 Mart. 1748 denen SEMINARIIS THEOLOGICIS FRATRUM zum Besten aufgefaßt und bis zur nochmaligen Revision des Autoris einstweilen mitgetheilt* [Görlitz: O. O. u. J., 1748; reprint, Hildesheim: Georg Olms, 1963], 95. "Nothing harms the Savior's deity, if one leaves his humanity quite human and small: for since we know that he is One Christ by the hypostatic union of God and the human being; so, the narrow circumstances of his humanity hinder nothing of the immensity of his deity."

14. Cf. ibid., 96–98: With this sentence in 1 Corinthians 15:24 about the surrender of the reign of the Son to the Father, Paul may have erred. Therefore, he was harshly chastised according to 2 Corinthians 12 so that "he was hit with fists by Satan's angels." Rather: "Whenever the Savior will begin to rule, He will not hand over the kingdom, but will rather dominate and rule the whole creation eternally. *He* must therefore rule, not the Savior, but the Father, until that (time) when he puts all enemies of the Savior at his (namely, Jesus') feet."

15. Evidence for this is quoted by J. A. Bengel, *Abriß der so genannten Brüdergemeine, in welchem die Lehre und die ganze Sache geprüft, das Gute und Böse dabei unterschieden und insonderheit die Spangenbergische Declaration erläutert wird* (Stuttgart: 1751; Berlin: 1858), 54.41ff. Inferred from the relation of Christ / the groom and the church / the bride, the title "Father-in-Law" (*Schwehr-Vater*) is also used for God the Father. For an understanding of the Holy Spirit as mother, cf. N. L. von Zinzendorf, *Eine Rede: Vom Mutteramte des heiligen Geistes*, in the appendix to his work *Der öffentlichen Gemein-Reden im Jahr 1747*, part 1 ([Barby?]: Zu finden in den Brüder-Gemeinen, 1748).

16. Relevant proof texts for this are offered by L. Hennig, *Kirche und Offenbarung bei Zinzendorf* (Zurich: n.p., 1939), 50–53.

the worship of the Father, possibly on the basis of the criticism of Bengel.[17] That's why Zinzendorf would probably agree with Barth.

Schmidt: The opinion about the Holy Spirit's office as Mother was abandoned soon after Zinzendorf, perhaps too soon. People were on the way to occupy themselves more with the human being. In this development, Zinzendorf and the *Brüdergemeine*, as Hirsch[18] sees it, had to be perceived as troublemakers. The unlucky man Zinzendorf spoiled the concept.

Barth: When I consider the confessional sentence "My Creator, my Savior," I am much more interested in the element of truth than in all the reservations. I would rather join with Zinzendorf in a few little errors than go along with Emanuel Hirsch and the "Father religion" of the eighteenth century.

Ruh: Here we probably must take into account that Zinzendorf thought in a manner that was more about perception than being.

Gärtner: Isn't Zinzendorf's talk about the Holy Spirit as the Mother still better than the current talk of the church as mother? Doesn't Zinzendorf's error appear more honorable from this oppositional framework?

Barth: I too do not like the talk of the church as mother, although one finds it even in Calvin.[19] Instead, should we now consider the Holy Spirit as mother? One should never commit oneself to things one says in confrontation. As the biblicist language of my father finally led me to liberalism, so liberalism had to be repelled again by me in the following period. For this reason I had to say then, for example, in my *Römerbrief:* Distance is needed![20] And so it had to come also in 1934 to my sharp "Nein" to Emil Brunner.[21] Later I brought in again the *theologia naturalis* through Christology;[22] today my critique would run as follows: one must say it, only differently—that is, christologically. Zinzendorf must certainly be understood from the antitheses. Yet with Goethe let us be warned: "Behold, my spirit calls to you from the cave: be a man and do not follow after it."[23] We do not have to share Zinzendorf's reactions, but we must seek to understand—and continue on.

Reichel: The statement "The Holy Spirit as Mother" is not intended to be an ontological statement (*Seinsaussage*) but is to be understood only as a picture, as a pictorial mode of expression, addressed only to the community (*Gemeine*). Zinzendorf was not an abstract thinker.

Gärtner: I see Zinzendorf's anthropomorphic speech as close to present-day psychology.

Schmidt: One could probably say that Zinzendorf was no "regular" theologian, but an "irregular" one.[24]

17. J. A. Bengel, *Abriß*, 29ff.
18. E. Hirsch, *Geschichte der neuern evangelischen Theologie im Zusammenhang mit den allgemeinen Bewegungen des europäischen Denkens*, vol. 2 (Gütersloh: Bertelsmann), 401–10.
19. J. Calvin, *Inst.* 4.1.4.
20. K. Barth, *Der Römerbrief*, 2nd ed., e.g., 18 (later ed., 16); 15th ed., 17: "He [God] acknowledges himself to be our God by creating and maintaining the distance by which we are separated from him" [Barth, *The Epistle to the Romans*, trans. E. C. Hoskyns (Oxford: Oxford University Press, 1968), 41].
21. K. Barth, *Nein! Antwort an Emil Brunner*, ThExh 14 (Munich: Kaiser, 1934). The "no" was related to natural theology. [ET: Karl Barth, "No!," in *Natural Theology: Comprising "Nature and Grace" by Emil Brunner and the Reply "No!" by Karl Barth*, trans. P. Fraenkel (Eugene, OR: Wipf & Stock, 2002), 70–128.]
22. Cf. *CD* IV/3.1:113–35 (*KD* 126–53).
23. Cf. the final lines of J. W. von Goethe's poem "Zu den Leiden des jungen Werthers" (1775): "Behold, his spirit beckoned me from the cave / Be a Man and do not follow me."
24. Cf. *CD* I/1:275 (*KD* 292): "There is a regular dogmatics and an irregular dogmatics." Under the examples for the latter, Zinzendorf is not mentioned.

Barth: Yes, yes. Let us have the sense of humor to put up with it, if we see what is right. But we need not so simply take over the picture of the mother.

Reichel: The Holy Spirit as mother is to be understood in the sense of the office, the *function* of mother (*Mutteramtes*), as a wet nurse and comforter of the child.

Ruh: In this context, I noticed that the functionary names of "mother" are predominantly expressed as verbs in Zinzendorf.

Barth: In one of the questions submitted to me, I have been asked whether the formula "My Creator, my Savior" could not serve as a help against interpretations of human life from a strictly biological or material point of view (*Biologismus und Materialismus*). Yes, I find it to be a wonderfully clear answer to dialectical materialism, which does not grasp and understand what this is all about. Spiritually speaking, preaching is probably easier in the DDR (East Germany) than in Basel, where the gospel is only all too well known. There in East Germany it is a good, new story,[25] a witness; here in Basel it is a theological opinion. Zinzendorf's preaching of the Savior is the best thing to preach in East Germany now.

3. The Meritorious Humanity of Jesus

Barth: In terms of the subject matter when Zinzendorf speaks of the meritorious humanity of Jesus, I can only say "yes." Jesus Christ is our justification, the enablement of our existence before God. Together with him as the Savior, we are right before God. However, the implications of the existence of the Savior for us do not exhaust themselves in this sentence about our justification in him. It is important to hear the *kai* (and) in 1 Corinthians 1:30. He has been made for us "righteousness *and* sanctification." The "and sanctification" (*kai hagiasmos*) must come along with it. Then even sanctification would not be our business, as the Pietists think, but rather the merit of Christ. However, the eschatological redemption (*apolytrōsis*) must also follow as a consequence. And in Zinzendorf this is perhaps not as clearly stated as something still unresolved.

Sanctification means being placed in the service of God. The human being, as a human being in Jesus Christ, is freed to be for God. And that is the point for Zinzendorf: our justification and sanctification are already accomplished in Jesus Christ. As the Son of God, he is also human. He lives his life and dies his death in obedience to God, and that is not only for himself, but also for us. That is what meritorious means. I would make the connection here with the concept of the covenant. God keeps the covenant. God is faithful to Israel, even without a reciprocal faithfulness. Israel is unfaithful. From God's side, nothing is lacking. From the human side, everything is lacking. In Jesus Christ the covenant is fulfilled. He reciprocates the faithfulness and thus closes the circle. "True God" (*vere Deus*) is now in the "true human" (*vere homo*). Jesus Christ fulfilled the definition, the essence of humanity: to be a servant of God (Isa. 53). He takes the place of Israel. He is the true Israelite who in the Old Testament would be

---

25. Quoting verse 1 of the hymn "Vom Himmel hoch da komm ich her [From heaven above to earth I come]," by Martin Luther (around 1538), *GERS* 115; *EKG* 16; *EG* 24: "Ich bring euch gute neue Mär [I bring to you good new news]."

waited for in vain. Now the authentic human being is finally and fully here. All the weight in Zinzendorf lies on the "It is finished" (*tetelestai*): It is finished (John 19:30), it is all fulfilled!

I stand fully and completely with this. All consideration of our sanctification and every ethical reflection must flow out from the statement that the goal already has been reached and fulfilled and that everything lies behind us. Kohlbrügge once was asked, "When did you convert?" Answer: "On Golgotha!"[26] Zinzendorf probably could have said the same thing.

Interjection: In the context of the penitential struggle (*Bußkampf*), he once said something similar![27]

Barth: If Paul is not mistaken in 1 Corinthians 1:30, then every act of humans starts at the goal and strives there no more. There begins every repentance, every obedience. There the life of the Christian begins. It is an entirely practical matter to accept that which Christ has done for us. I am allowed to accept this "for me," but really accept it, not merely gawk at it (*angaffen*). I am called to obedience, and I am taken in to it. We do not need to repeat sanctification any longer, but only to live it. The concept of [Christ's] representation (*Stellvertretung*) cannot be abandoned. It is the basis and essence of all ethics. The old orthodox only gawked at it (*gegafft*)! There is no comfort from being a spectator. He is now in my place. If he stands in my place, then there remains for me nothing else to do than to act according to this fact. Here one is equally distant from legalism and antinomianism. "Christ is our morality."[28] I should like to underscore this sentence three times, five times, even ten times! You must have love *for him*. Everything else will then fall into place. You must rejoice that he is here.

Now to the question that was also placed before me: "We Moravians probably have had to repeat over and over this testimony about the simultaneity of justification and sanctification as our contribution in the conversation with and within Pietism. May we continue to hold on to this?"

I say: Not only are you permitted to maintain it, but you ought to do so. Yes, indeed. Yes! That is not merely a contribution, not merely a complement or small little counterweight. It is important: this is the center. You must have the courage to stand by it. One must say it loudly like Zinzendorf did against Wesley.[29] Wesley also has his great merit, but at this point, please, do not deviate

---

26. Cf. H. Fr. Kohlbrügge, *Die Lehre des Heils, in Fragen und Antworten dargelegt*, with a foreword by P. Lütge (Elberfeld: Verlag der Niederländisch-reformierte Gemeinde, 1903), Question 316.

27. *Des Herrn Grafen Ludwig von Zinzendorff Sieben Letzte Reden So In der Gemeine, Vor seiner am 7. Aug. erfolgten abermahligen Abreise nach America, gehalten* (Büdingen: Stöhr, 1742/43), 116–17: "To whom does it come to endure the penitential struggle? And here I am of a sure opinion . . . that the Savior, the Lamb of God, has endured it for us all at one time."

28. Cf. N. L. von Zinzendorf, *Zwey und Dreyßig einzelne Homiliae Oder Gemein-Reden in denen Jahren 1744. 1745. 1746* (n.p.: Zu finden in denen Brüder-Gemeinen, 1746), 29: *Rede:* "There is absolutely no inner morality besides the Savior."

29. *An Extract of The Reverend Mr. John Wesley's Journal, from Nov. 1, 1739, to Sept. 3, 1741* (London: W. Strahan, 1744), 100 (quoted in S. Eberhard, *Kreuzes-theologie: Das reformatorische Anliegen in Zinzendorfs Verkündigung* [Munich: Kaiser, 1937], 123), offers the following version of the memorable discussion between Wesley and Zinzendorf: "*Wesley:* 'I think we are fighting over words. Is not every true believer holy?' *Zinzendorf:* 'Most assuredly. But holy in Christ, not in themselves.' *Wesley:* 'But, do they live in a holy manner?' *Zinzendorf:* 'Indeed, they live in a holy manner in everything.' *Wesley:* 'Don't they also have a holy heart?' *Zinzendorf:* 'Most certainly.' *Wesley:* 'Doesn't it follow that persons are holy in themselves?' *Zinzendorf:* 'No! No! They are holy only in Christ. They are not holy in themselves. They have no holiness at all in themselves.'" [W. Pugnamus, opinior, de verbis. Nonne omnis vere credens Sanctus est? Z. Maxime. Sed Sanctus in Christo, non in se. W. Sed nonne Sancte vivit? Z. Imo, sancte in omnibus vivit. W. Nonne, et cor sanctum habet? Z. Certissime. W. Nonne, ex

from Zinzendorf one finger's width! One must not take sanctification into one's own hands. That is a stumbling block to the "positive" Christians. That it led from time to time to antinomianism in the old *Brüdergemeine*—not only in the sifting period—must not lead to assigning the gospel the place after the law. An antinomian error may seem to be close at hand, but the sequence is valid at any cost: gospel, then law. *Abusus non tollit usum!* (Abuse does not take away use!) The Lutheran dogma of law and gospel is like a cat that falls again and again on its feet. Against this sequence it is important to give kindly priority to the gospel. In this, the *Brüdergemeine* will and must become a stumbling block in German Lutheranism—admittedly, in an entirely friendly way. You cannot do it in a quarrelsome manner!

My question to Zinzendorf would be this: Hasn't his thinking about this exemplary meritorious humanity of Christ been to a great extent abstract, and didn't he speak of Christ in such a way that the union of *vere Deus—vere homo* was really threatened? "Divinization of the creature," as I called it earlier, certainly was not what Zinzendorf wanted. I was too strong in my expression here.[30] But from the topic of the wounds,[31] a line via Schleiermacher and the new rationalism to the "historical Jesus" could emerge. In the talk about the humanity of Christ, perhaps one could recognize more of Calvin than Luther. Calvin also distinguishes rather strictly between the divinity and humanity of Christ. But that is only a question; perhaps . . .

It appears to me that at most the derivation of a work ethic from Jesus' faithfulness as a craftsman is possible.[32] But the derivation of a sexual ethics or marriage ethics[33] is very artificial, however, and must be set with a question mark. In any case, Jesus was not married.—But the crucial teaching on the meritoriousness of Jesus is to be applauded.

Günther: While every feature of Jesus' human personality has meritorious character for us, Zinzendorf sees every single feature of the life of Jesus bracketed by the cross. The derivation of a work ethic and sexual ethics shows the outermost extreme of this progress. Zinzendorf probably wants to say that the *vere homo* encompasses our entire life and therefore also the areas of work and sex. Zinzendorf simply expresses this in his own style.

Schmidt: An example is when he says that one should get ready for the sexual life up to the coital act by praying.[34] None would probably have the guts to preach this to the community today. Yet what remains to consider is the emphasis on holiness even in the sexual life. In his graphic talk about the wounds, the side hole, and the blood, it seems to me that Zinzendorf is inspired by Bengel, who says that the blood of Christ as a source for reconciliation can be "tapped into" again and again.[35] At this point the danger arose of too sharp a separation

---

consequenti, sanctus est in se? Z. Non, non. In Christum tantum. Non sanctus in se. Nullam omnino habet Sanctitatem in se.]"

30. Cf. *CD* I/2:137–38 (*KD* 150–51).

31. Allusion to the cult of blood and wounds with the hole in Christ's side. Cf. E. Beyreuther, "N. L. von Zinzendorf," in *RGG*[3], vol. 6, col. 1914.

32. N. L. von Zinzendorf, *Vier und Dreyzig Homiliae*, 120–27.

33. Cf. E. Beyreuther, *Ehe-Religion bei Zinzendorf*, in KuD 6 (1960): 276–305.

34. Cf. *Spangenbergs Apologetische Schlußschrift*, 607–8: "We do everything—including words and deeds—in his name, and . . . we praise God and his Father in the act and through the act."

35. J. A. Bengel, *Gnomon Novi Testamenti in quo ex native verborum vi simplicitas, profunditas, concinnitas, salubritas sensuum coelestium indicator* (Tübingen: Schramm, 1742), 967 (at Heb. 12:24). Bengel

between earthly nearness and heavenly distance of the meritorious Savior. No doubt Zinzendorf attempted to bring it together again.

Bintz: If one thinks of the hymn "Auf daß in jeder Eh' erschein / ein Bild von Ihm und der Gemein [So that in every marriage an image may appear of Him and the community],"[36] then it seems to me to be important for Zinzendorf's understanding of marriage that he sees in it a reflection of the relationship between the Exalted One and his church in the sense of Ephesians 5, a reflection of God's love. Tanner[37] appears to see something right here, when he—perhaps somewhat unguardedly—thinks that Zinzendorf's sexual ethics can be derived from the Trinity. Perhaps, Professor Barth, here one can even see a certain analogy to your own opinion (*Auffassung*).

Schmidt: In this context, I refer to Zinzendorf's own wedding song (*Hochzeitslied*)[38] and to the "Festival of the Marriage Choir" (*Ehechorfest*), still celebrated in the *Brüdergemeine* today.

Gärtner: Doesn't this opinion of marriage show that a piece of natural theology has been included here legitimately?

Barth: Yes, yes. Here the will expresses itself to integrate natural theology into doctrine via Christology.

Reichel: In the same way, in his work ethic, Zinzendorf's concern comes to expression to make the small and smallest worthy of honor for humankind.

Barth: That is certainly the truth content: we do it in *Christ's* authority.

Gärtner: With Zinzendorf and pietistic thought, hasn't sanctification been limited to the private realm? Do the attempts to form local church communities (*Ortsgemeinden*) not point in this direction along which the *Brüdergemeine* later got into a kind of dualistic doctrine of the two kingdoms and thus remained apolitical?

Barth: Before the twentieth century, there was no topic of political responsibility as part of what it means to be a Christian, and frequently it wasn't even discovered at all. For Zinzendorf the two-kingdoms doctrine was not yet a problem: temporal authority was simply there as a matter of course. It may have been different outside of Europe. The most significant attempt to go new ways was probably the formation of a community of living (*Lebensgemeinschaft*) in Bethlehem (Pennsylvania). This step must surely be understood in light of the particular situation.[39]

Erbe: Yes, the Brothers simply had to act in the muddled political situation. For example, Zinzendorf even approved a brother's dispatch into the Parliament of Pennsylvania. So Zinzendorf comments positively on the parliamentary form of government.

---

inserts an essay about the blood of Christ, which, always staying separate from him, remains preserved for ever and as such is applied to us and thus redeems us.

36. ". . . und in unsrer eh erscheine / Christi bild, und der gemeine, / Herr! Wir bitten, mache du [and that in our marriage the image of Christ and the community may appear, Lord! We pray, make it happen!]." Written as a poem by Zinzendorf in 1728, in *Herrnhuter Gesangbuch* (1735), no. 849.

37. Friedrich Tanner, *Die Ehe im Pietismus* (Zurich: Zwingli Verlag, 1952).

38. N. L. von Zinzendorf, "Die Seligkeiten Christi: An seinem Hochzeit-Tage, 7. Sept. 1722," in *Geistliche Gedichte des Grafen von Zinzendorf,* collected and arranged by A. Knapp (Stuttgart/Tübingen: Cotta, 1845), 30–31.

39. Cf. H. Erbe, *Bethlehem, Pa.: Eine kommunistische Herrnhuter Kolonie des 18. Jahrhunderts* (Stuttgart: Ausland & Heimat, 1929).

Schmidt: He could have agreed to the execution of Charles I for reasons other than puritanical, as he once expressed it.[40]

Barth: I can imagine that the doors were opened at least a tiny crack in the direction of political responsibility at that time and that, when it came to sanctification, Zinzendorf therefore thought not only in private terms but, at least incipiently, already in the direction of political responsibility. One could probably do even more along his line. In principle, the apolitical attitude of Pietism was probably overcome in Zinzendorf. As for the rest, he certainly was an incorrigible aristocrat and demanded shared political responsibility (*Mitverantwortung*) as Lord of the Estate (*als Standesherr*).

Theile: This aristocratic attitude shows itself also in his missionary activity. He preferred being a mission director to being a mission's messenger.

Schmidt: We probably could say that the rudiments of his theology of missions betray political-social thinking. This shows itself in that he goes to despised and vanishing peoples like the Hottentots and the Eskimos,[41] while the Pietists from Halle (*Hallenser*) wanted to prove their superiority over against the world religions in their missions to India and China.

Erbe: Inwardly, Zinzendorf was free for the demands of every different situation, so that he could act differently in America from the way he could in Europe. One must not turn his remarks into a political theory.

Schmidt: To draw our attention back to the theme of authority: Romans 13 is frequently present in Zinzendorf. One prays a great deal for the authorities.

Barth: I always like to pray for the press in the worship service, because they represent a good bit of political authority.[42] If anyone needs prayer, then it is the journalist. Political cooperation results from prayer for the authorities. If one prays for people, one must also work for them; one must also take an interest in their activity.[43]

Gärtner: And this especially in eastern Europe?

Barth: But not like Dibelius![44]

Gelzer: [Concerning the relationship of divinity and humanity in Christ:] Surely a warning against abstraction is in order, but it seems to me that there Zinzendorf was more a Lutheran than a Calvinist: he is concerned with God becoming a human.

---

40. Charles I of England, executed on January 30, 1649. According to a communication from H. Schmidt, Königsfeld, Zinzendorf expressed this opinion, as recorded in the minutes of the Gothaer Synodus (June 12–20, 1740).

41. Cf. K. Müller, *200 Jahre Brüdermission: Das erste Missionsjahrhundert* (Herrnhut: Verlag der Missionsbuchhandlung, 1931).

42. See K. Barth, *Predigten: 1954–1967*, ed. H. Stoevesandt (Zurich: Theologischer Verlag, 1979; 2nd ed., 1981), 71, 80, 89, 103, 120, 129, 137, 144, 162, 170, and passim.

43. According to the published notes of the conversation, one of those present apparently referred to the "Small Litany of the Church," by Zinzendorf. The "Small Litany of the Church" for the "Preaching Assembly" is found in the appendix of the *Gesangbuch der Evangelischen Brüdergemeine* (Hamburg: Wittig, 1967). It goes back to Zinzendorf: *Das Litanei-Büchlein nach der bey den Brüdern dermalen hauptsächlich gewöhnlichen Singe-Weise* (Barby: [Druckerei der Brüdergemeine,] 1757), 49ff.

44. Otto Dibelius expressed himself on the topic at hand in a brief private pamphlet, which stirred up considerable discussions within the Evangelical Church in Germany, in the following manner: "Calling rulers of a totalitarian regime 'authorities' [*Obrigkeit*] would be a mockery of the German language. Above all—and that is what must concern the theologian—it would be something completely different from what Paul wanted to say in Romans 13." *Kirchliches Jahrbuch 1959 für die evangelische Kirche in Deutschland* (Gütersloh: Gütersloher Verlagshaus, 1960), 128. Cf. also Barth, *Offene Briefe: 1945–1968*, ed. D. Koch (Zurich: Theologischer Verlag, 1984), 482n1.

Barth: My previous statement refers to the quote that was mentioned in the "draft notes": "He [Christ] has not conquered as God, but rather as a human being with powers with which we conquer. His father has stood by him, he stands by us. He did not have a power beyond that which he gives us. He has been like us in all things. Except for the one thing: that we are unfaithful people and he was a faithful heart."[45] Here, at any rate, I fear that a certain abstraction is present.

Schmidt: The meritoriousness of the humanity of Christ appears to me to be pressed too far in the idea of the "choirs" (*Choridee*).[46] It is well known that the young men were referred to the "carpenter," the married ones to Ephesians 5, while the widowed ones were to recognize themselves in the situation of the temporarily widowed community (*Gemeine*).The single sisters had no choice but to avail themselves of Mary.

Barth: That appears to me somewhat difficult to apply meaningfully. If one says in such an emphatic way that the community consists of men and women, then is this not a false separation, is not the body of Christ split in two? If I should tell you what I liked the least in your new Zinzendorf House, it is the two stairways and the two doors.[47] Are they not perhaps "hobbies"?

Reichel: I think behind that probably stands very strongly the idea of the family, the symbolic sign of the great family of God in which the individual Moravian families should be incorporated. By the way, the women in the *Brüdergemeine* had their solid place in the service of the care of souls.

Bintz: Zinzendorf's ethic is founded on the "Connection with the Savior."[48] He begins with a real, massive, often biblical picture. Is this picture an abstract fiction? How may we imagine this? Where is the connecting concrete thing? After all, God alone and the human alone are also abstractions. How do we handle this today in our pastoral care, Professor Barth? What can we do today?

Barth: There is no old and new knowledge here. We can only pray that the image of Jesus, the living Christ as true Man and true God in act, would actually stand before us again and again. With Zinzendorf it is not a different concern but rather the same. But we must say it in present-day language. I would even say: we must demythologize a little bit. However, . . . I know already! It was a mistaken development that Schleiermacher felt he had to leave the *Brüdergemeine.*[49] For him the *Brüdergemeine* was some kind of orthodoxy from

---

45. Zinzendorf, *Eine Sammlung Offentlicher Reden*, Pennsylvanische Reden 1:204.
46. For the *Choridee*, according to which the community lived in different "choirs"—children, singles, married, widows—cf. E. Beyreuther, *Zinzendorf und die sich allhier beisammen finden* (Marburg: Verlag der Francke-Buchhandlung, 1959), 221–28. Concerning the biblical themes (*topoi*) in the classification of individual "choirs," cf. *Christliches Gesang-Buch der Evangelischen Brüder-Gemeinen, zum dritten mal aufgelegt und durchaus revidirt* (n.p.: n.p., 1741), appendixes 1–12, esp. 2, likewise 3; ed. E. Beyreuther, G. Meyer, and G. Meyer-Hickel, new ed. (Hildesheim and New York: 1981), no. 1860, stanzas 2 and 18 (re the young ones); no. 2156 (re the married; ibid., stanza 5, re the widows); no. 2142 (re the single sisters).
47. These are to be used by men and women separately.
48. N. L. von Zinzendorf, *Einiger seit 1751. von dem Ordinario Fratrum zu London gehaltenen Predigten in dreyen Haupt-Abtheilungen edirter erster Band* (London and Barby: zu finden bey dem Seminario Theologico, 1756), 109: "Then what is the chief sum of all the Gospel . . . ? I call this according to my own personal way of expression, the personal connection with the Savior [*die persönliche connexion mit dem Heilande*]."
49. In the year 1787, the not quite 19-year-old Friedrich Schleiermacher cut himself loose from the Moravian Church and left their school (*Erziehungsanstalt*) at Barby because of doubts in Jesus' status as Son of God and the substitutionary atonement by Jesus' death. Cf. his correspondence with his father

which he had to free himself. With Zinzendorf it was not that way. Schleiermacher still has his best from Zinzendorf. The *Brüdergemeine* would simply have had to do a better job. With Spangenberg I do not hear any longer the direct language as in Zinzendorf.[50]

Gärtner: Zinzendorf called Christ the General-Elder (*den Generalältesten*) and the "Chief" (*Chef*);[51] doesn't that have concrete meaning for us today?

Barth: Yes, yes.

Marx: In the sermon, how can I proclaim Christ as the foundation of all ethics? I see the great difficulty if it does not stay with theological formulations but rather is proclamation with authority. How can we translate that? Doesn't it still require the community of saints?

Barth: The "how" depends on the "that." Is the "connection with the Savior" there? Then the "how" does follow from it! It is not to be had cheaply. You can't just shout out "Jesus!" The preacher must know of what she/he speaks. It is a matter of faith, of prayer and work. Theology also belongs to it. One cannot do without it. The name Jesus Christ must not be heard [just] verbally (*wörtlich*), but rather materially (*sachlich*) in the sermon. One must think further from him here and to him there, but not like the Bultmannians do, fleeing into existentiality! It is a spiritual issue, not an intellectual issue, that Jesus is being made audible.

Gärtner: Isn't there something similar to Zinzendorf in your theology, something like a "christological monism," as Althaus thinks he must accuse you of?[52] Or is there today really only either atheism or radical Christology?

Barth: If Christomonism means that sanctification does not join with justification, then No! However, if—as in Zinzendorf—justification and sanctification are connected and that is called Christomonism, then I accept the accusation of Christomonism. I will not be ashamed of it. Moreover, it appears to me that a justification-monism exists with the Lutherans, which leads to the dualism of Law and Gospel. On the other hand, there are voices in the Catholic realm who think that they can discern an overall agreement between my doctrine of justification and theirs, as it has happened in the book by Hans Küng, for example.[53] It is a very bold book. Directly under the nose of His Holiness, Küng has plowed through my *Church Dogmatics*. He must take responsibility for it; I told him that he is Catholic and I am Protestant (*evangelisch*). But he is convinced that his perspective will carry the day in Catholicism. I have asked him

from the beginning of the year 1787: *Aus Schleiermacher's Leben: In Briefen*, vol. 1 (Berlin: Reimer, 1858), 44–58, as well as an autobiographical text from 1794 (n.p.: n.p.), 11: "My concepts soon went so far from the system of the *Brüdergemeine* that I no longer believed I was able to remain a member of this same group with a clear conscience."

50. August Gottlieb Spangenberg (1704–92) was head of the *Brüdergemeine* after Zinzendorf's death in 1760. In his book *Idea fidei fratrum oder kurzer Begriff der christlichen Lehre in den evangelischen Brüdergemeinen* (Barby: Laux, 1779), new ed. (Gnadau: Pemsel, 1871), he blunted the peculiar edges of Zinzendorf's teaching.

51. On September 16, 1741, Jesus was proclaimed as "Chief-Elder" in the *Brüdergemeine*. Cf. the hymn, "Als Jesus das Ältestenamt übernahm [As Jesus Took Up the Office of Elder]," in *Geistliche Gedichte des Grafen Zinzendorf* (Stuttgart: Cotta, 1845), 288–89. Cf. further Zinzendorf, *Vier und Dreyßig HOMILIAE*, 357: "We look up to . . . the great Chief [*Chef*] of our confession."

52. Paul Althaus, *Die christliche Wahrheit: Lehrbuch der Dogmatik* (Gütersloh: Bertelsmann, 1947), 1:68–73.

53. H. Küng, *Rechtfertigung: Die Lehre Karl Barths und eine katholische Besinnung*, Sammlunge Horizonte, vol. 2 (Einsiedeln: Johannes Verlag, 1957).

whether he would still be saying the same thing if he were pope—after all, he is still a young man—and he responded, "Yes." We believe that the gospel also is powerful there. There are Catholic theologians with whom I much prefer to be in conversation than with some Protestant theologians.

Schmidt: Zinzendorf also befriended Cardinal Noailles.[54]

Barth: There is a secret ecumenism, which reaches further than that in Geneva. . . . [Likewise, I say once again]: I still prefer Zinzendorf's "hobbies" to some rather orthodox tediousness in other churches. At least Zinzendorf still possessed imagination.

4. The "Connection" with the Savior

Barth: Coming now to our third topic, we are concerned with the "Connection with the Savior" that is, with the bond (*connectere*) of the Christian with the living Jesus Christ.[55] Allow me to begin again with a Bible passage—with Ephesians 1:3–8. Our connection with the Savior is preceded by his connection with us. Our connection can only be an answer to the divine action. With this the problem of Father-Son surfaces again. The subject in Ephesians 1:3–[8] is indeed God the Father! Connection here will mean a life in concrete and conscious—fifty years ago the word was "experienced" (*erlebter*)—relation to Jesus Christ, in short, a Christian life in the best sense. This may and should be lived! It is the same as the "fellowship (*Umgang*) with the Savior," a life in the Holy Spirit or from the Word, in conversation with him as the superior. "He the Master, we the Brothers, He is ours and we are His."[56] He remains the *Kyrios*, the Lord. By definition discipleship means that someone walks in front. When we think about this sharply, two remain, that is, there exists no danger of a slide into mysticism; or, since it is two who remain in the connection, this would be genuine mysticism (Gal. 2:20!).

In this connection, I have been asked whether one might not do better, instead of saying, ". . . that you, invisible Master, can be felt by us to be so very near," to say, ". . . near us in faith."[57] That is a quiet tendency to move away from Zinzendorf. Thirty years ago I would have made the same point. But "feeling" is thought of here not as something sentimental, but rather as emphasizing that one is actively engaged. I would lay the emphasis not on that aspect, but some feeling will be present anyway; indeed, faith cannot be a callous affair! It is about a feeling that one has in faith. It is all right to get a little warm in the process! I would like to defend Zinzendorf against too-strict *Brüdergemeine* pastors. Certainly, the test of whether it is the right feeling, whether it is a feeling from faith, shows itself in that one keeps affirming, "Even though I feel nothing

---

54. Cf. Fritz Blanke, *Zinzendorf im Gespräch mit der römisch-katholischen Kirche (nach seinem Briefwechsel mit Kardinal Noailles, 1917–1929)*, in F. Blanke, *Zinzendorf und die Einheit der Kinder Gottes* (Basel: Majer, 1950), 5–27.
55. Cf. above, n. 48.
56. From verse 1 of the hymn by N. L. von Zinzendorf: "Herz und Herz vereint zusammen [Heart and Heart United Together]" (1725), *GERS* 327; *EKG* 217; *EG* 251. [ET: "Christian Hearts, in Love United."]
57. Ibid., verse 4.

of your power, you lead me to the goal, even through the night."[58] Feeling is secondary and can stop. One must not rely just on feeling. Feeling is the relative part of faith, not the absolute. But it is precisely in the relation that the relatedness shows itself. It is *only* relatedness, but even so it is *our* relatedness. A counterpart to Zinzendorf would be John of the Cross, with whom the triumph of the connection consists precisely in impassibility.[59]

In the connection (with the Savior), knowledge of sin finds its basis. The passage, which you have cited for me here, I find very nice. Yes, this is the way it must read: "This is a difference between an honest Pietist and an honest Herrnhuter (Moravian). The former has his misery before his eyes and glances at the wounds; the latter has the wounds before his eyes, and glances at the misery. The wounds comfort the former in his diffidence; the misery embarrasses the latter in his blessedness."[60] In light of the knowledge of what it has cost [Christ] to overcome our misery, one recognizes first one's own misery. Recognition in a void could only be the recognition of some kind of misery. This we can provide for ourselves. But it is not yet a recognition of sin and damnation. For that the gospel is necessary. And this recognition comes by itself in the "connection." In the process, keeping the correct order is important. But it would also be incorrect now to fall into arrogance and say, "I have it!" Even in the hymn we sang this morning, (the stanza) *"Hebe an . . . !"* ("Make your start . . . !") precedes (the stanza) *"Fahre fort . . ."* ("Continue on . . .") and was placed there by Zinzendorf.[61]

I would like to put in a good word for Zinzendorf's "It is this way for me" (*Es ist mir so*).[62] This phrase can also be understood correctly. In the context of the connection with the Savior, I find it entirely correct; there one can speak in that way. The emphasis lies then not on "It is this way *for me*," but rather it

---

58. From verse 3 of the hymn by Julie Hausmann, "So nimm denn meine Hände [So Take My Hands]," in several regional appendices for the *EKG* under various numbers; *EG* 376.

59. Cf. H. U. von Balthasar, *Herrlichkeit: Eine theologische Ästhetik*, vol. 2, *Fächer der Stile*, (Einsiedeln: Johannes-Verlag, 1962), 465–531, esp. 478–93.

60. Zinzendorf, *Vier und Dreyßig HOMILIAE*, 59. A similar quote is found in J. A. Bengel, *Abriß*, 315–16.

61. Zinzendorf took over stanzas 1 and 5 of the hymn, "Fahre fort, fahre fort," by Johann Eusebius Schmidt (*GERS* 351; *EKG* 213; not in the *EG*) and placed the following stanza of his own in front of them:

> Hebe an, hebe an, Zion heb im Elend an,
> An der Armuth, an dem Staube!
> Dann ist deine Sach' gethan;
> Habe gar nichts, aber Glaube,
> Daß der Herr, der treue Seelenmann,
> Helfen kann!
> [Make your start! Make your start!
> Zion make your start in misery,
> In destitution, in the dust!
> Then what you can do is done;
> Have nothing at all but faith,
> That the Lord, the faithful man of souls,
> Can help!]

—*Geistliche Gedichte des Grafen Zinzendorf* (Stuttgart: Cotta, 1845), 98.

62. Instances and a discussion of this phrase are found in J. A. Bengel, *Abriß*, 19ff. Cf. further K. Barth, *Das christliche Leben: Die Kirchliche Dogmatik IV/4, Fragmente aus dem Nachlaß, Vorlesung 1959–1961*, ed. H.-A. Drewes and E. Jüngel (Zurich: Theologischer Verlag, 1976); 2nd ed. (1979), 304–5n75; ET: *The Christian Life: Church Dogmatics IV/4, Lecture Fragments*, trans. G. W. Bromiley (Grand Rapids: Eerdmans, 1981), 180.

means "In Christ's presence the situation is such and such." The connection with him also forms the basis of the recognition "What should we do?" But this recognition will always depend on the moment. It is about the Christian *decision*, about the *life*, about the *way*, which must be walked. What we have is not an ethical *principle*. What matters is that I remain in the "connection," in the "feeling" *and* in the darkness, and then the connection will lead to this recognition time and again.

However, now I have a few questions again for Zinzendorf:

1. Where in Zinzendorf does the element of invoking the Father keep its place in the "connection" with the Savior? In the communion (*Verkehr*) with the Savior as "*Amtsgott*"[63] (the "officiating God"), we are asked to call on the Father! Isn't the Christian life only a response to the command "Call unto me in your trouble!" (Ps. 50:15)?[64] Even Jesus does that himself. With this invocation (*Anrufung*), all mystical danger is banished. In the invocation the two poles of the connection are maintained. I would not like to have the "Father" (*Patēr*) eliminated. Only in this way can the Christian life be correctly understood as a praying life. The Christian asks, seeks, knocks, then it is opened up for him (cf. Matt. 7:7). This all is demanded by the correctly understood "connection."

2. Zinzendorf does not make it clearly evident to what extent our present life in faith is not already a life in sight (cf. 2 Cor. 5:7). Is there more in Zinzendorf than an actualized eschatology (*aktuelle Eschatologie*)? Even if we feel it, it still remains a hope. The Christian still has to wait for something else—for the seeing! Christians hope—not as those who have not, but as those who someday will have the sight (*Schauen-Werdenden*). How far Zinzendorf has seen that is not entirely clear. He appears to stand in a certain proximity to Dodd's "realized eschatology."[65]

3. I see no sense in using the lot in the framework of the "connection with the Savior." Of course, the practice of casting lots was a widespread hobby in the eighteenth century. In Basel at that time, one cast lots for professorial positions.[66] Here Zinzendorf was probably only a child of his age, who expected—as others did—a mysterious stroke of fate from casting lots.[67] The lot, however, is not an essential element of the Christian life. One must not turn Acts 1:26 into a principle. At this point, I prefer the phrase "It is this way for me."

Motel: The fellowship (*Umgang*) with the Savior in Zinzendorf probably belongs to the things that are not found in express terms in the New Testament

---

63. Cf. S. Eberhard, *Kreuzes-Theologie*, 22–23: "Because God only acts with humans in Christ, Zinzendorf calls Christ also the *Amtsgott* (officiating God). It is only this God, who acts with humans, with whom they have to do in their knowledge of God." Cf. further *Büdingische Sammlung einiger in die Kirchen-Historie einschlagender, sonderlich neuerer Schriften*, vol. 1 (Büdingen: Stöhr, 1740), 408. [Trans. note: *Amtsgott* is a Moravian term that is translated in their literature as the "officiating God." For one example, see Henry Rimius, *A Candid Narrative of the Rise and Progress of the Herrnhuters, commonly called Moravians, or "Unitas Fratrum," with a short account of their Doctrines, drawn from their own Writings*, 2nd ed. (London: A. Linde, 1753), 113.]

64. Cf. Karl Barth, *KD* IV/4, *Das christliche Leben*, xi, 69.

65. C. H. Dodd, *The Parables of the Kingdom* (London: James Nisbet, 1935); also by Dodd, *The Apostolic Preaching and Its Developments: Three Lectures* (London: Hodder & Stoughton, 1936).

66. This procedure was introduced in Basel in the year 1718 to counteract the protectionism of families, which had become a common practice for the appointment of professors. Cf. E. Bonjour, *Die Universität Basel von den Anfängen bis zur Gegenwart, 1460–1960* (Basel: Helbing & Lichtenhahn, 1960), 247–49.

67. Cf. E. Beyreuther, *Zinzendorf*, 93–96.

but probably are Christian truths (cf. John 15; Gal. 2:20, "head and members" . . .). Blumhardt's slogan, "Jesus is Victor,"[68] also belongs here; it does not appear literally in the New Testament. Zinzendorf distinguishes, by the way, between a special and a general fellowship (*Umgang*) with the Savior, namely, the fellowship of the individual and of the community (*Gemeine*) with the Savior.[69] Between both there exists a polar relationship, a reciprocal relationship: one cannot exist without the other.

Barth: Yes, we are placed into the "we," for example, in the Our Father. I believe that in the New Testament the "we" predominates, but the "I" is also there. Paul also gladly makes use of the "we" when he speaks of himself. The contrast between collectivism and individualism is actually unbiblical, because the "we" consists of many "I's" and the "I's" are all members of the "we."

Bárczay: Surely in Zinzendorf Scripture serves as the criterion for the authenticity of the fellowship with the Savior, and in the process, according to him, the Holy Spirit has to be considered as well. But doesn't Zinzendorf have too graphic a picture of the Savior with whom he has fellowship, in contrast to which one misses the fellowship with Scripture?

Schmidt: Zinzendorf's fellowship with the Savior is inconceivable without his Bible reading. Zinzendorf himself possessed a rather good amount of scriptural knowledge. He underpinned his preaching with exegesis, even if he did not make exegesis accessible to his congregation as Bengel did. Now and then, Zinzendorf opposed Bengel's biblicism for very good reasons.[70]

Bárczay: Isn't the "historical Jesus" set too strongly in the foreground in Zinzendorf?

Schmidt: With Zinzendorf, fellowship with Scripture is a prerequisite for fellowship with the Savior. From this point of view, Zinzendorf criticizes the "inner light" of the Quakers.[71] One must not overlook the fact that Zinzendorf has pointed out a way for Christian research of the Gospels (*Evangelienforschung*). He says that one should not be afraid of the inconsistencies and errors of Scripture, for they show precisely the cruciformity of the Word.[72] Eberhard has described this in his book.[73]

Barth: What Zinzendorf surely would not have approved of would have been the attempt to seek a "historical Jesus" behind the Jesus of the New Testament! Zinzendorf cannot differentiate between a "historical Jesus" and a "preached Christ" (*Christus praedicatus*).

Bárczay: But for him, isn't the Jesus of the New Testament the "historical" (*historische*) one?

68. Cf. Fr. Zündel, *Johann Christoph Blumhardt: Ein Lebensbild* (Zurich: Höhr, 1880), 8th ed. (Gießen and Basel: Brunnen-Verlag, 1921), 109, 144.

69. N. L. von Zinzendorf, *Einiger seit 1751. von dem Ordinario Fratrum zu London gehaltenen Predigten*, 1:115: "As the holy Christian church *in genere* [in general] . . . is the object of the heart of Jesus; so again *in specie* [in particular] every human soul and He are the first and original community."

70. Generally, for drawing the lines against biblicism, cf. S. Eberhard, *Kreuzes-Theologie*, 6–18. For drawing the lines against Bengel's apocalypticism in particular, Eberhard quotes Zinzendorf: "The apocalyptic whims [*Grillen*] have ruined Bengel and so many others" (*Kreuzes-Theologie*, 213n193).

71. For this, cf. O. Uttendörfer, *Zinzendorf und die Mystik* (Berlin: Christlicher Zeitschriften Verlag, 1910), 130.

72. Zinzendorf, *Vier und Dreyßig HOMILIAE*, 140–51, esp. 144: "That the Scripture has so many errors as hardly any other book that comes out nowadays, is for me an irrefutable proof of its divinity."

73. S. Eberhard, *Kreuzes-Theologie*, 6–18.

Barth: Along with Kähler, he probably rather would have spoken about the "historic" (*geschichtlichen*) Jesus.[74] It was his concern to emphasize that God has become history (*Geschichte*).

Reichel: The fellowship with the Savior points to the Resurrected One, to the presence of the Savior *now!* From there I would see a bridge to prayer.

Bintz: Professor Barth, in your *Church Dogmatics*, the accentuation of the word and the work of Jesus Christ seem to me to be different from that in Zinzendorf. With Zinzendorf it was about a graphic conceptualization of the historical Jesus. He was totally unfamiliar with the quest for the "historical Jesus" of contemporary research. He imagined Jesus in a pictorial manner. Having read the *Church Dogmatics*, we are de-psychologized (*entpsychologisiert*). How does the fellowship with the Savior look like now? It is supposed to be personal; it is not about an abstract relation but a relation that is imaginable!

Gärtner: Zinzendorf thinks that we have the *eikōn*, the image, in Jesus himself. No crucifixes hang in the hall of the *Brüdergemeine!*[75] Zinzendorf refuses them on the grounds that the prohibition of images in the Old Testament is annulled in Jesus Christ as the *eikōn*. However, besides this image, one shall not have any other image. Zinzendorf says that the image of Jesus Christ should become observable (*anschaubar*) in his community. He also once says that the singular proof of the existence of God is the community (*Gemeinde*) of Jesus Christ.[76]

Barth: We certainly are exempt from manufacturing any image. If [we make] an image at all, then it should be of the one who was humbled. The crucifixion painting of Grünewald made a strong impression on me in my early days.[77] Perhaps some mistakes in my *Römerbrief* are due to Grünewald. I would not hang that painting in the church. It would not be good for the congregation. For the Risen One is not visible there. He is located on one of the wings in that strangely anthroposophical light. But precisely the Humbled One is also the Exalted One. For that reason alone, a picture is not meaningful because it cannot include everything.

---

74. Cf. M. Kähler, *Der sogenannte historische Jesus und der geschichtliche, biblische Christus* (Leipzig: Deichert, 1892), 2nd ed., ed. E. Wolf, ThB2 (Munich: Kaiser, 1956).

75. According to a communication from H. Reichel, Königsfeld, the absence of crucifixes in the worship rooms of the *Brüdergemeine* are primarily connected to the fact that for the Moravian Brothers crucifixes were signs of the Jesuits. According to S. Eberhard, Zinzendorf turned against the fashioning of the cross into jewelry, etc. (*Kreuzes-Theologie*, 105). H. Schmidt reported that he remembered, without being able to name the location, Zinzendorf's answer to a question why no crucifixes hang in the halls of the *Brüdergemeine*: "The cross shall shine out of the hearts of the Brethren through the Word."

76. N. L. von Zinzendorf, *Evangelische Gedanken: Gewißheit, Freude, Kraft*, collected by O. Uttendörfer, Hilfe für's Amt 14 (Berlin: Christlicher Zeitschriften Verlag, 1948), 178: "A community [*Gemeine*] is the sole proof against unbelief. No explanation is needed if only there is a community [*Gemeine*]." (A statement of Zinzendorf from September 16, 1749.)

77. Cf. K. Barth, *Der Römerbrief (Erste Fassung) 1919*, ed. H. Schmidt (Zurich: Theologischer Verlag, 1985), 164; also, "Biblische Fragen, Einsichten und Ausblicke" (1920), in *Das Wort Gottes und die Theologie: Gesammelte Vorträge* (Munich: Kaiser, 1924), 70–98; ET: "Biblical Questions, Insights and Vistas," in *The Word of God and the Word of Man*, trans. Douglas Horton (1928/1956), (Gloucester, MA: Peter Smith Publisher, 1978), 51–96; also, *Der Römerbrief*, 2nd ed., 108/137; later printings, 106/135; 15th ed., 116/147; also, "*Unterricht in der christlichen Religion*" (Zurich: Theologischer Verlag, 1924), vol. 1, ed. H. Reiffen (Zurich: Theologischer Verlag, 1985), 186–87; also, *Die christliche Dogmatik im Entwurf*, vol. 1 (1927), ed. G. Sauter 2 (Zurich: Theologischer Verlag, 1982), 341; and *CD* I/1:112 (*KD* 115/227); *CD* I/2:125 (*KD* 137–38).

Gelzer: There is a sermon of Zinzendorf about the second commandment in which he says that the image of God is now the Savior. We have him, nothing besides that.[78]

Günther: I do see a clear difference between your *Dogmatics*, Professor Barth, and Zinzendorf in the basic treatment of anthropology. With you the *eikōn* line is carried through in an entirely clear manner. [Christ] is human, and after and from this we are truly human.[79] With Zinzendorf this line is not carried through as clearly. With him the line of the incarnation emerges more strongly: [Christ] became what we are.

Preiswerk: In his own time, Zinzendorf was very impressed with the *Ecce Homo* painting by Domenico Feti, which had the caption: "This I have done for you; what will you do for me?"[80] In the intervening time it seems that people have moved away from the high evaluation of the significance of this painting for Zinzendorf.

Schmidt: This episode is somewhat demythologized nowadays. Zinzendorf himself said that to the second part of the caption, "What will you do for me?," he had nothing to respond.[81]

Motel: Concerning the question about eschatology in Zinzendorf, perhaps it may be pointed out that in any case it is found in connection with the church (*Gemeinde*).[82] For Zinzendorf, the visible church is the dawn of the coming kingdom of God. With a view to missions he speaks of the firstfruit community (*Erstlingsgemeine*). The Lord's Supper for him is a pre-eternity action (*Vor-Ewigkeits-Handlung*). The white clothing at the celebration is an indication of what is coming. Finally, a serious concern for eschatology is also found in connection with his ecumenical thinking: the kingdom of the cross of Christ in this world is pointing toward that which is to come.

Ruh: Eschatological thinking is also found, for example, in Zinzendorf's *Pennsylvanischen Reden*, where he speaks, for example, of eternity as the school for the right understanding of the Trinity.[83]

Theile: But Zinzendorf also says, "We are here together as if we were already in heaven."[84] And I noticed that in the entire section of the hymnbook *Warten und Wachen* (Waiting and Waking),[85] one cannot find even one verse from Zinzendorf!

---

78. A sermon by Zinzendorf specifically about the second commandment is unknown even to Zinzendorf experts. Cf., however, Zinzendorf, *Eine Sammlung Öffentlicher Reden*, Pennsylvanische Reden 2:216–17: In the New Testament "it no longer says: You shall make for yourself no graven image . . . , but rather, You shall imagine for yourself an image without end and without ceasing, . . . and that shall be Jesus."

79. *CD* III/2:141–42 (*KD* 158–59).

80. Cf. E. Beyreuther, *Der junge Zinzendorf* (Marburg: Verlag der Francke-Buchhandlung GmbH, 1957), 169–70.

81. Ibid. Zinzendorf wrote in his diary about the caption of the painting that he saw in Düsseldorf on May 22, 1719: ". . . that I would not be able to answer much here either, and I asked the Savior to wrest me into the communion of his suffering by force, if my sense refused to go in."

82. Concerning the eschatology of Zinzendorf, cf. W. Bettermann, *Theologie und Sprache bei Zinzendorf* (Gotha: Klotz, 1935), 123–47; further, see S. Eberhard, *Kreuzes-Theologie*, 211–26.

83. Cf. H. Ruh, *Christologische Begründung des 1. Artikels bei Zinzendorf* (Zurich: Evangelischer Verlag, 1967), 83–84.

84. Zinzendorf, *Vier und Dreyßig HOMILIAE*, 362: ". . . for we call the church, heaven . . ."

85. This is the heading for the collection of hymns 966–97 in the *Gesangbuch der evangelischen Brüdergemeine, ausgegeben im Erinnerungsjahr* (Gnadau, 1927).

Gärtner: Yet, next to the church here on earth, even the "church above" (*obere Gemeine*) does have its concrete eschatological significance for Zinzendorf.[86]

5. Zinzendorf's Concept of the Church and the Shape of the Brüdergemeine

Barth: I am sure you have noticed that I speak less of the church (*Kirche*) in my *Church Dogmatics* than I speak of the community (*Gemeinde*).The[87] church does not exist as an end in itself, but it exists in service to the world. The community has been sent out; from its very foundation, it is the community of mission. It is a community gathered, built, and then sent out by the Holy Spirit.[88] Perhaps one should rather say "created" instead of "gathered." Jesus Christ is the head of the community: there is only the community of Jesus Christ. He is the "chief" (*Chef*) and head (*Haupt*), from whom nothing can be abstracted. "He the master, we the brothers."[89] The church is his work. What counts is Matthew 18:20, "For where two or three are gathered in my name, I am there among them"; and Matthew 28:20, "Remember, I am with you always, to the end of the age." This "I," Jesus Christ, is constitutive for the concept of the church: otherwise it is a hollow nut. Ecclesiology is Christology and pneumatology unfolded.

The *Brüdergemeine* has come into being in the situation of an opposition between established Constantinian churches, which compete with one another, and a plethora of freely formed and free-flying spirit-churches, in other words, more or less sectarian communities, which stand in opposition to the official churches. Zinzendorf is not satisfied with the fact that "they exist." He founds the *Brüdergemeine*, which passes beyond this choice between large and small churches. Zinzendorf wants to bring into this situation the knowledge of what in every ecclesial form makes the church into the church, namely, the presence and the government of the living Christ as the head of the church. The Moravian Church was to be integrated into the ecclesial situation. Zinzendorf did not want Zinzendorfians, but he wanted the community of Jesus Christ. The description *ecclesiola in ecclesia* (a small church within the church)[90] seems unfortunate to me. There is only *ecclesia*. Even if there are only two or three, there is not *ecclesiola* but *ecclesia*. What does "in" mean? Would one not be better off to say "*ecclesia pro ecclesia* [a church for the church]"?! Is not that more along the lines of Zinzendorf? *Brüdergemeine* is church for the church and stands up for that which is so easily forgotten in the large and small churches and what

---

86. Cf. L. Hennig, *Kirche und Offenbarung bei Zinzendorf*, 92–93.

87. On this point in particular see *CD* IV/1:650–51 (*KD* 727–28).

88. According to these bullet points, the ecclesiology of Barth unfolds in *CD* IV/1:643–44 (*KD* 718–19); *CD* IV/2:614–15 (*KD* 695–96); *CD* IV/3:681–82 (*KD* 780–81).

89. Cf. above, nn. 51, 56.

90. Cf. Philipp J. Spener, *Theologische Bedencken, / Und andere Brieffliche Antworten auff geistliche / sonderlich zur erbauung gerichtete materien: zu unterschiedenen zeiten aufgesetzt / und auf langwiehriges Anhalten christlicher Freunde in einige Ordnung gebracht, und nun zum dritten mal herausgegeben* [3rd ed.], *Dritter Theil* [part 3] . . . (Halle: Waysen-Haus, 1715), 218–19: ". . . that we may gather . . . *Ecclesiolas* in our churches, which lead those who serve their God in truthful zeal to further growth so that they themselves become righteous Christians, worthy of the most worthy name, and also with their godly example . . . build up others at their side."

makes the churches [into] churches in the first place. What Zinzendorf wanted was an ecumenical church, rising visibly in Herrnhut, just as visible as the Lutheran or the Reformed Church, but precisely an ecumenical church! Ecumenism *in specie et nuce* (in its own form and in a nutshell)! The *Brüdergemeine* represents *in nuce* that which makes all (ecclesial communites) a church.

I find the following three types in the *Brüdergemeine*: [1] the local congregation; [2] the auxiliary type, lending support within the denominations [while] one remains denominational, whatever one is; [3] or the type that makes its appearance as an independent witness, especially on the mission fields. In my opinion, one type by itself would be one-sided. The side-by-side makeup is the irresolvable problem of the Moravians, and it will probably remain so; this threefold form is particularly characteristic of the sense and spirit of Zinzendorf.[91] Every form is legitimate, and none may be destroyed. The *Brüdergemeine* must continue to exist in this manifold shape. I would claim that this is truly a possibility in the New Testament, and therefore it is nothing to be ashamed of (*pudendum*). Just stick to it!

What is questionable for me in Zinzendorf is his teaching on the "tropes" (*Tropen*),[92] which claims that, according to God's plan of salvation, denominations (*die Religionen*) exist as *Tropen* (training methods) of the church. We must not resign ourselves to the fact that the body of Christ is divided in that way, by saying, like my colleague Staehelin,[93] that all churches are one big family. If anything, the *Brüdergemeine* shows that the split into denominations (*in die Konfessionen*) must be overcome. Concerning the written question presented by Pastor Gärtner, whether the *Brüdergemeine* has fulfilled its task, I say No! The problem with which Zinzendorf began still exists. The ecumenical movement, as it manifests itself in Amsterdam and Evanston,[94] is no replacement for the *Brüdergemeine*! The *Brüdergemeine* should be ecumenical for the sake of the ecumenical movement! It should be a living example of prophetic ecumenism with the limit: until the Lord comes! Then all this church bunkum comes to an end anyway.

I hear you speaking of a crisis in the peculiar consciousness (*Sonderbewußtsein*) of the *Brüdergemeine*. If I were a member of the *Brüdergemeine*, I would say this: our peculiar consciousness as a church consists in that we want to be

---

91. Cf. here K. Schuster, *Gruppe, Gemeinschaft, Kirche: Gruppenbildung bei Zinzendorf*, ThExh NS 85 (Munich: Kaiser, 1960). Further, L. Hennig, *Kirche und Offenbarung bei Zinzendorf*, 146–47. The author also speaks of a "three-tiered framework in Zinzendorf's concept of the church": (1) "Jerusalem above," to which the invisible church in the world belongs; (2) this church visible "through members connected in churches"; (3) the "religions" (= confessions) as the house in which the church of Christ dwells.

92. N. L. Zinzendorf, *Vier und Dreyßig HOMILIAE*, 163–65. Cf. L. Hennig, *Kirche und Offenbarung bei Zinzendorf*, 153–57. The *tropes* doctrine means this: In the denominations ("religions") the church of Christ is hidden, but in such a way that they are at the same time *tropes*, ways to educate people toward Christ (*tropoi paideias*). In the *Brüdergemeine* in which the church of Christ is visible at this time the members remain in their confessions/*tropes*, so that when the Spirit retreats from the church, everyone can return back into the "religion" out of which they came.

93. Cf. the somewhat later comment of Ernst Staehelin (1889–1980), professor of church history in Basel): ". . . and because the conditions of fallen creation are of decisive influence upon the formation of these orders and organizations, the church, when it gives itself an external form, splits with a certain necessity in individual parts, in confessions, denominations, sects, or however one would want to call the substructures." E. Staehelin, *Die Verkündigung des Reiches Gottes in der Kirche Jesu Christi*, vol. 7 (Basel: Reinhardt, 1965), 604–5.

94. The World Council of Churches conferences of Amsterdam (1948) and Evanston (1954) are meant.

a church exclusively in view of the real presence of Christ. The church lives under him. This peculiar consciousness, I hope, has not been caught up in a crisis. It is above all the church bunkum, which is in need to be demythologized. The *Brüdergemeine* can accomplish this, and it must do so. Again and again it is correct to begin anew to take Jesus Christ seriously as "chief." Here one must not ask, How would it be if we were a megachurch? "Big" and "small" are dumb questions. Gladly be what you are! Be happy for it! Then you will remain in the beneficial crisis. You do not have to participate in any idolatry. One must not be part of everything. The Lutheran insistence upon "law and gospel" and their conception of the sacraments, the insistence of the Reformed upon their doctrine of double predestination (*praedestinatio gemina*) and their presbyteral constitution . . . and all that Roman (stuff) . . .—you should not compete. You should strive, but not contend (Phil. 3)![95]

And then the Moravian bishops! . . . All right, let them exist. In Hungary there are even Reformed bishops. I would not be in favor of that. That, too, is something you could do without. It is not a capital offense, but it also is not advisable. Let your Chief Elder be enough for you![96]

You ask about success?[97] What does successful and unsuccessful mean? To be sure, in the book of Acts sometimes numbers are gleefully cited, yet not as a criterion for what is there and what is right, but as a sign of the goodness of God in the face of deficient human conduct. Success is not a criterion for the existence of the Christian church. Hold your gatherings, but in such a way that there is a shine toward the outside! Our purpose is only about sowing seeds [cf. Matt. 13:3–9].

Concerning the question about the "burnings" and the shedding of the superfluous,[98] I would dearly have loved just to say, "See to it yourselves!" [cf. Matt. 27:4]. Here I must be very cautious and can only bring up some timid questions: Is it clear to all that the *Brüdergemeine* here in Basel, for example, must be more than a "cozy, homey" family club with a Christian foundation? It is uncanny to me that we are not aware of this need even *more*. It must not be said that the *Brüdergemeine* fits well into bourgeois Basel. Where is the scandal that is the necessary result of the very existence of the *Brüdergemeine* so that the gospel would shine in this almost catastrophic manner as with Zinzendorf? Is the preaching of the *Brüdergemeine* noticeably different and distinct from other "positive" sermons? I would have a question for *Brüdergemeine* preachers: Does the ecumenical concern come to sufficient expression here? Do not be conformed to the church world! You might rather want to identify yourselves with the other world a little [cf. Rom. 12:2].

---

95. Esp. see Phil. 3:12–14; cf. Gal. 4:18.

96. Cf. n. 51 above.

97. On a sheet sent to Barth by H. Bintz, it says: "The 'successes' of the Moravian Church Missions [*Brüdermission*]—whose motivation for missions, I think, is more similar to Karl Barth's—have remained small in contrast to those of the new Pietists."

98. Fr. Gärtner, in his questions directed toward Barth, had written, among other things—using quotes from *CD* IV/1:684, rev. ed. (*KD* 764): "Believing that we may solely live because of Jesus' death, we would like to speak with Prof. Dr. Karl Barth about which 'kinds of burnings or at least revisions and modifications of our previous special positions,' and thus which 'liberations and renewals within our special existence' must happen among us. . . ."

Interjection: In the *Brüdergemeine,* pastors are called *Gemeinhelfer* (helpers of the community).[99]

Barth: That is nice! I would prefer addressing you pastors as *Gemeinhelfer.* That does not smell like church at all. *Gemeinhelfer* is better than the Constantinian term "pastor," which derives from *parochos.*[100] The title of pastor should be burned. If the *Brüdergemeine* would become somewhat more scandalous, then possibly more might happen in the direction of political responsibility, just as it happened symbolically many years ago through one out of your own in Bern concerning social tasks—a Brother Theodor Schmidt.[101]

Löw: To return once more to the question of bishops, I may point out that the bishop in the *Brüdergemeine* really has only pastoral functions.

Barth: But in the German realm the office of bishop has been magnified once again. Therefore, "Abstain from every form of evil!" [1 Thess. 5:22]. Never play with guns.[102] . . . I would let the bishops gradually vanish. Again, let us not keep talking about the bishop, but stay with the substantial issues. In this sense "Fahre fort, fahre fort / Continue on, continue on . . . !"[103]

Preiswerk: What would you think about the common double membership in the *Brüdergemeine* nowadays?[104]

Barth: I do not view it as something desirable. But why not? It can be this way, but one should not make a principle of it.

Marx: I would like to enter a plea on behalf of the idea of *tropes.*[105] Zinzendorf's warrant is the insight that nations and races are limited. Couldn't the *tropes* idea be an important aid for ecumenical understanding?

Barth: But can one think in this way on the basis of the New Testament? Isn't one church implied everywhere? Ephesians 4:3–6 should be visible, too. You [Moravians] can make it visible; it is not visible with the Lutherans and not with Pope John XXIII. There is division. Legitimizing the *tropes* idea is coming to terms with the circumstances prematurely. For me, your view smacks too much like philosophy of history. I would not want to play along with that.

Reichel: But as a working method, maybe it was historically justified. For example, at that time it served as a counterweight against the usual mutual accusations of heresy.

Theile: Mustn't the *tropoi paideias* (methods of training) be understood from Christ?

Schmidt: Similar to Paul's differentiation between Jews and Greeks . . . ?

Barth: But for Paul, Jews and Greeks were the *one* people (*Volk*). In the New Testament I do not see any legitimized heresies. And with the variety of

---

99. N. L. von Zinzendorf, *Theologische und dahin einschlagende Bedencken . . .* (Büdingen: Stöhr, 1742), 130.

100. Originally it was a Roman title for a governmental purveyor [*für einen staatlichen Lieferanten*]; then it became a church title for the "provider" of a parish [*für den "Versorger" einer Parochie*], of a diocese, of a benefice.

101. Cf. *Theodor Edmund Schmidt, 1870–1960: Ein Leben im Dienst der Brüdergemeine* (Herrnhut o. J.: [Winter,] 1960), 63–64. Schmidt was a preacher of the *Brüdersozietät* in Bern from 1904 until 1913. Inspired by H. Kutter and L. Ragaz, he came close to socialism. Incidentally he befriended Karl Barth's father, Fritz Barth.

102. A German proverb: "Never play with a gun, for it could be loaded!"

103. See n. 61 above.

104. Namely, simultaneously being a member in the *Brüdergemeine* and in one of the denominational evangelical churches [*Landeskirchen*], [which are legally accepted by the state as official churches].

105. See n. 92 above.

churches, the coziness stops when it comes to the Lord's Supper. If the pope would finally proclaim the correct doctrine of justification and otherwise affirm his being the pope for himself, I would call out to him: "Hello! Greetings!" (*Grüß Gott!*). But he is really aggressive!

Schmidt: For Zinzendorf, the confessions as "admirable fences"[106] signify a piece of thankfulness to the fathers. . . .

Barth: I do not become a Catholic or Lutheran either. But the disunity feels to me like a sickness. Do not let the fact be taken from you that Zinzendorf felt this sickness! Zinzendorf wanted to cure the sickness, but the *tropoi* probably point out a slight attempt on Zinzendorf's part to resign himself to the situation.

Marx: Nevertheless one can probably say that all churches and sects have a little piece of truth, even if it is in a one-sided, absolutized form.

Barth: Thanks to the gracious guidance of God, good can be found here and there. Splendid! The separated churches live on such special truths. But they are nothing more than special truths.

Preiswerk: Perhaps one can refer to the four Gospels as analogies for such differences.

Gärtner: They may be different, but they do not mutually accuse one another of heresy. . . .

Barth: And after all, there is no special Matthew-Church, and so on.

Löw: Professor Barth, I would like to express the thanks of a jurist for the fact that you understand the church (*Kirche*) as the community (*Gemeinde*) in your *Church Dogmatics.*

Bintz: Don't the sacraments belong to the right conception of the church, Herr Professor? As a rule, members of the local communities (*Sozietäten*) receive the sacraments in the main church (*Hauptkirche*).

Barth: Naturally, the community (*die Gemeinde*) must have its order. But do not embrace an all too sacramental thinking; rather consider the expressions of faith and of obedience as that which is desirable! By the way, *Church Dogmatics* IV/4 will probably cause considerable astonishment concerning the view of the sacrament.[107] Rejoice that you have room for the sacraments! But do it from the well-known Christian center. Concerning baptism, not every baptismal liturgy is useful. Who knows if infant baptism might not turn out to be an old humdrum routine! Unencumbered by other churches, the *Brüdergemeine* must go its new way. Do not leave the field to the others!*

---

106. N. L. von Zinzendorf, *Ein und zwanzig Discurse über die Augspurgische Confession,* 45: "Thus the Symbols are an admirable fence, if they remain in their order. . . ."

107. *CD* IV/4 (Fragment), 100–101 (*KD* 110–11): Baptism is "no sacrament" (*CD* IV/4:102 [*KD* 112]).

* Grant Henley, a professor of German at Wheaton College, and Sebastian Schmidgall, a graduate student who is a native of Germany, have assisted in helping translate some sections of this chapter.

13. Interview with Vernon Sproxton
1960

On October 15, 1960, Vernon Sproxton interviewed Karl Barth for two hours for BBC Television. The interview was broadcast on November 1, 1961, as a twenty-minute program, looking forward to Barth's seventy-fifth birthday on October 10, 1961. In an introduction made by John Thompson, editor of the magazine Time and Tide, *it was reported that Barth had refused to make himself available for an entire day for the recording. The following postcard from Barth was read, "If your demand is so urgent, it is my Christian duty to yield and to agree; I do it without guarantee for the success of the enterprise. And I ask you to give me in good time an idea of the content and character of the questions to whom I shall be confronted—not to forget the exact date of your arrival in my modest hut.... P.S.: Two hours, not more. I am busy with* Church Dogmatics, *the angels and the demons watching." The fact that the recorded material was larger than what was broadcast can be deduced in particular from Barth's response to the second question, where apparently answers to further uncited questions have been edited together so that the sections of this response don't seem to relate to each other very clearly.*

The original content of the interview was duplicated by BBC Television as a typescript titled "Viewpoint: Interview with Karl Barth, the great Swiss theologian (5 pages DIN A 4)." An edited version with corrections of the language was then published under the title "Karl Barth on the Christian Church Today: A Television Interview with Vernon Sproxton," in The Listener, *January 19, 1961, 137 and 141. Charlotte von Kirschbaum apparently made a German translation of this final text, which was published as "Ein britisches Fernseh-Interview mit Karl Barth [a British television interview with Karl Barth]," in the Protestant monthly* Junge Kirche 22 (1961): 275–78. *A further publication of excerpts, again with corrections of the language, appeared in the* Kirchenblatt für die reformierte Schweiz [Church Newspaper for Reformed Switzerland] *no. 117 (1961), 68–69. The English text provided here is the original version published by BBC Television.*

Sproxton: Professor Barth, you have been called the greatest theologian since Saint Thomas Aquinas. How does this statement affect you?

Barth: I simply don't like it, because such kind of comparisons can perhaps be made after some hundred years, but not now. I don't like to reflect upon my own position and significance in the history of the church. Let it to the angels.

Sproxton: If you had not become a theologian, what would you like to have been?

Barth: If I were not a theologian, I would like to be a traffic policeman. Look at these men, at their power and authority with which they direct twenty cars to one side and twenty to the other. That's real business and something necessary to be done. I would like to be such a man. And perhaps it wouldn't be so far from what I am doing now, *Church Dogmatics*, because dogmatics is also a kind of traffic police, showing where to go.

I think[1] a theologian has as much authority as the Word of God has given authority to him. If he listens and if he obeys, then he will also have some authority over against other human beings, but there is not such a thing as an authority that he had, thirty years ago, or has now, but that is a thing to be given to him.

A Christian[2] shouldn't be afraid either of psychology or of biology or of sociology or of Communism and things like that. There is one thing that counts: the fear of God. And if he is living in the fear of God, then he is not threatened.

Everything[3] can lead men away from God, the smallest and the greatest, it depends on him. The appearance of a mouse or fly can lead me away, and the biggest storm, a thunderstorm, cannot make me afraid. There is no such thing as a scale of greater or smaller dangers.

Sproxton: Do you think it is possible for modern man to hear the word of God clearly in the Bible?

Barth: It is not easier and it is not more difficult for modern man, because for all men, God is a stranger, and God can only be heard and understood insofar as he himself speaks to him. Now he speaks, but there will be a discontinuity on the side of man, not on the side of God, but on the side of man, and to that extent it is always an event, if men understand him. This event may happen in modern times as it happened in old times. I don't see a difference.

Sproxton: What about you and Emil Brunner?[4] Have you moved together or further apart?

Barth: Allow me to answer with a parable. Can you compare a whale, let us say Moby Dick, and an elephant?[5] The two of them are creatures of God, but they cannot meet, perhaps from far away, but not really meet; they cannot speak together; they cannot fight; they cannot conclude peace; that is so. My friend Brunner may decide whether he prefers to be the whale or the elephant. I hope the day will come when we will see and understand what has been planned—the idea of our good Lord to create these two, the elephant and the whale.

1. What follows presupposes an intervention by the interviewer along these lines: "Is the dogmatician a person of power and authority?"

2. What follows presupposes the inserting of a further question, along these lines: "Doesn't this authority diminish in view of the fact that Christian statements are opposed from so many directions today?"

3. It is possible that here as well a further question was posed somewhat like this: "And when the threat is so great that it leads a person away from God?

4. In the introduction of the interview, J. Thompson had remarked, "This [Barth's time in Bonn, 1930–35] is also the period of tremendous rivalry between Karl Barth and another Swiss theologian, Emil Brunner, who felt that Barth was not optimistic enough about the power of human reason; the controversy between Barth and Brunner dominated the whole of Protestant theology right up to the Second [World] War." A full month after recording the interview, on November 19, 1960, Barth did meet with Brunner in his home in Basel to attempt a reconciliation; see *Lebenslauf*, 465; *Biography*, 449.

5. On the metaphor of the whale and the elephant, see above, chap. 12, n. 3. "Moby Dick" refers to the white whale in the novel of the same name by Herman Melville. Its use as a reference to Barth's *Church Dogmatics* goes back to K. H. Miskotte, *Über Karl Barth's "Kirchliche Dogmatik": Kleine Präludien und Phantasien*, ThExh NS 89 (Munich: Kaiser, 1961), 10ff. It had already been in use in student circles as a "benevolently sarcastic term for the *CD*" (10).

Sproxton: What in your opinion have been the most important developments in the recent history of the church?

Barth: Is that a question of historical interest? Well, there have been certain important things—like the ecumenical movement, or the German church struggle, or some new relations between Roman Catholic and Protestant theology—that may be weighty. But if you ask me which are the spiritually important events, I am in trouble to decide because one never knows what will happen. It will be for a historian of later times to decide what have been the real important events of our time. Not for us.

Sproxton: What do you think is the church's greatest blindness at the moment?

Barth: Blindness?

Sproxton: What is the greatest shortcoming?

Barth: Ah, shortcoming. I think the task of the church is to stand in the middle between the message of the Bible and human life of every day. The church is often too less heavenly, and too less earthly, and the two of them should be realized, the heavenly God and the earthly God. And here we are and have to find the right way between.

Sproxton: Do you think it's possible for the church to have a proper existence in a totalitarian state?

Barth: They will have a troubled existence certainly. Perhaps the manner in which it will exist will more be a kind of dying than a kind of living. But perhaps a dying church is better than a living church if it proclaims the gospel, notwithstanding all the outward situation. And this thing is *done* in Eastern Germany, and the thing is *done* in Czechoslovakia, and the thing is *done* even in Russia. The real church cannot die. But what we call the church as an institution can die, and perhaps must die, even in our Western world.

Sproxton: In all these years has the figure of Jesus Christ changed for you in any way?

Barth: It has not changed, the figure of Christ, as such, but there has been a change in his importance for my thought. It was a time when I thought about him as, so to say, the prophet, or the messenger of the kingdom. Now I had to understand that he *is* the kingdom, not only the word of God, but also the work of God and, let me say, God himself acting among men and for men, for us all.

Sproxton: In terms of the Christian hope, what do you yourself look forward to?

Barth: Well, if you ask me concerning our eternal hope, what will be in the second coming of Christ, then my answer is [this]: what will be, what will come, is a general and definite and universal revelation, the revelation of what has happened in the first coming of Christ, what he did for the world, and what is the reality of the world, because our world is reconciled in Christ with God. That is hidden now, but that will be revealed sometime, and that is our hope.

And now, because we have an eternal hope, we have also a temporal hope. We are looking forward to see things a little better now. Look, for example, what happened last week[6] in the United Nations Meetings in New York. What was

---

6. Instead of the words "last week" in the original text, "recently" is in the text published by *The Listener* (which didn't appear until January 19, 1961), which paralleled the German translation made by Charlotte von Kirschbaum ("neulich"). Barth was referring to the negotiations in the United Nations

lacking? The real sight of things. Everybody knows what is meant by peace and justice and freedom and so on. But it was hidden to all these people, so there has been trouble and there will be always trouble because people don't see the reality of things. They hear words, great words, peace, freedom, and so on, but they are not able to see reality, which is there, which is given, but is hidden.

Sproxton: What do you do in your spare time?

Barth: In my spare time I like to read books of nontheological character, first of all historical books concerning modern political and war history. Have you read the whole of Churchill's books? I have, the whole lot. But not to forget, I like also to read detective novels. And for the rest, well, I like to listen to gramophone records, especially Mozart, because he is a pure musician, not a teacher and not a man like Beethoven, who tells me about his life and his heart, but who simply plays. And that is what I call music, playing, and that is what I find only with Wolfgang Amadeus Mozart.

Sproxton: What one word would you give to the church of Jesus Christ in this day? If you had only one word to speak, what would it be?

Barth: It would be [this]: Preach, proclaim the incarnation of the Word of God—of the Word of *God*, but *his* incarnation. And so there are two dimensions of the church: the Word of God and the flesh; the act of God and man living in [God's] world. And the church should be the bridge—no, the bridge is Jesus Christ himself—but in proclaiming Christ, the church proclaims that there is a bridge between God and man. The church has to stride back and forth on this bridge, which is the covenant between God and man. It should do that in the proper way, not forgetting the highness of God and not neglecting the deep sorrows of humanity, but bringing them both together.

General Assembly, which preceded the recording of the interview (on October 15, 1960) by a week, and which were addressing the controversial issue of the UN membership for the People's Republic of China, a process which moved the East-West conflicts back into the center of the negotiations. See *Archiv der Gegenwart* 30 (1960): 8676–82.

14. Interview by Marie-Claire Lescaze
1960

On November 26, 1960, Marie-Claire Lescaze interviewed Karl Barth for one hour concerning his view of demons and angels.* At that time, Barth was located in the Basel eye clinic. The interview was published under the title "Monsieur Karl Barth: Que pensez-vous du diable et des anges? [Mr. Karl Barth: What Do You Think about the Devil and Angels?]," in Jeunesse: Revue de la jeunesse de langue française *107, number 10 (Geneva/Paris/Mons, December 1960): 1. In the introduction to her interview with Barth, Marie-Claire Lescaze wrote the following: "He did not address himself to me as a doctor in theology, dry and full of dogmatics, but as a human being, a pastor enlivened by faith, by a radiancy and an extraordinary humanity. What is more, Karl Barth—whose vivacity of spirit and even combativeness are astonishing—possesses a sturdy common sense that never abandons him, even when he is engaged in purely abstract discussions."*

1. Concerning Demons and the Devil

Lescaze: What are demons? What is Satan? What is their role in the Bible and for us today?

Barth: They are puzzling explosions of Nothingness (*du néant*). Demons always gravitate in the vicinity of Christ as signs, as indicators of a type of "counterrevolution." But caution is required: they make their appearance only at the moment they are cast out. Actually, the New Testament is interested only in their suppression, and we should follow suit.

Satan is an indicator as well. He is the "impossible possibility."[1] Satan has not been created by God. He is a reality outside the "system"! Evil exists only in contradiction with creation, and one cannot "explain" this world of darkness—which incidentally is destined to vanish—neither by contrast nor affinity to it.

---

* This translation was made from the French interview; the introduction and notes were translated from the German edition.

1. With the concept of "impossible possibility," Barth in his beginning stage had described the reality created exclusively by God, such as grace, justification, new life, and so forth; see K. Barth, *Der Römerbrief*, 2nd ed. (Munich, Kaiser, 1922), 55, 83, 89–90, 116, 177, 188–89, 199, 213. [Later editions: 53, 81, 87–88, 114, 175, 186–87, 197, 211; 15th ed. (Zurich Theologischer Verlag, 1989), 58, 89, 96, 124, 191, 203–4, 215, 230]. In the *CD*, the concept serves on the contrary as the designation for the mode of reality of evil and sin; see chiefly *CD* III/3, esp. 349–68 [*KD* 402–28]. (Admittedly, on occasion the concept comes up already in the *Römerbrief* in this second sense: cf. 192; corresponding to 190 in the later edition, and to 207 in the 15th ed.: "I cannot see sin as a possibility next to grace, but rather only as the [*the* human!] possibility, which through the impossibility of grace itself becomes impossibility" [trans. rev.]).

The old dogmatics treated angels—good or evil—in a single chapter. . . .[2] I have always resisted this equal treatment,[3] in which the angels appear to be "first cousins" of the devil, so to speak. In 2 Peter as well as in Jude, one also finds the theory of the fall of angels and of Lucifer, a fallen angel (2 Pet. 2:4; Jude 6). I do not believe this because it is a theory that allows demons to be understood. Evil cannot be explained. But one must remember that the demons are already subjugated in heaven and will be likewise on earth at the return of Christ (Rev. 19:20; 20:10, 14).

Lescaze: I have read that Luther, at the time of all too great temptations, hurled his inkwell at the devil's head.[4] . . . Must we personify him then?

Barth: I like this realistic manner of fighting. But in the Middle Ages as well as in the time of the Reformation, the domain of demons often moved over into that of myth and Germanic legends. One must distinguish between the fundamental attitude of Luther and the influence of his century. But we certainly lack that energy with which Paul (cf. 2 Cor. 12:7) or Luther fought against Satan.

Lescaze: Nowadays, can one designate certain powers as demonic? What would be the criterion?

Barth: I do not like this question. . . . I prefer to talk politics in concrete terms. I remember a German who said to me after the war, "We have met the devil face-to-face." And I retorted, "It does not seem that it made much of an impression on him"[5] No, nowadays we know the reality of the devil only all too well. Today we need a certain sobriety in speech and writing. The Christian task is much rather to "demythologize" the demons than to hunt down still others. This fantastic notion must be reduced to its serious core. There is a divine reality and a reality of manifold darknesses. . . . This is our life down here on earth—to suffer and to fight while we receive help from above. And Paul has seen this correctly when he says, "I am certain that neither death nor life, neither angels nor principalities nor violent powers, neither things present not things future, neither height nor depth nor any other creature can separate us from the love of God, which is in Christ Jesus our Lord" (Rom. 8:38–39).

2. Concerning Angels

Lescaze: Let's get to the problem of angels! Who are they? Do they still play a role today?

Barth: The Greek word *angelos* means "one who is sent." The angels are therefore messengers or better yet a "trace of heaven" in our world. They are the sign that God acts from above in our world. There are—always in relation to the action and revelation of God—certain clues of the heavenly world, which is in the process of manifesting itself on the earth. However, the angel never has

---

2. Cf. HpB 159–73: *"de angelis bonis et malis"*; ET: RD 201–219; as well as under the title *"De angelis,"* in SchmP 134–49.

3. See *CD* III/3:519–21 [*KD* 609–10]. In his first dogmatics lectures in Göttingen (1924–25), however, Barth still followed the model of the "old dogmatics" formally: K. Barth, *Unterricht in der christlichen Religion*, ed. H. Stoevesandt, vol. 2 (Zurich: Theologischer Verlag, 1990), paragraph 21: "De angelis bonis et malis" (309–43).

4. Cf. on this above, 77 n. 9.

5. To this conversation between Barth and H. Thielicke, see *Lebenslauf*, 341; *Biography*, 328.

more than a subordinate, subservient role. He does not have his own personality; he speaks, but only on divine authority. In the New Testament, angels only appear, so to speak, at the beginning and at the end of the earthly life of Christ. There they underscore an event of universal scope. Through their presence they manifest the grandeur of revelation. Where God speaks, there is an entourage, and Christ *is* truly the incarnation of the Logos, the Word become flesh (John 1:14), and heaven in its entirety is present in him.

In the book of Revelation, the angel is also the one who interprets the visions and is a soldier of the heavenly army of Yahweh (cf. Rev 19:14).

Lescaze: Among many Christians, one finds the belief in a personal "guardian angel," a kind of "Jiminy Cricket" who deters Pinocchio from making foolish mistakes. . . .[6] Do you believe this is possible?

Barth: No, I do not believe it, but it must be said that in the sixteenth and seventeenth centuries this was a point of difference between Luther—who believed it—and the Reformed theologians, who were too rationalistic to believe this. . . .[7] I think that our Protestantism has become too poor in fantasy and imagination, and where it is far too serious, it is not very serious. . . . But, having said that parenthetically, I do not much like the idea of guardian angels and the representations one can create of them. I imagine a painting of a child on the edge of a precipice; the child is held back by his guardian angel. . . . Theological representations are dangerous, and this one in particular might be a source of superstition.

Yet I would never deny the existence of angels as a sign of the greatness and beauty of the revelation of God. I would even say that it is not impossible that in certain situations, a human being can be the representation of an angel.

Mademoiselle, I once taught an entire summer course of four hours per week on angels, and I only spoke for two hours on the devil and demons. . . .[8] You see, one must neither look at them nor study them too closely, out of fear of being contaminated through direct contact, but rather must fight them.

---

6. A figure from the children's book, *The Adventures of Pinocchio* [*Le avventure di Pinocchio*] by Carlo Collodi (Florence: R. Bemporad & Figlio, 1883). The name "Jiminy Cricket" was popularized by the 1940 movie version of the book by Walt Disney, in which the character was a cricket.

7. Cf. *CD* III/3:518–19 [*KD* 607–8].

8. Lecture course in the summer semester 1949; the text is printed in *CD* III/3:369–531 [*KD* 426–623]; concerning the devil and demons, *CD* 519–31 [*KD* 608–23].

15. Interview by *La Vie Protestante* 1961

On April 12, 1961, the first manned spaceflight took place with the Russian astronaut Yury Gagarin on board. On April 14, 1961, an opinion article appeared in the magazine La Vie Protestante *24, number 15 (Geneva), titled "Karl Barth and Man in Space." The article was prefaced by the statement of Bernhard Lovell, director of a British observatory: "We are in the presence of the greatest event of human history." There followed the remark of Jean Rostand: "We have become gods before we are capable of being humans." After these the opinion of Karl Barth on this subject was reported, which had been requested by telephone.*

Question: As a theologian, what do you say to the trip into outer space?

Barth: Is it really necessary to ask the opinion of a theologian? This is an event that counts in the field of science, politics, perhaps economics, but it does not count in the field of theology. Such an event does not change our relationship with God.

This poor fellow has orbited the earth—so much the better for him, or so much the worse! But one day he will die, and then what will be important for him—as for us—will not be his having orbited the earth, but rather what he will have made of his life.

To be sure, this event is important, even stirring, but we must not exaggerate its significance. The framework within which we live is changing, but we remain in the created order. A lot of things have changed since ancient times, and a lot of things will change again. But in the last analysis nothing changes.

16. Conversation with Methodist Preachers
1961

On May 16, 1961, at the spring district meeting of preachers from Methodist churches in Switzerland, at the retreat center Viktoria in Reute-Halisberg, Barth answered questions in morning and afternoon sessions for a total of four and one-half hours. A few years later Pastor Konrad Hell reworked his own handwritten notes from that meeting into typewritten minutes of the conversation with Barth. This account of the conversation was published in part in the periodical Schweizer Evangelist *13 (1966): 312–13, 328–30, 344–46, 359–61, under the title "Karl Barth Answers." The publication of the conversation that follows here reproduces the order followed by that typewritten account. That reproduction of the conversation at times consisted of catchwords, was at times unclear, and probably did not always reproduce well the sense of the dialogue. For this reason the present account has been reworked; the additions are marked by square brackets. In addition to this material, a short account of the conversation is also available from Pastor Hans Hauzenberger. Individual sentences from this account have been incorporated into the following text and may be identified by the presence of an asterisk (*) at the end of the sentence in question.*

In the printed text from K. Hell, a report from Wilfred Kloetzli is cited on page 321. This report reproduces the content of Kloetzli's talk with Barth while they traveled by car to and from Reute-Hasliberg. According to this account, Barth said in response to the mention of his eleven honorary doctorates, "Ah, you know, when I at some point enter heaven, if I ever get that far, then I will hand over all these many doctors' hats at the coat check outside. And I will also set aside all my books, including the thick volumes of the Church Dogmatics. *And then I will enter in without all these things only on the basis of the grace of my Lord Jesus Christ."*

1. Preliminary Remarks

Barth: Honored, dear gentlemen and brothers, I thank you for the invitation that has been extended to me to come to you. I thank you for the friendly words with which I have just now been greeted. Two years ago I was also with a group of preachers of the Community Movement in Basel, and as now also for a whole day.[1] At the end of the day we understood each other rather well. One year ago I met with a similar gathering, although not as large as this one: the preachers from the Moravian communities.[2] And today I am permitted to

---

1. See chap. 3 above.
2. See chap. 12 above.

be with you. As soon as I received your invitation, I was ready and pleased to accept it. So now we want to hope for the best from this gathering and especially that we will understand each other well. Questions have been sent to me, and so I want to turn to them now.

Question: Can you briefly describe for us the theological path you have taken?

Barth: I want to give an answer to this question only when we have nothing more intelligent to talk about. Of course, I could give you some particulars about this, but I have had to hear so much about myself over the last week since I turned seventy-five.[3] I have received over five hundred letters from all over the world; many newspaper articles have been written about me, especially in Germany; a whole series of radio broadcasts have been made about me; in short, I have heard and read so much about my theological path that I get quite "antsy."[4] I am not at all comfortable in this role. During the radio programs that have focused on me, I have often had to say to myself: the angels are listening to this, and what will they say about it all? So let us turn our attention then to the first serious question that you have posed to me! We want to ensure that we come through this great tunnel [of your substantial questions].

2. The Human Being as the Image of God

Question: What constitutes the image of God in human beings?

Barth: You will know that this question has three answers. One response goes like this: the image of God in humans relates to Genesis 1:28, where God says to the first couple, "Be fruitful and multiply, and fill the earth and subdue it." So then the human being as "the image of God on earth" lives as ruler under God![5] A second view on this question understands the image of God in humans to exist in human reason, in that this creature possesses spirit, conscience, and will, and therefore in analogy to the Spirit of God is a spirit-bearer. This is the answer that interested my friend Emil Brunner. It is from here that he developed his view about the "point of contact."[6] And as a third answer the Reformers said that the image of God consisted in the original righteousness of humans, in which they were created by God and which they lost in the fall.[7]

---

3. On May 10, 1961.

4. Swiss German expression for "touchy," "fidgety."

5. According to J. J. Stamm, "Die Imago-Lehre von Karl Barth und die altestamentliche Wissenschaft," in K. Barth, *Antwort: Karl Barth zum 70. Geburtstag am 10. Mai 1956* (Zollikon-Zurich: Evangelischer Verlag, 1956), 87, this view, e.g., was represented by L. Kohler and J. Hempel.

6. According to J. J. Stamm, ibid., this view is represented, e.g., by Fr. Delitzsch, E. König, and W. Eichrodt. Regarding E. Brunner's first proposed teaching on the "contact point for the divine message in humans," see his essay, "Die andere Aufgabe der Theologie [The Other Task of Theology]," in *Zwischen den Zeiten* 7 (1929): 255–76 (now in *Ein offenes Wort*, vol. 1, *Vorträge und Aufsätze: 1917–1962* [Zurich: Theologischer Verlag, 1981], 171–93). Cf. further E. Brunner, "Die Frage nach dem 'Anknüpfungspunkt' als Problem der Theologie [The Question about the Contact Point as a Problem in Theology]," in *Zwischen den Zeiten* 10 (1932): 505–32 (also in *Ein offenes Wort*, 1:239–67); and in *Natur und Gnade: Zum Gespräch mit Karl Barth* (Tübingen: Mohr; Zurich; Zwingli-Verlag, 1934–35), esp. 18–20; Emil Brunner and Karl Barth, *Natural Theology: Comprising "Nature and Grace" by Emil Brunner and the Reply "No!" by Karl Barth* (Eugene, OR: Wipf & Stock, 2002), esp. 31–33 (also in *Ein offenes Wort*, 1:333–75, esp. 348–50).

7. Cf. M. Luther, *Sermons on the First Book of Moses*, LW 51, Sermons 1; J. Calvin, *Inst.* 1.15.3.

There is much to be said for all three of these possibilities. But I myself could not be satisfied with any of these three understandings, simply from an attentive reading of the relevant Bible passages in which statements about the image of God in humans are found (from Gen. 1 right through to the passages in the New Testament that speak of Christ).[8]

Looking at the passage more closely, we see that Genesis 1:26 says, "Then God said, "Let us make humans in our image." And then it reads, "So God created the human in his image, in the image of God he created them; male and female he created them" (1:27). I would like to understand the text so that here human being and human being are facing one another. . . . This remarkable plural ("Let us make humans in our image!," Genesis 1:26) is noteworthy. The Bible never presents God as a hermit who exists in his own solitude; rather, it says that in God's self there is a plurality. God as Father, Son, and Spirit is the living, biblical God. God himself reasons with himself in his word and lives as Father and Son united through the Holy Spirit. Building on this, then one can pursue the line of thought in this way: the Bible is, at first in the Old Testament, the account of the story that God has with his people. He acts on behalf of his people and deals with his people. One of the most noteworthy pictures in the Old Testament is the one of Yahweh as the bridegroom and the people of Israel as the bride, a very unfaithful bride, but Yahweh is faithful.[9] God is the God of this communal existence: he is *with* his people. And now we find a word about this already in the creation story; indeed, the whole creation points to this, that God did not want to be alone. It is God's free love that moves him not to remain alone but rather to be with his creation.

And now human beings are created "in *his* image." It appears to me essential to see that in this text it states that a human being is created not as an isolated being but rather as male and female! This is, so to say, the prototype for human community. I by myself cannot in any way be a human being, as God has created me, without the other person. So this constitutes the image of God in the human being: as God does not exist on his own, so in the same way humans cannot and must not exist on their own. This is so important all the way through the Bible: "You shall love your neighbor as yourself" [Lev.19:18; Matt. 22:39]. "And created them male and female" is not just simply a little sentence added to the text: instead, it is enormously important. From this perspective the whole great truth about the image of God in humans gains its powerful and practical significance. Under the fatherly grace of God, I should be a human being, and this means to live with my fellow human being, to see the other as they are, to care for the other as they are, to live with them as they are, and not to think that they should exist in a way that suits me. I can only sketch all of this out now. I have developed it further in my *Church Dogmatics*.[10] Now I want to proceed in this way that I [after my answers] stop every now and then and ask whether you are in agreement with me. I want to be here with you as one person among other people. . . .

Question: Is the image of God in humans as you understand it not a burden?

8. Cf. Col. 1:15–18; 3:10; 1 Cor. 15:49; Rom. 8:29; Heb. 1:3.
9. Cf. Isa. 49:18; 62:5; Jer. 2:2; Hos. 2:19–20.
10. *CD* III/1:191–206 [*KD* 214–33].

Barth: Not only a burden. I have not yet said anything at all about Jesus. There the two are together [the burden and the advantage]: "Though he was in the form of God, [Christ Jesus] did not regard equality with God as something to be exploited, but emptied himself, taking the form of a slave, being born in human likeness. And being found in human form . . ." (Phil. 2:6–7).

[He, "like God," became "like a human," like us. He is with God and at the same time with us! He is the image of God and also the revelation of the image of God in humans!][11]

It would not be at all possible to believe in Christ if we could not, based on our belief in him, believe [also] in our own existence. Time and again we sin against this image of God because we are continually caught in a false movement: we want nothing to do with our fellow humans. We would like much more to exist for ourselves alone. Still, I remain the human creature made for life with other humans but cannot be this without the other ones.

Question: The idea that the image of God in human beings consists in the community of humans with each other is a wonderful thought. But when we think about the image of God in humans, we often think about the bestowal of the Spirit. The creation account speaks quite graphically that God breathed "the breath of life" into the human being (Gen. 2:7). Apparently then there exists an important difference between every other living creature and the human being since it is said only of the human that it received the "Spirit." So would not the bestowal of the Spirit as spoken of in Genesis 2:7 also be an essential part of the image of God in human beings?

Barth: That God breathed the Spirit into the first human being is stated in Genesis 2:7. There is no mention here in the second chapter of Genesis of the image of God in the human being. But I would say that the image of God in humans and the bestowal of the Spirit are not two different things. When we ask ourselves, What is the Spirit?, then we have to say, following the sense of Genesis 2:7, the "Spirit" is evidently the life that God gives to human beings precisely for the purpose that the human being live with another human being. The way I see it is that there exists a vital connection between the image of God in humans in Genesis 1 and God's bestowing of the Spirit according to Genesis 2. Both concepts bring to expression that the human being should belong to God, have fellowship with God, but also have fellowship with each other, with other human beings together. In this matter I also think of the text "The grace of the Lord Jesus Christ and the love of God and the fellowship of the Holy Spirit be with you all" [2 Cor. 13:13]. There it is all together. It is the same with the image of God in humans. I could not say that the bestowal of the Spirit would then involve a second, other thing.

Question: What really is the fall of the human being?

Barth: In the fall story, theology has its beginning. The serpent handles himself like a proper professor of theology. The serpent says, "Did God really say?" (Gen. 3:1). And with that the serpent gets itself into a discussion. And then it happens: the one created by God, the one who is brought into fellowship with God and who is also bound to the fellow human, wants "to be like God" (3:5).

---

11. Presumably at this point in the transcript of the conversation, the relevant comments have been lost, and so they need to be inserted in order to restore the logical connection between the Bible verse and the following sentence.

Theology proceeds in a similar way: Just a minute, human being, you must be able to distinguish between good and evil! The human being did not have the need to do this. The fall of man is a fall into the realm of the moral, into the place where the human being wants to be clever and on its own to know "what is good and what is evil" (3:5). This means, then, to want to be like God. Now we are precisely in this position and think that we can be "little gods." But this all will be set finally aside in eternal life.

3. Faith and Experience

Question: In Methodism the salvation experience has great significance. This relates to the fact that the Holy Spirit works in such a way in a human being that a person can come to a joyful certainty of the redemption that has been accomplished by Christ for that person and for the whole world. What is your position on the recognition of the psychological dimension experienced in salvation?

Barth: Here we are concerned about the joyful certainty of the salvation that Christ has accomplished for humans and for the whole world. The Holy Spirit brings about this joyous certainty, and it is not based upon something that *I* have accomplished and what *I* have apprehended. It is not something that somehow might have arisen in my heart, as it is spoken about in 1 Corinthians 2:9, but rather it is about something that could not have arisen in "the heart of anyone, what God has prepared for those who love him," specifically for me, this human being, *and* for the whole world, indeed not somehow just for me. The certainty here concerns something that lies completely and wholly outside of me, not within me. When I consider myself, what I feel, my little or big theology, my experience—yes, I have these, but what I am certain about [is not this experience]. I am not certain about my certainty; I do not believe in my own faith; rather, I believe in that which God has done in Christ. This is the great wonder, namely, that I am permitted to believe in something that stands high above me, something that came from God to me, never something that I have in my pocket. I can orient myself always and only on the cross on Golgotha.

With respect to what I can experience psychologically of salvation: naturally salvation is something that we can experience. I am a being who has been given a psychological dimension. Nevertheless, in this matter we must always clearly differentiate: What is an impulse of the mind? What is an impulse of the conscience and of the will? "We have this treasure in clay jars" [2 Cor. 4:7]. What there is on my human side, I will rejoice that I am permitted to have this treasure in this clay jar. But I do not want to confuse the treasure for the jar. I do not want to say, The Holy Ghost is present inside my little soul or my small head; rather, let us look to that place from which we may also live, namely, that which comes "from above," *anōthen*, and not in a way that there is still something to be found here below. What there is here below is what I am as the one who is addressed, the addressee. I want to be glad that I am the addressee to whom God directs his word, the Bible, this "letter." I will want to read the "letter" and be amazed over the fact that I am the one who may travel this path, this "theological path," about which you asked me in your first question [on which path I suddenly have the most wonderful thing occur, as Martin Luther put it]: "From heav'n above, I come down here. / I bring you tidings, good and new."[12]

I do not know whether what I have said here is "Methodist orthodoxy" or not. I do not deny the salvation experience. I wouldn't think of doing that! The salvation experience is that which happened on Golgotha. In contrast, my own experience is only a vessel. And now you have to contradict me. It's probably time for that.

Question: There was a time when you were not disposed to speak in this positive way about the experience of salvation. Considered on a purely psychological level, what has changed for you to bring this about?

Barth: I will give you an answer. I come [originally] out of the liberal theology stream, from Wilhelm Herrmann in Marburg and also from Adolf Harnack.[13] At that time I was [also] an assistant editor for the then famous journal *Christliche Welt* of Martin Rade.[14] In that little circle I heard no word as often as the word "experience." I absorbed all this, and for years I preached to my people in Safenwil[15] about this "experience." And then I discovered that behind this theology stood the great Schleiermacher. Then through my reading I also met up with Pietism. I noticed that before Friedrich Schleiermacher there was also a Philip Jakob Spener and an August Hermann Francke (back then I had not concerned myself so much with John Wesley). . . .

Then in the pulpit I had my breath taken away. I began to read the Bible more and so to look more attentively at what God has done. [And then it dawned on me: the] Bible does not [testify to] "experience," rather to the acts of God.* And then as it happens in these matters, there has to be a 180-degree turn made, from pious humans to God himself, who has done everything in Christ that was needed to redeem the world. Then I began to write books.[16] I read a great deal [for this task], including many Pietist biographies,[17] and in this activity I said to myself: wait a minute, it does *not* work *like that!* Pietism and rationalism are brothers: they [both think in] human-centered [ways].* In *Romans* and in my early writings about forty years ago, I offered people some very tough things to swallow. Whenever I even heard the word "Pietism" or just had the inkling that it was close by, I believed that I had to engage it strongly.[18] So it happened that

12. The first lines of the Christmas carol by Martin Luther (around 1538), GERS 115; EKG 16; EG 24: "Vom Himmel hoch, da komm ich her. / Ich bring' euch gute, neue Mär'."

13. Barth studied with A. von Harnack (1851–1930) in the winter of 1906–7 in Berlin and with W. Herrmann (1846–1922) from spring 1908 until fall 1909.

14. From fall 1908 until summer of 1909. Prof. Martin Rade (1857–1940) in Marburg was the editor of the journal from its founding.

15. From 1911 to 1921 Barth was a pastor in the Aargau town of Safenwil.

16. The first edition of Barth's work *Der Römerbrief* [*The Epistle to the Romans*], written in 1916–18, appeared in 1919 (Bern: G. A. Bäschlin); ed. H. Schmidt in a new ed. (Zurich: Theologischer Verlag, 1985); the 2nd ed., written 1920/21, came out in 1922 in Munich; cf. the 15th ed. (Zurich: Theologischer Verlag, 1989).

17. According to K. Barth and E. Thurneysen, Bw.Th. 1:138–39, 199–200, 203–4, 215–16, 218–19, 221–22. In 1916–17 Barth read a series of biographies from the revival period of the 19th century. According to the same source (1:149) he likewise used Spener, presumably Ph. J. Spener, *Auslegung des Briefes Pauli an die Römer*, 4th ed. (Halle: Schott, 1861).

18. In fact, Barth addressed himself aggressively against Pietism only in his first exposition of Romans, not because of its emphasis on the experience of salvation, but rather because of its individualism. In the second Romans exegesis, Barth did negatively address the issue of experience, but in that

with the position I took against the experientiality of salvation, I gave offense to many good, pious people.

Now I have become somewhat older, and now I can speak tenderly as well with this part of Jerusalem [cf. Isa. 40:2]. Now I do not have to turn so fiercely against this expression of faith.

Interjected comment: Our critique of your position on this has proved to be of some use then!

Barth: I hope so . . . many people were expecting [in fact], that things should develop exactly this way further through my life, [namely, to push the critical boundaries further]. No, it has been so for me that doors and windows have opened in a variety of directions. I do not have to take back anything. At that time, it was right, and these things had to be said. And it would probably be good if this or that group would still today read my *Romans*.

Interjected comment: Thank you so much for describing this part of your "theological path"!

Barth: I think you have noticed that I am not completely without feeling.

4. Repentance and Conversion

Question: Should the church, in its proclamation to modern people, follow the example of Jesus and quite decisively call them to *metanoia* (repentance) as the first conscious step that initiates discipleship to Christ?

Barth: Certainly, this question causes some upset. But to my knowledge Jesus called the *pious* people of his time to *metanoia*. These people were the theologians, the scribes, the Pharisees (the Pietists back then and maybe as well the Methodists just a little bit), and then the Sadducees (these were the liberals). And so it makes me uncomfortable when this picture emerges: the church stands here, and over there are modern people—and now we, the Christians, call for *metanoia*. Is not *metanoia* something above all else that we must call *ourselves* to do, us and those like us? I would say this about our established church. I do not know if this is different in the Methodist church. But it is precisely the church that actually has need of *metanoia*! This is an enormous word, this *metanoia* [the recognition of how much we depend on having to pray]: "Hallowed be your name. Your kingdom come. Your will be done on earth as it is in heaven [Matt. 6:9–10]! Would it not be urgently needed that we before everything else sweep clean the step before our own door and only then step before modern people, not as those who do this as though [we ourselves had no more need to repent?]. Have we called ourselves enough to turning around so that we can in turn preach it? So, we never have this *metanoia* behind us. Martin Luther [spoke about] "daily repentance."[19] Do you not believe with respect to this modern person, this person "come of age"—with his existentialism, with his sport activities, with his wholly curious superficiality—this very person, who

---

discussion he did not name Pietism. Cf. E. Busch, *Karl Barth und die Pietisten: Die Pietismuskritik des jungen Karl Barth und ihre Erwiderung* (Munich: Kaiser, 1978) esp. 50–54, 98–116 [ET: *Karl Barth and the Pietists*, trans. D. W. Bloesch (Downers Grove, IL: InterVarsity Press, 2004), 40–45, 88–105].

19. Cf. Luther's Theses against Indulgences (1517), thesis 1, in WA 1:233.10–11.

would rather go to the movies than to church, that everything would depend upon our being able to make this *metanoia* visible in our own lives? And *then* we could also speak about it authoritatively to that modern person. But only after we have said it first to *ourselves*!

Yes, indeed, naturally this proclamation involves a "conscious step." But we cannot be clear enough to ourselves what this conscious step means. To me it is simply a curious thing [if it somehow leads me to think,] I, the Christian, presume to know, and modern people do not yet [know this]. It comes out as a friend/enemy relationship. And when the world notices this—here come some people who assume that they have the goods or have it figured out—it will react negatively. As Christians we cannot be open-minded enough. Those others, the people in the movie theaters and on the sports field, these are our brothers and sisters, whom we can invite to take this great step into discipleship to Christ only out of our solidarity with them. Would that it might be given us before everything else to shout (this message) into our own circles (!), into the circles of the holy ones, of the justified, of the honest Christians, who want to be Christians in earnest.[20] [Then we would learn finally once again,] What is authority in the biblical sense? And then we would have to make use of this authority in solidarity with the people. If we do not want to be the "foremost" among sinners [cf. 1 Tim. 1:15], then we have nothing to say to the other sinners!

Question: We have to admit that in the best of cases we are handling things badly as far as being Christians goes. But regardless of this, are we not given the commission to serve the world?

Barth: It is out of the question that we in any way withhold the gospel from modern people. Despite our failure [we still have to say it]. Of course, the church is not at all the church if it is not an evangelization church. But we must take the lead with the others in this *metanoia* conviction, and this cannot happen too often. I do not want to call back or hinder anyone [from evangelizing]; rather, I want to remind us of Jesus' saying: "For which of you, intending to build a tower, does not first sit down and estimate the cost, to see whether he has enough to complete it? . . . Or what king, going out to wage war against another king, will not sit down first and consider whether he is able with ten thousand to oppose the one who comes against him with twenty thousand?" (Luke 14:28–31). I want to ask: *have we* determined that "we can carry this out"?

Question: Still, does the accent in the New Testament not lie more on evangelization?

Barth: The Gospels speak of repentance in no other way than this: "Believe in the gospel"; Mark 1:15, "Repent and believe in the gospel"! There is no other doing of repentance and no other turning around than that which orients itself to the gospel. This holds true as well within one's own ranks. There are so many sad Christians. They have absolutely no fun with regard to the gospel. Within their ranks one finds nothing like "My heart goes forth in leaps and it cannot be

---

20. Cf. M. Luther, *German Mass and Order of Service* (1526), in WA 19:75, lines 3–8: "The third kind of service should be a truly evangelical order and should not be held in a public place for all sorts of people. But those who want to be Christians in earnest and who profess the gospel with hand and mouth should sign their names and meet alone in a house somewhere to pray, to read, to baptize, to receive the sacrament, and to do other Christian works." ET from Luther's Works 53, *Liturgy and Hymns* (Philadelphia: Fortress, 1965), 63–64.

sad."[21] Christians themselves have need of the joyous message, and this is the presupposition for their going out into the world.

Question: For quite some time now our practice in the Methodist churches has been for us to conduct so-called "evangelization meetings" and "evangelization weeks" as a special attempt to present the Christian message to the people of today. Is this the best possible way to do this? At this time great efforts are expended in campaigns of this kind. What do you think about this kind of "evangelizing"?

Barth: Well, if I am to give you a good answer, then I have to make sure I have heard how you evangelize! I guard myself from making a general judgment. Evangelization today is necessary and commanded. Those among you who have read in my *Church Dogmatics* what is said about the task of the church know that I have spoken there about evangelization as a necessary task.[22] It all depends upon how it is done. It is the same with the church's preaching. Unfortunately, one cannot say either "if only it were preached!" or "if only evangelization were done!"

I have heard Billy Graham, and I have also gotten to know him personally.[23] In personal conversations I have come to clarity with him. When I heard him preach, I said, That was not good news; that was "gunfire." There was pressure in the appeal to people: you must, you should! It was a [legalistic] pushing I could not go along with and could not agree that this was truly "*evangelization.*" It was preaching the *law,* not a joy-inspiring message. He wanted to shock the people. Threatening always makes an impression. People like much more to be shocked than made to rejoice. The hotter one makes hell for them, the more they "run."[24] I must say this because the name of Billy Graham is mentioned in the questions posed to me. I am not speaking against his personal sincerity, [but is it not so] that in America, as I have heard, evangelization has been made into a tremendous business? But can one "market" the gospel as though it were like any other marketable product? We need to allow dear God himself the freedom to carry out his work. But when I am asked whether I think that this is a good thing—this way and method [to evangelize] including this calling forward at the conclusion of the event (which one can repeat a fourth or a sixth time!) and with the filling out of decision cards . . . —I hope you evangelize better!

Question: Is it not so that the word must be made visible by means of the proclamation?[25] What is the criterion for this?

21. Stanza 10 of the hymn "Ist Gott für mich, so trete gleich alles wider mich [If God himself be for me, I may a host defy]," by P. Gerhardt (1653): *GERS* 259; *EKG* 250 (stanza 13); *EG* 351 (stanza 13); "Mein Herze geht in Sprüngen und kann nicht traurig sein [My heart does go in leaps and cannot now be sad]."
22. *CD* III/3, 87–90; *KD* 999–1002.
23. The American evangelist Billy Graham visited Barth in August 1960 during Barth's vacation in his son Markus Barth's chalet in the canton of Valais and then in Barth's house in Basel on August 30, 1960. On the evening of the same day in Basel, Barth attended the Graham evangelization campaign event at St. Jacob's Stadium. According to the letter dated September 18, 1960, written by Karl Barth to Christoph and Marie-Claire Barth (in the Karl Barth Archive in Basel), Barth had a positive impression of Graham from his personal conversations with him, whereas the evangelistic event was very disappointing for Barth. Cf. E. Busch, *Lebenslauf*, 462; *Biography*, 446.
24. The term for "religious pilgrimage" to evangelization gatherings etc.; cf. Bw.Th. 1:163.
25. Perhaps the original question was "Must not the proclaimed Word be made visible in life?"

Barth: The proclamation of the gospel must be based on solidarity with the sinners. However the evangelist speaks, this must stand behind it. Forty or fifty years ago it was said, Doctrine is not a concern; what is important alone is living.[26] Then the younger generation came along and said, Doctrine is important, not life.[27] Yes indeed, doctrine is important to be sure, but the *lived doctrine* is important above all else. We are not permitted to tear apart faith and works.

Question: When I was at the Billy Graham gatherings, what impressed me was the stillness of all the people listening. To be sure the "gunfire" in his proclamation was there, but is it not conceivable that in these gatherings the Spirit of God is operative? Naturally, I am not in agreement with all of the practices of the Graham team. But I am thinking that God can still nevertheless be at work in this way.

Barth: The Holy Spirit does make use of the human spirit as a means. God can work even by means of weak and imperfect instruments—[if only] God's Spirit [through this] [is] not distilled—God works right through human weaknesses.* It is wonderful that God does not become tired of making such compromises. It works the same with Billy Graham as with us all. But if we are asking how we can evangelize in a good way, then we are confronted with the question Do we also want to do it in this way? Do we also want to set up a kind of gunfire? Are other ways not better? Should not the joyous message actually be proclaimed? These are the questions one can and must pose in the light of the Billy Graham type of evangelization.

Question: What is your view of the evangelists Dwight L. Moody and Charles G. Finney?[28]

Barth: This is difficult to answer in a general way [and with this distance from them]. Moody is less known to me; I do not want to allow myself a judgment on this. From what I have heard, it must have been a serious matter back then. Still, I have also heard different things. Let us leave Moody, Finney, and Graham aside! It cannot be about whether we praise or criticize these people, rather only about how we do our work with the proper mind-set. And then we will first see how enormous the task is. Our time is no longer the time of Finney and Moody, and we are not Americans.

Question: You have explained to us that we as messengers to modern people should meet the other person, our neighbors, with our lives, with our own

26. Barth became acquainted with this way of thinking through his teacher Wilhelm Herrmann for the most part in the latter's battle for "the personal and living Christianity . . . , which is unattainable by the binding law of doctrine." W. Herrmann, *Der Verkehr des Christen mit Gott* (Stuttgart: Cotta, 1886); 7th ed. (Tübingen: Mohr, 1921), 9 [ET: *The Communion of the Christian with God* (London: Williams & Norgate, 1895), 9]. Following in Herrmann's footsteps, Barth was still thinking in this schema when he wrote his book *Der Römerbrief* (Bern: G. A. Bäschlin, 1919): cf., e.g., 264 there and as found in the new edition by H. Schmidt (Zurich: Theologischer Verlag, 1985), 356.

27. In the 1920s Barth belonged to this "younger generation," and with this came, as much caused by him, that higher valuation of and emphasis on "doctrine." Compare some of the following sentences from Barth in his debate with W. Herrmann, such as K. Barth, "Die dogmatische Prinzipienlehre bei Wilhelm Herrmann," in *Vorträge und kleinere Arbeiten, 1922–25,* ed. H. Finze (Zurich: Theologischer Verlag, 1990), 602: "The Church should certainly present revelation to people consistently as 'doctrine' (what else could it be . . . ?) and certainly with the claim that this doctrine is *to be held as true* (how else could it be viewed . . . ?). Would to God that our doctrine was so believable that it *must* be held as true!"

28. Dwight L. Moody (1837–99) and Charles Grandison Finney (1792–1876) were the speakers and organizers of revival campaigns and mass evangelization in the USA.

personal Christian existence. Some have accused you, or perhaps more your followers, that for you the concern is more for the "theological existence"[29] and less about the other person. After we have heard you today, one can no longer maintain this. It would even seem to resemble slander.

Barth: Actually, as Christians and as theologians we are human beings just like everyone else. Christians and theologians are often "inhuman."* Our existence as Christians and our living as human beings must be a unity. Any person on the street must notice: here is someone like us. They must not be left with the impression: here comes someone dressed up in black, scary!—and now wants to preach and to convert me. Christian existence must emerge out of human existence.

5. The Understanding of Sanctification

Question: With respect to the sanctification of the human being, how do the two sides, the objective side (that is God's gift) and the subjective side (human activity) relate to each other?

Barth: It is good to have it said expressly that in a human's sanctification there is an objective side. I would go even further and say directly: sanctification in the New Testament sense is wholly a work of God. There is no way that human beings sanctify themselves. A person *is made* holy and thus has the task of giving an answer to what God does. It is the Word, that is, the living word of God, the word that is alive though the Holy Spirit, that sanctifies a person. "You have already been cleansed by the word that I have spoken to you" (John 15:3). Pardon me, but when that is said, a person cannot sit around and take it easy. You need to take it as the word for you, and this brings about human action. God's work then corresponds to human work and human faith, obedience, love, hope, and before all else one's *metanoia*, a person's turning around. And then in this connection baptism comes in as the answer to the word of grace from God that is spoken to humans. Sanctification is in the Bible: God lays a claim on humans. He takes them to his side and into his service. He wants to make use of human beings so that they operate with their lives in the service of God's work, of God's name, of the kingdom, and of the will of God. This is sanctification, and it is described as a work of God. No prophet or apostle called himself—that is, if the calling was authentic. It happens the way it was with the conversion of Paul [Acts 9:1–19]. This character, who did not want it, is not told, "You must begin a new life"; rather, what he hears is "I have need of you." Sanctification is this placing into immediate service. And then Paul begins to run [cf. Gal. 2:2]—you know the saying "Ya gotta do what ya gotta do."[30] He runs through country after country and this all as his answer to how God dealt with him.

Question: If Paul then went throughout the whole world, must not we also be about the same "running"?

29. A play on the title of a famous pamphlet *Theologische Existenz heute!* [Theological Existence Today!] (Munich: Kaiser, 1933) and then of a series (or journal) edited by K. Barth and others from then onward (Munich: Kaiser).

30. A Swiss German expression, literally, "What you can, that you have!"

Barth: Paul ran toward the *Lord* and was very active in this, [but it was toward the Lord]! We [also] want to be doing this. But we do not want to boast of it and begin to think that [now we are such magnificent Christians,] we only have to die, and then everything will work out [with the encounter with the eternal Judge]! Yes, that totally unsanctified human being must yet still die. Even old Tholuck in the last weeks of his life had to experience the most wrenching challenges to his faith.[31] We all must be prepared for something like this. And in that time nothing helps other than this: "My God, I beseech Thee by the blood of Christ, bring me to a good end!"[32] By the blood of Christ!—not by that which I have built up! The time will come when we will all rejoice to be saved by the sheer, pure grace of God.

Question: How do justification and sanctification relate to each other? Are we dealing with both as one and the same event? Do they relate as things that work together at the same time, or does one follow the other?

Barth: Justification in the Bible, "the righteousness that is valid before God," literally, "the righteousness of God," *dikaiosynē theou* [Rom. 1:17; 3:26], appears to stand in a particular relationship with the fact that a person is a sinner. When God justifies a person, this is what happens: God, with his own righteousness, steps into the life of an unrighteous human being. Why does God do this? Because God needs this person! Each person is to be made holy. And to that end the mortal should and must be someone who is allowed to know "My sins are forgiven" [cf. Luke 7:48]. My righteousness will never consist of our saying or thinking that I as preacher, as human being, as theologian, am really a fine chap! No, we are always in need of the justification of God. And, thank God! God makes right what I am doing badly "even in the best lived life."[33] Without this justification, there is no sanctification. There is only *one* action of God that has this double aspect: forgiveness of sins and renewal for service. "Do they relate as something that works together at the same time, or does one follow the other?" (as you asked earlier). I cannot well imagine that this involves a following one after the other. There is only this free and gracious action of God regarding us that contains both moments.

Question: What we Methodists have understood as the justification experience, we have conceived as a beginning. Can one not actually think about the justification experience in such a way that it is a beginning for a person, an experience, that can signify something for the individual when considered in relation to one's past? Sanctification is something central for Methodism. You have said that sanctification is a being-taken-into-service by God. But you are probably also aware that we Methodists have understood and still today understand sanctification as the perfected love! [More precisely,] sanctification has the sense of a growing, an increasing, in no way a becoming sinless, but rather as a constantly increasing work of the Holy Spirit in us with the purpose of perfected love, as John Wesley already saw. Our forefathers, also in

---

31. Cf. L. Witte, *Das Leben D. Friedrich August Gottreu Tholucks,* vol. 2 (Bielefeld and Leipzig: Velhagen & Klasing, 1886), 505–9.

32. The refrain from the hymn "Wer weiss, wie nahe mir mein Ende [Who Knows How Close My End Is]," by Ämiliane Juliane von Schwarzburg-Rudolstadt (1688), in *GERS* 379; *EKG* 331; *EG* 530.

33. "Es ist doch unser Tun umsonst, auch in dem besten Leben [Our efforts amount to nothing, even in the best lived life]," stanza 2 of the hymn by Martin Luther "Aus tiefer Not schrei ich zu dir [Out of the Depth I Cry to Thee]" (1524), in *GERS* 37; *EKG* 195; *EG* 299.

continental Methodism, still said, "We are not aware that we had committed any sin at such and such a time. We were able to overcome sin for such and such a length of time." It is a concern for us "to spread sanctification across the land," as John Wesley expressed it.[34] Is sanctification also something that grows, a something that comes steadily closer to its goal?

Barth: It would be sad if one did not grow a little, if one were always to remain a beginner and had nothing more to learn. "Perfected love" is a wonderful thing, *if* it is not just an expression. I am certainly in favor of speaking about this concern and taking it seriously. I am thankful with respect to myself that I am no longer such a young pup, as I was when I was twenty years old. I am thankful that some small refinement has taken place and that for me a few new lamps have been lit.

But when you read the New Testament, it is still true with everyone there, including Paul and all the others, that they are running toward a goal, namely, the epiphany, the appearance of Jesus Christ. *This day* will be the day of the "perfected love." And this day is *on the other side* of the four or five months "in which I was able to overcome sin," the other side of all of these perfectifizations. Paul says that he struggles to be a runner in the race [1 Cor. 9:24–26], and then he concedes, "Not that I have already obtained this or have already reached the goal; but I press on to make it my own" [Phil. 3:12]. I do not want to carry on any polemics against the classic Methodist teaching on holiness. But I ask you to consider this: when the New Testament speaks of all that God has done, then the consequence is expressed in this way: "Since all these things are to be dissolved, what sort of persons ought you to be in leading lives of holiness and godliness, *waiting for and hastening the coming of the day of God*" (2 Pet. 3:11–12).

A little while back I was shocked as we sang the hymn by Hans Jakob Breiter: "Ein volles Heil für jeden Schaden, / für jedes Herz ein volles Heil (A complete healing for every hurt, / for every heart a full salvation)."[35] I am afraid that there are a few heresies contained in those stanzas. "A complete healing for every hurt"; "Redemption in the present time"; "No, now Jesus comes to you gladly, / with him the whole of heaven enters in!" At this point I am no longer comfortable. I ask you, is this consistent with the New Testament? "Eternity already present in this time"? This is how Schleiermacher spoke.[36] According to this hymn there is no Christian hope. It says to the people that they can have all of it now already. I would never concede to the idea that we slowly slide into the eschaton with our sanctification. I would rather say, "Whoever *believes* in the Son has eternal life" (John 3:36). But he has it *in eternal life*. According to this hymn it would appear as though we already have it. It would be better

---

34. With respect to the above-mentioned teaching of J. Wesley (1703–91), the founder of Methodism, compare H. Lindström, *Wesley und die Heiligung* (Frankfurt: Anker-Verlag, 1961); ET: H. Lindström, *Wesley and Sanctification: A Study in the Doctrine of Salvation* (Stockholm: Nya bokförlags aktiebolaget; Wilmore, KY: Asbury, 1946).

35. The beginning of the first stanza of the hymn by H. J. Breiter (1845–93) in the *Gesangbuch für die Evangelisch-methodistische Kirche* [Hymnal for the Evangelical Methodist Church], 2nd ed. (Zurich: Christliche Vereinsbuchhandlung, 1969), no. 391. The other quotations in the following sentences are from stanza 3.

36. End of the second speech: F. Schleiermacher, *Über die Religion: Reden an die Gebildeten unter ihren Verächtern* (Berlin: J. F. Unger, 1799), 133; ed. R. Otto, 2nd ed. (Göttingen: Vandenhoeck & Ruprecht, 1906), 83; ET: F. Schleiermacher, *On Religion: Addresses in Response to Its Cultured Critics*, trans. T. Tice (Richmond: John Knox Press, 1969), 157: "In the midst of finitude to become one with the infinite—and to be eternal in every instant—this is the immortality of religion."

for you not to say it that way! This way of expressing it cannot be helpful to anyone. Yes, marching, hastening forward, "waiting for a new heaven and a new earth" [2 Pet. 3:13]—and then we will be dealing with the "perfected love" when Christ himself will appear. "Redemption in the present"?[37] Yes, indeed, in the New Testament both of these are together, the "already" and the "not yet" [cf. 1 John 3:2]. Neither the one nor the other is allowed to be expressed in isolation. I would see the boundary at this point: "We walk by faith, not by sight" [2 Cor. 5:7]. Let us be thankful that we are permitted to walk in faith and to say: "I believe; help my unbelief" [Mark 9:24]. This applies certainly as well for the Methodists.

Question: When the proclamation is divided between the indicative (the offer of salvation by God) and the imperative (the acceptance by man), how then should the imperative in the view of the New Testament be made visible in the community? Should not the imperative again today be more emphasized in the sermon?

Barth: The sense of the indicative and the imperative as it is presented in the question posed has been very familiar to me for decades. One cannot, however, use such formulas so as to make a sharp and clean distinction and say, "This is the indicative and that is the imperative." Consider the Christmas story! There the angel says to the shepherds in the field: "I am bringing you good news of great joy for all the people: to you is born this day . . . a Savior" [Luke 2:10–11]. This is an indicative that had its immediate effect as an imperative, because they said at once: "Let us go now to Bethlehem and see this thing that has taken place" [2:15]. If the indicative is a proclamation of the "mighty works of God" in Jesus Christ [cf. Acts 2:11], then there is no stronger imperative than this indicative. So I would not talk in this way: we have now heard about the indicative, namely, the salvation offer from God; let us now come to the acceptance of salvation, to the imperative! Suddenly one has moved from the gospel to the law again. We would gain a great deal if we would never speak about the imperative other than by articulating the indicative, and on the other hand never about the indicative other than by allowing the indicative to show its edge to people and meet them as invitation, and calling. [The] gift of God always brings along with it [a] task.*

6. The Question of "Universal Salvation"

Question: The main thesis in the *Church Dogmatics* II/2 states: "Jesus Christ is the electing God—Jesus Christ is the elected human being."[38] "Election is that election which is accomplished by and through Jesus Christ, and it is the election that happened in him."[39] Does not then the future fate of human beings

---

37. Stanza 3 in the hymn referred to in n. 35 above.

38. *CD* II/2:94 [*KD* 101], (where the title of the first section in paragraph 33 is) "Jesus Christ, Electing and Elected"; 103, "Jesus Christ Is the Electing God"; 116, "Jesus Christ Is the Elected Human Being."

39. A summary according to the content of the theses referred to in ibid. Cf. ibid., 115: "Jesus Christ *reveals* to us our election as . . . made *by him*": trans. note: the German original of this footnote in the *Gespräche* has "seine Erwählung [his election]," whereas *KD* II/2:124 [*CD* 115] has "unsere Erwählung [our election]"; 117, ". . . of the election of Jesus Christ . . . it must be said . . . that [it is] the original and all-inclusive election. . . . Of none other of the elect can that be said . . ."

depend upon their decision of faith? Will all people be saved (universal salvation)? Is there a hell?

Barth: "Does not the future fate of human beings depend upon their decision of faith?" I do not like the term "fate." It should not come up in Christian language. There is no "fate" that stands before us—[rather,] "providential occurrences," if you wish.

Does our eternal future depend upon our decision of faith? I would never say that. Our temporal and eternal future does not depend upon our decision but rather upon that which happened on Golgotha, and our decision of faith is our response to it. But one cannot now take our response to this event and make it a *condition* for our salvation's becoming real. As soon as the question is posed in such a way that now my faith is brought in and becomes, so to speak, an achievement, with the result that it makes true for me what happened on Golgotha, then the whole affair becomes almost blasphemous. My goodness, my little bit of faith, with which I should now make it possible that salvation is also mine—this cannot be! This is precisely what we cannot say! We can only leave ourselves open to being summoned by this call, that Christ is my salvation just as he is salvation for all people.

"Are all people going to be saved (universal salvation)?" Also, one cannot pose a question like this. We cannot place ourselves alongside the salvation in Christ, of whom Scripture says: "In Christ, God was reconciling the world to himself" [2 Cor. 5:19], and then look about and ask, Will all people be saved? Like someone observing a building under construction, and then asking How will this come out? Let this be the word to us that we should proclaim: Christ is the Savior of the world! With that we shall have our hands full. With that alone we are also given a tremendous vision of the future. Surely it will be a huge affair so that we will open our eyes and ears wide indeed! But "universal salvation"—such a curious term! In Colossians 1:20 we do hear about something like this; nevertheless, I am not fond of the concept. I was good friends with Inspector Imberg in Gümlingen.[40] He was such a preacher of universal salvation. I said to him once: "I do not believe in universal salvation, but I do believe in Jesus Christ the universal Savior." Yes indeed, I believe in Christ, the *sotēr tou kosmou* [John 4:42; 1 John 4:14], the Savior of the world. I cannot even say about myself whether I am saved. That will be God's free grace.

The title of the book *The Triumph of Grace*, which was written about me,[41] should be better named *The Triumph of Jesus*. The hymn by Friedrich Traub that we sang earlier this morning is a good hymn: "Jesus lebet, Jesus siegt (Jesus lives, Jesus is victorious), Hallelujah, Amen!"[42] Very interesting!

Question: Before a preacher is admitted into full connection in the Methodist Church by the Annual Conference, the candidate, according to our church ordinances, must answer eighteen questions, and among them are these: "(2) Will you pursue perfection? (3) Do you expect to become perfected in love in this

40. Richard Imberg (died 1958) was the Director of the Deaconess Home Siloah in Gümmlingen, Bern, of whom Barth said, "whose warm humanity opened up to me a whole new side of the community movement." *CD* IV/3:xiii [*KD* ix].

41. G. C. Berkouwer, *The Triumph of Grace in the Theology of Karl Barth* (London: Paternoster, 1956).

42. Friedrich Traub (1873–1906). The hymn may be found in *Philadelphia-Hymns*, published by the Old Pietist Community Association in Württemburg, Reutlingen (1935), no. 659.

life? (4) Do you strive earnestly for this?"[43] Bishop Sigg[44] proceeds with the young preachers by not posing the individual questions to them but rather by posing them all together.

Barth: This would work better.

Question: The message of perfection was an important concern of John Wesley.[45] Can you help us to properly understand this perfection as Christ [cf. Matt. 5:48] and Paul taught it [cf. Col. 1:28; 2:10]?

Barth: This is the genuine perfection: that I find myself within this body [of Christ]. . . . What we read in the original text of Matthew 5:48 is part of a very specific context. This is almost universal salvation. The Zurich Bible translation renders the text as "Ihr sollt nun vollkommen sein, wie euer himmlischer Vater vollkommen ist (You should be perfect then as your Father in heaven is perfect)." The Greek word for "perfect" is *teleios*, and this word signifies "oriented toward the goal." When we render the word with "perfect," it brings another emphasis to the meaning. God goes for the whole thing, for the goal—this is what *teleios* means. Precisely this word must not be torn out of its context. [In its context it means] you should act [in this regard] as God's children, in the same way as God acts with you. And the "you should be," *esesthe*, actually means "you shall be." "You should be" is also not the correct translation. The goal is the kingdom of God. This is God's *teleios*. If I were a Methodist myself, I would propose that the ordination question "Do you expect to become perfected in love in this life?" be changed. . . .

Is there a hell? This is as though I were to ask, Is there a God? In such cases I say, No, there is not. God is not "something" that "is." Plums and cakes are, but one cannot say that God "is." One can and must say: God has spoken; God has acted. Likewise, one cannot say about hell that it exists. One can only say that it looks as though it does. The heavenly places are full of principalities and powers of darkness [cf. Eph. 2:2; 6:12]. But it also says in Scripture that hell is locked, overcome; it now is Christ's.[46] It is certainly true that "Jesus is victor!"[47] "In Christ, God was reconciling the world to himself" [2 Cor. 5:19]. It is not a good Christian interest that asks whether hell exists. The whole New Testament bears witness much more to this: "Heaven is open" [cf. John 1:51]. It also says that we are called out, taken out of the kingdom of darkness [1 Pet. 2:9; Col. 1:13]—a right turnabout, with eyes set straight toward Jerusalem![48] It is this

43. *Kirchenordnung der Methodistenkirche* [Liturgy of the Methodist Church], shortened German ed. (Zurich: Christliche Vereinsbuchhandlung, 1958), 100–102, §103. These questions, which originated with Wesley, are required to be responded to by every Methodist preacher "after serious fasting and prayer" before being received into the pastoral ministry. According to *The Book of Discipline of the United Methodist Church* (Nashville: Methodist Publishing House, 1968), §334, these questions are valid for every Methodist preacher in the United Methodist Church.

44. Ferdinand Sigg (1922–65), Swiss Methodist bishop.

45. Cf. C. W. Williams, *John Wesley's Theology Today* (Nashville: Abingdon Press, 1960), 167–90, esp. 167, ". . . for the sake of propagating this [namely, this doctrine] chiefly he [God] appeared to have raised us [Methodists] up."

46. Cf. 1 Cor. 15:55–57; Rev. 1:18; 11:15; 20:1–3.

47. The watchword of Johann Christoph Blumhardt (1805–80) that he encountered in his struggle with the ill Gottliebin Dittus, who uttered the saying. Cf. Fr. Zündel, *Pfarrer Joh. Christoph Blumhardt: Ein Lebensbild* (Heilbronn: Henninger; Zurich: Höhr, 1880), 138; 8th ed. (Giesen and Basel: Brunnen, 1921), 144.

48. Following stanza 2 of the hymn "Kommt Kinder, lasst uns gehen [Come, Children, Let Us Go]," by G. Tersteegen, in *GERS* 325; *EKG* 272: "Ein jeder sein Gesichte / mit ganzer Wendung richte / hin nach Jerusalem (Let each one direct his face / with a full turn / toward Jerusalem)"; A. Knapp,

movement that we need to make; it is the proper eschatological movement. I just read in your "order for worship" that in your services the Lord's Prayer is prayed in unison.[49] This is the best answer to this question!

7. The Doctrine of the Virgin Birth

Question: Is the doctrine of the virgin birth biblical, or can we, on good grounds, abandon it?

Barth: I say yes to Jesus' virgin birth, but I am not particularly proud of this. I simply understand the biblical testimony that Jesus had a human mother but no human father to be a strong expression for this truth: the man Jesus from Nazareth does not come out of human history, of the history men have made. World history is a history of men, and that's well and good! But the man Jesus is no product of world history, even though, of course, he is an actual man who has a mother who represents humanity, although not the active "deed-ful" humanity. I've always tried to understand Jesus' virgin birth from this point of view. In relation to this, my conscience is clear concerning the minimal New Testament discussion of the virgin birth. The virgin birth is, for me, no nuisance, rather a true statement. Even my long since departed father, Professor Fritz Barth, who was a good positive theologian, rejected the virgin birth, and this denial twice cost him a professorship (in Halle and Greifswald).[50] The orthodox there said, "We have no use for this man: he denies the virgin birth." I, as his son, found no difficulty with the virgin birth. But I would never make it a *conditio sine qua non* so that I would say, "You must believe in the virgin birth, whether you like it or not."[51] I would say, "I have the freedom to say yes even here." It should be added that I have noticed, when I discount my father, that those who reject the virgin birth incline toward natural theology. . . . The divine sonship of Jesus does not depend on the virgin birth. The virgin birth is better understood as a sign of this, his divine sonship. As Jesus' healing of the paralytic was a sign of his divine authority to forgive sins (Matt. 9:6), so the virgin birth is a sign of

---

Evangelischer Liederschatz, 2nd ed. (Stuttgart and Tübingen: Cotta, 1850), no. 1131 says, ". . . fest nach Jerusalem [steadfastly toward Jerusalem]"; as also *EG* 393; T. Klein, *Gerhard Tersteegen: Eine Auswahl aus seinen Schriften, Liedern und Sprüchen* (Munich: Kaiser, 1925), no. 324 says, ". . . steif nach Jerusalem [steadily toward Jerusalem]." The first version is correct, according to G. *Tersteegen's Geistliches Blumgärtlein inniger Seelen, nebst der Frommen Lotterie, nach der Ausgabe letzter Hand berichtigt und mit einigen Zusätzen vermehrt, sammt dem Lebenslauf des sel. Verfassers* [Spiritual Flower Garden of Tender Souls, Together with the Spiritual Lottery, according to his last corrected edition with certain additions, along with a life of the same author], new ed. (Stuttgart: Steinkopf, 1969), 328.

49. *Liturgie der Methodistenkirche, herausgegeben auf Anordnung der Jährlichen Konferenz der Methodistenkirche in der Schweiz* [Liturgy of the Methodist Church, published by order of the Annual Conference of the Methodist Church in Switzerland] (Zurich: Christliche Vereinsbuchhandlung, 1956), 10: "Die stehende Gemeinde soll das Gebet des Herrn laut mitbeten (the congregation shall stand and say the Lord's Prayer aloud in unison)."

50. Fr. Barth, *Die Hauptprobleme des Lebens Jesu* (Gütersloh: Bertelsmann, 1899), 3rd ed. (1907), 271–300. Cf. *Lebenslauf*, 22; *Biography*, 12.

51. Barth here makes reference to Bonhoeffer's criticism in his *Widerstand und Ergebung: Briefe und Aufzeichnungen aus der Haft* (Munich: Kaiser, 1951), 9th ed. (1959), 184; ET: *Letters and Papers from Prison* (Minneapolis: Fortress, 2010), 373: "Barth was the first theologian—to his great and lasting credit—to begin the critique of religion, but then he put in its place a positivist doctrine of revelation that says, in effect, 'like it or lump it.' Whether it's the virgin birth, the Trinity, or anything else, all are equally significant and necessary parts of the whole, which must swallowed whole or not at all."

Jesus' divine sonship. We ought to accept this sign. I think I have good reasons not to discard Jesus' virgin birth. But when someone is offended by it, I would not say, "You are, therefore, not a Christian." Faith is not a shop full of truths.*

Question: When Paul says, "God's grace toward me has not been in vain" (1 Cor. 15:10), he seems to suggest that there are people who do receive the grace of the Lord in vain. Therefore, I cannot simply say that everything is a fait accompli. The reaction of the human to God's offered grace still seems to be decisive. It cannot be unimportant whether I accept or reject the salvation created and offered by God. The question always remains: how do I react to it?

Barth: The question here is not fait accompli or not? Whenever God's grace becomes revealed and proclaimed to us, this is already the strongest call to us to begin our movement toward God. When that does not occur, we have not heard the word of grace. Right hearing is as well itself grace. For Paul, everything is governed by grace. We find no trace of the thinking that I have also contributed something to salvation. I am, however, not finished with this question. One can never be finished with this question.

8. Infant or Adult Baptism?

Question: On Christian baptism: ought it be infant or adult baptism?

Barth: For me, what is important regarding the question of baptism is this: ought baptism be administered to people who are mature or immature, who are responsible or are not yet shouldering responsibility? In Göttingen, it once happened to me that a Jewish Privatdozent came to me and said: "I am in a big predicament. My nine-year-old son says that he wants to become a Christian and to get baptized. I do not know what I should do." I said to him: "Send him in to me." Soon the young boy came marching in. He then told me that he goes to school with Christian children and had read in their school Bible the stories of the Old and New Testaments. As a result of this reading, he had recognized that this Jesus, about whom the New Testament stories report, was the Messiah for whom the Israel of the Old Testament had waited. "Therefore," he said, "if I am a Jew, I must become a Christian." I said to him, "My boy, you are going to be baptized! You have understood the decisive point of the Bible; you have grasped the center of the biblical message." And after that, I baptized him—a nine-year-old child![52] I hope that I have done the right thing. That is the process when I think about Christian baptism. When someone says *that*, confesses their faith in that way, then they ought to be baptized. But today the situation when we baptize is this: they are all baptizands who were *not* asked by anyone and of whom one cannot expect that they are able to answer. With *confirmation* as corroboration of the baptismal vow, it is the same situation. Everything is sick here. But one should not take this matter lightly, for this system generates the mass Christianity of our church. "Church" in the sense of the New Testament,

52. Hans Hermann Fränkel was born in 1916 to Dr. Hermann Fränkel and his wife, Lilli, born Fraenkel. The father was a Privatdozent from 1920 onward before serving from 1925–35 (until his emigration to Stanford in California) as a professor of classical philology in Göttingen. The baptism occurred on June 21, 1925, administered by Barth and recorded in the baptismal register of the Reformed Church in Göttingen.

however, means a community of living members who voluntarily have confessed Christ as their Lord. I want to understand baptism, basically, in this way: not as a bestowal of grace, as a "means of grace" (there is only one means of grace: that is Jesus Christ, and there are no other such "actions" beside him!), but as a response of the trust, the hope, the obedience, the readiness, and the μετάνοια [*metanoia*], by both the church *and* the baptizand as a free and responsible action. You (Methodists) are a free church. You could much more easily undertake a renewal of baptismal practice, which then might amount to a true renewal. Get to work!

Question: But in the Baptist practice, will not the action of baptism easily be understood as the baptizand's making a small contribution to salvation? And this is very dangerous. . . .

Barth: Yes, of course!

Questioner: . . . With baptism, when we baptize a child, we erect a sign of God's gracious act. We accept with thanks what God offers us.

Barth: But the latter could be accomplished by other means than by baptism. Baptism is a sign of the beginning of a new life; this cannot be erected without the person in question. With infant baptism, the central participant lies on a pillow and cries. I was formerly a supporter of infant baptism. I was always glad when a child cried during baptism. This crying seemed to me to be a reminder of the free grace [which is being directed to the resistant person]. But reading the New Testament, I had to say to myself more and more that we cannot do it this way. Rather, we must here think of the eunuch who said to Philip: "Look, here is water! What is to prevent me from being baptized?" (Acts 8:36). Of course, [such is] not in order to make any contribution to salvation by means of this baptism and being baptized! No, no, certainly not. What is irritating about the Baptists is that they dream of such a baptismal grace.[53] For me, baptism belongs to ethics.[54] It is the first, representational, symbolic demonstration of the obedience, which in the person who believes breaks forth and leads to participation in the Christian life and the life of the Christian community.

Question: Couldn't the practice of infant baptism be justified by reference to the mission situation of early Christianity?

Barth: Well, that depends. Naturally, it had a role to play. But we must consider John 1:13: ". . . who were born, not of blood or of the will of the flesh or of the will of man, but of God." One does not become a Christian through birth, through Christian parents. God's children are not born "of the will of the flesh or of man," but rather of God. This beginning of being a Christian is something special. We ought not to blur it with the existence of a person in a Christian environment. I certainly do not want to minimize the latter. But both must

---

53. It is not clear from where Barth derived his knowledge of the Baptist understanding of baptism. Prof. Thorwald Lorenzen, of the Baptist Theological Seminary in Rüschlikon, suspected, in a letter to the editor, that Barth informed himself by consulting the study by the New Testament scholar Johannes Schneider titled *Die Taufe im Neuen Testament* (Stuttgart: Kohlhammer, 1952), which may be read as suggesting that baptism belongs to the reception of salvation (cf. 79). However, Schneider's book is not considered as representative of the Baptist position; cf. *Rechenschaft vom Glauben*, ed. Bund der Baptistengemeinden in der Schweiz (Basel, 1977), esp. 9.

54. Cf. *CD* IV/4 (Fragment), e.g., 107 [*KD*, passim but esp. 118]: The meaning of baptism must be understood "as the *ethical* meaning of an action which, though it comes from Jesus Christ and hastens towards Him, is still a genuinely human action" (107).

be distinguished. I am afraid that, while the first generation of Christians in the young mission churches are certainly baptized responsibly, already by the second generation that is no longer the case. Then what we hear in the warm mom-and-pop atmosphere is "Come on in; you will also be baptized!" And it is not a responsible attitude that the church simply says yes to this situation and turns into a big family club.

9. On the Newer Theology

Question: Should one endorse the endeavor advocated by Bultmann to abandon certain scriptural statements that are conditioned by their contemporary historical setting (e.g., worldview, Karl Heim)? Where do we draw the line here?

Barth: I do not at all agree with Rudolf Bultmann. I have written a booklet with the title *Rudolf Bultmann: An Attempt to Understand Him.*[55] I am at home elsewhere. On this question of "abandoning certain scriptural statements that are conditioned by their contemporary historical setting," however, he is misunderstood. He did not want to abandon certain statements, but wants to "interpret" everything, to be understood in the framework of its contemporary historical setting and its language, and by doing so show that everything, including the virgin birth of Jesus, has an existential sense, a connection to human life.[56] So he understands that the scriptural statements are expressions or perspectives in which the people of that time described their relationship to the cosmos and to their fellow humans. The error that I see here is that Bultmann wants everything to be centered upon human existence. The New Testament simply does not only speak of that which concerns me. Naturally, it also speaks about this, but there is still an objective proclamation that I, first of all, have to acknowledge and that cannot be translated into statements about myself.

Question: Does not theological liberalism, once seemingly overcome, now exist in the church in a new and much more dangerous form than earlier on? What should be done today to overcome it?

Barth: It is certainly true, and I see it widely in theology: liberalism is returning. What I mean by this is a theology in which the theme is somehow personal piety or the Christian religion. The Erlangen theologian Hofmann stated it thus: "I, as a Christian, am for me as a theologian the actual object of my science."[57]

---

55. K. Barth, *Rudolf Bultmann: Ein Versuch, ihn zu verstehen*, ThSt 34 (Zollikon: Evangelischer Verlag, 1953) [ET: "Rudolf Bultmann: An Attempt to Understand Him," in *Kerygma and Myth: A Theological Debate*, ed. H.-W. Bartsch, 2nd ed. (London: SPCK, 1962), 83–132].

56. Cf., e.g., R. Bultmann, *Jesus Christus und die Mythologie: Das Neue Testament im Licht der Bibelkritik* (Hamburg: Furche-Verlag, 1964), 50 [ET: *Jesus Christ and Mythology* (London: SCM, 1964), 50: "Demythologizing is a hermeneutical method, that is, a method of interpretation, a method of exegesis." Bultmann, *Das Urchristentum im Rahmen der antiken Religionen*, rde 157–58 (Hamburg: Rowohlt, 1962), 8 [ET: *Primitive Christianity in its Contemporary Setting* (New York: Meridian Books, 1972), 12): "His, the historian's, task is to interpret the phenomena of the earlier history out of the existential understandings of human possibilities."

57. J. Chr. K. von Hofmann, *Theologische Ethik* (Nördlingen: Beck, 1878), 17: "I, the Christian, am for me the theologian the object of knowledge." Hofmann, *Der Schriftbeweis: Ein theologischer Versuch*, vol. 1 (Nördlingen: Beck, 1852), 10: "Theology is only a free science . . . when I, the Christian, am for me, the theologian, the most proper material of my science."

Although he was a positive theologian, he succeeded in pumping out the positive. That is liberalism in principle. And it all comes around again. In Germany, a retrograde movement has occurred in connection with Martin Heidegger, Karl Jaspers, and Rudolf Bultmann. Bultmann made the first serious attempt to draw existentialism into theology. If I had to choose between the liberalism of Friedrich Schleiermacher and that of Bultmann, I would, without hesitation, return to Schleiermacher. If liberalism at all, then let it be as Schleiermacher understood it! There was still an "intuition of the universe,"[58] whereas today's existentialism is an arid affair. My goodness! Boring, eternal repetition! And if you ask me whether this is more dangerous than earlier on, then the old liberalism was more dangerous because it was more beautiful. The young theologians today find no joy in preaching. The followers of Schleiermacher glowed when they preached. Schleiermacher himself preached with delight and he preached so beautifully that he himself was in tears.[59] I have read many of Schleiermacher's sermons.[60] When I see how the man himself was moved, I cannot read them without being moved.

10. Other Forms of Church's Services

Question: Which form of a community's evangelistic services (besides the Sunday service) would you consider as most appropriate for our present circumstances?

Barth: I know two unusual students, very good theologians, who completed their doctorates with scholarly distinction and went into the service of the church.[61] Both live in industrial congregations in the Rhineland. They constantly have today's factory workers in mind—living in mass accommodations, standing on the conveyer belt, [struggling] with their working conditions and with the little free time left after their work, when they return home exhausted. And now both these young pastors, who came from Basel, are powerfully aware of the question What does preaching to these people mean? Is it enough that one wins one or two? Must we not take a very great detour in order to reach the modern person at all? Must evangelization not begin with us standing by their sides and joining them? And, as a consequence, both these doctors of theology have become simple workers, standing together with the other workers at the factory's conveyer belt, living together with them in the tenements—a

---

58. F. Schleiermacher, *Über die Religion*, 32 [ET: *On Religion*, 22]: The essence of religion is "neither thinking nor acting, but intuition and feeling. It wishes to intuit the universe, wishes devoutly to overhear the universe's own manifestations and actions, longs to be grasped and filled by the universe's immediate influences in childlike passivity."

59. Cf. E. Willich, *Aus Schleiermachers Hause: Jugenderinnerungen seines Stiefsohnes Ehrenfried von Willich* (Berlin: Reimer, 1909), 82: "In great calm, he always began to develop his ideas clearly and simply, but his sentiment involuntarily increased so that his language became more vivid and warmer. And when a moment came where he could no longer restrain his emotions which, for a while and with considerable effort, he tried to keep in check, his voice would collapse and you could see tears in his eyes, then the impression on his hearers was overwhelming."

60. In his lecture course on Schleiermacher in Göttingen, Barth attempted to interpret Schleiermacher on the basis of his sermons: K. Barth, *Die Theologie Schleiermachers: Vorlesung Göttingen Wintersemester 1923/24*, ed. D. Ritschl (Zurich: Theologischer Verlag, 1978), 13–243 [ET: *The Theology of Schleiermacher: Lectures at Göttingen, Winter Semester of 1923–24*, ed. D. Ritschl (Grand Rapids: Eerdmans, 1982)].

61. Barth's students Ekkehard Börsch and Holger Samson.

Protestant parallel to the French worker-priests of the Roman Catholic Church.[62] In their environment they also try to form Christian circles. The prerequisite for such "evangelizing" is that one does not live outside the life of the modern man, his work, and his free time. They must know from their own experience what such a workday means, for eight hours always doing the same work, making the same motions. Naturally there are workers who say to these Christians, "You are moles, you are spies!" But these young theologians did not let themselves be deterred by this. I would propose considering whether or not something along *this* line ought to happen, whether *this* might not be a form of the community's evangelistic service that imposes itself in the contemporary situation, that Christians connect with the people not only with words, not only with their message, but [also] by living together with them. The church ought to offer the possibility that one might be a pastor in this way as well. For these young theologians want to be pastors not only in the manse or from their writing desk, but rather by living the gospel.

Question: On the [worker-]calling of the two pastors: all of us had such a calling also, but there remains relatively little time for counseling and preaching. It would be wonderful if our congregation members each in their place evangelized, and we preachers could provide them with instruction and preparation from the pulpit. How is it that there are so many Christians living in their snail-shells, that so many Christians fail to live out the message of Christ [vis-à-vis the modern person] in the daily front line joyfully, but stand disheartened and timid?

Barth: Actually, I do not like to hear the phrase "modern man." I do not like it when one makes an idol out of him, so to speak—[often even citing] Dietrich Bonhoeffer's phrase, the "world come of age!"[63]—[only to then complain] how horribly difficult it is to approach the people of today. I say "modern man" in quotes, because I believe that the human has always remained the same. And I object that one [then proceeds to give theologians instructions] and talks about "the Word—arriving." As if *we* were able to control God's Word arriving, as a train arrives at a station!

Question: From the vantage point of the gospel, what specifically is to be said about the practice of many evangelists to testify to the initiation of a change of heart through the raising of hands or the altar call? Should one express one's "repentance" right on the spot?

Barth: One cannot simply reject making visible an active decision in front of other people. There may be situations where it is perfectly necessary for me to raise my hand. But it is fatal if this practice becomes an institution. To my knowledge, we do not find it in the New Testament, but rather Christian baptism was this gesture. It was an enormous thing if someone wanted to be baptized. Christian baptism is the visible form of μετάνοια [*metanoia*]. And it is wonderful when conversion does not remain only a mental matter, but that the word at baptism is "into the water!" Hand raising is no longer needed. It has

---

62. See, e.g., H. Perrin, *Journal d'un Prêtre ouvrier en Allemagne 1943/44* (Paris: Éditions du Seuil, 1945); German: *Tagebuch eines Arbeiterpriesters* (Munich: Kösel, 1955; Hamburg: Furche-Verlag, 1964); further, H. Godin and Y. Daniel, *France, pays de Mission* (Paris: Éditions du Cerf, 1943).

63. D. Bonhoeffer, *Widerstand und Ergebung*, 216–17, 221, 230–31, passim [ET: *Letters and Papers*, 426, 431, 450–51 passim].

happened once for all that the baptizand has made their confession as a Christian. It is dreadful that we have so emptied baptism that we no longer have any idea of what its actual essence is. And that leads to these "demonstrations," such as the raising of hands and answering altar calls and the like, which one can repeat at will in the next and succeeding evangelization services. In this situation, the act has lost all credibility. Nevertheless, I would be the last who wants to say that everything must remain internal. No, it must also be external. If we follow the New Testament, baptism would be this "demonstration."

Question: Might we make use of the gospel image of "casting out the net" and "bringing it back in" (cf. Matt. 13:47; Luke 5:5) for our evangelistic method?

Barth: I am no specialist on fishing techniques. Throw out the net, pull it in! Yes, yes, but one ought not to force the parables of Jesus; rather, they must be taken in their entirety (i.e., one must always pay attention to the particular point).

11. On the Free Church

Question: State church and free church: which form is most appropriate to the New Testament status?

Barth: I would prefer to reformulate the question. Instead of "state church and free church," I would like to say, state church, established church (*Volkskirche*), megachurch and confessing church. For me, I incline toward the free church. The state church is always something bad, like the church in the Cantons of Bern and Zurich, where it is an organ, a "department" of the state, which in an earlier period proved disastrous.[64] No, better not this! Ultimately it does not depend on a national church or a free church. A state church can be a confessing church (I prefer to say "confessing church" rather than confessional church, because a confession is only on paper, while confessing is an action!). Confessing might occur in the realm of a state church, and it might fail to occur in a free church. It ultimately depends not on the church's form, but that here and there the gospel is preached, believed, and witnessed to.

Question: In your opinion, does the Methodist church in its proclamation and its existence exhibit deviations from the gospel from which it must be recalled?

Barth: Are you aware that there is a relationship between the problem of liberalism and the problem of John Wesley? With Wesley, one can become a very good liberal. In America, Methodism is quite liberal. This is the case when one is about to make the human being the point of focus. You (the Methodists!) may not declare yourselves free of guilt or solidarity with liberalism as the point of departure. A great anthropocentric train is at the doorstep. "Do you imagine, whoever you are, that when you judge those who do such things and yet do them yourself, you will escape the judgment of God?" (Rom. 2:3). That is the only thing that I want to say to you. I will not say that you are

---

64. W. Hadorn, *Kirchengeschichte der reformierten Schweiz* (Zurich: Schultheß, 1907), 187, speaks about the "relentless repression of all dissenting views," of "the misuse of religion as the means of preserving and enhancing power," etc., as a consequence of the old state church system, in which the pastors were appointed to their position and paid as officials and thus were supporters of the state's ethical codes (*Sittenmandate*) and of its laws.

becoming deviant, but the danger is there! As a good friend, I would advise you: Be careful! Place the emphasis more on Christ and less on the experience of salvation! Then it will not happen to you as it has with your American brethren who are caught up in liberalism. The overemphasis on the salvation experience resembles a person finding oneself on a downhill track, not knowing which way the ball rolls. One cannot discuss either Christ's resurrection or the virgin birth or eschatology if the starting point is wrong. When the human and his experience are decisive, everything begins to wobble and one finds oneself on boggy ground, so to speak. Liberalism has entered this boggy ground. It is not its denial [of this or that doctrine] that is bad, but that it has stepped onto this ground.

12. An Ecumenical Question

Question: On the coming general assembly of the World Council of Churches in New Delhi:[65] what do you hope for from the integration of the International Missionary Council into the World Council of Churches?

Barth: This is good, in principle. It must be understood that the church is not a church if it is not a missionary church. The church is, as such, a missionary church. If this understanding undergirds the union, it is a good thing. Hopefully, it does not mean that mission becomes paralyzed!

Question: What do you make of the ecumenical council planned by the Catholic Church? Are we to take seriously the interconfessional dialogues initiated by the Catholic Church?

Barth: On the first part of your question: I have submitted this question to a Catholic theologian friend from Strasbourg and asked him, "What do you, as a Christian and a theologian,[66] think of what we Protestants should make of this planned council?" And he gave me a spontaneous answer: "We expect you Protestants to pray for this council!" The planned council, really only a Catholic affair, is a Christian attempt, not only for a better unification, but also for the renewal of the Catholic Church. Hans Küng, a Catholic who has written a book on justification and one on the council,[67] described the purpose of Vatican II to me with the words "in order to unite the church through renewal." I said to him, "but renewal means reformation," whereupon he answered, "Yes, yes." When one talks with these men, we find ourselves drawing very close. What Rome intends and does with the council is an inscrutable matter. The Catholics themselves do not know. This apparatus in the Vatican is something

---

65. The International Missionary Council merged with the World Council of Churches at its third assembly held between November 18 and December 12 in New Delhi, India. Cf. W. A. Visser 't Hooft, ed., *Neu-Delhi spricht: Das Wort der Vollversammlung des Ökumenischen Rates zu den Hauptthemen Zeugnis, Dienst, Einheit* (Stuttgart: Evangelischer Missionsverlag, 1962) [ET: *New Delhi Speaks about Christian Witness, Service, and Unity: The Message, Appeal, and Section Reports* (New York: Association Press, 1962)].

66. Barth probably posed this question orally to Yves Congar, OP, at a meeting held in Strasbourg on November 22, 1959 (cf. chap. 6 above). Pope John XXIII announced the Council on January 25, 1959.

67. H. Küng, *Rechtfertigung: Die Lehre Karl Barths und eine katholische Besinnung* (Einsiedeln: Johannes Verlag, 1957) [ET: *Justification: The Doctrine of Karl Barth and a Catholic Reflection* (Philadelphia: Westminster Press, 1981)]; Küng, *Konzil und Wiedervereinigung: Erneuerung als Ruf in die Einheit* (Freiburg et al.: Herder, 1960) [ET: *The Council and Reunion* (London: Sheed & Ward, 1961)].

mysterious, almost as mysterious as that in the Kremlin. When I prayed for the pope during the public prayer in one of my services in Basel's prison,[68] the word went around: "He has prayed for the pope." I said in response, "Yes, and he really needs it!" [As to the second part of your question on the "inter-confessional dialogues,"] yes, we are to take them seriously. It is always good when Catholics and Protestants speak in a sincere and honest manner with one another. This kind of thing should generally occur more often in the church. It is a good aspect of the ecumenical movement that one can come together and speak with one another. Not every Catholic is a lackey of the pope, a devotee of Mary, and a servant of the sacraments; they also have a concern for Jesus Christ! I spoke with a Catholic friend from Paris[69] about Catholicism, and he all of a sudden said, "Let's not talk any more of the pope; let us talk of Jesus Christ!" Under this sign one can very well engage in interconfessional dialogue. [For it generally applies in the] relationship of the churches to one another: the nearer to Christ, the nearer to one another!*

13. On the East/West Issue

Question: Where should the church stand today in the confrontation between East and West?

Barth: One can burn one's fingers on this question. The *Neuer Zürcher Zeitung* and the *Basler Nachrichten* have bestowed a "lovely" title upon me because of my opinion in this matter.[70] But the Christian church cannot participate in this fight between East and West. It is true [that] God "makes his sun rise on the evil and on the good, and sends rain on the righteous and on the unrighteous" [Matt. 5:45]. What is going on here? There are two blocks of powers and ideologies opposing and wrestling with one another. Under no circumstances is this a situation in which one as a Christian should pick a side, must be for or against. It is an interesting fact that on either side, whether they are more or less Christian Americans or more or less un-Christian Russians, it is a matter of people who are God's creatures, poor sinners for whom Jesus Christ has died. Coming from the message of Jesus, we cannot opt for one side or another. The church here in the West must always think the best of the people in the East, and the East ought not take part in this silly talk of capitalism, colonialism, and so forth. Everywhere, we Christians must be on guard and remain calm. This too shall pass.[71] Meanwhile the church must be the place of peace and not join the chorus of hatred and competition. With the latter, we do not help anyone at all. Did all the railing against this Russian despotism help in the Hungarian crisis?[72] It has not helped a single Hungarian in the slightest, bringing only

---

68. Barth prayed for Pope John XXIII in connection with his sermon preached on March 29, 1959. See *Pr. 1954–1967*, 244; *Lebenslauf*, 456; *Biography*, 440.

69. Augustin-J. Maydieu, OP.

70. Cf. *O.Br. 1945–1968*, 481.

71. Cf. the comment by Athanasius about his fourth banishment from his bishop's see in the year 362, as conveyed by Eusebius, *Ecclesiastical History* 10.35, in *GCS* 9.2, on 995: "Do not be disturbed, my children. This is a small cloud, and it will pass [nolite, inquit, o filii, conturbari, quia nubicula est et cito pertransit]."

72. The Hungarian uprising began on October 23, 1956.

panic and hatred. We have better things to do. If you ask me, "Where ought the church stand?," then I answer, "In the middle and over it!" And yet we stand under the burden of this opposition [as well], but really as the church and not as a little piece of state power, whether here or there. On both sides the temptation is extremely great.

17. Conversation with Zurich Pastors
1961

According to an entry in Barth's calendar, he met for a discussion with twenty pastors from Zurich on August 21, 1961, in the Bruderholz Restaurant in Basel. Pastor H. O. Kühner had previously sent him questions from the group participants (see Kühner's accompanying letter of August 12, 1961, in the Karl Barth Archive). The total of twenty-seven questions deal with Church Dogmatics *IV/1, §62.2, "The Being of the Community," and IV/3, §71, "The Vocation of Man." The conversation is documented in four pages, which contain these questions and the short abbreviated notes for his answers. Of the twenty-seven questions, the following eighteen are those for which Barth made notes. The page numbers in parentheses next to questions all refer to the Barth volumes under discussion; the first (lower) number is for the English edition; the second refers to the original German edition,* Kirchliche Dogmatik; *they are divided by =.*

The Being of the Community [CD IV/1]

Question: (CD 657 = KD 734) You speak of the sword that hangs over the *ecclesia visibilis* [visible church]. Do you also see this sword with us in Switzerland? Aren't our insistence on and our pride in our territorial and state churches perhaps very suspect?

Barth: [no doubt referring to the word "sword"] = instead of witness: revelation.[1]

Question: (660 = 737) How can we in the Swiss church still risk speaking publicly in the authority of faith? Who will speak this word of the church? The preacher from the pulpit? The church council?

Barth: [addition to "authority of faith"] + of obedience. [To the entire question:] No danger, if it is *this* authority.

Question: (671 = 749) If the existence of the synagogue is a wound in the body of Christ, how can this wound be healed and removed? What do you see as practical possibilities (if "mission to the Jews" cannot be considered)?

Barth: According to Romans 11[:25–32], [the healing of this wound] is eschatological hope. But in the meantime: proclamation of the God of *Israel*: Romans 9:4–5.

---

1. In the cited passage in *CD* IV/1, Barth says: On the question whether the church in its visible form wants to be more than the witness of its "invisible being," that is, of its head, Jesus Christ, whether it would like to be equated with him or not, its being "unserviceable" hangs in the balance ("stands on the razor's edge" [sword!]).

Question: (678 = 757) Conversations with the Catholic Church: We know that this conversation among theologians has been taken up with great seriousness. Where do you see the possibilities that, at the level of the local congregation, such conversations can also be carried out that could have more than just "the form of various common understandings" [ibid.]?

Barth: We should take the Catholics at their word with their confession of X [Christ]!

Question: (684 = 764) Where in our Reformed Swiss Church would changes be necessary? And where should we take care of our own legacy with new faithfulness?[2] "*Credo unam eccl[esiam]* [I believe in one church]."

Barth: Changes: Mystery (worship!) Our o[wn]: Directness.[3]

Question: (668–75 = 746–53) Why is ecumenicity not expressly mentioned here? Is there a theological locus for ecumenicity, and if so, which locus or loci?

Barth: Ecclesia oecumenica = catholica[4] > "movement."[5]

Question: How could we overcome in practice the dividedness of the church, and what does "penitence" mean here for the church concretely?

Barth: In all the churches the One/oneness (Eph. 4:1–[6]) [is to be believed and sought].

Question: What are the "*signa ecclesiae*" [signs of the church]? Are established churches and confessing churches such things in themselves, or do they overlap with these concepts? "Credo *sanctam* ecclesiam" [I believe in the holy church].

Barth: Church in its particularity (pure, *recte, congregatio*)[6] → world.[7]

Question: Is a nonconforming separation in some circumstances legitimate (e.g., "sects," but also the Reformation), and if so, what would these circumstances be? If not, what does that mean for our relationship with Rome?

Barth: [referring to the word "separation"]: avant-garde, vanguard. [To the entire question] Are we also the same?[8]

---

2. *CD* IV/1:684 [*KD* 764–65] declares that the question of the one church is decided by hearing the voice of its Lord. In hearing it, the church will no doubt have to "revise or modify its particular constitution." "Note that it is not true to *itself* if at bottom it tries to resist this. Or it may be that much that is proper to it will now prove for the first time to be right, that it will be committed to the cherishing and continuance of it. . . . "

3. What Barth might have meant with these terms could be illustrated in his description of the Reformed distinctiveness of the Swiss church and theology—[as] in his essay "Reformierte Theologie in der Schweiz," in *Ex auditu verbi* [Festschrift for G. C. Berkouwer] (Kampen: Kok, 1965), 27–36. See, e.g., on 31 the characterization of Swiss theology as "unceremonious [*unfeierlich*]," "clearly organized and lacking in mystery," with the danger that revelation becomes "manipulable"; and on 34, "Our great strength has always lain in the field of ethics," in a thinking oriented "less toward meditation and aesthetics and more toward the practical life."

4. See *CD* IV/1.1:703 [*KD* 785]: "'Catholic' had, therefore, and in the first instance still has, the narrower sense of 'ecumenical,' i.e., identical in the whole inhabited world, in all parts of the globe where men live and where it [may] exist as the church."

5. See *CD* IV/3.1:36 [*KD* 38]: We only moved beyond the "neutral point" [*toter Punkt*)] of an ecumenicity as an "end in itself," "where the union of the Churches [began] to be conceived in *teleological and dynamic* terms as a union which derives *from* Jesus Christ and is thus union *for* Him, namely, for the attestation of His work in the world and for the world."

6. Allusion to the *Confessio Augustana,* art. 7, according to which the church is defined as "congregatio sanctorum, in qua evangelium pure docetur et recte administrantur sacramenta [the congregation of saints in which the gospel is purely taught and the sacraments are rightly administered]" (*BSLK* §61, on 1–6).

7. See *CD* IV/3.2:771–72 [*KD* 883], rev., where it is stated that with regard to the existence of the church, its turning to the world has "to do with a true *nota ecclesiae* [mark of the church], the lack of which is an impossibility for the actual community of Jesus Christ."

8. The question probably refers to sentences such as these in *CD* IV.1:675 [*KD* 754]: "There may be good grounds for the rise of these divisions. There may be serious obstacles to their removal, . . . but

Question: (697–98 = 779) What should we think of church discipline, and in connection with that, also of confirmation (as "admission")?[9] "Credo *catholicam ecclesiam* [I believe in the catholic church]."

Barth: [referring to the words "church discipline"] cure of souls, grace, and crisis.[10]

Question: (701–2 = 784) What is the difference between heretical, apostate, and schismatic?

Barth: ["heretical" =] mistaken belief; ["apostate" =] unbelief; ["schismatic" =] dissenting belief. All are *borderline* terms.[11]

Question: (704 = 786–87) Is a retreat from a specific ch[urch] tradition to be seen as positive—as a movement toward the *ecc[lesia] cath[olica]*?

Barth: Always a *problem*!

Question: (704–5 = 787) What is the significance of the individual (Kierkegaard!) in faith?

Barth: [In faith the individual is] presupposition + goal—*not a criterion!*[12]

Question: (719 = 803) To what degree may we simply take over the commission given to the apostles (e.g., power of the keys)?

Barth: What else is possible? = question 24.[13]

Question: (724–25 = 809) Why do we take on the commission of preaching and mission without question, but not the commission to heal [Mark 16:17–18]?

Barth: ?! *Healing* as sign.

Question: (716–17 = 800–801) Is the gift of the Holy Spirit that which is essential for the apostle rather than the witness to the resurrection of Christ (Acts 1!)?

Barth: [Both are] identical!

Question: (517 = 577) Why is "moral rearmament" not a spiritual process? We would appreciate a more convincing argument.

Barth: Because ["moral rearmament"] as such is merely an abstract "light" without connection to the Light.

Question: (587–88 = 655) Are the commissioned apostles truly "examples" for all Christians?

Barth: See question 16.[14]

---

this does not alter the fact that every division as such is a deep riddle, a scandal." The word "also [*auch*]" in Barth's note above might possibly be read instead as "still [*noch*]."

9. Old Swiss expression for "Confirmation," which designates the "admission" to the Lord's Supper.

10. See *CD* IV/3.2:836 [*KD* 1015]: "Cure of souls . . . is thus a legitimate exercise of the church discipline which in the past has been a more painful than profitable undertaking on the part of the Christian church. Here in the cure of souls there can and should be *confession* with the promise of the remission of sins, and the invitation to the resultant amendment of life . . . as an *event.*"

11. That is no doubt meant in the sense of the exposition by K. Barth, *Die protestantische Theologie im 19. Jahrhundert: Ihre Vorgeschichte und ihre Geschichte* (Zollikon: Theologischer Verlag, 1947), 6th ed., 1994), 3; ET: *Protestant Theology in the 19th Century: Its Background and History*, trans. B. Cozens and J. Bowden (London: SCM, 1972; Grand Rapids: Eerdmans, 2002), 3: "Only the heretic, indeed only the arch-heretic, the one who is totally lost even for God's invisible Church, could really belong to the past and have nothing more to say to us. And we are in no position to identify such arch-heresy."

12. See *CD* IV/1:705 [*KD* 787]: "The Christian is first a member of the Christian community and only then, and as such, this individual Christian in their particular Christian being and nature and presence. And this means that the Christian faith is first the faith of the Christian community, and only then and as such is affirmed and shared by them, the faith of the people united in it. It does not have in them, as it were, its original and normative form."

13. Refers to the last question printed below.

14. See n. 13 above.

18. Conversation with Catholic Students of Theology from Paderborn
1961

When a group of Catholic students of theology from Paderborn on an ecumenical study tour of multiple European countries conducted by their teacher, Professor Albert Brandenburg, reached Basel, they managed a previously unplanned, improvised visit with Karl Barth at his home on October 2, 1961. Participants subsequently recalled: "From a telephone booth, Professor Brandenburg called Karl Barth and promptly received an invitation. . . . As for topics, we discussed the announced council and the already detectible traces of renewal in the Catholic Church. Professor Brandenburg [made reference] to a review he had written about Karl Barth's Epistle to the Romans. However, Barth was not acquainted with his review; he stated with a smile that for a long time already he had not read any more reviews of his works. Another participant remembers that Karl Barth also heavily criticized the sitting government of the Federal Republic of Germany." (Letter from Dr. Hans Jörg Urban to the editor on December 21, 1988.) There are no known transcripts of the conversation.

19. Questions and Answers in the Basel Prison
1961

At the invitation of his friend Martin Schwarz, at that time pastor in the Basel Prison, Karl Barth, during the years 1954–64, used to fill in for him occasionally as preacher and pastor. Compare M. Schwarz, editor, Karl Barth in der Strafanstalt: Bericht des evangelischen Strafanstaltpfarrers *(Karl Barth in Prison: Report of the Protestant Prison Chaplain), Basel, 1968. On October 19, 1961, Barth arrived at the same place to answer a number of questions that ten prisoners had submitted before the meeting. M. Schwarz wrote about this event in the* Jahresbericht des evangelischen Strafanstaltspfarrers, 1961 *(Annual Report of the Protestant Prison Chaplain), Basel, 1961: "During his interview, Karl Barth probed, as it were, behind the questions, that is, he turned the matter around and put the individual questioner before the question directed by the gospel to him. This was a Thursday evening in which everyone, the most complex to the most primitive, knew that he had been addressed and understood directly and to the core. On this evening it once again became clear how happy and thankful the inmates of the Basel prison are for 'their' Karl Barth, who comes so readily and faithfully to them." Preserved from the conversation are voluminous pages filled with the prisoners' questions as well as a DIN A4 sheet with Barth's handwritten notes. Only the latter are published below. The top half of this sheet is filled with keywords that serve as a memory aid to the submitted questions; the bottom half of the sheet contains biblical questions for the discussion session. The order of these latter questions in what is published here has been reorganized according to the numeration of Barth himself.*

Personal

Mixed marriage? Inhibitions in *prayer*, how to overcome them? "Shipwreck" by accident?[1] Expiation without a temporal limit? Retribution? Future with the help of white lie?[2]

---

1. The question was "Are there for us Christians so-called 'accidents' in our lives? To what extent is our shipwreck predestined?"

2. The question was "Can a Christian tell a white lie for valid reasons?" The question was introduced with the following description: "Fortunately, we also are concerned about our future. . . . We imagine that we will encounter relatives, friends, and employers from whom we will conceal our transgressions and imprisonment; we would even like to explain our last months or even years with a prefabricated excuse or a white lie."

Church

Whether membership necessary? Which is correct? Bible ambiguous or churches unsympathetic and insensitive?
Why so little done for the evangelization of the imprisoned?
Japanese Non-Church Movement? Whether a model, because modern?
Council. Its purpose? Its effect on non-Catholics? How organized?
Sects, anxiety?
Jehovah's Witnesses?
Christian Science?
For [?] fellow believers in the East?
Church Rally [*Kirchentag*] in East Germany?
Youth dedication [*Jugendweihe*]?[3]

Bible

Gen[esis] 1—natural science? "Outdated?" "I would like a biblical answer."

Contemporary Issues

Technology—superficiality—in former times was there still the experience of the deeper meaning of life? Should the church adapt?

Doctrine

Is there a Trinity?
Do human beings have an immortal soul?
Why does Christianity support military service?

Mostly important . . . questions. Answers behind them [determined already]?
Still to be posed and answered calmly
In the Bible, *different* . . .
Shocking, because cannot be answered on a human level [?]:

Humanity before God
Dependent on his answer
To break through!

I. O man, indeed, who are you to argue with God? R[omans] 9:20
Lord, who shall stand? Psalm 130:3

---

3. The questions on the three key words were "What is the Reformed Church doing for their oppressed brethren in the East? Is the National German Church Congress [*Allgemeine Deutsche Kirchentag*] held only for demonstrative reasons in East Germany? What is the Reformed Church's view of the introduction of a so-called youth dedication in place of confirmation?" [Trans. note: *Jugendweihe* is a secular ritual developed to replace confirmation and practiced in Communist East Germany.]

Lord, who is it? [John 13:25; 21:20]

Who are you, that you judge another man's servant? R[omans] 14:4

If God be for us, who . . . ? [Romans 8:31]

Why does your teacher eat with tax collectors and sinners? [Matthew 9:11 and parallels]

Why are you cast down[?] . . . Hope in God, for I will still give him thanks. Psalms 42–43

Who will separate us from the love of God? [Romans 8:35]

II. O wretched man that I am, who saves me . . . ? R[omans] 7:24]

    1. Why have you done this? [Genesis 3:13]

        a. What is man that you . . . ? [Job 7:17; Psalms 8:4; 144:3]

        b. Why have you forsaken me? Psalm 22:1!

        c. Why do you not forgive me my transgression? Job 7:21

        d. When will you finally look away from me, and give me rest, if only for a moment? Job 7:19

    2. Where is your brother Abel? [Genesis 4:9]

    3. Why are you afraid?

    Are you so fearful? [Matthew 8:26; Mark 4:40]

    Do you doubt? [Matthew 14:31]

    Who can discern how often he errs? Psalm 19:12

20. Interview with Joachim Berger
1961

Dr. Joachim Berger of (East) Berlin conducted this interview on December 15, 1961, with Karl Barth at the Barth home on Bruderholzallee in Basel. Berger published it under the title "Gespräch mit Karl Barth" in two parts in Evangelisches Pfarrerblatt, *edited by the Bund Evangelischer Pfarrer in der DDR (e. V.), 1962, 67–69, 73, and 83–85. Shortly after the publication Barth distanced himself from the report in a letter dated March 28, 1962, to Wolf-Dieter Zimmermann, Member of the Consistory, with the following words: "[The report] is consistent neither with the spirit nor the wording of what the author heard from me. . . . I must resolutely decline joint responsibility for this publication." The letter can be found in K. Barth,* Briefe: 1961–1968, *edited by J. Fangmeier and H. Stoevesandt (Zurich: Theologischer Verlag, 1975), 49 [ET:* Letters: 1961–1968, *translated by G. Bromiley (Grand Rapids: Eerdmans, 1981), 37].*

21. Conversation in the Basel St. Elizabeth Church
1962

The conversation took place on March 6, 1962, at the initiative of the St. Elizabeth Church in Basel. At that time, the Bruderholz neighborhood in which Karl Barth was living formed part of the parish of the St. Elizabeth Church, which is located in the city center. All that is retained from the conversation are the questions submitted to Barth in advance and his handwritten notes about them.

Question: Is the second beatitude in the Sermon on the Mount ("Blessed are those who mourn, for they shall be comforted" [Matt. 5:4]) directed above all to those mourning a relative or rather or even exclusively to those who feel inconsolable about their guilt? Or to both at the same time? Does this promise apply to life in this world [underlined by Barth]?

Barth: [The comfort is directed to those who mourn] about [the] power of evil in the world.

Question: Does the Word of God in 2 Cor[inthians] 12:9, "My grace is sufficient for you," apply only to Paul, the patient sufferer and fighter, or also to us? If to us, why is it so difficult for us contemporary [underlined by Barth] people to accept this admonition and accordingly to live in its comfort?

Barth: Human beings should always [trust] *more* in "grace," *less* in "human strength."

Question: How do you assess the question of factions in our church?[1] According to the gospel of Jesus Christ, how should members of the positive school relate to the members of the liberal school?

Barth: "Factions":

Good, if different "gifts" (1 Cor. 12:4–11).

Not good, if conflict among people, groups, and such.

Really bad, if division is over the First Commandment

God of the Bible in h[is] deeds—or *Universal* God [Allerweltsgott]?

Positive?   Liberal?

Positive? Liberal? 1933.[2] Do not judge prematurely! [1 Cor. 4:5.] In the worst case: [the opinion: everything is arbitrarily possible in a] national church

---

1. In the Swiss church tradition, this refers to the opposition between two different church groups that arose in the nineteenth century: the "Bible believing," orthodox or pietistic, "positive" school—and the modernistic, "liberal" school. Both groups maintained parallel administrative structures in many Reformed congregations until late into the second half of the twentieth century.

2. Barth must have been recalling his experience in the struggle in 1933 against the German Christians, who aimed to overrun the church with the application of the National Socialist ideology. During this struggle, the structure of such oppositional factions was fading in importance since

[*Volkskirche*]! [One does not know what a truly free church is until one first knows what is called a binding] confession.

---

representatives of both schools stood on both sides of the struggle and thus fought not only against one another, but also with one another. Cf. J. Beckmann, ed., *Rheinische Bekenntnissynoden im Kirchen-kampf: Eine Dokumentation aus den Jahren 1933–1945* (Neukirchen-Vluyn: Neukirchener Verlag, 1975), 40; see also: *Lebenslauf*, 241; *Biography*, 227–28.

22. Interview with John Elson
1962

On April 2, 1962, John Elson, Religion Editor of Time *Magazine, interviewed Barth for a cover story in his magazine. This was preceded by several visits with Barth made by the reporter Mr. Blandon at Barth's vacation site in Ticino, beginning March 20, 1962. The article that resulted was published in the magazine in volume 79, number 16 (April 20, 1962): 59–65, under the title "Witness to an Ancient Truth." A large amount of the answers and comments that Barth had given apparently flowed into the text, reflected in a series of verbatim citations. It is not possible, however, to sort out where the interview materials and the reporters' findings from research elsewhere served as the sources for their draft. The citations presumably derived from the interviews are drawn together here from the larger text of this article.*

At the University of Berlin . . . he could study under the best known of Protestant church historians, Adolf von Harnack.[1] "I was so enthusiastic about him that I missed going to concerts and museums. In the midst of Berlin, I saw little of the city, doing only my work."

(About the) "German Christian" churches in which National Socialist political theories were given the same sanctity as theological dogma: "This was a nationalist heresy, a confusion between God and the spirit of the German nation."

He refused to take an oath of allegiance to the Führer or open his classes with the Nazi salute. It would be bad taste, he told them, "to begin a commentary on the Sermon on the Mount with *Heil Hitler.*"

At the end of 1934, Barth was brought before a Nazi court and found guilty of "seducing the minds" of German students.[2] For his defense, Barth pulled a copy of Plato's *Apology* from his pocket, read Socrates's argument to the court of Athens. . . .[3] "It seemed like a good idea before going into court, but it made no impression on the judges."

---

1. In the winter of 1906–7.

2. On the court proceedings in Cologne on December 20, 1934, in which Barth was deposed from his academic appointment, see H. Prolingheuer, *Der Fall Karl Barth: Chronographie einer Vertreibung 1934–1935*, 2nd ed. (Neukirchen-Vluyn: Neukirchener Verlag, 1984), 286–96.

3. Barth read the following passage from Plato's *Defense [Apology] of Socrates* (Plato, *Sämtliche Werke*, vol. 1 [Hamburg: Rowohlt, 1957], 20–21): "I am well-minded and friendly toward you Athenians, but I will obey the god more than you. . . . Therefore I am also now very far, you Athenians, from defending myself for my own sake, which one might certainly have thought, but rather for your sake so that you might not sin against the gift of god by your condemnation of me. . . . For my part, I believe that there never was a greater goodness done for the state than this service that I perform for the god."

In many respects the Barth of the *Church Dogmatics* is "wholly other" than the angry evangelist who wrote the *Epistle to the Romans* after World War I.[4] In that early work, "I had to show that the Bible dealt with an encounter between God and man. I thought only of the apartness of God. What I had to learn after that was the togetherness of man and God—a union of two totally different kinds of beings."

Barth feels free to reject the writings of the church fathers where he feels they have mistaken the meaning of God's Word; even his admitted master, John Calvin, is not exempt. Once, when someone questioned the unorthodox way in which he was commenting on Calvin, Barth retorted: "Calvin is in Heaven and has had time to ponder where he went wrong in his teachings. Doubtless he is pleased that I am setting him aright." Calvin argued that God has already determined both those who will be saved at the last judgment and those who will suffer the eternal pangs of hell. Barth says that this belief does not pay sufficient heed to the fact that Christ's death was intended for all men: Man's ultimate fate is shrouded in mystery, but Barth believes that Christ, the loving Judge, could indeed reconcile all the world to the Father. "I do not preach universal salvation. What I say is that I cannot exclude the possibility that God would save all men at the judgment."

The foundation of the *Church Dogmatics* is the faith held by the Christian churches: faith in the God who revealed himself through the Scriptures in the person of Jesus Christ. Faith, Barth says, is not an idea about God; it is man's humble, total acceptance of God brought on by God, "the consequences in man of the action of God himself." And God is not an idea, "not a banner for human ideas and intentions. For many people Christianity is a kind of moral, religious, and political idea, against what they call an atheistic idea."

To Barth, the capitalist West is as materialistic as the Communist East—and represents a serious temptation to the church since it tries to cloak its political ambitions in religious and moral terms. He has asked the West to give up nuclear weapons unilaterally; such a gesture would help the West regain the "confidence" of the Soviet Union, and start it on the road toward a peaceful democratic regime. The vast majority of U.S. theologians regard such views as politically naive at best and irresponsible at worst. . . . On other days, Barth would undoubtedly have hit back at such criticism. . . . "I was hard then. Now that I am older, I am softer."

For many years, Barth's only preaching has consisted of occasional sermons to the prisoners in the Basel jail. He takes great pride in this spiritual work, writing out the prayers for the service and choosing hymns for the prisoners. "When I come before these men, I do not have to explain that we are all sinners. They have committed every sin there is. All I have to tell them is that I, too, am a sinner."

Does Barthian theology have anything to tell a world in which persistent doubt seems to be man's real condition? Barth himself believes his work contains "a missionary call." It provides no easy, immediate, specific answers to

---

4. K. Barth, *Der Römerbrief*, 2nd ed. (Munich: Kaiser, 1922) [trans. note: In 1933 Sir Edwyn Hoskyns's ET of the 6th German ed. was published in London by Oxford University Press].

man's daily worries, but summons him to learn that all questions are ultimately theological and that the ultimate theological answer has been given.

Barth . . . disowns the idea of a school, "except for my two sons," meaning Markus, a New Testament scholar at the University of Chicago, and Christoph, who teaches Old Testament in Djakarta.

He usually retires early, lying awake to read military history or detective stories, from which he first learned English at the age of forty. "My friends claim that I have a criminal vocabulary."

Barth has little taste for modern novels, poetry, or art. "What I object to is the disappearance of the object. In art, as in theology, it is the object that counts, not the subject."

Barth has always insisted that dogma is important, that theology is not philosophy, that Christianity is not the spiritual side of politics. The mysteries of God's Word are hard ones, but they cannot be made more palatable to nonbelievers or to the lukewarm faithful by hiding them in the language formed by man's own wishful thinking. God speaks; man must listen. And Barth summons Goethe to warn the church: "Long, long ago the Truth was found, / A company of men it bound. / Grasp firmly, then, that ancient Truth!"[5]

5. From the poem by J. W. von Goethe, "Vermächtnis" [legacy], second strophe.

23. Interview with Mr. Lemon
1962

During Barth's trip to the United States, there appeared on April 23, 1962, a report in Newsweek Magazine (64–65) with the title "Barth in America." In the article there is a series of Barth quotations as well as direct answers to questions. These passages, which apparently result from a conversation with the reporter, Mr. Lemon, on April 11, 1962, in Chicago and make up about one-half of the article, are printed here.

. . . Along with his other controversial traits, Barth won a reputation for anti-Americanism by denouncing "those fleshpots of Egypt that symbolize the American way of life."[1] He never visited this country. . . . Last week, after years of staying put while Americans came to the mountain, the mountain at last paid a visit to America. . . . The professor's personal reason for coming was "to see and to listen and to learn." . . . His first impressions, says his son,[2] were "awfully positive." The supposed detractor of the U[nited] S[tates] found only two things he disliked here: (1) The plight of Negroes in nearby slums and (2) the fact that commercial sponsors have a large influence on television programming.

Barth has said he sometimes feels that he exists in English-speaking nations only in the form of "certain hoary summations" in the fantasies "of even the best men." . . . American Protestants have difficulty understanding precisely what Barth means by "Word of God." Barth himself isn't surprised at their bafflement. "The Word of God has always been a puzzle for man," he said last week. "That is not an especially American problem." . . .

Despite the exalted purity of his theology, Barth has no use for the ivory tower ("Private Christianity is no Christianity at all"). . . . Since the war, however, he has been vigorously neutral in world politics. "In the beginning, National Socialism was a danger because the souls who spoke against it were in a small minority," he said last week, in explanation of his stand against Hitler. "But now everyone is convinced that Communism is a bad thing. It does not help if I take part in this great storm. So I remain silent. I dislike Communism. But one cannot always speak when one dislikes something."

As for his personal mode of living, his son Markus says: "He has never made war on materialism. He likes life too much." In Basel, he frequently goes to the movies and to cabarets. He is a Civil War buff and plans to tour Gettysburg. . . .[3]

---

1. K. Barth, "Brief an einen Pfarrer in der Deutschen Demokratischen Republik (1958)," in *O.Br. 1945–1968*, 430; see also 404–12 [ET in K. Barth and J. Hamel, *How to Serve God in a Marxist Land* (New York: Association Press, 1959)].

2. Markus Barth, at that time professor in Chicago.

3. The Civil War between the southern and northern states of the USA, 1861–65, turned against the South with the victory of the northern states at the Battle of Gettysburg, July 1–3, 1863.

Regarding the current eagerness to communicate the Christian message, did he detect any slackness about what was being communicated?

"Yes, certainly. In sermons, ministers have neglected the question of what should be said for how it should be said. That's a snake biting its own tail.

"The whole question," Barth observed, "is whether the task of the church is to cultivate religion, or whether its task is to announce the good Word of God. Even the word 'religion' should disappear in this discussion. Religion means man going around and around with higher aspirations, but that's not what counts. What counts is the encounter between God and man. And that's another thing."

"In the nineteenth century, the progress of science intimidated us. Theologians sought to provide a place for the church within the area of human activity. They said there was art and science . . . and religion. Religion became a kind of Indian Reservation where God and Christ and the Holy Spirit might be cultivated. And beginning with this Indian Reservation, the cause was lost. The difference between the nineteenth and twentieth centuries is that there is now a counterattack, so to speak."

What does Barth consider the greatest failure of contemporary Protestantism? "How shall I formulate it . . . ?" he asked himself. "The true thing in the original Protestantism was God's word to man, and then man's response to it. Modern Protestantism has lost its character as a response. If Protestantism is only a fight for individual liberties, [for] freedom of the soul, then its cause is lost. Man is left alone with himself."

Did he, nonetheless, feel that the church had increased in vigor in recent years? "Yes, yes," he said. "If I compare the role of the church today and the role of the church when I was a youngster, the church has definitely become stronger and more important. But that's not enough. When there is great danger, men go to church. On a deeper level, it can be said that the optimistic outlook on man is vanishing. Thus there is existentialism. People are looking for something greater than man. Because of this need, the church has greater appeal."

"But if I am right, this doesn't mean a real progress for the cause of the church; it is only a manifestation of man's *need*. Because now we have a pessimistic trend. And there is no real change if we are trading optimism for pessimism. Because pessimism and optimism are brothers."

Next week, when Barth emerges from relative seclusion to deliver his lectures,[4] American Protestants will have a fresh chance to examine his theology. The first five lectures as written are the most lucid exposition of his dogmatics yet made. The sixth, to be delivered only at Princeton, is a striking introduction of a new theme: The function of the Holy Spirit[5] in transmitting to men Barth's difficult, transcendent "Word of God."

---

4. In Chicago from April 23 to 27, 1962, Barth repeated in English the first five hours of the lectures that he had delivered in the winter semester of 1961–62: *Einführung in die evangelische Theologie* (Zurich: Evangelischer Verlag, 1962) [ET: *Evangelical Theology: An Introduction* (New York: Holt, Rinehart & Winston, 1963)].

5. Error of the reporter: in Princeton from April 29 to May 3 he delivered the same five lectures that he had given in Chicago. The lecture on the Holy Spirit was the fifth one and was presented in both sites.

24. Press Conference in Chicago
1962

During his trip to America from April to June, 1962, Barth participated in a press con-
ference that took place in Swift Hall of the University of Chicago on Thursday, April
19. He was accompanied by Dr. Jerald C. Brauer, the dean of the Divinity School. Press
reports from the conference appeared in [the following papers]:
1. Chicago Daily News, *April 19, 1962: "Godlessness All around Us: Barth,*
Noted Theologian, Doubts Nations Are Much Different," by Dave Meade.
2. Chicago Daily Tribune, *April 20, 1962: "Theologian Karl Barth Finds Clergy*
Often in Error," by Richard Philbrick.
3. Chicago Sun Times, *April 20, 1962: "Theologian Karl Barth Explains Beliefs*
Here," by Dolores McCahill.
4. Chicago Daily News, *April 21, 1962: "Too Little Love in Christian Church:*
Barth, Famed Theologian, Chides Clergymen," by Dave Meade.
These reports are reprinted here in the above order, after editing out general remarks
about Barth's person, life story, and work.

1. Chicago Daily News

He was asked, "How is it possible for God to live in a godless country—such as the Soviet Union?

Without hesitating, he spoke quietly. ". . . God Himself lives in a godless country," he said.

Then he asked, "Are Switzerland [and] perhaps also the United States less godless than Soviet Russia—really?"

He said it's a great mystery the way "everywhere God deals with the ungodly." "We all are ungodly," he said, but in the West "we are allowed to believe in [God]."

In an earlier interview, Professor Karl Barth compared ways of life of West and East. "I prefer ours," he said. "But we shouldn't be proud of it."

"And if we are so afraid of them, that's a sign that we are not sure of ourselves. It's a sign of a bad conscience. Men of good conscience wouldn't be afraid."

He said he feels people have misunderstood his past criticisms of the West. "In no way have I more sympathy for the East," he declared. "I think the best use we can make of the freedom, or liberty, which we have in the West is to see our own faults. But it doesn't mean to take sides for the East." . . .

In the interview, he predicted that unity between Roman Catholic and Protestant churches is "far away," but "better understanding" between the two groups will continue.

2. Chicago Daily Tribune

Yesterday Dr. Karl Barth . . . accused clergymen of getting in the way between God and man. There is a place for the clergy in Christianity, he said at a press conference at the University of Chicago, yet pastors "should regard themselves not as lords but as servants." They are obstructing the path between God and man, in his opinion, not only by what they are doing but also by what they are not doing. . . .

The seventy-five-year-old scholar said ministers today worry overly much about finding the right words to use in communicating with modern man. That is not as important, he explained, as determining what should be taught. "My experience," he said, "shows that men will understand regardless of words if the message is proclaimed simply and clearly."

Clergymen fail, he believes, when instead of "accepting humanity and the fact that it is loved by God, they separate sheep and goats." "God will do that," he declared.

The judgment of God, Dr. Barth pointed out, is especially important in relation to Communism. "Everywhere, God deals with the ungodly," he said. "The godliness [godlessness][1] of Communism is peculiar but not entirely unlike the godliness of Switzerland and the United States."

"Our approach to the difference that is involved must be with love," Dr. Barth asserted.

Asked what the aim of his writing and lecturing is, Dr. Barth replied, "My task is to teach what the real nature of the gospel is."

Before he could undertake it, he added, "I had to understand that Christianity means a covenant, an encounter between God and man, and now the problem is to understand God and man without mixing them up."

In explanation he referred to the concept for which he is noted, that God is always first, that man must wait upon and do God's will.

Asked about several religious topics of current interest, Dr. Barth commented:

1. On the coming Vatican council to be held this fall in Rome: "I am not a prophet. I cannot discuss things I cannot foresee. We must wait and see."

2. On papal infallibility as an obstacle to Christian unity: "In a broad sense there is a tendency toward papal infallibility within Protestantism. The pope in Rome is only one example of it. If the pope would recognize that there is only one infallible head of the church, then there would be no more trouble."

3. On Evangelist Billy Graham and the mass evangelism he conducts: "I like him as a good fellow. As a speaker it [mass evangelism] is not for me. I will also admit that the gospel can be preached in a football stadium."

4. On the doctrine of the priesthood of all believers: "I would not restrict the administration of the sacraments to a segment within the church."

---

1. In this sentence the English text uses the term "godliness" twice, but it must certainly be "godlessness." See also the first sentences in the previous section for the correct usage.

5. On the doctrines of the virgin birth and the second coming of Christ: "If you ask me as though you were pointing a pistol at me, yes, I believe them, but there is much more to be said about each."

3. Chicago Sun Times

Dr. Barth doesn't like the word "neo-orthodox," which has been used to identify English translations of his work in this country. He also rejects the term Barthianism. Years ago he sometimes called it "neoconfessionalism,"[2] a theological approach rising above the rigid doctrinal statements left by past generations of church leaders. Now he calls it "evangelical theology."

Trying to summarize his lifetime's work for reporters, Dr. Barth described it as an effort to counterbalance the humanism of the nineteenth century, when men were overconfident in their own ability to run the world, by a return to the Bible, in which God talks to men.

"The problem," he said, "was how to understand God, how to understand man, and the encounter of God and man, yet not to mix them up. I had to show that God is Lord over men."

He further observed: "There are many interesting and serious attempts to show young clergymen how to deal with man and the modern world. In straining this 'how,' the 'what' has often been forgotten. I stress the 'what,' the real nature of the gospel to be proclaimed. When people realize what is the matter with the world, they will find the way to deal with it."

Many clergymen, Dr. Barth said, "are too much troubled by learning humanity instead of trying to learn what God tells us in the Bible and giving the simple message of God."

This[3] message does not allow us to accept as human reality that humanity is left alone by God in "faults, misery, hostility, and atheism." There is a tendency in the thinking of many clergymen "to separate between sheep and goats, good men and bad ones, pious and nonpious, instead of seeing them together in their common misery and the common grace given for all in Jesus Christ."

With a chuckle, he added: "That's what I have tried to explain in thousands and thousands of words."

After parrying questions on Christian unity, his thought soared to pinpoint Christian-Jewish relationships as "the fundamental issue of the ecumenical movement."

"It is a good thing," he said, "to seek union between Presbyterians and Episcopalians and so on, and between Eastern Orthodox and Roman Catholics, but the big thing is our fundamental unity with the synagogue, because we all came from Israel. Christ was a Jew, and so long as we understand Judaism only

---

2. It is difficult to imagine Barth ever referring to his theology positively as "neo-confessional." If he ever said something along these lines, then it will have related to the movement to confession linked to the Theological Declaration of Barmen (May 1934).

3. This sentence as it stands in the English text is garbled and actually states the opposite of what Barth asserts. The German editor revised the sentence to read as above, replacing the following wording in the original English text: "Instead of accepting as a fact of humanity that men are left by God in faults, misery, hostility, and atheism, he said, there is a tendency . . ."

as another kind of religion, there will be something lacking at the root of the ecumenical movement."

Dr. Barth refused to be drawn into a comparison of the relative "godlessness" of Switzerland, America, and Soviet Russia, or an evaluation of either Dr. Paul Tillich, leading U.S. theologian, or evangelist Billy Graham—both of whom he termed "likable persons."

4. Chicago Daily News

One of Protestantism's great living theologians said this Easter season that a big weakness of the Christian Church is "too little love."

Dr. Karl Barth said he meant "love . . . in the Christian sense of the word." Lack of enough of this kind of love, he indicated, is one of the human frailties of the clergy.

What is most needed now, the Rev. Dr. Barth explained, is for the church and its ministers to "simply accept the fact that (all humans) are loved ones, loved by God even with their faults, miseries, hostilities." He said that God's love includes atheists.

Barth warned against the church "separating men, . . . good and bad, religious and nonreligious, pious and nonpious."

Too often, he added, the clergy try to "separate between sheep and goats," an activity reserved for God alone, whereas they should see men together in their "common misery and common grace for all in Jesus Christ."

In an interview, he noted that the "task of the church is to listen to the whole message, . . . all of the New Testament."

He said priests and ministers should look upon themselves "not as lords but as servants."

And, he added, "I wouldn't limit the task of preaching and offering the sacraments . . . to a restricted number of persons within the church."

Professor Barth was asked for his views of the Roman Catholic doctrine of papal infallibility. He answered, as is often his habit, by using the method of self-criticism. Papal infallibility, he noted, is also to be seen in Protestantism. "Everywhere there is a tendency among theologians and clergy to become small popes who believe themselves to be infallible," he said. "The pope (in Rome) is only one example."

He asserted that much of the trouble of disunity among Christians would be cleared up if all would recognize Christ as the "one infallible authority, the Lord of the church."

25. Podium Discussion in Chicago
1962

The discussion reported in what follows took place during Barth's American trip in the context of his visiting lectures at the Divinity School of the University of Chicago. The discussion took place in two parts on April 25 and 26 in the large Rockefeller Memorial Chapel of the university before the largest audience that Barth had ever experienced. C. Stinson ("Karl Barth," in Commonweal, *June 1, 1962, 246) spoke of "the overflow crowd of 2,200 who had come from all over the Midwest and South and from as far as Canada and the Pacific Coast." Facing the audience and seated at a long table next to Barth were his son Markus and the moderator, Professor Jaroslav Pelikan, along with six younger theologians of diverse backgrounds and origins, all of whom participated in a discussion to which the audience listened. The great interest in Barth's presence and presentations there led to the comment in the* New York Times *of April 30, 1962, that "to hear him and to see him in the flesh . . . is to ecclesiastics what a personal appearance of Sir Winston Churchill would be in the House of Representatives."*

Regarding Barth's English, H. D. Friberg ("Reflections on Karl Barth's Lectures," Christianity Today, *May 25, 1962, 847) thought that, in comparison with the presentation of his lectures, "He is even better at the free play of dialogue." Dr. Mackay, who had been Barth's first English teacher in the 1930s in Bonn, said, "My student has become a master of the English language" (*New York Times, *May 1, 1962), whereas C. Stinson (loc. cit., 246) described Barth's language as "triumphantly Teutonic English," and F. L. Filas ("Barth as a Seeker of God's Truth," in* The Christian Century, *May 30, 1962, 685) reported, "I was to become accustomed to 'ziss' and 'zat,' and to learn to recognize the quotation 'from face-to-face' as St. Paul's 'from faith to faith' in Jesus Christ." H. D. Friberg finally stated (loc. cit.), "His delivery, with its strongly German accent, deliberative pace, and uncommonly sensitive management of voice inflection—particularly a circumflexion of tone at the critical point, which gave his speech a certain ingenuousness that pulled the hearer into acquiescence—was extraordinarily effective and had an almost oracular character."*

The English version of the conversation was printed under the title "Introduction to Theology: Questions and Discussion with Dr. Karl Barth," in Criterion: A Publication of the Divinity School of the University of Chicago 2, no. 1 (1963): 3–11, 18–24. *Barth's answers and comments at this conversation, together with those from the conversation in Princeton (chap. 27 in this volume), were also published in recorded form: K. Barth:* Evangelical Theology; His American Lectures at the University of Chicago and Princeton Theological Seminary, Including the Discussions Following the Lectures, *edited by Markus Barth, audio recordings (Waco: Word Records). The text of the Chicago conversations was quietly corrected at some points based upon these recordings, as was the German translation that also resulted.*

[Trans.: German translations of all the conversations in languages other than German are included in Gespräche, 1959–1962.*] Preceding the account of the conversations below are the handwritten notes with which Karl Barth prepared for the discussion of the submitted questions.*[1]

A. Barth's Handwritten Notes for the Podium Discussion

1. To the Questions of S. M. Ogden

1. Misunderstanding: "Ecl[ecticism]" does not imply a selection between "mythical elements" but between diff[erent] kinds of worldviews. None of these have to be absolutely accepted or rejected. Elements of every one of them may become dangerous if understood as particulars of a system claiming ultimate reality and truth. Elements of every one of them may be used as analogy of the real[ity] and truth of God's revelation (see parables!). Principle of selection: can the witness to Christ (the way . . .) be borne by the use of them?

2. In no sense! The work of the theologian is necessarily and by nature independent from that of the philosopher. I wonder how you came to ask *me that* question: From the beginning, . . . to procure *independence!* For what reason? Phil[osophy] deals with man and his possibilities, tendencies, needs, . . . including "religion," asks man's questions, works out, pretends to have *them* answered. Theol[ogy] deals with God in his encounter with man, with man responding to God's approach (remember lect[ures] 1, 2, 3!). Stud[y] of Phil[osophy] is necessary for the theologian in a double meaning—positively: may learn about the nature of a consistent manner of thought and speech (dependence?); negatively: may be warned of the traps into which he is not supposed to fall (traps: absolute worldviews, built upon a preconceived ontology or anthropology).

2. To the Questions of H. W. Frei

1. What concerns Anselm, I am sure—not so sure what concerns Thomas. Can his proof be understood as a reflecting explanation . . . ? "by faith unto faith." If so, all is very well: Certainly there is a presence of God in external structures (heaven and earth, soul and body, man and woman, history of the Jews!, Negroes and Whites!, Mozart) and not only to intellect. But: that's for the psalmist and for Paul (Rom 1; Act 17) to *recognize* and to *proclaim*. Is that the reasoning of Thomas? This I leave to the Thomists to decide!

2. Even in Nazi Germany, there were no "clear-cut political issues" except inasmuch as the task of the church became problematic under the impact of the demands of the totalitarian state (for political conformity). Is a distinction between situations in which it is easy or not easy to preach the gospel, really possible? Not the same, but similar totalitarian demands are made also in Switzerland (—America?). Stringfellow! Description of relation: Bible—congregation is

---

1. The questions to which Barth's notes refer are printed below in Section B, each in relation to its content.

mine also. No abstractions on either side! Read and explain Bible as witness of Christ given to a church in a specific situation! There the situation may become "clear-cut"! (Gospel does it!)

3. To the Questions of B. Cooke

1. Man's destiny as God's creature: to be his covenant-partner, to be able to grasp his revelation. De jure he is it! But de facto—like one who has legs to walk but cannot do so, because they are (in Adam's fall) broken—he is still *capax* [capacious] (destined!) to walk but finds himself incapacitated: practically cannot grasp God's word. The healing for the poor patient following the Bible [is] the work and the gift of the Holy Spirit. By the Spirit (as new man) he will fulfill his destiny.

2. While you seem to grant an *essential* (!) difference between . . . (even: *of* God . . . *about* God!), you presuppose the *identity* of the "gods," perceived by these two methods? *Are* they identical? If yes: why in the Old and the New Test[aments] the insuperable conflict between the alleged knowledge of gods, deities, heavenly powers . . . and the faithful knowledge of those to whom God has spoken as the God of Abraham . . . and as the Father of J[esus] C[hrist]? If not: then "nat[ural] theol[ogy]" and Christian theol[ogy] cannot be integrated in one system. Does this mean disruption between faith and reason? No: it makes *good* sense; it is the appropriate use of reason to be faithful to the one good Lord and not at the same time try to serve Yahweh and Baal, God and Mammon.

4. To the Questions of E. J. Carnell

1. I have always "stressed" (emphasized) the ob[ective] char[acter] of the inspiration of Scripture insofar as Scripture is the *unique*, for good and all, [and] given witness to that work of God whose content is the reconciliation (atonement) realized for all men. By objective char[acter] of inspiration, I understand: the one work of the one Holy Spirit, in which [the Spirit] evokes and instructs the prophets and the apostles to be witnesses to God's work and word and . . . discloses to hearers and readers of the Bible the meaning and the irresistible challenge of the testimony of the proph[ets] and apostles. As much as the reconciling work of Christ has immediate bearing upon the existence of all men, so the biblical Word is in its objective character an event of immediate bearing upon all men.

1a. Is there such a thing as real freedom for disobedience?! "If the Son makes you free, you are indeed free" [John 8:36]—not otherwise. This does neither imply nor exclude tacit universalism. Not imply: because God is not compelled be any "ism" to give freedom to any or all. Not excludes: because God's grace cannot be thought as limited. Who believes, to be saved himself by this grace, cannot imagine that grace should be irresistible for him, [yet] resistible for others. (Preach the freedom of God's grace and the real human freedom: to obey him!) The biblical passages to which you refer are to be understood as warnings rather than as a historiography of the future.

1b. The Bible has proved and will prove itself as a true and fitting instrument to point man to God, who alone is infallible. The Bible did and does so—as a human document, bound by temporal views of nature, history, ideas, values, . . . insofar it is not sinless like J[esus] C[hrist] himself and thus not infallible like God. No wonder that, seen from the viewpoint [of] the worldviews of other ages, the question may rise whether we have not to reckon with the occurrence of certain tensions, contradictions, and maybe "errors" on the level of its time-bound statements.

2a. "False thinking" in the Bible means to live a lie—a terrible practical, not only theoretical, mistake!

2b. They have an "ontological being" of its own kind: to be described only in negative terms. Therefore: I believe? No! Can and dare we "believe" in the objectivity of the devil, since he is a liar from the beginning and since Christ saw him falling from heaven? He can only be treated with horror, contempt, resistance, and even humor: God certainly laughs at him.

5. To the Questions of J. J. Petuchowski

1. You compare me with "other Christian theologians" and state that you have "no great difficulties" of communicating and coexisting with them. Nevertheless you speak of "a certain grandeur" of my "uncompromising christological claims." Is that only a kind of *apple-polishing* (compliment) concerned with a *formal* quality of my work? Or do you feel yourself *materially* nearer to me than to those "other Chr[istian] theologians"?

2. There *is* a *way* for communication between Jewish and Christian theologians as myself. We read the same *Law*, *Prophets*, and *Writings*, from which we are not permitted to deviate. When we read these documents *together*, we should be able to arrive at a common understanding of *their problem:* Since God's revelation through prophets seems (in Israel's history) to be *restricted* to a given period, the *end* of prophecy points *either* to vacuum and chaos *or* to the event in which the New Testament writers saw the fulfillment of both the law and the promises. In our *dialogue* we should deal with the question of how far the apostles and evangelists of the New Testament *truly* affirm fulfillment of the law and the promises.

3. Jews should not understand themselves abstractedly as representing to the Christians the *godless!* Rather, we Christians have to learn from the Jews again and again the indelible election of the contender against God to be a Jehoudah = the man who gives God the glory among all gentiles.

4. I consider the creation of the modern state of Israel (omitting all other explanations: insofar as it is to be considered in the context of the fulfillment of Old Testament prophecy) another sign of the electing and providentially ruling grace and faithfulness to the seed of Abraham. After the horrors of the Hitler-Time, the reappearance of Israel as a nation even in the political realm may well be called a *miracle* for all who have eyes to see. Remember the answer to Frederick the Great of Prussia, when he asked for a proof for God's existence: "Your majesty, the Jews!" The Jews have always owed their existence to the power of God alone and not to their own or their history's might. So also they do today!

6. To the Questions of F. W. Stringfellow

(Who are the principalities and powers?)

Money, sport, traditions, fashion, religion, unconscious, reason, sex. Good creatures. Alienated subject[s].

(What is their relation to the claim that Christ is Lord of history?)

What does this mean? In [Christ's] death man—as sinner, as alienated from himself, as a prey of death—is done in. In [Christ's] resurrection, man, free from the yoke of pseudo-gods, has appeared in the flesh (therefore *bodily* resurrection!!) as God's new creature: the beginning of a new heaven and a new earth that will be universally and definitely revealed and vindicated in the last Parousia of the Lord.

(What practical freedom does a Christian have from the dominion of these powers?)

To look back to the first—to look forward to the last coming of the Lord, to look upon his presence. That is freedom, that is life. Looking to him means to be equipped with that Spirit who is potent to stand and to fight the ghosts!

B. Podium Discussion on Wednesday Evening

1. Greeting

Dean Brauer: Ladies and Gentlemen, for the past three days, including today, we have been treated to three provocative and stimulating lectures by Professor Karl Barth.[2] This evening we have planned a special program because we hoped not only to hear Professor Barth deliver his formal lectures, but in addition to hear several young theologians address questions to Professor Barth and engage him in discussion. The panel this evening was selected with great deliberation. Most of us, as theologians, and some of you, after reading *Time* and *Newsweek*, know fairly well what theologians such as Niebuhr, Tillich, and Buber think concerning Professor Barth.[3]

It was our conviction that the impact of Professor Barth upon the American theological scene, while dependent upon many factors, is also dependent upon the impact he has made and will make upon younger theologians. For our discussion this evening we therefore have selected a panel of six theologians and one lay theologian, each of them under forty-five years of age and holding key positions in the American scene. The moderator for this evening is Professor Jaroslav Pelikan, professor of historical theology in the Divinity School of the University of Chicago. I am pleased to present this panel to you tonight. I shall now turn the program over to Professor Pelikan.

Pelikan: In one of Karl Barth's favorite scenes from one of Karl Barth's favorite operas, by Karl Barth's favorite composer, Papageno the bird catcher and Monostatos the Moor chase each other around, half hoping to catch the other and half afraid that they might.[4] That is not our situation tonight, for we have caught the bird catcher, we have heard his magic flute, and we have been

2. See above, chap. 23, n. 4.
3. Brauer is referring to the interviews with the two newspapers published in chaps. 22–23 above.
4. W. A. Mozart, *The Magic Flute* (KV 620), act 1, entry 9.

entranced by it. Indeed, to be serious for a moment, I am sure I am speaking for most of those present, both in the audience and on the panel, when I say that to Karl Barth, as probably to no other living theologian, we may, without blasphemy or exaggeration, apply the words of the Fourth Evangelist, "And of his fullness have we all received, grace for grace" [John 1:16]. We are what we are, theologically, because of him; and it is in reaction to him that our own theological movement has moved as it has. It is also in reaction to him that we have met this evening.

My colleagues on this panel, whom I shall introduce to you in a moment, have prepared questions for Professor Barth. These I shall read one at a time. Professor Barth will then present his answer, to which the panel in turn will respond. Beginning on the far left, with the Jesuit member of the panel, is Father Cooke, chairman of the department of theology of Marquette University, Milwaukee, Wisconsin. Next to him, Professor Hans Frei, assistant professor of religion, Yale University, New Haven, Connecticut. Next to him, Mr. Frank William Stringfellow, attorney, New York City. Next to Professor Barth is Karl Markus Barth, my colleague in the Divinity School of the University of Chicago. Next to him is Professor Edward J. Carnell, professor of ethics and philosophy of religion, Fuller Theological Seminary, Pasadena, California. Next to Professor Carnell is Rabbi Jakob Petuchowski, associate professor of rabbinics, Hebrew Union College, Cincinnati, Ohio, and at the far right is Professor Shubert Ogden of Perkins School of Theology, Southern Methodist University, Dallas, Texas.

We shall begin at the far right then, and I shall put to Professor Barth the questions that have been prepared ahead of time by my colleagues on the panel, beginning with Professor Ogden. Question number one from Professor Ogden to Professor Barth:

[Ogden:] If, as you have said (*Church Dogmatics*, III/2:447 = *KD*, III/2:536–37), the preferable procedure for theology is to deal with the mythical elements in the New Testament "eclectically" (instead of, as with Bultmann, either to accept or reject such elements as a whole), what is the "principle of selection" for determining which elements are to be retained and which eliminated?

Barth: Ladies and Gentlemen, let me begin with two general preliminary remarks. First, my handling and pronunciation of the English language, which is a foreign one for me, will be rather weak, but do not be sorry; don't be sad[5] if I have some trouble with my words.

The second remark: My books are said to be big, not to say "fat." This evening I will give short answers. I hope that those among you who may complain about the shortness of my answers will be kind enough to go back to the big volumes, where they will find explicit and well-expounded data and statements that I cannot give you here in this place.

2. On the Problem of the Interpretation of the Kerygma

I begin with this first question of my colleague, Dr. Ogden. My dear colleague, first of all I must tell you that there is a misunderstanding in your question. The

---

5. English folk song: "Don't be sorry, don't be sad, / think, what a lovely time we've had."

eclecticism of which you speak does not imply a selection between mythological elements, but between different kinds of worldviews or world conceptions. None of these worldviews, old or modern, has to be absolutely accepted or absolutely rejected. Elements of every one of them may become dangerous if understood as particulars of a system claiming ultimate reality and truth. On the other side, every one of these elements of worldviews may be used as an analogy of the reality and truth of God's revelation.

Think, for example, of the parables and the Gospels.[6] You ask me about principles of selection between the elements of certain worldviews. My answer is that the criterion of selection will be the question Can the witness to Christ as the way, the life, and the light [cf. John 14:6; 8:12] be borne by the use of such and such an element out of a very old worldview, or let us say, out of the worldview of the Middle Ages or the worldview of more modern times, or the worldview of our technical age? That is a vital question. Can it be used? Is it helpful? Does it clarify something? Then it can be used. If it does not help, if it hinders, well then, it is no good to use it. That is my answer.

Pelikan: Mr. Ogden, do you wish to respond?

Ogden: Yes. I welcome the clarification. As far as I am concerned, the answer that you have given to the question, as you have restated it, meets very well the intent of my question. That is, I feel that you have responded to what I wanted you to speak to. Not that I am altogether in agreement with your answer or accept it fully, but it seems to me that there is no serious problem in misunderstanding between us at the point of the question itself. I think that I should agree that the principle of selection of the criterion for determining the selection or rejection, as the case may be, of these elements is the kerygma, the witness to Jesus Christ, and the question always is to what extent these elements serve to proclaim this witness more or less appropriately. The question that comes to mind in this connection, however, grows out of your lecture this morning, where you were at some pains to point out to us that the preoccupation on the part of certain contemporary theologians with the problem of communication, of making the kerygma understandable to the modern man—that this preoccupation seems to rest upon the assumption that the kerygma can be easily defined, that it is self-evident.[7] Now, my question to you would be this: if the criterion for determining the relative appropriateness of these elements from the different world conceptions is the witness to Christ, the kerygma, then must one not have defined that witness in order to apply it as a criterion in making the selection in the sense in which you have indicated?

Pelikan: And is not the witness involved in the very elements that one is trying to select—is that what you mean?

---

6. Correction of presumably a typographical error or verbal slip: "the parables in the Gospels."

7. K. Barth, *Einführung in die evangelische Theologie* (Zurich: Evangelischer Verlag, 1962), 43–44; ET: K. Barth, *Evangelical Theology: An Introduction*, trans. G. Foley (New York: Holt, Rinehart & Winston, 1963), 35: "Nowadays, of course, the 'exegetical-theological' task is often said to consist in the translation of biblical assertions out of the speech of a past time into the language of modern man. The remarkable assumption behind this project, however, seems to be that the content, meaning, and point of biblical assertions are relatively easy to ascertain and may afterward be presupposed as self-evident. . . . The truth of the matter, however, is that the central affirmations of the Bible are not self-evident; the Word of God itself, as witnessed to in the Bible, is not immediately obvious in any of its chapters or verses. On the contrary, the truth of the Word must be sought. . . ."

Ogden: Yes.

Barth: I should speak to two things: finding out the true content of the kerygma of which I spoke this very morning, and the selection of the useful words, these are not separate things. They go together. What I deny is the idea that first we can have a quite certain understanding of what the kerygma means and then the only problem remaining is how to tell it to one's children.

Ogden: To pick up this point, it seems to me that as you have stated it this evening, I could accept it wholeheartedly. My trouble with your statement this morning, as in other statements that you have made to the same effect, is that when you put it the way you did, it is a secondary concern, not a primary one. This again seems to me to separate these two things in a way that violates the point you have just made, namely, that they belong together. That the task of determining what kerygma is, and what the appropriate elements are through which it can be proclaimed, is one task with two aspects, perhaps, but these cannot be artificially separated, neither in one way nor in the other.

Barth: I agree that they cannot be separated; but there is an order: the task to find out the truth of the gospel itself is the primary task, and this order cannot be reversed. The task of interpretation and of translation, this task can only follow the other, but they belong together.

3. Theology and Philosophy

Pelikan: Professor Ogden's second question:

[Ogden:] As you know, Heinrich Ott has claimed to be in fundamental agreement with you in his view that theology and philosophy alike serve and express "one universal truth."[8] In what sense, if any, then, is Christian theology properly understood as "philosophical theology"? Or alternatively, is there any sense in which the work of the theologian is of necessity dependent on that of the philosopher, and if there is, in what sense?

Barth: Let me first tell you that I can take upon myself no responsibility for what Heinrich Ott has said and will say. But now in response to your question, Is there any sense in which the work of the theologian is dependent on that of the philosopher?, I must clearly answer, "In no sense." The work of a theologian is of necessity and by nature independent from that of the philosopher. I wonder, Mr. Ogden, how you came to ask me that question, because from the very beginning of my theological work it was my primary intention, or one of my primary intentions, to procure freedom and independence for theology over against philosophy. For what reason? Well, philosophy deals with man— with man and his possibilities, tendencies, needs, and problems, including religion. Philosophy asks man's questions and works out some answers to them. It pretends to help man or to give him answers. Theology deals with God in his encounter with man, with man responding to God's approval. Remember what I have said in lectures I, II, and III.[9]

The study of philosophy is certainly necessary for the theologian, and I should say in a double way. First, positively, the theologian may learn from the

---

8. H. Ott, *Denken und Sein: Der Weg Martin Heideggers und der Weg der Theologie* (Zollikon: Evangelischer Verlag, 1959), 20.
9. See n. 2 above.

philosopher a lot of things about the nature of the manner of consistent thought and speech; many theologians miss that teaching of philosophy. But, negatively, the theologian must study philosophy in order to warn of the traps into which he is not supposed to fall. As to the traps, I think of worldviews making themselves absolute as ultimate reality and truth, systems built up (before theology begins) of preconceived ontology or anthropology. In order not to fall into those traps, a theologian must earnestly study philosophy.

Ogden: The reason for raising the question springs, I must confess, from my concern to clarify a matter on which I've held an opinion very like your own, Dr. Barth. I have likewise been convinced that your answer to this question would be exactly the answer that you have just given, but I have been assured by some of your American followers, with whom I have been in conversation, that I was in this respect being unfair to you and that your attitude toward the question of the relation of philosophy and theology allowed for a much more positive dependence between them than you have just indicated is allowable; and they have, in this connection, referred me to your recent contribution to the Festschrift for your brother;[10] and having read it myself, it seems to me that the answer you have just given summarizes very well the answer that I have found there. So frankly, I had an ulterior motive in raising this question. It seems to me that Heinrich Ott's eagerness to appeal to you in support of his own concern to make use of the work of the late Martin Heidegger, and to make it fruitful for theological work—that his appeal to you in this connection may perhaps be forcing you to say something you would not be quite as willing to say as he indicates. I think I have been satisfied on this point by your answer.

Barth: The important point is, I ask the assembly, "Have you heard out of my answer something like the dependence of theology upon philosophy? Dependence—that is what I fight against. Dependence is . . . ."

Pelikan: I think that is what Mr. Ogden means, that you have made it clear that there is no dependence of theology upon philosophy or anything substantive. Whatever theology can learn in a positive way is in the realm of method rather than in the realm of content.

Barth: Aha! That implies that I make use of it as a kind of tool. Take this glass of water, for example: I am not dependent upon this glass of water.

Pelikan: But you are dependent upon water in general, if not this particular glass. We now turn to a theologian from Yale University, Hans Frei. This is Professor Frei's first question: It is rather long, but if you follow it, I think that the point will become clear.

4. The Ontological and Cosmological Proof for the Existence of God

[Frei:] For a long time you have been recorded as an opponent of all theological endeavors to prove God's existence. However, a number of years ago you suggested, in a book on St. Anselm's *Proslogion*, chapters 2–4,[11] that a proof

---

10. K. Barth, "Philosophie und Theologie," in *Philosophie und christliche Existenz: Festschrift für Heinrich Barth; Zum 70. Geburtstag am 3.2.1960* (Basel: Helbing & Lichtenhahn, 1960), 93–106.

11. K. Barth, *Fides quaerens intellectum: Anselms Beweis der Existenz Gottes im Zusammenhang seines theologischen Programms* (München: C. Kaiser, 1931); 2nd ed. (1958); new edition, E. Jüngel and I. U. Dalferth, eds. (Zurich: Theologischer Verlag, 1981); 2nd ed. (1986).

of a certain kind may in reality also be a testimony of faith. Do you think that the same thing could be said of the cosmological argument, either in the form St. Thomas Aquinas gave it, or some other?[12]

By way of explanation: In your book *Fides Quaerens Intellectum*, you suggested that Anselm's proof is a kind of analogical circumscription of God's name. It is not a proof in the usual sense of demonstrating a theorem or the actuality of something possible. Instead it does three things: [1] Negatively, it reduces to absurdity the notion of God as merely existing in the intellect. [2] Positively, it is a reflecting [*nach-denkende*] explication of the self-revelation in Jesus Christ of that God who, in revealing himself, makes it impossible for us to conceive of him as not existing. [3] In both respects, it is explication, that is, faith's rational exploration of itself as divinely given before and during the exploration.

St. Thomas's five ways, the proof usually called the cosmological, is a procedure that starts with reflection upon the presence of God to external structure rather than to the intellect. St. Thomas believes also that his proof is a circumscription of God's revealed Name ("He Who Is"[13]). Is it possible to conceive of this proof, like Anselm's, as a reflecting explication of God's self-revelation, that is, as an exploration by faith into faith by means of the structures of being?

Barth: My answer: As to Anselm's proof (the so-called ontological proof for the existence of God), I have studied the argument, and I am sure of what concerns Anselm. I have also studied Thomas, but I am not so sure about what he is saying. Can his so-called cosmological proof be understood as reflecting an explanation of God's self-revelation *by* faith *into* faith? Can it be understood that way? If so, all is very well, because certainly there is presence and, even objectively speaking, a disclosure of God in external structures, and not only to the intellect. Certainly!

Let us think about the biblical relation of heaven and earth, the relation of body and soul, or the relation of man and woman. These are structures, external structures, cosmological structures, so to speak. In history we may think, for example, of the historical fact of the history of the Jews. You perhaps remember what has been told of Frederick the Great of Prussia, who asked his doctor one day, "Can you give me a certain proof for the existence of God?" And this doctor answered, "Your majesty, the Jews."[14] Certainly a cosmological factor.

I could add to this indication a thing I have seen the last two Sundays here in Chicago, visiting a service in a church in which Negroes and whites sat peacefully together, worshiped, heard the Word of God, sang, and prayed together. White men and black men!—a fact, an external structure of the cosmos, and in this case, we may say, a remarkable proof for the existence of God. And if you allow me only to mention the music of Wolfgang Mozart . . . !

12. Thomas Aquinas, *Summa Theologica* I q. 2 a. 2 and 3.

13. According to the Greek translation of the Old Testament name of God, the Tetragrammaton, YAHWEH [יהוה], in Exod. 3:14.

14. The doctor was Johann Georg von Zimmermann (1728–95). According to Fr. Frh. von Lipperheide, *Spruchwörterbuch* (Berlin: Lipperheide, 1907), 428, it was Voltaire who responded to Friedrich II's question about a persuasive proof of Christianity by saying, "Les juifs!" Lipperheide cites Zimmermann without providing the location.

BUT—now comes the great BUT! You see, to find the presence of such cosmological proofs within the surroundings of nature and history presupposes God's revelation where he has revealed himself directly, and then also presupposes man's place in it. I think of the reflectors on the highways where the cars are going back and forth. These reflectors in themselves are dark, but when cars shine their headlights, then these reflectors shine, also. You see a revelation only in the event of their encounter. There is a relation between God's actual and unique work in Jesus Christ and such possibilities within the cosmos that may become reflecting lights. But they only reflect afterward. Now my question to Professor Frei is the reasoning of Thomas Aquinas—this is what I am not sure of. Is my reasoning the same as Thomas's? This I leave to colleague Frei and to the Thomists to decide.

Pelikan: Professor Frei, do you wish to respond?

Frei: Well, just let me say very shortly that as a matter of fact, I certainly am not at all sure either. That is why I have said that I wondered if the argument could not be understood in that way, even if St. Thomas himself was not clear that it should be understood in that way.

Pelikan: You mean no clearer than was St. Anselm about where he put his argument?

Frei: Perhaps.

Barth: Concerning Anselm, I am sure he must be understood in this way. But here I am not sure, and it seems that you are not sure either. . . . So we agree.

Pelikan: Father Cooke, would you like to speak for St. Thomas?

Cooke: I would like to say that until you spoke, I had not realized the possible area of agreement that lies there. If I do not misunderstand you, I think what you are saying is that as one encounters reality and creative form, one can find a certain mirroring of the divine reality. There is a certain sort of contemplative approach—sort of an insight—into reality that is there. Personally, I think that at least a certain understanding of St. Thomas's proofs can coincide with that. I think that they are, in the ultimate analysis, an insight into the creatureliness of creatures.

Pelikan: But there is a matter of priority. Professor Barth is indicating that there is a priority of the knowledge obtained by revelation, which then enables one to recognize these structures, and not the other way around.

Cooke: Let me just add this one word. So far as I am concerned, I did not mean to consider this proof apart from a christological theology. It exists only *if* it can be understood on the basis of christological theology. Does one not then have a possibility concerning which Professor Ogden was also asking, namely, that the theologian now makes substantive, rather than merely formal, use of philosophy?

Barth: Substantive use? Take care. I have never made substantive use of Mozart. And I could not do it in all the cases mentioned before. What can be said is only that there are possibilities, also, of a presence of God, even of a revelation. But this is not to say that all people have met him. But the apostle says, "And now I will *tell you* about the God whom you seem to know, but as it seems only" [cf. Acts 17:23]. Nowhere in his Epistles does Paul build up a natural theology, not even in Romans 1 or Acts 17. He didn't—and he knew why.

5. Preaching and the Political Situation

Pelikan: Professor Frei's second question is of another order, raising the question of the nature and implications of Christian proclamation:

[*Frei:*] Here as everywhere in the church, the minister faces the task of preaching. He seeks to expound the Word of God in the hearing of the congregation. In some ways the situation in which he preaches here is a very difficult one. Unlike the church in Nazi Germany, the church in this country faces no absolutely clear-cut political issues. Again, it is difficult to preach in a society that is at once thoroughly sated and affluent and yet restless and uneasy. Obviously you may not, as a visitor to these shores, want to comment on our domestic situation. What I wonder about is this: Can one perhaps provisionally specify the sort of exegetical principles that will at once be faithful to the Bible and pertinent to the congregation? The sermon is object-directed; that is, it points toward the gracious God. Does this pointing, of itself, make the sermon pertinent to the congregation in the situation where there are no clear-cut political issues?

Barth: It may be that you overrate the situation in Nazi Germany for the church. Even in Nazi Germany, there were no clear-cut political issues, as you presuppose. Except, inasmuch as the tasks of the church became problematic under the impact of the totalitarian state's demands. I mean the demands for political conformity of the church. And now, allow me to ask you a question. Is a distinction between situations in which it is easy or not easy to preach the gospel really possible? Not the same, but similar totalitarian demands are made to the church, to Christianity, also in Switzerland, and perhaps also in the United States of America. At this point, I would like to ask Mr. Stringfellow to tell us something about his outlook on this question. That would be a good thing; it would help me to answer your question.

Stringfellow: I would have to say that the thing that disturbed me about the question was the fact that I never saw any clear-cut political issue, with the possible exception of some very erratically conservative Republicans, who thought they could see some clear-cut political issues.

Pelikan: And thus become one.

Stringfellow: I do not understand the meaning of preaching as you seem to imply it here and wonder if you have not confused the task of preaching (that is to say, of exposing the Word of God, laying bare the Word of God, within the congregation, so that it may be enjoyed, so that it may be praised for itself and celebrated) with the work of prophetism, which may not necessarily be joined at any given time with preaching in a congregation or with the work of the preacher. The second query is about that.

Finally and more directly, as far as I can see in this country the church and Christians are accorded, on the whole, only two kinds of freedom: to speak publicly or to act publicly. In the first instance, the church surrenders to the notion, so popular in this country, that religion is supposed to have only to do with religion—perhaps in some instances also with the lives of children, but never with the lives of adults or never with the great issues of the nation. Then the church is tolerated, and then it is allowed to publicly assemble and meet and carry on its esoteric life.

In the second case, where the church is still permitted in this country to intervene in public life, it is only so long as it intervenes on the side that protects the national unity and solidarity and the stated public policy at a given time.

To be concrete about it, a few years ago we had a rather ridiculous controversy involving a study document published by the National Council of Churches respecting Red China and its relation to the United States.[15] This was not an official stand of the council. It was not as forthright as that, but it was a conscientious report from a study conference. This has been, and still is being, attributed to the churches as an unhappy example of their meddling in politics and of their hostile relationship to the national interest—misused, I think, largely by opponents of the policy in question in this way.

Notice the reaction of the churches to this attack. There will never be another study document of that kind, or even of that moderate degree of criticism and forthrightness. For the last five years or so, since that study document came out, the National Council of Churches has been at great pains to explain that it was not an official pronouncement, and also at great pains to try to recover the substantial economic losses it suffered because the study document was circulated. In other words, I think that more and more the public freedom of the church to say anything (even assuming it is informed) is suffocated.

One other example was most interesting. You remember the sit-in demonstrations a few years ago at the time both national political conventions met.[16] Both conventions made statements in effect endorsing the sit-in movement, principally in the South in this country. Both political parties through their own conventions, which are the most conservative forms of political voice within the party structures in this country, in principle approved the sit-in movement. Shortly after the convention, the General Board of the National Council, and also the General Assembly of the Presbyterian Church, among a host of church bodies who were silent, made statements about it, which were much more modest, much more restrained and much more cautious in their comments and much more equivocal concerning the sit-in movements than either of the great political conventions. That is how stifled we are, in my view.

Barth: Well, thank you; I will go on to answer your question, Mr. Frei. I agree with your conception and description of the relation between the Bible and confronting the congregation. This concept is also mine. The trouble always is that we may not make abstractions on either side. The sermon cannot be a purely biblical one, and it cannot be a purely congregational address. But there is a sequence; there is a gift from the Bible to the congregation and through the congregation out into the world; that is a principle for a good sermon, that it has this gift. My view would be to read and explain the Bible as the witness of Christ, given to a church—to your church, to this or to that church—in a specific situation. Then necessarily out of the words of God, out of the words of the

---

15. The editor could not document this account.

16. These demonstrations, which soon spread across the country, began in February 1960 in North Carolina and pursued the goal of the legally guaranteed equality of blacks in American society. In the presidential campaign of that summer, this theme was also engaged in the conventions of the two opposing parties, the Republicans and the Democrats. See S. B. Oates, *Let the Trumpet Sound: The Life of Martin Luther King* (New York: Harper & Row, 1982), 151; D. J. Garrow, *Bearing the Cross* (New York: W. Morrow, 1986), 127–40.

prophets and the apostles, will directly or indirectly come those applications to the life of this congregation and its life within this present world. It is then that the situation *may become* clear-cut. There are no clear-cut situations, as you said before. The situation could become clear-cut, but then it is not our work that makes it clear: it is the gospel that does it. You know, our task is to testify to the gospel.

6. Faith and Reason, Revelation and Nature

Pelikan: Now we move to the third questioner, Father Cooke of Marquette with his first question. Perhaps this question should be prefaced by Professor Barth's own observation that some of the most discerning insights into, comments upon, and criticisms of, his theological position have come not from his fellow Protestants, but from his—alas, primarily European—Roman Catholic interpreters.[17] First question:

[*Cooke:*] If knowledge in faith involves some encounter with God, if revelation is given us so we can grasp it, does this mean that the Christian is *capax Dei?* And if so what is the root of this capacity?

Barth: Well, Father Cooke, let me begin with a statement: Man's destiny as God's creature, the destiny given to him as a created being, is to be God's covenant partner; he is created to be able to grasp God's words, God's revelation, de jure not de facto. But again—BUT the situation is like that of a fellow who has two legs with which to walk, but he cannot do so because, unfortunately, they are broken. What happened in Adam's fall? He is still *capax*-destined, this is certain. His legs are there, but it is a pity that he finds himself incapacitated for doing what he could do. Practically, he cannot grasp God's revelation. Poor patient. His healing is described in the events of the Bible. This healing is the work of the Holy Spirit. The Spirit creates a new bond, a new man. Man will fulfill his destiny. He will not only be able to grasp God's revelation: he will do it. That is my answer.

Cooke: If I might pursue just a little of that question: there is still in my mind a certain vagueness in this area. I can see that once man has been harmed by sin, he must have the entry of the action of the Holy Spirit. But my question would rather center on this: Does the Holy Spirit do something to man, making him once more capable of this encounter, or is man just there with the Spirit working in him, and is it, as it were, the Spirit and God who encounter each other, or is man himself once more transformed by the action of the Spirit so that he has this capacity?

Pelikan: Does the Holy Spirit believe for us, or in what sense is it said that man also believes?

Barth: Oh, no! Oh, no! The Holy Spirit does not believe for us. No—but [the Spirit] gives us the freedom to believe, and then this gift as a gift, you see, is our own freedom to believe. The freedom of this newborn man.

Pelikan: And that is the restoration to authentic humanity?

Barth: Yes—authentic humanity.

---

17. See no. 4, "Interview with Kristeligt Dagblad," in Karl Barth, *Gespräche: 1963,* ed. E. Busch (Zurich: Theologischer Verlag, 2005), fn. 13.

Carnell: Dr. Barth, in this connection might I ask if I could assert that I encounter God by listening to Mozart while reading the telephone book? What observation would you have in regard to that claim?

Pelikan: In other words, what difference does it make where one encounters? Is it purely arbitrary choice, like having a taste for olives, that one says one encounters God here rather than there? Why in this particular situation, rather than another?

Carnell: Yes. You have world religions of various species where similar dogmatic claims are made. A person may encounter God through the Analects of Confucius, so he says, and you say that the Logos is the Word of God. Now, if an assertion is made that God, in fact, meets me elsewhere on Sunday morning, especially when I am listening to Mozart at 11:00 o'clock, not in church but at home, and here I encounter God through this particular work of the Spirit of God . . .

Barth: Well, now I think we come to the question: What do we mean when we speak of God? There are different kinds and sets of "Gods." We speak of God as revealed, acting, and speaking in Jesus Christ, not of another one. And then I wonder whether you can say, "Oh, I am reaching him here and there and there and so on." Is that so? Maybe, but it is not so certain as you seem to think. But I think we come back to that question, the second question of Father Cooke. . . .

Pelikan: Father Cooke's second question is related to the second question of Professor Ogden and the first question of Professor Frei. But it is put in another context:

[Cooke:] Granted the essential difference between that knowledge of God arrived at in faith and that knowledge about God attained in natural theology (i.e., a philosophical approach to a transcendent being), is it not possible to bring these two knowledges to bear on one another and so enter into an integrated act of theologizing? (Actually, the question I am trying to raise here is that of the relation between faith and reason.)

Barth: Father Cooke, you seem to grant (and I like it), you seem to grant an *essential*—that is your word—difference between that knowledge of God arrived at in faith and the knowledge about God attained in natural theology: *an essential difference.* And more than that, you made an interesting distinction: you spoke of the knowledge *of God*, arrived at in faith, and then of knowledge *about God*. I think it is not accidental that you said *of God* and *about God*. I love you for that.

Yet you presuppose the identity of the Gods perceived by these two methods. My counterquestion is [this]: Are they identical? If yes, why then in the Old and in the New Testaments that are in your Bible is there conflict between the knowledge of gods, deities, heavenly powers, principalities, and so forth, and the revealed and faithful knowledge of those to whom God has spoken as the God of Abraham, Isaac, and of Jacob [cf. Exod. 3:6], who is not the God of the philosophers?[18] Why does the Bible make this difference? If there is a

---

18. According to the *Memorial* of Blaise Pascal (1654): "Fire. 'God of Abraham, God of Isaac, God of Jacob,' not of the philosophers and scholars: Certainty, Sensibility: Joy, Peace." Cited according to *Pascal*, selected and introduced by R. Schneider (Frankfurt and Hamburg: Fischer, 1954), 3rd ed. (1957), 122.

distinction, it excludes identity. If there is [a distinction], then natural theology (as it is called and as also you call it) and Christian theology cannot be integrated in one system. Does this mean a disruption between faith and reason? No, it doesn't. It makes good sense. It is appropriate that the people of God made use of reason to be faithful to the one good Lord and did not at the same time attempt to serve Yahweh and Baal, God and mammon [cf. Matt. 6:24].

Pelikan: Then the God to whom natural theology attains is always an idol?

Barth: The Bible says so.

Pelikan: Or does it, Father? John Calvin did not think so, did he?

Petuchowski: I have a question in my mind. St. Paul, speaking in Athens, said to the Athenians who worshiped the unknown God that that unknown God whom they worshiped was the very one whom he, Paul, was preaching to them [Acts 17:23]. It seems to me that Paul made some kind of identification there, and it would be rather strange if he would now be guilty of the kind of idolatry, of mixing up Baal with Yahweh, of which we have just heard. I would appreciate some clarification of that.

Barth: I wonder that a Jewish theologian should say such a thing to me.

Pelikan: You quoted his Bible—now he can quote yours.

Barth: Yes, yes. If you go on and study the apostle Paul, you will find no place, no one verse in which he puts the Father of Jesus Christ together with the Greek or other ideas about God. His approach to these people at Athens was a very sharp, dialectical one. He saw their attitude of adoration, and he said to them, "I will tell you about the true God that you are cultivating" [cf. Acts 17:23], and he told them about Jesus Christ risen from the dead [17:31]. You know the sequence of the story. This story has often been used by Christian and other theologians as an example of good apologetics; but if, then, Paul was an apologist, there in Athens he was a failure, because they laughed at him. When they heard him speaking of Christ risen from the dead, then they walked away, saying, as we may say this very evening, "Let us hear something another day" [cf. Acts 17:32], perhaps tomorrow.

Pelikan: I am sure that I express the sentiments of all of you when I articulate—to Professor Barth, above all, and to our colleagues on the panel—our gratitude for the candor, the freedom, the humor, and the goodwill with which this dialogue has been carried on, and when I invite all of you to tune in at the same time, same station, for the second half of this conversation.

Thursday Evening

7. Introduction

Dean Brauer: This evening I would like to take the opportunity to express the gratitude of the University of Chicago, the Divinity School, and of the vast audience (I should say, audiences) that have come to hear Professor Barth. He has endeared himself to the hearts of his listeners. He has stimulated us. He has provoked us. He has intrigued us. Those of us who had read his works or part of them, now have a whole new dimension in terms of which we can understand him, for now we have seen him in action. We have been impressed by his humor, his good grace, his curiosity, and above all, by his wisdom. Continuing the procedure that was employed last evening, to introduce the panel and to moderate the discussion, I should like to present Professor Jaroslav Pelikan, professor of historical theology in the Divinity School of the University of Chicago.

Pelikan: Anyone who earns his groceries, as I do, teaching about the theology of the church fathers, must find it a signal but strange honor to meet a church father in person, and then to preside over a panel discussion with him, and then in English rather than Greek. But as I said to last night's audience, and I think it bears repeating in all seriousness but more in gratitude, I am sure I speak for all of you when I say that from my own twenty years of preoccupation with him, that to Karl Barth, as to no other living theologian, and to very few of the theologians of the church's past, I find myself able without any exaggeration to apply the words of the Fourth Gospel: "And of his fullness have we all received, and grace for grace" [John 1:16].

I cannot resist the observation that most of last night's questions, and indeed of tonight's, deal with the relation between what Father Daniélou has called "God and the ways of knowing,"[19] or what the professional in theology calls "prolegomena," theology and . . . or theology versus philosophy, faith and reason, authority, and related issues. No question has raised the problem of the doctrine of the Trinity, the restatement of which may be one of Professor Barth's greatest and most lasting theological achievements. None has dealt with the doctrine of the atonement, the person of Christ, or with the sacraments. None has dealt with our unity in Christ and our disunity as churches. This probably says something about American theology. Perhaps it says something about the theology of Professor Barth as well. But the questions last night, and even more Professor Barth's answers, manifest, as I think all of you who were here yesterday would agree, the two fundamental virtues of all responsible theological inquiry: First, a seriousness about the truth; and second, a reverence before the majesty of God and before nothing else. In this spirit, then, let us begin. Tonight we start tonight with Professor Carnell's questions.

8. *Questions to the* Church Dogmatics

(On the Inspiration of the Bible, the Freedom of the Human, Universalism)

[Carnell:] First, I realize that it is all a matter of *stress*, but if Dr. Barth had a chance to rewrite the *Dogmatics*, would he be more inclined to stress the objective character of the inspiration of Scripture[20] in the same way that he has expressed the objective character of the atonement against the rationalism of Rudolf Bultmann?[21]

Barth: Dear colleague Carnell, do you think also that I have not always stressed and emphasized the objective character of the inspiration of the

---

19. This formulation summarizes Daniélou's view that the revelation of God, although and in that it has its fullness in Christ, remains open for diverse ways of knowing, including from the various religions. See J. Daniélou, *Wege zu Christus* (Mainz: Matthias-Grünewald, 1962); Daniélou, *Vom Heil der Völker* (Frankfurt: Knecht, 1952).

20. See *CD* I/2:512–27 [*KD* 568–85].

21. See *CD* IV/1, passim, esp. 284–85 [*KD* 313], and the implicit debate, 223–28 [*KD* 245–50].

Scripture? And that there is need for a change in another edition of my *Dogmatics*? Insofar as Scripture is the unique witness for that work of God whose content is the covenant of Jesus Christ (the work of reconciliation—one can also say atonement), it realizes for all men the character of its inspiration. I understand the one work of the one Holy Spirit to be that of invoking and instructing the prophets and the apostles to be witnesses to God's work and word in which he discloses to hearers and readers of the Bible the meaning and the irresistible challenge of the testimony of the prophets and of the Bible. That is what I understand—speaking of the objective character of inspiration. This double work of the Holy Spirit, of God the Holy Spirit, as much as the reconciling work of Christ, has immediate bearing upon the existence of all men; so the biblical word is in its objective character an event of immediate bearing to all men—all men. That is what I have to say to your first question.

Pelikan: Response, Mr. Carnell?

Carnell: I would like to thank Dr. Barth very sincerely for this answer. I suppose I could lay aside the problem that is turning inside me, and yet I want you to know that I am searching for the truth rather than trying to criticize. I would ask, How would you reconcile your judgment, expressed in I/2 of the *Dogmatics*, that the Word of God is sullied with errors and inconsistencies, even in theological matters,[22] with your extensive appeal to Scripture as a normative source for evangelical theology? How do these fit together?

Barth: I think that I will deal with this special issue in answering your third question.

Pelikan: Let me then go on to the next question, continuing Dr. Carnell's basic inquiry into what Professor Barth would do if he had to rewrite his *Dogmatics*.

[Carnell:] Dr. Barth contends that man does not have freedom to choose between obedience or disobedience in following Christ.[23] Does this imply a tacit universalism? And what about those verses in the Epistles and in the Gospels prophesying that some will be lost? Would Dr. Barth express himself differently if he had a chance to write the *Dogmatics* over again?

Barth: I do not think that I would express myself substantially differently if I had a chance to write the *Dogmatics* over again. But let us come to your point. I like to answer in the form of a question, and now I ask you, Is there such a thing as real freedom for disobedience, as you seem to presuppose? Freedom for disobedience? In my Bible I read, "If the Son makes you free, you are indeed free" [cf. John 8:36]. Indeed free, not otherwise. Disobedience does not mean a kind of freedom, but imprisonment. This neither implies nor excludes what you call tacit universalism. It does not imply [universalism] because God is not compelled; God is not forced by an ism, such as the isms of Origen,[24] to give freedom to any or to all. God is not bound to do it, and thereby my thesis cannot imply universalism. On the other side, I see no possibility of excluding

22. *CD* I/2:507–12 [*KD* 563–68].

23. For example, *CD* IV/1:745–46 [*KD* 833–34]: "The whole idea of a possibility of faith confronted by that of unbelief, the whole conception of man as a Hercules at the crossroads able to choose between faith and sin (and therefore unbelief) is an illusion."

24. Barth apparently means here chiefly the "universalism" of Origen, whose "monism" in his doctrine of God and his doctrine of the eternal preexistence of souls (moving him close to "emanatism") results in a doctrine of *apokatastasis*.

it because God's grace cannot be thought to be limited. Who believes himself to be saved by God's grace cannot imagine that grace should be irresistible for him, yet resistible for others. Let us preach and teach the freedom of God's grace and the real human freedom that he gives us in his grace to obey him, the real freedom to obey him. The biblical passages to which you refer are,[25] if I am right, to be understood as very strong warnings rather than as historiography of the eternal future. That is my answer. Are you satisfied?

Pelikan: Then would it be appropriate, Dr. Barth, to say that it is the implication of the Christian tradition that there must be a hell, and we hope there is no one in it?

Barth: What you have said just now I heard in the same phrases from a very famous Roman Catholic theologian (I will not tell his name).[26]

Pelikan: Continuing with Professor Carnell's questions, and tying this next in with the first of them:

[Carnell:] In this connection how does Dr. Barth harmonize his appeal to Scripture, as the objective Word of God, with his admission that Scripture is, indeed, sullied by errors, theological as well as historical or factual?[27]

Pelikan: This is a problem for me, too, I cheerfully confess.

Barth: The Bible has proved and will prove itself to be a true and fitting instrument to point man to God and his work and his words, to God who alone is infallible. Since the Bible is a human instrument and document, bound and conditioned by the temporal views of nature, of history, of ideas, of values, it to that extent is not sinless, like Jesus Christ himself, and thus not infallible, like God. No wonder that seen from the perspective of the worldviews and the concepts of other ages; the question may arise whether we have to conclude that the Bible is not solid. I should never say such a thing, but would admit rather the occurrence of certain, let us say, tensions, contradictions, and maybe if you prefer, "errors," in its time-bound human statements. Is that enough to encourage you to continue to cheerfully confess that here is a problem also for you?

Pelikan: That is just another way of saying, "Welcome to the Club." Dr. Carnell, do you wish to respond?

Carnell: Thank you, sincerely, Dr. Barth.

9. The Reality of Evil

Pelikan: We now come to Dr. Carnell's second category of question. The first involved several implications, and the second, in a sense, deals with quite another matter: the relation between the definitions of "good" in relation to God, and the definition of evil in the relation to that which is not.

[Carnell:] Dr. Barth asserts that evil is nonbeing.[28] Evil is the possibility that God passed by and despised, a chaos that no longer exists. But in Christ and

25. What is meant are passages such as those that speak of "perishing," such as John 3:16; 1 Cor.1:18; or such as those who speak of the "twofold outcome" of the day of judgment, as in the three parables in Matt. 25.
26. Barth knew this saying through Hans Urs von Balthasar; see *Biography*, 362; *Lebenslauf*, 375–76.
27. See n. 22 above.
28. *CD* III/1:108–10 [*KD* 119–21]; *CD* III/3:351–53 [*KD* 405–7].

since Christ, it stands revealed as nothing, as having no objective existence. But man is man, not God.

Hence, is sin only an ontological mistake borne in false thinking? Do sin and evil have ontological being, so that they can genuinely be spoken of as existing, fearful forces? I think it was Billy Sunday who once said, "I believe in the objectivity of the devil for two reasons: first, his existence is taught in Scripture; second, I have done business with him."[29]

Barth: Let me begin with the historical remark that what I say concerning the existence and essence of evil is not the same as the Greek church fathers said.[30] But let us not dispute this scientific point: it simply is not the same. My answer to the question of Dr. Carnell can be very short this time. Certainly sin is a question of false thinking. It is only an ontological mistake born in false thinking. Yes, you are right. I think so, but mark this point: I think that false thinking in the Bible does not always imply solely a theoretical mistake and error. False thinking in the Bible means to live a lie, and so it is something very practical and something very real in its kind. It is a terribly practical, not only theoretical, mistake if man sins. That may be enough to this point.

To go on to the next point, my answer is that sin and evil have an ontological being of their very peculiar own kind, a kind of being that can only be described in purely negative terms. As, for example, I should say sin and evil, and the devil himself, are impossible possibilities. Or, if you prefer, unreal realities. It cannot be helped: that is their nature because sinning means living a lie. You can describe a lie only in terms of a lie.

Now, I do not like the sayings of this Billy Sunday because he begins with the words "I believe in the objectivity of the devil . . ." and then gives two reasons, and so on. Can and dare we believe such a thing? Since the devil is certainly, following Scripture, a liar from the beginning [cf. John 8:44], and since Christ saw him falling from heaven [cf. Luke 10:18], can we believe in him? Believe in a liar? *No!* The devil has a possibility and reality, that I do not deny—in which form you have heard. The devil can only be treated with horror, with contempt, with resistance, and even with humor.

Pelikan: And with the sign of the cross?

Barth: It is too good for him.

Pelikan: That is why it drives him away.

Barth: God certainly laughs at him. Is that enough?

Carnell: I have a rather extensive collection of collateral questions here, but I will end, as I began, with sincere thanks to you, Dr. Barth, for the time you devoted to your answers and the illumination you have given, and I hope that I can draw therefrom. Thank you.

---

29. William ("Billy") Ashley Sunday (1863–1935), Presbyterian minister, in matters both theological and social an extremely conservative revival preacher in the USA. See W. T. Ellis, *Billy Sunday: The Man and His Message* (Chicago: Moody Press, 1959), 104: "I know there is a devil for two reasons; first, the Bible declares it, and second, I have done business with him."

30. The Neoplatonic view of evil, first advocated by Plotinus, as "nonbeing," as a mere *privatio boni* [privation of good], was then taken up and adapted by Origen, Basil the Great, Gregory of Nyssa, and Augustine—as argued by J. Müller, *Die christliche Lehre von der Sünde*, vol. 1 (Breslau: Max & Camp, 1844), 338–40.

10. Jews and Christians

Pelikan: I move now from Dr. Carnell's questions to those of the next speaker, from Fuller Theological Seminary in Pasadena to Hebrew Union College in Cincinnati. [Here is] the first of Rabbi Petuchowski's questions:

[Petuchowski:] There is a certain ambivalence that must mark a Jew's approach to Karl Barth. On the one hand, the central theme of God's sovereignty is not foreign to the Jew. Your treatment of it with such prophetic earnestness shows that in the Hebrew Bible we have a firm common ground. On the other hand, you strike at least this Jew as being one of the most Christian, in the traditional sense of that term, theologians of all. There are other Christian theologians behind whose christological vocabulary I am able to detect a common human nature. When they speak of creation, of revelation and redemption, or even of the Christ, I have no great difficulty in finding similar or at least corresponding categories within my own Jewish universe of discourse. In this way, therefore, a dialogue becomes possible. There is even a possibility of a peaceful coexistence, with a mutual recognition of the other side's raison d'être, between, let us say, the heirs of Sinai and those of Calvary—as, for example, both Franz Rosenzweig and James Parkes have shown.[31] In Karl Barth's writings, however, the Jew is confronted by the same uncompromising christological claims with which the apostle Paul confronted his ancestors. There is a certain grandeur about it that I am able to appreciate.

Barth: May I begin with an introductory remark to your exposé "theologia." Without naming names, you compare me to some other Christian theologians behind whose christological vocabulary you are able to detect a common human concern and have no great difficulty in finding similar or corresponding categories, and so on. You have no great difficulty, as you state, of communicating and coexisting with them. So far, so good. Nevertheless, now you speak of a certain grandeur of what you call *my* (they are not mine) uncompromising christological claims, and you go on to speak of certain dangers; but now comes my question to you. Is the reference to the so-called grandeur in my christological claims, is that only a kind of, let us say, apple-polishing? A compliment concerned with a formal quality of my way of thinking and speaking—a formal quality? Or do you feel yourself materially nearer to me than to those unnamed other Christian theologians? Can you give me an answer to my question?

Petuchowski: I shall try, Professor Barth. When I speak about the grandeur that marks your approach to this question, the central question, what I have in mind is that in your writings the reader can be in no doubt as to what you mean precisely, and that when you speak of revelation you are referring to the incarnation of the Word. Now, in a way, this emphasis lends, shall we say, authority, definiteness, decisiveness to your system. But to the same extent, it does point out precisely the gulf that separates any Jew from your particular position. By

31. See Fr. Rosenzweig, *Der Stern der Erlösung* (Frankfurt: Kaufmann, 1921), 3rd ed. (Heidelberg: Schneider, 1954) [ET: *The Star of Redemption*, trans. W. W. Hallo (Notre Dame: University of Notre Dame Press, 1985)]; J. W. Parkes, *The Jew and His Neighbour* (London: SCM, 1930); Parkes, *The Conflict of the Church and the Synagogue* (London: Soncino Press, 1934); Parkes, *Judaism and Christianity* (Chicago: University of Chicago Press, 1948).

contemplating this towering christological position, I—who am unable to share it—can nevertheless appreciate the grandeur with which it is expressed. That was the implication of my statement.

Pelikan: Perhaps, Rabbi Petuchowski, your elaboration of this in the second question will make the misgiving you express more explicit.

Barth: I regret that you did not say a little more. But let us go on.

Pelikan: Rabbi Petuchowski continues.

[Petuchowski:] There is a danger that we might not be able to communicate. Thus, with all of Karl Barth's appreciation of Martin Buber, Karl Barth is compelled by the logic of his position to note that even Buber has not penetrated to the idea of the Suffering Servant in the fifty-third chapter of the book of Isaiah, as the one who already has come, who is present, and who is to come again. In a word, quoting Professor Barth, "Buber has not penetrated to Jesus Christ."[32] In other words, you would really expect Buber to take the position of the Ethiopian eunuch in the eighth chapter of the book of Acts, who, you recall, was reading Isaiah 53 until Philip asked him, "Do you understand what you read?" [Acts 8:30], and then Philip, on the basis of the text that this associate of the Ethiopian queen was reading, explained that what was described in the fifty-third chapter of Isaiah had now become historical fact in Jesus. Similarly, what you say about biblical Israel, about the covenant and the election, and even about anti-Semitism,[33] contains much that can be of help to the Jew in the clarification of his own religious heritage; and yet revelation culminates in the existence of Jesus of Nazareth. And the existence of the synagogue alongside the church is based upon the denial of Jesus Christ, and on a powerless continuation of Israelite history, which entered upon fullness long ago.[34] And all you are able to see in the synagogue is the shadow-picture of the church.[35] I am personally not offended by this, since I realize it is but the logical outcome of your biblical theology. What does intrigue me, however, and this is the real point of the question, is the problem of how you would communicate with the Jew? How would you attempt to convince *him* that revelation culminates in the existence of Jesus of Nazareth? Would that not involve you necessarily, [during] this confrontation with a Jew, in the discussion of those very questions of history, biblical

32. See K. Barth, "Möglichkeiten liberaler Theologie heute," in *Schweizerische Theologische Umschau* 30 (Bern, 1960): 99–100: "Here Martin Buber has broken through from the unambiguous I-Thou theology of the Old Testament prophets, but certainly not arrived at the Servant of God of Isaiah 53, who has come, is coming, and will come. He has not reached the *one* cohuman in whom the God who is gracious to humans discloses himself to *us*, that is, to the neighbor with me and to me together with my neighbor, as *our* Father, as *our* liberator, delivering himself to us, giving himself to us; thus he has not arrived at Jesus Christ—but, all the same, to the fellow human who has undeniably been ordained to humanity as boundary and definition, as law and sense-making, because God as I first speaks with him and says Thou to him. . . ."

33. See, in *KD, Registerband,* ed. H Krause (Zurich: Evangelischer Verlag, 1970) [ET: *Church Dogmatics, Index Volume with Aids for the Preacher,* ed. G. W. Bromiley and T. F. Torrance (Edinburgh: T&T Clark, 1977)] the references to the terms Anti-Semitism, Covenant, Israel, Judaism, Synagogue.

34. See *CD* II/2:262–63 [*KD* 289]; *CD* IV/3:877 [*KD* 1006]: "Meantime the Synagogue became and was and still is the organization of a group of men which hastens towards a future that is empty now that He has come who should come, which is still without consolation, which clings to a Word of God that is still unfulfilled."

35. See *CD* III/3:211 [*KD* 239]: "The definitive destruction of the old form of Israel was the negative side of the death of Jesus as a saving event, the shadow thrown by that event in the wider sphere of world history generally." *CD* III/3:218 [*KD* 248]: ". . . It is this whole shadow of the history of the covenant and salvation and its fulfillment which the Jews embody and reveal." See *CD* II/2:505 [*KD* 561].

criticism, and even worldviews? Those very questions that within your own
dogmatic system you have relegated so far into the background! How would
you bring the truth, which stands by itself, to the attention and, if possible, to
the assent of the unbelieving Jew?

Barth: There is a way open for communication between Jewish theologians
and Christian theologians such as myself. We have a point of contact, and a
very big one, because we read the same law, the same prophets, and the same
writings from which we—you and me—are not permitted to deviate; insofar as we read them, we are together. We communicate. When we read these
documents, what we Christians call the Old Testament, Law, Prophets, and
Writings—when we now read these documents together, we should be able to
arrive at a common understanding. I should not speak too quickly of convincing one another, but of coming to a common understanding of the problem of
these documents. What is their problem? God's revelation through Moses and
the prophets is in Israel's history, as it is described in those writings, restricted
to a given period, and this prophetic period ends; therefore we, both you and I,
have to reckon with the end of Moses and the prophets, of their acts and deeds.
This end of prophecy points either to some sort of vacuum—perhaps even to
chaos—or this end of prophecy points to the event in which the New Testament
writers saw the fulfillment of the law and the promises of the same, one God.
And now we should deal with the question, and I think that it could be done, of
how far the apostles and evangelists of the New Testament truly affirm, as I do,
the laws and promises—and thus the fulfillment of Israel's history—or of how
far they do not. That would be some material for discussion.

Petuchowski: I am very grateful, Professor Barth, for your clarification of this.
We are not meeting here tonight to engage in the kind of dialogue that would
be desirable and, I am sure, pleasurable. I may just mention in passing that as
far as my particular religious tradition is concerned, due to the teachings of the
Pharisees and the rabbis, we do not believe that God has stopped revealing
himself and that God has stopped speaking.

The point of my question, however, is something quite different. Trying to
anticipate this kind of dialogue, trying to answer just the very question that
you, Professor Barth, have raised, namely, "Was Jesus of Nazareth the Messiah?" "Did the disciples and the apostles witness the fulfillment of messianic
prophecies, as understood by the Hebrew Bible?" Would we then not really—
you and I, as twentieth-century people—would we not have to deal with questions of historical scholarship in order to make that identification? And if so,
would it not be necessary, in order for us to communicate, for you to move
historical questions more directly to the center of the stage? That was the intent
of my question.

Pelikan: I think that in view of the fact that many of the prophecies of the
Hebrew Scripture were regarded by the Christians as having not been fulfilled
in the first coming, that they were rather postponed to the second. So that they
had already begun the process that you described.

Barth: I have never denied that if we have to explain texts, that criticism—
literary criticism—must have its place; and certainly if this dialogue should
take place, we would have to undertake very earnest common research. That is
for me not a question, certainly.

Petuchowski: I am grateful for this information; certainly I am glad to hear you say that. I must have misread those aspects of your writings that have come to my attention. I was under the impression that what matters to you is the fact of revelation, rather than the demonstration of the historical accuracy of the facts described.

Barth: Well, I cannot make such a separation because the fact of revelation, which is the really great thing for you and for me, is for both of us witnessed in these texts; and then—insofar as historical questions may arise—we have to take them seriously.

Pelikan: How many people left in the exodus and that sort of thing.

Barth: Yes.

Petuchowski: I am very grateful for the clarification.

Barth: I think it could be done. I do not know with what result. That is not the question. But my point is that we are not so separated by what you call my christological point that there is not a possibility for a real discussion. I should say no, on the contrary, there is even the necessity of having such a discussion.

Petuchowski: I am very gratified to hear that.

Pelikan: One of the implications of the question that Rabbi Petuchowski just raised, I think, is the question of the problem raised for Christian theology by the sheer continuation, or if you like, the durability of the community of Israel beyond the life and death of Jesus of Nazareth, and therefore the next question:

[Petuchowski:] And finally, speaking from a Christian rather than from a Jewish perspective, may not this be the true task of the divinely ordained function of Israel, as the shadow picture of the church, to provoke and compel the Christians in every generation into an *Auseinandersetzung*, a controversy, in which they unite themselves with and relate to such people both from Israel as from the heathen world, who—differently than the Christians as Professor Barth sees them—are seeking to get to the root of everything and to understand the existence of things by proceeding from themselves, and, with or without God, to arrive at a generally valid way of seeing things.

Barth: My answer to this set of your remarks is as follows: Jews should not understand themselves as abstractly representing the godless to the Christian. I do not like it, and you should not. Rather, we Christians have to learn from the Jews again and again the indelible election of Israel, indeed, as the contender against God [cf. Gen. 32:24–32]. Yes, of the godless, but as the contender against God, the man who gives God the glory among Gentiles. This is my concept of Judaism.

Petuchowski: Professor, this is a much more beautiful concept, and may I say, a more acceptable concept from my point of view than the associations one would get from the shadow-picture of the church. It looks like something more positive, as reformulated by you now.

Barth: Yes, but there is no contradiction. I mean the same thing as the shadow-picture. As you know, the shadows are always in what we call "the church."

11. On the Theological Understanding of the State of Israel

Pelikan: Bringing this now into the present situation, including the present political situation, Rabbi Petuchowski has asked a question which has, from a Christian point of view, been phrased also by Mr. Stringfellow, and I hope that the audience will bear with me as I develop the question of the implication of the establishment of the State of Israel as it has been put first by Dr. Petuchowski, speaking from the viewpoint of Jewish theology, and then by Mr. Stringfellow, speaking from the viewpoint of Christian thought. For surely, anyone who is concerned, as Professor Barth is, about the relation of Israel to Christianity, must also be concerned about what meaning, if any, there is in the undeniable empirical fact that the Jewish nation has a political form for the first time in almost two millennia. Beginning now with Rabbi Petuchowski's formulation of the question:

[Petuchowski:] One of the questions with which modern Jewish theology has yet to deal effectively is the creation of the State of Israel. In the destruction of the temple and the state in the year 70 CE, nineteenth-century Reformed Judaism had seen a clear sign of the divinely terminated political phase of Israel's temporal existence, and according to Reformed Judaism in the nineteenth century, the fulfillment of Israel's mission—now that this political phase, the possession of the land, was over—was now to lie in the Dispersion, in the Diaspora, and the relation between Judaism and the several nations within which it was dispersed. Secular Zionism (and so forth) was, in any case, not very much concerned with the religious implications of the return; meanwhile Orthodox Judaism was, at least at first, quite opposed to any human efforts at national restoration without the leadership of the Messiah sent by God. This latter position is still maintained within the State of Israel by the *Neturé Karta* group[36] in Jerusalem. On the other hand, there are signs that in some Orthodox Jewish circles, the creation of the State of Israel is given some messianic significance, even though the *complete* "fulfillment" is recognized to involve not only the rebuilding of the temple, but also the coming of the personal Messiah. Such an interim view is aided within Judaism by the availability of the concept in Hebrew[37] of *athhalta di-gaullah*, "the beginning of redemption."

Within Christianity, there are indications that some of the more fundamentalist Christian sects hail the establishment of the State of Israel as an inevitable step leading toward the speedy second coming of Christ. On the other hand, one realizes how—from the traditional Christian point of view, which sees the destruction of Jerusalem in 70 CE as a punishment for Israel's rejection of the Christ—there must be certain difficulties in coming to terms with the existence of the modern State of Israel. Likewise, mutatis mutandis, Reform Judaism is at present involved in the difficult task of reconciling the nineteenth-century ideology with twentieth-century reality. It would be of great interest to hear how you, sir, view the establishment of the State of Israel, particularly in the light of your seeing in Jesus the fulfillment of Old Testament prophecy, and of your description of the synagogue as existing on a "powerless continuation of Israelite history."[38]

[Pelikan:] And now the question is put with a different kind of piquancy by Mr. Stringfellow, from the viewpoint of a Christian believer:

---

36. *Neturé Karta* (Aramaic) means, literally, "Watchman of the City": an anti-Zionist, ultrareligious group of extremists who battle the secularism of the State of Israel. See the *Encyclopaedia Judaica*, vol. 12, *Min–O* (Jerusalem: Encyclopaedia Judaica, 1972), cols. 1002–3.
37. More accurate: Aramaic.
38. See n. 34 above.

[*Stringfellow:*] In terms of the relationship between the Israel of the Old Testament and the new Israel, which is Jesus Christ, of what significance is the establishment of the present State of Israel as a secular nation for the apologetic, evangelistic, and ecumenical tasks of the church of Christ, particularly in a pluralistic society, like the United States of America, in which there dwell many people of no specific religious belief, or of individualistic religious or pseudo-religious beliefs, alongside Christians of all sorts and denominations and Jews of several sects, under the overarching ethics of a society that disapproves of proselytizing or apologetics in the name of the Christian faith or of religion as disruptive of a cooperative spirit and mutual accommodation among the people, as hostile to the national unity and purpose and as threatening the survival of democracy in the nation? Specifically, what is the significance of Christians in American society clearly acquiescing to the Jews and atheists and agnostics' rejection of Jesus Christ?

Barth: Answering the question of Petuchowski, I shall consider the creation of the modern State of Israel in the context of the fulfillment of the Old Testament. A possible explanation is that it is another and new sign of the electing and providentially ruling grace and faithfulness of God to that seed of Abraham, a very visible sign, visible for every reader of the papers, the whole world, a sign that is not to be overlooked. After the horrors of Hitler's time, the reappearance of Israel, now as a nation in the political realm, even as a state, may well be called a miracle for all who have eyes to see this evidence [cf. Matt. 11:15], and a scandal for all those who have not eyes to see. Remember the answer, mentioned yesterday, given to Frederick the Great: "The proof for God's existence, your majesty, are the Jews."[39] And we could now add today, "your majesty, the State of Israel." The Jews have always owed their existence to the power of God alone and not to their own force or to the might of their history. And here we have another case of this kind of existence for Israel. God alone can help it to exist, and it seems that he will do so. Now, I do not know, Mr. Stringfellow, if that response given to our Jewish friend is also an answer to your question. You have asked your question in some other way, in the context of your whole outlook on the American scene, and perhaps it is not enough what I have said to him.

Stringfellow: I think that I am mainly concerned with the (I will say) practical impact of the vocation of the political state and the historic nation Israel upon a nation like the United States, within which there is a significant, partly secularized Jewish community—partly, that is, as I would understand it, having lost or renounced their vocation—in relation to the given tasks of the church to defend Jesus Christ, to defend the faith in and of Jesus Christ, to do the work of evangelism, and to be the church within the structure of this nation and within the structures and conflicts of all nations. It is only, therefore, about the impact of the existence of the old but now new nation of Israel upon the given tasks of the church that I still have a further question.

Barth: Maybe I cannot answer this question in your sense. I don't like to speak here for Americans. That's what Americans must tell to Americans and not something that a poor man coming from Switzerland can tell you.

39. See n. 14 above.

Pelikan: Mr. Stringfellow, I think, presses you to speak from within your own setting in a way that we can hear by the next question he has put to you:

12. Romans 13

[Stringfellow:] In the United States, the many and divided churches live in a society that constitutionally professes the freedom of public worship and the public practice of religion in a formal sense. That is, attendance at services, public preaching, representation of the religious and ecclesiastical authorities and institutions in public life, and the like. It increasingly appears, however, that the use of that freedom—the only use that is socially approved, at least—is confined to either the mere formalities of religious observance and the preservation of some religious causes, or the use of religion to rationalize, to serve, or to sanctify the national self-interest—the use of religion and of jargon and images of religion for the preservation and perhaps the aggrandizement of the nation. Consequently, the churches do not commonly exercise a vitally critical attitude toward politics, public policy, or the nation's actual life and culture.

Pelikan: Now, with this observation as a preface, Mr. Stringfellow asks you, sir,

[Stringfellow:] to comment upon how the church and the churches can maintain the freedom of the gospel to proclaim the gospel in such a society in which the churches seem to be constantly tempted to forswear the gospel in order to protect our freedom as external institutions in society. What bearing do the words of St. Paul in the thirteenth chapter of Romans [13:1–7] have upon churches in such a position within such a society? If it seems appropriate to you, sir, would you compare the relationship of the churches and the state in the United States and in, for example, the German Democratic Republic of East Germany with respect to the freedom that the state practically—not just on paper, but in fact—affords to the churches and the freedom that churches in fact have to proclaim and to represent the gospel, that freedom that the gospel assures to the churches? (This question specifically arises out of your correspondence with those East German pastors who sought your counsel.)[40]

Barth: I am troubled. What I have read and heard are statements with which I am in sympathy. I like to hear you speak as you do, but statements rather than answers I could only whisper to you. But why only whisper? Because your concern is over this country, America, and I have, so to say, sworn not to enter criticisms of the American scene into the record: I cannot enter America in order to criticize you.

Perhaps I could answer one very special point. You have asked what bearing Romans 13 has upon churches in such a position in such a society. Romans 13 is a very important and very difficult and even disturbing chapter in the Bible. Romans 13 has played a great role in Germany till today, and not only for the Lutherans. Paul speaks of the powers that be, and he means the state, and he speaks of the Christian, who should be subject to these powers [Rom 13:1]. But if I understand this chapter rightly, the most important term in it, "being

---

40. K. Barth, "Brief an einen Pfarrer in der Deutschen Demokratischen Republik (1958)," *O.Br. 1945–1968,* 401–39; ET: K. Barth and J. Hamel, *How to Serve God in a Marxist Land* (New York: Association Press, 1959).

subject," must be understood in a more concrete way than it has been. Being subject—the Greek word ὑποτάσσεσθαι [*hypotassesthai*] does not mean only that "you have to obey: here is the power, we are under it, and let us submit to it." But the term ὑποτάσσεσθαι includes the meaning: τάξις [*taxis*]. And τάξις is an order and ὑποτάσσεσθαι means, You have to put yourself within the rule of this order. And what does it mean then? In other places, speaking also of the political orders, the New Testament says you have to pray for those who are in power. Paul does not say it; but it is said in other places, "Pray for them" [cf. 1 Tim 2:1–2]. Well, if we have to pray for those who are in power—in the old time for the empires and kings and so in the New Testament and maybe [today for] the president and so on—well, if we pray for them, then we make ourselves responsible for them. Romans 13 cannot be explained without this notion of responsibility. The Christian has to bear the task of the state, and that is what is lacking within many Christian circles; we are only spectators of political life. We look on as things happen and take them as they come, but we should feel ourselves asked to do our part. That is one question for us Christians: "Are we willing and able to take upon us our whole responsibility and not leave it to others to manage political affairs?"

Pelikan: You say that submission as such is not really all that this chapter imposes upon us, but in addition it is an active, essential responsibility?

Barth: Yes, yes. Because it is submission to an order; and if we submit to an order, we go within the realm of this order: we take our place, and as human beings we become responsible for what is done in this order.

Stringfellow: Just a very concrete question in reference to your point, as I understand it, that to be subject to the civil authority does not mean merely an automatic obedience, but a variety of actions.

Barth: Yes, because even the term "obedience" reminds us that there is no true obedience where there is not free obedience. Not only an outward obedience, but also an inner obedience that is a free act.

Stringfellow: My question is, then, "When Pontius Pilate consigns Jesus Christ to be crucified, this is an expression on the part of Jesus Christ of his subjection to civil authority. Is that the case?"

Barth: Yes. Certainly, certainly. He does it out of his own freedom. He subjects himself.

Pelikan: There is no power given Pilate, except that it be from above [cf. John 19:11]?

Stringfellow: Our freedom riders must remember this.

13. Principalities and Powers

Pelikan: Mr. Stringfellow's final question:

[Stringfellow:] It appears to be widely believed, both within and, for that matter, outside the churches of the United States, that the history of redemption is encompassed merely by the saga of relationships in history between God and man. At the same time, at least in American Protestantism, it is commonplace to distinguish the biblical identification and discussion of the angelic powers present in the world as nothing more than archaic imagery. What there is of Protestant moral theology in America almost utterly ignores the attempt

to account for, explicate, and relate one's self to the principalities and powers. Yet empirically, more and more, the principalities and powers seem to have an aggressive and indeed possessive ascendancy in American life, including, alas, the life of the American churches. Who are these principalities and powers? What is their significance in the creation and in the fall? What significance do they have with respect to merely human sin? What is their relation to the claim that Christ is the Lord of history? What is the relation of the power and presence of death in history to the principalities and powers? And therefore, practically speaking, what freedom does a Christian have from the dominion of all of these principalities and powers?

Barth: Well, that is a very large question. You are right to emphasize that in the New Testament there is not only speech about personal sin and personal salvation, but also about the powers that are ruling the world, and of salvation as our liberation from the kingdom or empire of these powers. You are right: the New Testament speaks very seriously of these things. Now, your question—I must be short, but I will try to say something. You ask me, "Who are the principalities and powers" today in our world? I will mention only some of them. Everywhere that an ideology is ruling, there is such a power: a Communist or anti-Communist ideology; money is such a power. No need to give a description. Sport is such a power. Traditions of all kinds are such angelic powers. Fashion for men and women is also a power. What we call religion, in all kinds of expression, is also a world of powers. Angelic powers, the thing unconscious within us, that is a real power. But also what we call reason is such a power. And let us not forget sex. Now you ask me what is their significance in the creation and in the fall? What significance do they have for human sin? I think that all these powers represent certain human possibilities that are given in the very nature of man, as he is, and are given as a part, as an appearance, of God's good creation in man. None of these things is bad, necessarily; but now we have to deal with the man who has separated himself from God and from his neighbor. In doing so, he becomes and is alienated also from himself. He sees his natural possibilities, his powers, become isolated over against him; and instead of being the Lord of them, man becomes their servant. Yes, he must now obey himself; and work and all his powers are kings and princes and emperors and führers of all kinds. We pray, "Thy kingdom come" [Matt. 6:10], and the kingdom is Jesus Christ because in him, as the Lord, man as a sinning man is replaced by a new man; what binds him in these powers is driven away, and in the coming of the kingdom he becomes free over against these powers. In Christ's death, man as sinner, man as alienated from himself, man as prey to death, is done in, finished. In [Christ's] resurrection, man has appeared in the flesh as man, as God's new creature, as the beginning of "a new heaven and a new earth" [cf. 2 Pet. 3:13; Rev. 21:1], which will be universally and definitely revealed and vindicated in the last Parousia of the Lord. Now you ask me, What practical freedom does the Christian have from the dominion of these powers? His freedom lies in Jesus Christ, in his death and in his resurrection. But you ask me what practical freedom we have? In him and through him we have the freedom to look back to his first coming and to look forward to his last coming, and to look upon him as present and as he will come. That is freedom. That is life, the life of the children of God within the realm of his presence.

Looking to him means to be concrete with that Spirit, that one true Spirit, which is potent and mighty. In order to stand, to fight these gods, we need his power.

14. Theology of Freedom

Pelikan: Professor Barth, colleagues, and ladies and gentlemen, after so eloquent and moving a proclamation and demonstration in the Spirit and the Power, it would, I am sure, be undue magnification of the office of moderator were I to do any more than the following:

First of all, to express the thanks of all of you—of those who have come from New England, New York, Ohio, Wisconsin, Texas, and California; from Judaism, Roman Catholicism, and Protestantism—for having the opportunity to speak with and to hear Professor Barth; above all to express to Professor Barth the accumulated debt we have owed him for so many years and on behalf of the university, to articulate our gratitude that his analysis of theological science has at the same time enriched our lives, for that is the motto of this University, "Crescat Scientia, Vita Excolatur [Let knowledge grow from more to more and so be human life enriched]."

Barth: I would like to make some concluding remarks: First of all, to say "thank you": thank you to the faculty of the Divinity School in Chicago for your invitation, your kind invitation to come here to give these lectures, and a special thanks to the indefatigable dean of this faculty. Never in my life have I spoken before such a big audience as here in Chicago. It was an event in my life. I would thank you especially for the kind attention with which you have followed the lectures and discussions here.

Now, I have been here in Chicago for nearly three weeks, and I have met many kinds of American people: I had a series of good evening meetings with Christians, Jews, also atheists—there are some in Chicago—with Protestants, and also an evening with some Roman Catholic scholars. I have seen The Second City, as you may have noticed in *Time Magazine*.[41] But I have also listened to a very beautiful performance of Handel's *Messiah* here in this chapel, which has shown me the high standard of musical art in Chicago. And on these evenings I have met other members of this panel, and I have enjoyed discussions with all of them. I do not think that in Switzerland I could have had an opportunity to engage in a discussion with liberals, Jews, and even Roman Catholic theologians together. That was something very new for me. It was an experience that I enjoyed having.

Now a concluding word: If I myself were an American citizen and a Christian and a theologian, then I would try to elaborate a theology of freedom—a theology of freedom from, let us say, from any inferiority complex over against good old Europe, from whence you all came, or your fathers. You do not need to have such an inferiority complex. That is what I have learned these weeks. You may also have freedom from a superiority complex, let us say, over against Asia and Africa. That's a complex without reason. Then I may add, your theology should also be marked by freedom from fear of Communism, Russia, inevitable

---

41. "Second City" is a theater group in Chicago that was famous for its critical statements on political themes in free improvisation on stage. There is a photo of Barth with the members of this group in *Time*, April 20, 1962, 48.

nuclear warfare, and generally speaking, from all the aforementioned principalities and powers. The freedom for which you would stand would be the freedom for—I like to say a single word—humanity. Being an American theologian, I would then look at the Statue of Liberty in the New York Harbor. I have not seen that lady, except in pictures. Next week I shall see her in person. That lady needs a little or, perhaps, a good bit of demythologization. Nevertheless, maybe she may also be seen and interpreted and understood as a symbol of a true theology, not of liberty, but of freedom. Well, it would be necessarily a theology of freedom. Of that freedom to which the Son frees us [cf. John 8:36], and which as his gift, is the one real human freedom.

My last question for this evening is this: Will such a specific American theology one day arise? I hope so.

26. Press Conference in New York
1962

In the middle of Barth's seven-week trip to the USA, at the beginning of May 1962, his English lectures—the first five from his course in Basel the previous winter titled "Introduction to Evangelical Theology"—were now behind him, and their repetition at Princeton Theological Seminary was imminent. In the offices of the publisher Holt, Rinehart, and Winston in New York, who published the English version the following year, Karl Barth met with the press on May 1, 1962, at 11:15 a.m. The moderator was A. Cohen, the director of the religious department of the publisher. Daniel Poling, who raised questions toward the end of the encounter, was the publisher of the journal The Christian Herald. *After returning home from his trip, Barth described something that on the journey appeared to him to be "fantastic": the "pertinent and sometimes impertinent curiosity and descriptive power of the American reporter" [see* Biography, *458].*

The English text of the press conference is located in the Karl Barth Archives in Basel, in typewritten and duplicated form, titled "Rough Transcript of the Press Conference with Professor Karl Barth, May 1." It is possible that this text is not a verbatim account of the press conference but rather a summary based on the electronic recording of the session or on someone's notes. The text below is based on excerpts from the report of the press conference that appeared on the front page of the New York Herald Tribune *on May 2, 1962, with the title "Karl Barth—a Study of Understanding." The content below focuses upon the parts of the article that contain statements made by Barth during the press conference.*

Cohen: Professor Barth has come to the United States for the first time in his life. He is the guest of honor of the Princeton Theological Seminary, at their 150th Anniversary. He is accompanied at the meeting here today by "his own theological faculty," his two sons, Markus, professor at the University of Chicago Divinity School, New Testament; and Christoph, Old Testament, who has come from Indonesia for this reunion with his father. Professor Karl Barth's assistant during several decades, Miss von Kirschbaum, is also in the audience.

The meeting today also serves to inaugurate officially Holt, Rinehart and Winston's new religious department. Karl Barth's Princeton lectures, expanded and revised, will be the department's first book on a promising new list. Its title, *Evangelical Theology: An Introduction,* is to be published in January.

Question: What is your attitude on nuclear testing?[1]

Barth: I do not like nuclear testing at all; not if the Russians do it, and not if the West practices it.

Question: What are your feelings on the church, the synagogue, and the State of Israel?

Barth: (In reply, Professor Barth told an anecdote of the great Prussian king, Frederick II, who was known to have been an atheist and who allegedly said, when asked whether there was any living proof of God's existence, "Yes, there is one: namely, the Jews.")[2] And now we have the State of Israel, which is an affirmation of this proof.

Question: What is your reaction to Reinhold Niebuhr's criticism of your writings as "irrelevant to American theology"? Further, as "infinitely imaginative and irresponsible"?[3]

Barth: It would be a pity if it were so. I don't think I teach irresponsibility. What I try to teach is responsibility, toward God simply.

Question: You have been called the greatest theologian of the twentieth century. How do you feel about this statement?

Barth: My reaction? I do not like it at all. Who will be the judge? I know my name has now become quite famous, particularly, it seems, in America. But attention passes on to another object very quickly here. Who will speak of me next month, and in a year, who knows? I have also been called a giant. Just look at me; I am only a simple, normal human being.

Question: What is your opinion of the position of religion behind the Iron Curtain?

Barth: The position of Christians behind the Iron Curtain is in some ways more difficult than ours; in some ways it is also easier. Where there is so much oppression, the great issues of Christianity become clearer, and I have heard some of my theological friends on the other side of the Curtain express the view that they would not like to exchange their lot for a better life in the free West because "now we know what it means to be a Christian. . . ."

Question: What are your thoughts on Christianity in an affluent society, as opposed to behind the Iron Curtain?

Barth: Here, where we can speak freely, it is an easy thing to have (Christianity). But Christianity is not an easy thing, since Christ has been nailed to the cross. Here we are not challenged enough to become martyrs.

Question: Have you found your teachings to be of value to children?

Barth: I cannot judge the relevance of my teachings respecting children's education. Ask the teachers who have read my writings. It is for them to decide what use they can make of my books in teaching children. I cannot be my own judge.

Question: What is your opinion of the Eichmann Trial?[4]

Die UNO-Studie: Kernwaffen (Vollständiger Bericht des Generalsekretärs der Vereinten Nationen) (Munich: Beck, 1982).

2. See above, chap. 25, n. 14.

3. This statement by Niebuhr is cited in the article about Barth titled "Witness to an Ancient Truth," in *Time* 89, no. 16 (April 20, 1962). See above, chap. 22, and especially its introduction.

4. The trial of Adolf Eichmann, the organizer of the National Socialist annihilation of the Jews, took place in the second half of 1961 in Jerusalem, and it ended on December 15, 1961, with his death sentence. On March 22, 1962, the trying of his appeal commenced. This review confirmed his death sentence on May 29, 1962, and he was executed on May 31, 1962.

Barth: I feel it is a good thing that it all came out into the open, that Hitler's atrocities were made known to the world. It would be a fact of relevance for the whole world if it were decided in Israel that the sentence will not be carried out.

Question: What is your attitude on the Vatican Ecumenical Council?[5]

Barth: I am not the pope. Nobody knows exactly what he has in mind. There are different opinions. It is always good if Christians meet. Why should they not do so? But the outcome—I am not a prophet. I believe that even the most important Catholic thinkers do not know something exact about this matter. So I am cautious. There is no clear goal. Is the issue a universal society of churches, or a kind of new reformation of the Roman Catholic Church, or is it only on certain liturgical teachings, or whether there will be a new dogma perhaps? All things are possible.

Question: What would you like to see?

Barth: If I were the pope, I would try to give a proclamation for all churches and would help to give the people a simple truth, a message, a gospel. But the pope has not asked me about my opinion.

Question: What problems have Catholics raised in their conversations with you?

Barth: I have many Roman Catholic friends, and they tell me that even they do not know more about this.[6] Perhaps somebody here is Catholic and can enlighten us.

Question: To come back to an earlier question, would you further discuss Christianity in an affluent society? Did I understand you right? Were you saying that Christians behind the Iron Curtain are better Christians than we are here?

Barth: I did not say better. Better—that is a judgment that cannot be made.

Question: What is your stand on church and state?

Barth: I think that they should be separate. Especially for the church, it is better not to be involved in political arrangements. My idea is a free church within a free state.

Question: Will you see the president?

Barth: I don't think he needs to listen to me.[7]

Question: In view of the fact that you insist upon the relation of dogmatics and ethics, how could you assume a position of apparent neutrality toward the East-West conflict, in which ethical questions are certainly involved?

Barth: Theology speaks of the grace of God. If you take this meaning seriously, it means gratitude. Gratitude means obedience. Obedience means the same for every man in his own country. Neutrality—I have never spoken of neutrality, but I have spoken of the need to understand one another better than

5. In the *Motu proprio* of Pope John XXIII, *"Concilium"* of February 2, 1962, the beginning of the Second Vatican Council was established as October 11, 1962.

6. There appears to be a misunderstanding here. Barth is discussing the fact that he does not know which questions are, in fact, going to be dealt with at the [Vatican] Council, whereas the point of the question was what Catholics were saying about what they would like to have happen.

7. On the evening of May 7, 1962, Barth met in the home of Mr. Lefever with a group of men from President John F. Kennedy's staff. The primary conversation partners were A. Schlesinger and G. Bundy. The evening's conversation themes included East-West relationships (anti-Communism), with a particular focus upon the role of the Federal Republic of Germany (rearmament). The conversation was lively and engaging. (Based upon Markus Barth's written communication by letter to the editor.)

we do now. We should not think in terms of systems, as we do now, but we should think in human terms. Behind the Iron Curtain, there are human beings, not Russian automatons. If I look upon the situation of today, it seems to me that, if we had more people who refuse to think in terms of systems, but instead in terms of humanity, an approach to what is commonly called peace could be made on a broad basis. I have not joined in the general chorus. It seems to me that, if a whole population cries out, my little voice is not needed.

Question: What about Niebuhr's criticism of your silence in the face of the Hungarian suppression and uprising in 1956?[8]

Barth: I was silent because there was such an uproar in the whole world. I don't need to join in this general uproar. I have good friends in Hungary, also among those who have joined in the revolution. What could I do for them? Certainly nothing by crying out. But if I have been silent, I have been able to free two of my friends from prison.[9] The Hungarian authorities listened to me, just because I had not cried out against them. In my opinion, it was more important that I could help save two lives than join in the general outcry.

Question: Niebuhr criticized your not speaking out against Communism (in Hungary), but you took a stand against Hitlerism. Could you explain?

Barth: That was another case. I was directly involved. I was up against the Nazis. I lived in Germany and in Switzerland. Hitler was an adversary to fight. I could help by fighting, and I fought. It was a practical issue where I had to take my stand, and I did. . . . In the case of the Eastern world, the Communist world as such, crying does not help. Obedience does not mean that it has no application to a system. Obedience is to God, and applied to men, it means How can I help somebody?

Question: What about your attitude toward America? Is it true that you have said that you approve of American history, but not of our way of life?

Barth: It is not true. The American way of life is a human way of life.

Question: What are your impressions of America?

Barth: This is my first visit. I have been here for only three weeks. I have made up my mind, when I came here: "I will be silent. I will open my eyes and my ears. I will have no prejudices, no preformed ideas. I will be silent." I have my impressions. I don't think it is necessary to explain them to you. They are not yet ripe. Perhaps they will never be. This country is so vast, a whole world. How can I, in six or seven weeks, say something certain about America?

Cohen: [Do] you mean you will not return to Europe and write a book about us?

Question: Is music a part of your theology, or is it a matter apart?

---

8. Reinhold Niebuhr, "Why Is Barth Silent on Hungary?," in *Christian Century* 74 (1957): 108–10, 236, 303–4, 453–55.

9. On March 11, 1957, Dr. Marcel Pradervand, General Secretary of the World Alliance of Reformed Churches in Geneva, sent a telegram signed by both of them to the president of the Hungary State Office for Church Affairs in Budapest, J. Horvath: "Deeply concerned about the arrest and confinement of Reformed pastors and urgently request the government to practice forbearance. Stop. Pradervand will telephone you on March 12" (copy in the Karl Barth Archives). On March 16, 1957, Barth, at his vacation house in Brione near Locarno, received the following telegraphed reply: "In response to your telegram I am informing you of the following: As a result of my mediation Prof. Barnabas Nagy and Pastor Sándor Jóo will rejoin their families within the next twenty-four hours. With my highest regards, Janos Horvath, President of the State Office for Church Affairs" (the original was written in Hungarian).

Barth: I have written about Mozart,[10] and if you read my book, you will have an answer. Mozart's music, for me, is a kind of parable of the kingdom, but that is not a dogma. I am less dogmatic than you think.

Question: Despite Niebuhr's view that your teachings are bad for America, do you have a special message for America?

Barth: Generally speaking, the problem is the same everywhere. We have forgotten the simplest and most important thing. Christianity has become an affair of ideology or of religion. Christianity is no religion. We no longer listen to a message from God. That should be learned here and everywhere. If we did, we would be more able and willing to speak out about the affairs of the world's politics. Now we lack the courage to say what should be said.

(Professor Barth then asked the chairman's permission to "ask a question."): I am interested in prisons. Sometimes I preach to prisoners.[11] I therefore asked for permission to visit an American prison. I will not give you its name. It was called a "cell-house." But they were not even cells; they were cages. Tiny cages for two human beings, without a view, without a bath, without floor space. It was a terrible shock for me to see these conditions. Prisons in Switzerland are a paradise compared to this. These small cages were, for me, the sight of Dante's *Inferno* on Earth. Now my question: I was informed that the price of a trip to the moon and return, including a stay of eight to ten days up there, would be about 13 billion dollars. The cost of building a prison is approximately $10,000 per inmate. For the cost of one such moon shot, a prison could be build to encompass about twice the entire American population. Why not spend a fraction of the moon shot's cost on humane prisons? Why are the churches silent? Roman Catholics, the Protestants, and the synagogue, all should raise their voices against this condition. This is in contradiction to the wonderful message on your Statue of Liberty. We dare not condemn the Russians for their inhumanity as long as such conditions prevail in the West.

Daniel Poling: The prison you saw is an exception. We have better prisons everywhere in the country, also around New York. What you saw is not typical.

Question: To return to your message to America . . .

Barth: I have given the same lectures here in America as I did in Basel. There is nothing special to add for Americans. Except the prisons.

Question: How many more books do you intend to write?

Barth: I am no prophet. At present, the pressure of teaching is very great. When it relaxes, and if I can carry out my plans, I would want to write at least two more volumes of my *Dogmatik*. I hope I have given no offense.

New York Herald Tribune

Karl Barth, the eminent Swiss theologian, refused yesterday to be drawn into the Cold War. Christian practice, he indicated, does not require such an

---

10. K. Barth, *Wolfgang Amadeus Mozart: 1756/1956* (Zollikon: Evangelischer Verlag, 1956), 10th ed. (Zurich: Theologischer Verlag, 1978).

11. With a few exceptions, Barth's sermons at the prison in Basel during the years 1954–1964 first appeared in two collections: *Den Gefangenen Befreiung: Predigten aus den Jahren 1954–59* (Zollikon: Evangelischer Verlag, 1959) [ET: *Deliverance to the Captives*, trans. Marguerite Wieser (New York: Harper & Row, 1961)]; *Rufe mich an! Neue Predigten aus der Strafanstalt Basel* (Zurich: EVZ-Verlag, 1965). Both collections are found in *Predigten 1954–1967* (Zurich: TVZ, 1977).

involvement. Long accused of being a neutralist, or even soft on Communism, Dr. Barth said he had never spoken of neutrality, "but of the need to understand one another better than we do now."

"What is needed at present," he continued, "is not to think in terms of Systems—capitalism, democracy, Communism—but in human terms. In Moscow, there are human beings, not automatons. As I look at the scene today," he said, "if we had more people who refused to think in terms of systems, . . . then an approach to what is commonly called peace could be made on a broad basis. That is why I refuse to join in a blanket condemnation of the East. Condemnation will not help. There should be more comprehension. . . . The word of God is helping people."

Now on his first visit to the United States, Dr. Barth said he had asked to visit one of our prisons, as he regularly does in his home city of Basel. What he saw here, he said, "was a sight out of Dante's hell. Human beings who had been sentenced, and some not yet sentenced, were kept not in cells," he said, "but in cages—small for two persons, behind bars, utterly without privacy." He declined to name the prison but said it was a major one. "Why are the churches silent?" he asked. "The churches, all of them, should be crying out against such things."

Asked for his impression of the United States, Dr. Barth said, "I see the advantage of your way of life, but there are others. I will keep an open mind, look, hear, listen, and learn."

Dr. Barth, who was among the first of the Protestant theologians to defy Adolf Hitler in 1933, was asked at a press conference how he reconciled that defiance with his silence on the Soviet suppression of the Hungarian people's revolt in 1956. "I did not join in the general outcry on Hungary," he replied. "With so many shouting, my poor voice was not needed. But I did think about what I could do for the Hungarian people. By remaining silent at that time I was later able to help two people to get out of a Hungarian prison. Two people free is better than a condemnation."

27. Conversation in Princeton I
1962

During his trip to America, Barth also visited Princeton in early May of 1962. On the occasion of the 150th anniversary of the founding of Princeton Theological Seminary, he repeated the lectures he had given in Chicago, "Introduction to Evangelical Theology," now as the Warfield Lectures. On May 2, 1962, he also responded to questions from students. The text below is reproduced from the tape recording made of that conversation in Princeton.

Moderator: (I would like) to welcome the Reverend Dr. Karl Barth.

Barth: Now, ladies and gentlemen, I thank you for this warm reception. I have been asked to sit here among you in order to give some answers, if I can, to your questions; to hear you; to listen; to learn what are your opinions. And now, please do what you can and will do. As an introductory remark, I can only say what I always say when I'm at home in Basel together with new students of mine. I tell them, "You may speak quite freely, quite openly; I'm not a man to be feared." In a long life I have learned to accept even blows if it's necessary to do so. And you may speak as you like, ask me questions, tell me perhaps also your criticism. Perhaps you have something to [re]act to what you have heard or read from me. Do so, and now I'm listening and prepared. Everybody may open his mind so that we do not lose more time.

Moderator: Okay, thank you. We will entertain questions. The questions will be repeated by myself after they have been given, and then Dr. Barth will give the answers.

1. God's Revelation and Hiddenness

Question 1: My question may be a little bit long to repeat it or to be repeated, but I hope it will be clear. In the light of this I will try to shorten it: God reveals himself in the gospel. The gospel is the good news of his Son and of the coming of his Son, Jesus Christ, through God the Father. This is the revelation of God without reserve. There was no reserve in the true revelation of God. Just so, however, his glory remains undiminished, his counsel inscrutable, his mystery high above us, not because he withholds them partially or wholly from us, but because his glory, counsel, and mystery are nothing other than his disposition of himself for our benefit, to the uttermost depths of our weakness and misery, in Jesus Christ and him crucified. . . .

Moderator: I wish I could repeat the question!

198

Barth: I ask you only to tell me exactly the point of the question.

Student: The point of the question is that the revelation of God in Jesus Christ is without reserve.

Barth: Certainly, yes, there is no reserve. But if God reveals himself, well, he remains God. And as God he is high above our intellect, our comprehensional ideas, and so on. And so in revealing himself as God, he remains, and even he becomes a new mystery for us. Look, that's the point in the question of revelation. In his revelation God shows himself as the God who over against all men is and remains a hidden God. But as such he reveals himself so that we have to deal with him as he is in his majesty and also in his condescension toward us. Is that enough for you, or would you like to hear some more comments upon . . .

Student: Well, if I could be free to do so, yes. I was trying to say that in giving us unreservedly his Son, he indeed is and becomes our Lord.

Barth: Yes.

Student: And as such is and becomes mysterious, high above us, and glorious. But he's not hidden from us any longer. He was once hidden from us.

Barth: He is no more an alien for us. We know him now. He became even our neighbor, but as the one he is who he is—as God. And in so far as Lord, well, he remains also high above us.

Moderator: Could we have another question?

Question 2: Sir, in his young years Dietrich Bonhoeffer wrote *Akt und Sein*,[1] and it seems to me that in *Akt und Sein* he offered epistemologists a very excellent way to understand the very special idea of transcendence, which he thought influenced a great deal of your theology and certainly did of his. Many years later he said, "Transcendence of God has nothing to do with epistemology."[2] I wonder, Was he correct in the first case, in the second case, or in neither case?

Barth: I do not remember the second stage that you mentioned, what was meant by denying the transcendence of God. Look, I also do not like these terms: neither immanence nor transcendence—all such philosophical terms. I can't remember that Bonhoeffer did completely leave behind himself his earlier standpoint. Did he really?

Student: This statement was reproduced for us in a recent summary of Bonhoeffer during his prison years.

Barth: Is there any Bonhoeffer specialist in this assembly? Do you think of his last book?

Student: I had the misfortune to come across this at secondhand in somebody else's report upon it.

Barth: As a quote?

Question 3: Dr. Barth, a number of years ago, in your book on the resurrection of the dead, you wrote that exactly in the place of that which makes me a man—a human soul—is set that which makes God [to be] God.[3] This was speaking of resurrected man. And my question to yourself would be: First,

---

1. D. Bonhoeffer, *Akt un Sein: Transzendentalphilosophie und Ontologie in der systematischen Theologie* (Gütersloh: Bertelsmann, 1931), 2nd ed., ThB 5 (Munich: Kaiser, 1956) [ET: *Act and Being: Transcendental Philosophy and Ontology in Systematic Theology*, trans. M. Rumscheidt (Minneapolis: Fortress, 1996)].

2. See D. Bonhoeffer, *Widerstand und Ergebung: Briefe und Aufzeichnungen aus der Haft*, ed. E. Bethge (Munich: Kaiser, 1951), 141 [ET: *Letters and Papers from Prison*, ed. E. Bethge (London: SCM, 1967), 155].

3. K. Barth, *Die Auferstehung der Toten: Eine akademische Vorlesung über 1. Kor. 15* (Munich: Kaiser, 1924), 4th ed. (Zollikon-Zurich: Evangelischer Verlag, 1953), 118: "It is exactly at the place of that

whether you would still hold this view and, second, whether this would not make resurrected humanity no real humanity at all? A radical discontinuity but no continuity.

Barth: Another question that is difficult for me to answer because it is so long ago [that] I have written this book. And I remember that there are some sentences which I can no longer uphold. Will you kindly repeat this particular phrase? I will look what I can make out of it.

Student: "Exactly in the place of that which makes me a man—a human soul—is set that which makes God God."

Barth: Can you tell me what I may have meant? I can only say it sounds very strange to me. I should also have the German original before me. Often in the translation there are mistakes. But look, at that time I was strongly influenced, always influenced, by Platonic philosophy. And as in the *Römerbrief,*[4] so also in this book on resurrection, there are traces of Plato. And I stopped being a Platonist later on. Maybe also this little sinister-looking phrase may have its ground in this connection.

Question: Were you speaking in the context of *imago Dei* at that point in the book?

Barth: In this particular phrase? I don't think so, no, no.

2. The Understanding of Analogy and of the Knowledge of God

Question 4: Dr. Barth, in your volume in the *Dogmatics* on the "Doctrine of God," in your denial of natural theology, can you honestly deny any *analogia entis*? But later in the same volume you introduced the idea of *analogia entis* when you discussed the speech of God and the human speech about God.[5] So I must admit that my question is Will you explain fully to us the modified use of *analogia entis* in the context of grace, which you use later?

Barth: Yes. Exactly speaking, it is true that in the first volume of *Church Dogmatics* I said something very nasty about *analogia entis*. I said it was the invention of the antichrist.[6] Later I began to see that the notion of analogy cannot totally be suppressed in theology. At first I didn't speak of *analogia entis*. I spoke of *analogia relationis*[7] and then in a more biblical way of the analogy of faith.[8] Then some of my critics said, "Well, after all, an *analogia relationis* is also some kind of *analogia entis*."[9] And I couldn't deny it completely. I said: Well, after all,

---

which makes me a man—a human soul—is set that which makes God God." [ET: *The Resurrection of the Dead*, trans. H. J. Stenning (London: Hodder & Stoughton, 1933).]

4. K. Barth, *Der Römerbrief*, 3rd ed. (Munich: Kaiser, 1923). In the foreword Barth speaks of the influence of Plato on him.

5. In *CD* II/1:75–85 [*KD* 82–93], Barth rejects the *analogia entis* in the context of his repudiation of "natural theology." In *CD* II/1:225–43 [*KD* 254–75] he makes positive mention of the concept of analogy in the framework of the question of the human knowledge of God, but he still retains his rejection of *analogia entis*.

6. *CD* I/1:xiii [*KD* viii].

7. *CD* III/2:220–22, 326 [*KD* 262–64, 390–91].

8. According to Rom. 12:6; *CD* I/1: 243–44, 437 [*KD* 257–58, 459–60].

9. See H. U. von Balthasar, *Karl Barth: Darstellung und Deutung seiner Theologie* (Cologne: Hegner, 1951), 177–81. See also the formulation by G. Söhngen in the title of his essay, "Analogia entis in analogia fidei," in K. Barth, *Antwort: Karl Barth zum siebzigsten Geburtstag am 10. Mai 1956* (Zollikon-Zurich: Evangelischer Verlag, 1956), 226–27.

if *analogia entis* is interpreted as *analogia relationis* or analogy of faith, well, then I will no longer say nasty things about *analogia entis*. But I understand it in *this way*. So I have not changed my mind. My criticism over against *analogia entis* was that—as Thomas has understood it[10]—it was spoken of a common ground between God and man, and the ground was found in the notion of "being." God is. Man is also. Insofar as there is an analogy of God and man, and so on. And against that notion I had to fight. But if analogy is understood as analogy between two marks or two points in the doings of God and the doings of man, then it is acceptable, and I think it is necessary to speak of it. For example, if we speak of God's grace, of God's behavior as a graceful God, and if we then think of man as the partner in the covenant over against God and speak of man, who is destined to be thankful to God, and if we then translate these two terms "grace of God" and "thankfulness of man" into Greek, then we see χάρις [*charis*] on the one side and εὐχαριστία [*eucharistia*] on man's side. Here you have an example of *analogia relationis*, you see, between these two behaviors of God and man. Well, if now somebody will say, "But in being graceful and in being thankful God and man *are*, and so the notion of 'being' reenters the scene," I will not resist. But the point is that the relation between God and man is a question of common history between God and man—something that happens from God's side and then should also happen from man's side. That's the point, and not a simple "being-God" and "being-man." Do you understand? Do you see the point?

Question: Yes, sir. Are you saying—and I thought I may have understood you as saying—that this *analogia* is created by the act of God's grace?

Barth: Good so! Yes, yes, good so!

Question 5: Dr. Barth, in your volume on the "Knowledge of God," you state that the one who knows is similar to that which he knows, that he is one with what is known, that he is becoming like that which he knows.[11] I would like to know from what philosophical source you have drawn these conclusions.

Barth: I don't think that it is an introitus from any philosophical sources. You have said—and you are right—you have said, "A man in knowing God comes into a relation with God." Certainly—if knowledge is understood as the Bible understands it. *Gnōsis* in the New Testament means certainly a real connection between God and man, a connection that is grounded in God's doing, which is not to be re-separated from God's revealing himself. As I say now in the lectures, "God works, and in working God also speaks."[12] Well, and if he does so and if he *is*, [and if] what he works and does is apprehended from human side, then a real connection exists between God and man. Is that your question? I never thought of any philosophy in this relation.

Student: It was pointed out in our study of this section that there were strong Platonic and Kantian overtones to the knower being similar to that which is known—becoming one with what is known.

10. Barth debates the concept of analogy of Thomas Aquinas in *CD* I/1:41, 239, 437 [*KD* 40, 252–53, 459–60].

11. *CD* I/1:189–90 [*KD* 211–12].

12. K. Barth, *Einführung in die evangelische Theologie* (Zurich: Evangelischer Verlag, 1962), 27 [ET: *Evangelical Theology: An Introduction* (New York: Holt, Rinehart & Winston, 1963), 19].

Barth: Not becoming *one*, which would be saying too much, but being connected with, entering into a relation with him. Man doesn't become God in knowing God, but he becomes acquainted with him, and in becoming obedient and in becoming thankful to him, he enters into this relation of God's grace, which is also his grace of making himself known, and then again, there is a history that happens between these two, and so there is a bond between them. You see? A bond is enough. You don't need identity or something like that. That would be philosophy and a bad philosophy.

Question 6: Dr. Barth, if it would not be unfair to ask you another question about something you wrote some time ago, I would like to ask you a question about your *Römerbrief* similar to the one that was asked about your book on the resurrection. When I studied your *Römerbrief*, it struck me that a number of things would fall into place, would fall into a coherent pattern and be intelligible, if what you said about Christ being "my existential 'I' or 'ego'" were interpreted—I'm aware you don't believe this now—in terms of something like Absolute Ideal even almost on the pattern of Fichte. And I said this to my teacher, and he was very skeptical because he thought it didn't sound like you. I would like to know whether you can recollect whether I am right or wrong.

Barth: I recollect that I have said such things. Look, ladies and gentlemen, I have been allowed to have a long life and to begin, approximately in your condition now, to begin my theological way, and I have been allowed to grow. What I say now is not quite—well, in substance it is—the same thing, but my form of thinking has changed and changed again and is . . . At this very moment I'm always changing forms of thinking concerning the same thing, the same reality. And then, look, that was forty years ago. Think, forty years! Nobody of you was born at that time when I wrote these pages. Well, and then I was under the influence, well, from Plato, from Kant, from Dostoyevsky, from Kierkegaard, and so on. And I was in a bitter fight against my liberal fathers. And then in order to strike them, I said such things as there is mentioned in order to be clear and to be strong. Well, later on I saw that this phrase can no longer be used. I meant it well, but I had to go on and say no more such audacious things as I said. All of you will make the same experience. I hope that you will also be allowed to begin with a strong impact and then, day by day and year by year, you will have to learn. And then life becomes a pleasure. Look, it would be dull if I had written a book forty years ago and now [declare,] "It is stated! No more change!" Not so! A man is—how to be a man—is a living being who goes on his way, and he remains always the same, but the scene, also the intellectual and spiritual scene, in which he lives changes. And insofar as it is easy—yes, I understand, that when you read my old books, you find contradictions and so on. There may be. Don't be disturbed by it, but try to go forward with me.

3. On the Church and Its Practice

Question 7: Dr. Barth, I wonder if you would say a word about your position on infant baptism.

Barth: Here sits my son who has written a big book on baptism.[13] He knows more about it than I myself. Well, I can say it in some phrases, short phrases. I think, first of all, that it is difficult or even impossible to give a reason for infant baptism out of the New Testament. In the New Testament, so far as I can see, baptism is understood as an act, certainly an act of the church, but of the church together with a certain man who is now confessing his sins, declaring his readiness to believe, confessing his hope in Christ, and now he is, so to say, signed or sealed in his attitude by the act of baptism. But I think for such an act—and I see it done no other way in the New Testament—for such an act it needs a creature who is able to decide. I shouldn't overrate the necessity of reason, but to decide to say, "I believe, I have heard, I accept the word, and now it is my earnest proposition to become a Christian." And then he is baptized. I think that what we have now as children-baptism is, excuse the harsh expression, a caricature of a true baptism. And maybe it will be one of the big questions of Christian and ecclesiastical life in the future whether a change must not be made. Think it over.

Question 8: Dr. Barth, I'm a senior in seminary, and most of my colleagues will be going out this next June into the pastorate. I wonder if, out of your experience—I know you yourself were a pastor—whether you would give us young men some advice on the calling of the pastor; just what would you tell a young man going out into the pastorate in this day and age? Could you perhaps expand upon this? It's a rather general question. . . . This, sir, is not a theological question.

Barth: No, but this is also a theological question! Couldn't you perhaps put your question into a little more concrete form? What are you worried about?

Questioner: What am I worried about? Perhaps I can narrow it down somewhat. What one thing, sir, would you tell a young pastor today if you were asked about the pastoral ministry? What one thing above all else is necessary in this day and age for the church?

Barth: That's the whole question of theology, don't you see? It's a big question. I should say I hope that during your studies you have busied yourself earnestly with the message of the Old and the New Testaments, and not only with this message but also with the object and with the subject of this message. And I would ask you, Are you through it [able] to busy not only yourself now but also a congregation with what you have learned out of the Bible and out of church history and dogmatics and so on? Do you have something to say? Do you have *that thing* to say?

And then [comes] the other question: Are you willing now to deal with humanity as it is? Humanity in the twentieth century with all its patience and sufferings and errors and so on? Now you come with that biblical message. Do you like them, these people on the streets? Not the good Christians only, these also, but do you like people as they are? People in their weakness and wickedness also? Do you like them? Do you love them? And are you willing to tell them the message that God is not against them, but for them? That's the

---

13. M. Barth, *Die Taufe: ein Sakrament? Ein exegetischer Beitrag zum Gespräch über die kirchliche Taufe* (Zollikon-Zurich: Evangelischer Verlag, 1951).

one real thing in pastoral service, and that's the question for you if you go into ministry, to do that work in great modesty. It will be a difficult work but also a beautiful work to do. That's what I would say, as you asked me, in short words. If I had to begin anew for myself, if I were a young pastor, I would tell myself every morning: Well, here I am, a very poor creature. But by God's grace I have heard something. I will need forgiveness of my sins every day anew, and I would pray God that he will give me the light, his light, shining in the Bible and his light shining into the world in which humanity is living today. And then do my duty. Simple. Is that, first of all, enough?

4. The Gospel for Humanity

Question 9: Dr. Barth, I wonder if you can tell us what your thoughts are on universal salvation. Who or what is included in salvation?

Barth: If you have read some of my books, you will have found out that I have never taught universal salvation. And that cannot be done. I understand universal salvation to be what Origen has told people, that in the end all will be good, all will be saved, and even the devil is coming home.[14] That's too easy, and we are not allowed to say such a thing because salvation is an act and a decision of God's free grace. And if we proclaim, well, we are all saved, we all will end in a pleasant way, and thus we take away God's freedom to do it. We can only believe, we can only hope, we can only pray that not only we but also others may be saved, you see, and all others. And now, I should say, it is neces-sary that we think so. If we understand Jesus Christ and his work, we cannot avoid looking for, yes, looking for universal salvation. Not to proclaim it, but to look for [it] and to deal with every man in the light of the fact that Christ has died for him. If I believe that I myself have a Savior in him, then I cannot think of other people as if they had no Savior. It is, insofar, a look upon the salvation of all without proclaiming, "All shall and will be saved," because it's always God's free grace and above all God's grace, when *I* will be saved, not to speak of the whole humanity. Do you understand?

Student: Yes, I think [so].

Question 10: Dr. Barth, you have mentioned the fact that your thinking had naturally changed over the years. This question is in the light of this fact: Do you now believe that the church can be true to its witness to Christ by being involved in political movements of the day, that is, by giving support to one particular political program, as over against another that it believes to be right?

Barth: I will try to answer. The gospel deals not with systems of any kind, neither with an intellectual system nor with a moral system nor with an aes-thetic system nor with a political system. And we are always in error if we think that the gospel is identical with this or that system of thought. Now in the political realm we have the different systems, the isms, and indeed they are important and interesting and we must deal with them, but not identify the gospel with any of these subjects. The gospel deals not with systems but with

---

14. See above, chap. 10, n. 8, on Origen.

men—that makes the whole difference—with men living under such and such conditions and in the realm of such and such systems. Yet what counts is not these structures, but what counts is these and these men all over the world.

Question 11: Dr. Barth, the first question is Do you accept the validity of revelation in other religions besides Christianity?

Barth: In other religions? The answer is *no!*

Question: The second question is How would you explain the text in the Bible "Yet he did not leave himself without witness," Acts 14:17?

Barth: Certainly, Acts 14, "I have not left you without witnesses," means "without signs of my presence," whereof Paul speaks also in Romans 1, whereof Paul speaks in Acts 17, certainly, but it's quite another question if there is *revelation*, because revelation does not mean only that there are signs of God's presence, but rather that God himself is speaking, revealing himself to men. Certainly we are in a world created by God, in which we are surrounded by signs of God's presence and actions. But the question is whether they are shown to us, whether God makes himself understandable. And if you ask me about revelation and say [to] me, well, there are religions, [then I reply,] in the Bible, in the Old and New Testaments, the religions of the surrounding peoples, surrounding Israel, and those of the world surrounding the first Christian community, well, these religions are not dealt with as a kind of revelation. On the contrary, Israel had to fight against these religions. And so the New Testament writers didn't think of teaching, "Well, the world is full of religions and now go on with it and then at some point you will reach Jesus Christ." But on the contrary, in the Old and New Testaments we have a fight of God revealing himself over against what is called "religion." The gospel is not a religion, a kind of religion, but the gospel is God's word toward humanity, which is living not in its best but in its worst when it becomes religious. Because becoming religious means man trying to understand some deity out of his own mind and then making even oneself divine and then trying to deal with these deities. The worst thing in the world is religion, and the Bible is against religion and not for religion. And you shouldn't mix up religion with revelation. According to my first answer, which was *no*, I could say that even Christianity, insofar as also Christianity has become a kind of religion, is not revelation, certainly not. But God's speaking in the gospel and in his doings, well, there is revelation over against the whole Christian and non-Christian world, with all this religious fuss that we make. That's the point to be understood—do you understand?—this principally new thing that is meant in the Bible when it so speaks, not as a pious man [merely] out of his religion: "Thus says the LORD." And then comes something strange and new and graceful and helpful, and not the old things in our heads and in our hearts and whatnot. Isn't it so?

5. On Theological Method

Question 12: Would you comment, sir, on the validity of Anders Nygren's motif-research methodology in theology?[15]

15. See A. Nygren, *Eros und Agape* (London: SPCK, 1953).

Barth: Tell me in short terms what for you is Nygren's point that is interesting for you, his thesis, so that I can take a stand.

Question: Do you feel that this admittedly philosophical approach to the New Testament is valid?

Barth: Yes, but I would like to hear something about Nygren now. Give an example!

Question: His handling of the idea of agape and eros. Is his approach worthwhile . . . ?

Barth: I know this book, about eros and agape, you mean?

Student: Yes.

Barth: Well, it's an interesting book. Yes, earnestly speaking, very interesting. And I found many good points in it.[16] But what I don't like in his book is that in the end all ways of God are ending with Martin Luther. He speaks about eros and agape, tries to show they all were wrong, always the new agape was mixed up with eros, and then happily in the sixteenth century came Martin Luther as the one who has understood true agape. When I read a book of this kind that narrows things in such a way, then I become unhappy. And that's my grievance over against him. But I have not fought against the great merits of his doings. But perhaps you have another point which could have interested you?

Question: Do you object to this philosophical approach, or do you think that Nygren did essentially have a philosophical approach to theology, and what would you comment about that today—or do you consider your own position a philosophical approach to theology?

Barth: Well, there is a philosophical approach, but if I remember well he is not one of the worst. And so on this point I have no special fight against this very honorable man.

Question 13: Dr. Barth, outside the city of Tel Aviv there sits in a lonely cell a man condemned for his part in World War II.[17] I wonder if you can comment on the trial and conviction of this man and whether it has absolved the issue of man's general guilt in World War II. Second, can we kill him and then just wash our hands of war guilt? And last, is the State of Israel duly justified in the supreme verdict that was handed down?

Moderator: I think, H., we will let you narrow that down just a little bit first, and we will go on to another question right now and take yours next.

Barth: Yes, narrow it down to one special point. I will answer that question. I'm also interested in the Eichmann case, but we'll go on, and we'll come back to yours.

Question 14: Sir, would you comment briefly on or tell us the names of some of the schools in Europe that are actively engaged in hermeneutics, and what we may expect, if anything important, in the future from this discipline?

Barth: The situation has become more and more obscured. The theme of hermeneutics has come up, more and more people speak of hermeneutics— every young man in a different way—and I regret that in discussing hermeneutics, the texts themselves come up short, you see? They are discussing the question of language, of translation, of application, and so on. I have always

---

16. *CD*, IV/2:737–38, 740–41, 747–48, 751, 795, 827 [*KD* 837, 840–41, 848, 853, 902, 919].
17. On Adolf Eichmann see above, chap. 26, n. 4.

preferred *to do* the thing, to try to explain, to understand texts. And now they are fighting, especially in the different schools of the Bultmannians, because there are different Bultmann schools now, and they are fighting on this methodological basis. I can't like this thing, I'm not involved in it; I look, I see, I read it, but I would prefer that they would write commentaries or deliver sermons or write, let us say, a good theology of the New Testament, a better one, yes. Instead of that, they are thinking round and round on *how* we understand instead of trying to understand and then making a jump into the water and seeing if they are able to swim!

6. Questions of Concrete Political Responsibility

Question 13: Does this issue [re Eichmann] absolve the issue of man's general guilt in World War II? And can we just wash our hands of the war guilt, and is the State of Israel justified in the supreme verdict which it has handed down?

Barth: No, certainly that's quite impossible to say: "Our guilt is laid upon the shoulders of this poor Eichmann." Our guilt is laid upon quite another man's shoulders. That shouldn't be done. And this, I think, is a kind of escape when people now believe, "Now we have him and he shall die, this man for the whole people" [cf. John 11:50]. Not so! Maybe it's a good thing that this trial has taken place in order to show again what happened and to show it, so to speak, in a documented way that everybody may know what was done. But now they have tried him, they have sentenced him to death, and the question is whether this sentence will be executed. And I hope that the Israelis will be, what I shall say, wise enough—yes, it would be wisdom not to execute him. In front of all his terrible deeds, they can't release him, certainly not, but not to kill him. Perhaps it would be a sign of more than political weight and importance if in that very place, Jerusalem, this person Eichmann would not be executed and something like pardon, forgiveness of sin, would take place—significant, symbolic, so to say, over against this whole terrible thing that happened. But I wonder whether the Jewish people will be wise enough to do that. In their place, I would do it. I would not execute him.

Question 15: Dr. Barth, Reinhold Niebuhr was very critical of your position on the Hungarian revolution. Would you comment on this?

Barth: Yes, again and again. Reinhold Niebuhr complained, asking, "Why?" His point was "Why is Karl Barth silent about Hungary?"[18] It was in the year of our Lord 1956 when this thing happened in Hungary. And the whole Western world was crying aloud against the Russians, yes, what they did in Hungary. Everybody. In Switzerland, not only the great papers but also every association, let us say, of butchers or of bakers and so on had its own protest meeting against the Hungarian horror. And in Switzerland even people claimed that now in each place of Switzerland the play of Schiller, *William Tell,* should be played, . . . freedom against tyranny, and so on. Well, I was silent. I didn't say a word for the Russians, but I was silent. And what happened in the world? None of the Western nations believed it necessary to do something for the

18. See above, chap. 26, n. 8.

Hungarians. Why was it not done by the United States of America? Why didn't they forbid the Russians to do what they did in Hungary? We all know why. There probably would be another world war. But be that as it may, there was no resolution *to do* something about [it], but the general resolution to say, to speak, to cry, to affirm freedom against tyranny, and so on. And, I can't help it, I was not allowed to join in the ranks of these singers because they were only singers, not doers. And so I was silent. I couldn't help anybody in Hungary when I had also said something. And it seems to me that certainly for Christians the big question in every occasion must be "Can what I do now or what I say now, can it be some help for others?" And crying against the Russians doesn't help anybody behind the Iron Curtain. And so long as we can do nothing about [it], I think it would probably be more reasonable to be silent. That was my point which . . . please?

Question: Many people . . . I have heard many people who have talked about this, what you have said, that they felt that because of your *theological* position of a hesitancy to use a particular theory or system, [also your theological interests,] to keep a great distance between theology and this [event], would probably help to make understandable your hesitancy or your qualms to say something specific or particular at this time. Could you relate what you have said to this point?

Barth: Yes, the point is simple: we have to do and we have to [say] something if it has importance and if it helps the sake of humanity or human existence. When we can help somebody, then we must do or say something. But if we can't do that, if we are only affirming a system, a theory, let us say democracy over against totalitarianism, then it doesn't help. I think I'm a good democrat for my person. But what does it help when I proclaim myself to be a democrat and hate totalitarianism? Yet maybe I can be of some help for people who are behind the Iron Curtain and tell them something that is a help for them. And in a very modest way I have been able to be of some help for men, for persons in Hungary.[19] And that's what I did. I couldn't speak, I couldn't proclaim it, I couldn't tell it to good Reinhold Niebuhr: Now I also do my thing, because in the systematical question, so to say, I was silent because I had better things to do.

---

19. See above, chap. 26, n. 9.

28. Conversation in Princeton II
1962

During his visit to Princeton Theological Seminary, Barth participated on May 4, 1962, in a podium discussion similar to the one in Chicago. There were 2,200 people in attendance. The discussion was published in Theology Today *19 (1962): 171–77, under the title "A Theological Dialogue." The text below reproduces that report.*

The written draft of the questions for the discussion had been given to Barth in advance. He prepared handwritten notes for his answers in English. These notes are inserted below before the actual transcript, including the questions that were discussed as well as those that were not addressed. As an "appendix," a statement was attached to the list of questions to the effect that "the questions concerning the interpretation of Augustine, Bonhoeffer, Küng, and hell are not to be answered in this context." Barth supplemented this sentence by adding "and Communism" after "hell."

Barth's Notes for the Conversation

1. Simplicity and Mystery of the Center of Theology

That Jesus Christ is the central content of the biblical witness is *easily* seen and stated. So the confession "Jesus = the Lord" is clear in itself and *easily* to be pronounced, accepted, and understood. Yet that statement and that confession merely as such would be *void* and *meaningless*. It has to be filled and explained. *Fides quaerens intellectum!* [Faith seeking understanding!] Jesus Christ is a *living person* (in the Bible and for us)—it's a mystery (although it has an analogy in all our relations to our factually well-known human neighbor (Jesus Christ = *the* neighbor).

The easy statement (confession) *that . . .* becomes *not so easy*—a task with which we have to deal every morning *anew:* in what way is he, what is he? His revelation and knowledge thereof: a continual series of encounters between God and man, man and God.

2. God in Christ

Statements about God (*and* about man) must, in order to be trustworthy and practically valuable, be grounded in solid knowledge. Statements of that kind made apart from Jesus Christ may be based upon interesting theories, hypotheses, opinions, speculations. In Jesus Christ, *God* and (by God's grace) also *man* have spoken themselves, giving ground for *knowledge*. In order to *know* about

209

God and man, we have to look on Jesus Christ. "Statements" about both (God and man), if made in *knowledge* of both, are indirectly christological statements.

3. Christomonism?

Sound theology cannot be dualistic or monistic, but only unionistic. "Christomonism" (an awful catchword invented by . . . !) would mean that Christ *alone* is real—all other men only apparently [real]. That would be in contradiction to the union between God and man, which is not made alone in him, but in him for the benefit of all other men, represented in him. Jesus Christ is true God and true man as the servant of *God* and of all other *men*. "Christomonism" is excluded by the very meaning and goal of God's and man's union made in Jesus Christ.

4. Creation and Redemption

In this context *significat* and *est* are *not mine*, but Regin Prenter's words. I feel no obligation to explain myself in those strange terms.

The relation between creation and redemption:

- *Creation* [is] not an end in itself, but rather the institution of the *theatrum Dei gloriae* [theater of God's glory], the natural ground of redemption.
- *Redemption* [is] the end of God's way with the world, his glory in the realization of his mercy—the spiritual ground of creation.

5. Analogies to the Covenant?

Analogy: a created picture, following its original in some similarity:

Analogies of the covenant:	man and his neighbor
(= relation!)	heaven and earth

6. Eschatology as Point of Departure for Doctrine of Reconciliation and Ethics

Old rule: no rule concerning the sequence of the theological topics: *Methodus est arbitraria* [method is arbitrary].

- Each topic is to be understood as a point on the periphery of a *circle* pointing to the same center.
- [It is] well treated if it is clearly such a pointing finger.

Why not begin with *eschatology*? (Schleiermacher?!). But beware of all systematization also of this kind! Advantage of the traditional sequence: its lack of a claim for control over the whole!

7. Salvation History and World History

[Question:] Connected to the question concerning the relation between creation and redemption is the question whether your theology gives enough weight to history: God's work in history and the various manifestations of his redemptive purpose in the historical process. Would you indicate, then, what you think of the *Heilsgeschichte* emphasis that reaches from Bengel through von Hofmann to Cullmann, Otto Piper, and von Rad?

[*Barth:*] Have I *really not* given enough weight to *history* (= God's work, speaking his word as such)? I speak (with Bengel . . .) not of the general process of world history, but of that very *special, particular* history of reconciliation and revelation, which is

- *centered* in the fact of God's Word becoming flesh (history of Jesus Christ).
- *foreshadowed* in God's promise given to his people.
- *followed* by its testification (church, Holy Spirit) over against the whole world.

Development? historical process? (Cocceius, Bengel . . .) *No*, in all times, in various forms the same thing: the covenant and its fulfillment.

8. The Truth of Revelation? Criteria for Truth and for Understanding the Scriptures?

[*Question:*] In view of the life-and-death character of the problem of "the truth," what criteria do you employ to determine "the truth" of Christian revelation? If your answer is in terms of (a) Scripture, or (b) the belief-ful response of the Christian, what are the criteria for determining *these*?

[*Barth:*] No "criterion" different from God's own judgment, becoming event anew and anew through the testimony of the Holy Spirit. Truth subjected to any other "criterion" (superseded, controlled, supported by it) would not be *God's* truth. *Dieu parle bien de Dieu.*[1] God alone (revealed, witnessed, preached, heard) speaks well (efficiently, authoritatively, infallibly) of himself.

9. Dialectics?

[*Question:*] What is the place of dialectics in Christian or *Church Dogmatics*; and how much or how far has your approach to theology been influenced by a dialectical thinking?

[*Barth:*] *Dialectics:* the inevitable *togetherness* of two seemingly *opposite* Statements, to be understood

- as different *aspects* of the same truth (mountain).[2]
- as different moments
    a. in the movement of its reality
    b. of its knowledge

---

1. B. Pascal, *Pensées et opuscules*, ed. L. Braunschweig (Paris: Hachette, 1946), 700 (pensé 799); Pascal, *Oeuvres Complètes*, Bibliothèque de la Pléïde 34 (Paris : Gallimard, 1969), 1317 (no. 743) [ET: *The Thoughts, Letters and Opuscules of Blaise Pascal*, trans. O. W. Wight (New York: Derby & Jackson, 1859), no. 743].
2. The term "mountain" presumably implies a metaphor that Barth wanted to use: The diverse aspects of the truth may be compared with the views of a mountain, which differ in relation to the side from which it is being viewed.

Examples:
  Question 1
    very easy: that question!
    not so easy: to what extent
  God's
    judgment
    grace
  God's
    hiddenness
    revelation
  Jesus Christ
    true God
    true Man

= paradoxical character of the theological language. Do not insist on these *terms!* [My use of these terms] was "influenced" by the problem itself

10. Use of Reason and Feeling for the Better or for the Worse?

[Question:] I take it that you would agree that in some sense faith is a human decision as God's decision, that to some extent this human decision involves human responsibility as well as divine responsibility, and that in part it involves human thinking that can be understood as such. In view of your repudiation of natural theology, how do you understand such thinking? How are reasons, feelings, and so forth involved in it? In such thinking, is there a difference between good and bad reasons, appropriate and inappropriate feelings, and if so, what is it?

[Barth:] Faith is an *answer* (a human decision corresponding) to God's Word (as *his* decision). No identity (monism!) but union. *Human response* is *called for, awakened* by God's address to man. Human reasons, resolutions, [and] feelings become involved in this response. [All these are] good, appropriate to this action insofar as they *are useful* (not out of their *inner* quality!). [It is] for the object (subject = God) to decide *whether* they are useful. [It is] for us to do our *best* in harmony with the meaning of our doing and speaking of [God].

11. Rebirth as a Surrender?

[Question:] How do you preach the new birth? Must the recipient surrender his will? How does one surrender his will?

[Barth:] New birth happened at Christmas, on Calvary, in the Easter event = God's own surrender *to us.* That certainly means surrender ("an unconditional surrender")[3] also on our side: we surrender to God's own surrender for our sake!! Take it for granted that the surrender has happened. This means *faith,* never as a completed act, but as an act that must happen anew, insofar as [we]

---

3. At their meeting in Casablanca, January 14–26, 1943, British Prime Minister Winston Churchill and U.S. President F. D. Roosevelt agreed that the military goal of the Allies was the "unconditional surrender" of the German Empire [Third Reich, Nazi regime] and its allies.

always [live] in the prayer "Thy will be done on earth, as [it is in heaven]" [Matt. 6:10].

12. Christian Faith and Culture

Christian faith: "In God *we* trust"—we Christians living as members of the people of God, as such in and for the surrounding *world*, to whom we owe our witness, with whom we live together. We trust, being entrusted to cultivate that "garden," being obedient in this service, insofar as faith → culture as a task: "Christian culture."

13. Theology—Eschatology—Ethics—Politics—Action

Politics: (a part of culture:) the human attempt to create, to uphold, and to enter *some* order and *some* peace in the world, to realize in some degree a human commonwealth. Since evangelical theology deals with *God's* practiced and revealed *justice*, it *confronts* all humans with superior justice. It does so by elucidating man's destination realized in Jesus Christ's act as the *King* who *came* and *will come* again (sanctification + eschatology). Since it does so, it is not only related to politics, but also in itself is a political action.

14. Theology and Church Unity

Evangelical theology has to remind any church-union movement that *real* church union cannot be sought and found by means of mutual understanding and tolerance, nor by means of compromises (e.g., concerning episcopalian + presbyterial church order, or emphasis upon sermon—sacrament), but only by a common effort toward the Head and Lord of the Church, to be realized by a common research of the biblical message.

[Second Vatican] Council? Who knows with what it will be concerned? Whether and what kind of decisions are placed? Whether we non-Catholics are invited to busy ourselves with its interiors?

15. Christian Dogmatics, Church Dogmatics, and Evangelical Theology

Movement toward a
   less formal, more *material*   } *formulation*
   less abstract, more *concrete*   J

Christocentric Theology

Question: You said in your third lecture,[4] Professor Barth, that the central content of the biblical witness is not easy to ascertain but must always be sought after by theology. But have you not been telling us all along that the

---

4. As in Chicago, Barth presented in Princeton the first five lectures from his *Einführung in die evangelische Theologie* (Zurich: Evangelischer Verlag, 1962), 43 [ET: *Evangelical Theology: An Introduction* (New York: Holt, Rinehart & Winston, 1963), 35]. There he defined his stance against the view that "the

Word of God is Jesus Christ, who is easily identified as the central content of the apostolic *kerygma* and *paradosis*. Where, then, is the mystery?

Barth: The fact that Jesus Christ is the central content of the biblical witness is easy to see and easy to state, as every student of the Bible knows. And the corresponding confession, "Jesus is Lord," is also clear and easily understood. Yet that statement or that confession by itself would be void and meaningless. It has to be interpreted and explained. I have been speaking of *fides quaerens intellectum* (faith seeking understanding),[5] and the statement and confession about Jesus Christ needs understanding. Jesus Christ is a living person, both in the Bible and in us, for God and for men. So in our relation to him and his relation to us, there is a mystery, analogous to our relation with our all-too-human neighbor. And Jesus Christ is *the* neighbor! So the confession that Jesus is Lord is not so easy after all and involves a task with which we have to deal anew each day if we would understand who and what he is.

Question: To what extent do you hold that statements about God are either reducible to or deducible from statements about Jesus Christ?

Barth: Statements of some kind about God and about man that are made apart from Jesus Christ may be based on more or less interesting and important theories, hypotheses, opinions, speculations. In Jesus Christ, God has spoken for himself (and also for man, by God's grace) and not only for theories, hypotheses, opinions, speculations. In order to know about God (and man), we have to listen where God has spoken, and so we have to look at Jesus Christ. Statements about God (and man) are therefore of necessity indirectly christological statements.

Question: In what specific way, Professor Barth, does your theology avoid being Christomonistic?

Barth: Sound theology cannot be either dualistic or monistic. The gospel defies all "isms," including dualism and monism. Sound theology can only be "unionistic," uniting God and man. "Christomonism" (that's an awful catchword!) was invented by an old friend of mine whose name I will not mention.[6] Christomonism would mean that Christ alone is real and that all other men are only apparently real. But that would be in contradiction with what the name of Jesus Christ means, namely, union between God and man. This union between God and man has not been made only in Jesus Christ but also in him as our representative for the benefit of all men. Jesus Christ as God's servant is true God and true man, but at the same time also our servant and the servant of all

---

content, meaning, and point of biblical assertions are relatively easy to ascertain and may afterward be presupposed as self-evident."

5. K. Barth, *Einführung*, 51, 54 [ET: *Evangelical Theology*, 42–43, 45–46]. The formulation goes back to Anselm of Canterbury, *Proslogion*, *Prooemium*, in *S. Anselmi Cantuariensis archiepiscopi opera Omnia*, ed. Fr. S. Schmitt, vol. 1 (Seccovii: Abbatia, 1938), 94, line 7 [ET: *Prosologion*, in *The Major Works*, ed. B. Davies and G. R. Evans (Oxford: Oxford University Press, 2008), 82–83]. See also K. Barth, *Fides quaerens intellectum: Anselms Beweis der Existenz Gottes im Zusammenhang seines theologischen Programms* (Munich: Kaiser, 1931) [ET: *Fides quaerens intellectum: Anselm's Proof of the Existence of God in His Theological Scheme*, trans. I. W. Robertson (London: SCM, 1960)].

6. According to G. C. Berkouwer, *Der Triumph der Gnade in der Theologie Karl Barths* (Neukirchen: Verlag der Buchhandlung des Erziehungsvereins, 1957), 4 [ET: *The Triumph of Grace in the Theology of Karl Barth*, trans. H. R. Boer (Grand Rapids: Eerdmans, 1956), 12], this term was used by E. Brunner, P. Althaus, and Berkouwer himself. On Althaus, see also E. Wolf, *Barmen: Kirche zwischen Versuchung und Gnade*, 3rd ed. (Munich: Kaiser, 1984), 96–97.

men. Christomonism is excluded by the very meaning and goal of God's and man's union in Jesus Christ.

Question: Regin Prenter criticizes your theology for not giving adequate emphasis to creation.[7] He says you let the word *significat* stand over creation, but never the word *est*. Would you indicate, then, what you conceive to be the relation between creation and redemption in the gospel?

Barth: These words *significat* and *est* in this context[8] are not mine but Regin Prenter's, and it is easy to detect that he is a good Lutheran! The relation between creation and redemption as I understand it is as follows: Creation is not an end in itself but the area and ground of God's great final work of redemption. Calvin said that the world as God created it is the *theatrum gloriae Dei*,[9] the theater of God's glory. God's glory is what he does in the world, but in order to do what he does, he must have this theater, this place and realm: heaven and earth, creation, the creature, man himself. That's the relation between creation and redemption seen from the side of creation. From the side of redemption, I would say that redemption is the end and goal of God's will for the world and creation. Redemption is God's glory in the realization of his mercy toward his creation and his creature. Creation is the natural ground for redemption, and redemption is the spiritual ground of creation.[10]

Question: How can we explain the covenant of God with man analogically, and what type of analogy would you consider appropriate for an evangelical theology?

Barth: What is meant in theology by analogy? I would say that an analogy is a created picture, an image, that involves both similarity and dissimilarity. In the picture or image, if we have eyes to see, the original itself is mirrored. The "original" of Scripture is the covenant between God and man: this relation, this story, this happening between God and man. Are there analogies to this central biblical content? One can only say that there are more or less enlightening analogies, more or less adequate analogies. For example, the relation of man and his neighbor is an analogy of God and man in the covenant. This is not *my* invention since the Bible tells us so.[11] Husband and wife and their togetherness is such an image. They are created together, and in their togetherness they reflect something of the relation between God and man. Man is not God. Certainly not! But in his relation to woman, he reflects—Paul says it [Eph. 5:21–33],

---

7. R. Prenter, "Die Einheit von Schöpfung und Erlösung: Zur Schöpfungslehre Karl Barths," in *TZ* 2 (1946): 161–82, esp. 171, 176, 180–81.

8. The question of *est* and *significat* is located in terms of the history of theology, in relationship with the question about properly understanding the words of the institution of the Lord's Supper. This was one of the major points of contention between Luther and Zwingli at the Marburg Disputation of October 1–3, 1529.

9. J. Calvin, *De aeterna Dei praedestinatione* (Geneva: Ioannes Crispinus, 1552), CR 36 (= Calvini opera 8), col. 294: "Ergo hoc axioma retinendum: Sic Deo fuisse curae salutem nostrum, ut sui non oblitus, gloriam suam primo loco haberet, adeoque totum mundum hoc fine condidisse, ut gloriae suae theatrum foret" ["Hence the principle must be held fast: God had such regard to our salvation as not to forget Himself but to set His own glory in the first place, and the whole world is constituted for the end of being a theatre of His glory"; J. Calvin, *Concerning the Eternal Predestination of God*, trans. J. K. S. Reid (London: James Clarke & Son, 1961), 97].

10. Here Barth gives a variation of his thesis from *CD* III/1: "Creation as the External Basis of the Covenant" (*CD* III/1:94 [*KD* 103], and "The Covenant as the Internal Basis of Creation" (*CD* III/1:228 [*KD* 258].

11. This is the import of Gen. 1:26–27, according to Barth's exposition in *CD* III/1:182–205 [*KD* 204–31] and in *CD* III/2:323–24 [*KD* 390–91].

not I—something of the glory of Christ and of God himself. Another kind of analogy would be heaven and earth; heaven above, earth below. It is a picture; God is not heaven, and heaven is not God, but this relation is an analogy of the covenant. Another may be the relation between man's soul and body. Why not? And another might be faith and obedience. Faith precedes and comes first, but obedience must follow; they are inseparable and are, as such, a picture or analogy of the covenant. There are many more that may help us to understand, but there is no such analogy that can explain or reveal the original itself unless we already know something of the original, for example, of Jesus Christ. Then we may detect him also in such reflections, in such mirroring. Please do not say, "Now he is going to erect a natural theology." It has nothing to do with that.

The Theme of Theology and the Theological Themes

Question: In the traditional sequence of theology, eschatology comes at the end. If end means τέλος (*telos*) as well as *finis*, what would it mean to study the doctrine of the church and the Christian life, that is, soteriology, from the perspective of Christian hope, that is, eschatology?

Barth: Let us first remember an old hermeneutical rule that says there is no law concerning the sequence of theological topics.[12] You can begin theology anywhere, however you like. We are allowed to begin here, or there. Let us hope that we do not do it arbitrarily, but it can be done! Each specific doctrine or topic in theology is to be understood, let us say, as a point on the periphery of a circle, a point that points to the focus and common center. So you can begin here or here or here, and you always have the same subject matter with which to deal. Each doctrine or topic can be treated and explained adequately if it is clearly such a finger pointing toward the center. The criterion is that a point must point! If we look here and here and here but not at the same center, then all is wrong everywhere.

As to the concrete question, Why not begin with eschatology? It would be possible. In the latter years of his life, the great Schleiermacher, as he worked on a revision of his *Glaubenslehre*,[13] wrote to a friend, "I have asked myself, Why not begin with eschatology?"[14] He didn't, and I wonder what would have happened if Schleiermacher had written his *Glaubenslehre* beginning with eschatology! It was in his mind to do so. Why not? Systematization is always the enemy of true theology. It is not allowed to make one of the points of theology the center but only a pointer to the center. If we would make eschatology the center and explain everything else from that point, then we would be wrong. That is not allowable.

---

12. The rule *methodus est arbitraria* is often cited by Barth and applied to the ordering of the contents of dogmatics, esp. in *CD* I/2:860–61 [*KD* 962–63].

13. Fr. Schleiermacher, *Der christliche Glaube nach den Grundsätzen der evangelischen Kirche im Zusammenhange dargestellt*, 2 vols. (Berlin: Reimer, 1821–22); 2nd ed. (1830–31) [ET: *The Christian Faith*, ed. H. R. Mackintosh and J. S. Stewart (Edinburgh: T&T Clark, 1976)].

14. *Schleiermachers Sendschreiben über seine Glaubenslehre an Lücke* (1829); ed. H. Mulert, new ed. (Giessen: Töpelmann, 1908), 30: "When I first set about working on the book, I went back and forth for a long time about whether I should arrange the various themes in the order which they now have, . . . or should I change them around. . . . The first definitive statement about God would have been that he renewed humanity through his sending of Christ and established his spiritual realm in him."

I think the traditional sequence has an advantage because it has no systematic claims. It deals with God, creation, man, sin, and so on, but there is no secret mystery in this sequence. Its advantage lies in its modesty, in its renunciation of being governed by one point in the whole structure; sensing the advantage of this traditional method, I have followed it myself.[15] I have not chosen to begin with eschatology or the church or the sacraments or creation, but have simply followed what has been done since the days of Peter Lombard and Thomas Aquinas: this is the line I have followed.

The Relationship of Theology to History, Culture, and Politics

Question: Does your theology give enough weight to history, to God's work in history, and the various manifestations of his redemptive purpose in the historical process? In this connection, what do you think of the *Heilsgeschichte* emphasis in modern theology?[16]

Barth: Have I really not given enough weight to history? I think in every one of these lectures,[17] which I have given in this place, I mentioned the context of God's word as God's work. To speak of God's word as God's work is to speak of the history, the story, the content of the biblical message and witness. What more? I don't think we are invited by the biblical witness to speak of the general processes of world history, but we must think and speak about that very special, very particular history of reconciliation and of revelation. That history, of course, was in the context of general world history, but the sacredness of that history is in the fact of God's Word becoming flesh [John 1:14]. As history of salvation and revelation, it is in one word *Heilsgeschichte*. The Lord in the flesh, the history of Jesus Christ, together with the foreshadowing promise to Israel and followed by its testification in the church over against the world—this whole as such can be called *Heilsgeschichte*.

Are we to think of a kind of special history within this history, of a historical process, so to say? Some theologians have thought so. The Dutch theologian Cocceius, who was the founder of a big, important school of theology,[18] and also Bengel[19] thought in terms of events following one another on a line, and so this became for them a kind of philosophy of sacred history. I personally cannot follow this way because the history in question is a "history" that not only happened but also happens and will happen in all times as the same history. It should not be divided into different steps and phases: it is one history. We are always at one with the prophets of the Old Testament;[20] we are always invited

---

15. See *CD* I/2:869–70 [*KD* 972–73].

16. What the questioner was concretely thinking about is made clear in the more extensive information on the question that is found under §7 of Barth's preparatory notes above.

17. See n. 4 above.

18. Johannes Cocceius (1603–69). See his work *Summa doctrinae de Foedere et Testamento Dei* (1648). On the entire theme, see G. Schrenk, *Gottesreich und Bund im älteren Protestantismus vornehmlich bei Johannes Coccejus: Zugleich ein Beitrag zur Geschichte des Pietismus und der heilsgeschichtlichen Theologie* (Gütersloh: Bertelsmann, 1923); rev. ed. (Giessen: Brunner-Verlag, 1985).

19. Johann Albrecht Bengel (1687–1752). His scattered thinking is drawn together and ordered in R. B. Evenhuis, *De biblicistisch-eschatologische theologie van Johann Albrecht Bengel* (Wageningen: Veenman, 1931); see also G. Mälzer, *Johann Albert Bengel: Leben und Werk* (Stuttgart: Calwer-Verlag, 1970), esp. 311–35.

20. It's possible that a clause is lacking: "and with the apostles of the New Testament."

to be witnesses of Christ's presence in this life; and in history we are always called to live in and with them as secondary witnesses.[21]

Question: To what extent is a Christian culture the goal or fruit of Christian faith?

Barth: What is Christian faith? Christian faith means "In God We Trust."[22] [Do] you know that motto? I have learned this beautiful definition, and it is a great thing that in God we trust. We Christians live as members of the people of God in the world. Living in the world—to which we must witness and with which we must live in a responsible way—we trust, having ourselves been entrusted. But to what? Why not say that we are entrusted to cultivate God's wonderful garden, perhaps "The Garden State"?[23] Wherever there are human needs and miseries, obedience and desires, and so on—well, that is the garden of God, and we have to cultivate it. I don't very much like the term "Christian culture"; do you?

Question: Would you elucidate how "evangelical theology"[24] is related to politics? How are eschatology and sanctification related to political action?

Barth: What do we mean when we speak of politics? Politics is an aspect of what we have just called culture. Politics means the human attempt to create and uphold some sort of order and peace in the world. Even at best, politics will create only *some* order or *some* peace, no more. The purpose of politics is to realize something like a human commonwealth in some degree. Now since "evangelical theology" deals with God's justice (God has revealed the justice of the covenant in Jesus Christ), it confronts all human attempts to create justice, order, peace, and so on with this superior justice. Thus there is an encounter here, and to this extent "evangelical theology" has to do with politics.

Now, we also say that Jesus Christ is a King who came once and who will come again. If we look at the fact that he came, then we understand our sanctification. He came; and since he came, we are sanctified for the service of this King. But he will come again: here then we have eschatology. Christians look forward in hope to the new coming of the same King. So from both sides—from sanctification completed in Jesus Christ's death and resurrection on to eschatology or his second coming in glory—Christianity has to do with politics. If Christians serve the King of kings, then politics is something straightforward. Thus theology is itself political action. There is no theological word, no theological reflection or elucidation, there is no sermon and even no catechism for children that does not imply political meaning and as such enter into the world as a little bit of political reality. You cannot believe in the kingdom that came and will come without also being a politician. Every Christian is a politician, and the church proclaiming the kingdom of Jesus Christ is itself a political reality.

---

21. See K. Barth, *Einführung*, 34–44, 45–46, 58 [ET: *Evangelical Theology*, 21–30, 31–32, 43–44], where Barth distinguishes between the authors of Holy Scripture and the members of the communities as between primary and secondary witnesses, the "original" witnesses, or the "witnesses of the first order" and "witnesses of the second order."

22. Inscription on American currency.

23. The motto of the American state of New Jersey, within which Princeton is located.

24. A reference to the title of the lecture series that Barth presented in the USA (see n. 4 above).

Ecumenical Movement and Council

Question: What is the vocation of "evangelical theology" in the face of the interest in the unity of the church today? Would you be so kind as to relate your reply to the ecumenical movement and to the forthcoming Ecumenical Council of the Roman Catholic Church?

Barth: I would very willingly be "so kind," but it is not an easy question to answer! "*Evangelical theology,*" generally speaking, must remind any church or church union movements that real church unity cannot be founded only on mutual understanding and tolerance. Being together in large conferences, greeting one another, this may be very nice, but this is not church unity. Nor is compromise—for example, a compromise between Episcopalian and Presbyterian Orders whereby bishops are surrounded by presbyters and presbyters by bishops—real church union. This can only be realized, and this is what "evangelical theology" must remind us, by our common movement toward the Head and Lord of the church. And that would come about only as a result of our common obedience to the biblical message. I think that reading the Bible together is the most that can be done for church union!

Now, as to the famous Ecumenical Council of the Roman Catholic Church,[25] I am somewhat embarrassed because who knows with what this forthcoming council will be concerned? My impression is that even the pope himself does not know exactly! How then shall *we* know! We don't know whether some new decisions or dogmas will be defined. We don't know whether non-Catholics will be invited. So we can only wait and see what will happen next October in Rome. Maybe it will be very interesting, maybe not. But as for now, I can't take a stand one way or the other.

"Progress" in Barth's Thought

Question: When you first began writing dogmatics, you called it "Christian Dogmatics."[26] Then you changed it to "Church Dogmatics."[27] Now you've given these lectures under the title of "Evangelical Theology."[28] Do these changes indicate changes in your thinking about the task or place of theology?

Barth: Well, let me try to give a thoughtful answer to this question. Here we have a good example of a theologian who is clearly a human being and who lives in time and moves with the time. Why not? It would be a dull sort of theology if I had stayed simply in the 1920s or in the 1930s. No, I *must* grow old, and so here in this question you have an illustration of the movement through which I have gone as a theologian. From "Christian Dogmatics" to

---

25. The Second Vatican Council, as it was called, was announced by Pope John XXIII on January 25, 1962, and opened on October 11, 1962.

26. Karl Barth, *Die christliche Dogmatik im Entwurf*, vol. 1, *Die Lehre vom Worte Gottes: Prolegomena zur christlichen Dogmatik* (Munich: Kaiser, 1927); ed. G. Sauter (Zurich: Theologischer Verlag, 1982).

27. K. Barth, *Die kirchliche Dogmatik* (Munich: Kaiser, 1932–; Zollikon-Zurich: Theologischer Verlag, 1938–67) [ET: *Church Dogmatics* (Edinburgh: T&T Clark, 1936–69)].

28. See n. 4 above.

"Church Dogmatics" and now "Evangelical Theology"; I ask you to see this movement as one toward a less formal, more material, less abstract, more concrete kind of thinking. I don't know whether I will ever find a fourth way! This certainly is not the last word, but I think for the moment it is a satisfactory word.

29. Questions and Answers in Washington
1962

Barth visited the capital city, Washington, D.C., from the evening of May 5 to the morning of May 8. On the midday of May 7 he took part in a lunch at George Washington University and American University to which fifty prominent church leaders in the capital city were invited (according to the Evening Star: *forty-five Protestants, two Catholic priests, two rabbis). On this occasion he responded to questions placed by the participants.*

There were two press reports of this gathering: (1) Myra McPherson, "Theologian Barth Sees New Field for Niebuhr," in The Evening Star, *Washington, D.C., May 2, 1962; (2) "Highlights of Barth's Visit to the United States," in* Christianity Today, *May 25, 1962, 26–27. These two reports are printed in abbreviated form below; the focus here is upon Barth's actual comments in response to the questions raised at the lunch.*

The Evening Star

Dr. Karl Barth . . . yesterday challenged Reinhold Niebuhr to do something about what Dr. Barth terms the inhuman conditions in United States prisons. . . . A reference had been made to Dr. Niebuhr's critical comments that came when Dr. Barth refused in 1956 to condemn publicly the Communist repression in Hungary.[1]

"'Why is Karl Barth silent about Hungary?' I can answer with a question of my own. Why is Reinhold Niebuhr silent about American prisons? Wouldn't it be wiser if he thought of things nearer to him than farther away? . . ."

Asked what he thought of Paul Tillich and Dr. Emil Brunner, two theologians who share an opposing view, Dr. Barth with a soft sigh said that he was friends with them both. "But I have the biggest difficulty understanding him (Tillich) as a theologian. Here lies a great problem for me. Even at the end of a seminar, I didn't reach a point where I could understand him. . . ."[2] Asked if "certain sacred events" such as the "resurrection of Christ" could have been covered by newsmen if they had been around at the time, he paused, then said: "Newsmen? Including photographers?"

The question, designed to get an indirect comment about the fundamentalist approach to the Bible, which is that all events in the book actually took place,

1. See above, chap. 26, n. 8.
2. The theme of Barth's seminar in the winter semester 1958–59 at the University of Basel was "Paul Tillich, Systematic Theology I."

was further parried by Dr. Barth. "You are asking whether it happened in time or space: would it have been understood as an historical event? It was an apparition of the living Christ to his disciples, but not to the Roman soldiers. By its nature, not everybody would be a witness of it. It needs a living Christ to see a living Christ."[3]

Christianity Today

At a luncheon in Washington, . . . Barth had some choice remarks about his theological contemporaries Brunner, Tillich, and Niebuhr. His comments were prodded by a remark that he had once made that he and Brunner were "like trains traveling in different directions. . . . We hail each other along the way."[4]

"He remains my friend," said Barth. . . . "In human relations we are amicable and on good terms. But as to theology nothing is changed." . . . In a BBC television interview in 1960,[5] Barth likened his relation to Brunner to that of an elephant and a whale. "In his good creation, God saw fit to create such diverse creatures. Each has his own function and purpose.". . . With a broad smile Barth repeated to his Washington hearers his previously stated preference to be considered the whale, which "can traverse the whole creation."

Barth now says that it was Brunner who came out "with the notion of the new Barth."[6] Barth recalls that in the late 1920s and early 1930s he said "no" to Brunner's view of general revelation.[7] "But I could not eternally say 'no,'" he adds. "I circled around and from a 'christological' starting point (which was not Brunner's), I took up the idea of general revelation. Then Brunner spoke of 'the new Barth.'"[8]

The Washington luncheon . . . also saw Barth challenge Reinhold Niebuhr, who has criticized the Swiss theologian's silence on Red repression of the Hungarian revolt. "That is a closed chapter," Barth said. "I ask why Niebuhr is silent about American prisons. When he speaks out on this, I will speak out on Hungary."

As for Tillich, Barth said, "I have great difficulty understanding him as a theologian, but I can understand him 'as a philosopher.'"

Editor Carl F. H. Henry of *Christianity Today*, noting that newsmen were present, asked if the saving events of the first century, particularly the bodily resurrection and virgin birth, were of such a nature that newsmen would have been responsible for reporting them as news—that is, whether they were events in the sense that the ordinary man understands the happenings of history. Barth

---

3. In the report of the *Evening Star*, the text, which is certainly erroneous, states "It needs a living Christ. . . ." Either Barth spoke of "a living Christian" or the parallel account from *Christianity Today* contains the correct wording, which, however, does not fit well in the context.

4. Barth once used the same image to characterize his relationship with L. Ragaz; see M. Mattmüller, *Leonhard Ragaz und der religiöse Sozialismus: Eine Biographie*, vol. 2 (Zurich: EVZ Verlag, 1968), 229.

5. Chapter 13. The citation is not verbatim.

6. E. Brunner, "Der neue Barth; Bemerkungen zu Karl Barth's Lehre vom Menschen," *ZTK* 48, (1951): 89–100.

7. K. Barth, "Nein! Antwort an Emil Brunner" ThExh 14 (1934); ET: *Natural Theology, Comprising "Nature and Grace" by Emil Brunner and "No!" by Karl Barth*, trans. P. Fraenkel (London: Centenary Press, 1946).

8. Brunner's essay is a discussion of *CD* III/2.

replied that the bodily resurrection did not convince the soldiers at the tomb, but had significance only for Christ's disciples. "It takes the living Christ to reveal the living Christ," he said. Barth thus shied away from emphasis upon apologetic evidences and refused to defend the facticity of the saving events independently of the prior faith of the observers. . . .

30. Conversation at Union Theological Seminary
1962

On May 9, 1962, Barth repeated the first of the lectures from his "Introduction to Evangelical Theology" during a visit to Union Theological Seminary in Richmond. In that context a discussion also took place. The next day there was a report on the event in the Richmond News Leader, *on the page devoted to "Area News." The article was titled "Swiss Theologian Blessing Church Unity Move in Visit Here." The article was written by Mary Moore Mason. The following account carries the passages that refer to the actual discussion; it is translated from the German rendering of the original English version.*

Dr. Karl Barth . . . gave his blessing to the movement toward the unity of the church. It was a movement through which one could hear the "voice of the good shepherd, who is calling his sheep together." With his arms held wide as in a paternal blessing, this Swiss "theologian of theologians," as he has been called, described this movement as "good, hopeful, and helpful."

"The ground of the gospel is not a lonely God who is content with himself and is limited to himself. He is not separated off from everything else," said Dr. Barth. "He has a sincere interest in human existence. He exists neither next to humanity nor merely above it, but rather much more with it and for it."

Barth continued by stressing that God not an inhuman and rejecting God. Nor does he have anything to do with a "theology that isn't going anywhere." Rather, "he discloses himself again and again in new ways." Theology makes an error, he warned, when it attempts to bind God to humans rather than binding the human to God. At this controversial point he contradicts liberal theology, which asserts that the New Testament is an "inspiration" for Christians on how one could lead a good life. Rather, it is the documentation of God's unique intervention in human history.

He also rejects the idea that Western civilization and Christianity are synonymous. "Christianity should not be regarded as part of a culture," he said. If Western culture and Christianity were seen as one and the same thing, he said, then the fate of Christianity would be completely interwoven with Western culture and would disappear some day along with Western culture.

As [Barth] pulled out of his pocket two bullet shells from the American Civil War, he spoke of Abraham Lincoln and the Civil War.[1] "The birth of modern America" emerged out of this Civil War, he said, because it was a "struggle

---

1. See above, chap. 23, n. 3.

between two different ideas about what the state should be." "Abraham Lincoln," he added, "was the first modern American" because he anticipated what America would one day be, and how it would become a "world power."

31. Press Conference in San Francisco
1962

On May 14, 1962, Barth's trip through the United States brought him to California. There on May 15 in the Press and Union League Club in San Francisco, he conducted a press conference that was moderated by Dr. Theodore A. Gill, president of San Francisco Theological Seminary in San Anselmo. Several newspapers reported on this press conference on May 16, 1962: (1) The San Francisco Examiner, under the title "Hidden Paganism—Target of Barth: Theologian Visits Here"; (2) San Francisco Chronicle, under the title "Karl Barth Here: Theologian Brings a Simple Message." An abbreviated version of the second report, under the title "Karl Barth Here: Serene Message from An Eminent Theologian," which also lists Carolyn Anpacher as the author, appeared in a further unnamed newspaper (there is a clipping without the newspaper's header in the Karl Barth Archives). Here we reproduce the first two reports, leaving out the general information about Barth's life, work, and person.

San Francisco Examiner

The Christian churches should begin their mission by combating open and hidden paganism within their own churches at home, Dr. Karl Barth said here yesterday. The Swiss theologian said that while the day might come when Buddhism and Islam might join with Christianity in some form of religious unity, "the real task of religion today is within the strange Christian world of invisible idols."

"Today's problems are in no way different from the problems man has always faced," said the scholar. "Nor is the church's task different. It is simply to tell man that he has not been left alone, that God is with him, not against him."

"Disaster doesn't bring mankind closer to truth. It has never made any one listen to God's word." With a smile, he asked: "Do you think that earthquake here changed the behavior of the residents?"[1]

With his hands out to each son,[2] Doctor Barth said, "I've never believed in a division of Old and New Testament. You can't think of Israel without thinking of Christ, or think of Christ without Israel. Having a son in each has solved the problem for me."

---

1. The San Francisco earthquake in 1906.
2. Christoph and Markus Barth, professors of Old and New Testament respectively.

Speaking of Billy Graham, Doctor Barth said he held him in strong affection. "But I can't hopefully accept his work," he said. "I don't think the Christian doctrine should be held like a pistol at man's breast. Christian faith begins with joy and not with fear. Mr. Graham begins by making people afraid."

Doctor Barth said the ecumenical approach would be successful only if unity sprang out of common understanding.

"Mutual kindness is not enough," he said, and added that no one should hanker for the church to be "acceptable" or "successful" like a big business.

San Francisco Chronicle

Dr. Karl Barth . . . brought a rare and simple message to San Francisco yesterday. The seventy-six-year-old Swiss theologian said this: "What God wills for man is a helpful, healing, uplifting work, and what [God] does with him brings peace and joy." . . . "The God of the gospel is the God who mercifully dedicates and delivers himself to the life of all men—helping, healing, uplifting, bringing peace and joy."

Dr. Barth made it clear that he considers man's problems in the modern world much the same as they have been since the beginning of time. . . . He told reporters that the function of the church today is to announce simply and clearly the doctrine of God's love for man, not man's love for God. The message, he said, is that man is not left alone, that God is not apart from him or against him, but forever with him.

Dr. Barth . . . does not believe that external conditions, either fear or imminent peril, bring man closer to the word of God. "There have been disasters since the beginning of the world," he said gently. "Did your earthquake here in San Francisco change the population? Did two world wars in Europe change the people?" . . . True evangelism begins with joy rather than fear, and it is for this reason that he takes issue with Billy Graham's evangelistic techniques. "I know Billy Graham," he said. "I like him. He is a good man. But the word 'evangelical' doesn't mean to me what it means to him."

Dr. Barth said he does not believe that the Christian gospel should be announced as a "command call" with a "pistol at a man's breast." The beginning, said Dr. Barth, is not the pistol. It is kindness, and out of kindness comes the kind of spiritual and intellectual unity in which men, together, seek and find truth. There is, he said, a strange world within the Christian world, filled with what he described as "invisible idols" and "paganism," and it is for this reason that he believes the "missionary fight must begin at home."

Dr. Barth . . . believes all men can be united regardless of theologies. Similarly, he cannot bring himself to condemn Communism but pleads only for "comprehension." "If we in the West are stronger," he said, "we should not react in fear or condemn it. We must simply stay where we are, with Western culture and civilization, being sure we are right. If we are sure, very sure, we do not need to fight." "If we are truly living as a community—a religious and political community in which every man has dignity and receives his right of coexistence—then no one is alone." "The Communists give the impression, perhaps the false impression, of building such a society. We should do better than they in every way. . . ."

As a visitor in the United States, said Dr. Barth, it is not for him to discuss this country's resumption of nuclear testing, nor its rearming of Germany and Japan. "I asked why in Washington," he said a little wryly, "but I got no satisfying answer. But I asked only. I made no statement." "But if I were in Switzerland, I would say in a loud voice what I think. Here I am an old man and cautious."

Similarly, he carefully ducked questions about his impressions of the United States. "I have been here five weeks," he said. "It is so big, and there are so many different kinds of people. Let us say only, I have some good impressions—and some less good ones."

32. Questions and Answers in San Quentin
1962

On May 25, 1962, the newspaper The San Quentin News *reported on Barth's visit to San Quentin State Prison under the title "Dr. Barth Tours San Quentin: Will Lecture in the States." "One of the greatest theologians of this century, Dr. Karl Barth visited San Quentin on Wednesday morning, May 16. As the guest of Senior Chaplain Byron E. Eshelman, Dr. Barth traveled to this institution and heard a special concert that was presented by the forty-voice New Chapel Choir. . . . Dr. Barth, a citizen of Basel in Switzerland, has written more than two hundred books, articles, and sermons. Especially noteworthy among these works are* Faith of the Church, The Word of God and the Word of Man, *and* Christ and Adam. *All of them can be found in the church library. Dr. Barth, who speaks an exact English, rejects the Calvinist theory of predestination—that the human is subordinated to the moods of an unknown God who is infinitely far away in his majesty. He said: 'The true meaning of predestination is to be recognized in how Jesus Christ lived. Through him we recognize God. For that reason we may accept [our] life and fate as based on the eternal will of God. That is how we come to know what we are to do in our life.'"*

33. Interview in the United Nations
1962

During his trip through the USA, Barth also visited the United Nations in New York, on May 24, 1962. There he responded to questions from reporters. One of his responses was reprinted in the article "Highlights of Barth's Visit to the United States," in Christianity Today, *May 25, 1962, 26.*

Barth said that the international organization could be an "earthly parable of the kingdom of heaven." "In any event," he added, "the true peace will not be made here—although what happens here can move us closer to it—but by God himself at the end of all things."

34. Conversation with Protestant Book Dealers
1962

The conversation was conducted on the evening of June 24, 1962, in the Alpine village of Flims, in the canton of Grisons, as the conclusion to the multiday Annual Meeting of the Association of Protestant Book Dealers and Publishers. Chairing the discussion was Walter Weitbrecht, president of the association, and at the time proprietor of the E. F. Steinkopf Verlag in Stuttgart. Over three hundred participants attended the conversation with Barth. In his remarks, Barth alludes to some other events of the conference: the address of the bishop of the Swiss Methodist Church, Dr. Ferdinand Sigg ("The Christian in a Democracy"), a sermon by Pastor Walter Lüthi, and a group chairlift excursion, during which the participants heard alphorn players and saw a flag-waving show.

The conversation was recorded on audiotape. The transcript printed here follows that recording. Extracts of the conversation also appeared in print under the title "Professor Dr. Karl Barth antwortet," in Mitteilungen der Vereinigung Evangelischer Buchhändler *(Stuttgart, November 1962), 4–5. The text, complete but with errors, is available in the form of typed and duplicated minutes of the conference: "Hauptversammlung 1962 in Flims-Waldhaus" (arranged and edited by E. Schwarzenbach). A report of the conversation appeared under the title "Das Verhör [The Interrogation]," in* Sonntagsblatt für die evangelisch-lutherische Kirche in Bayern *17, no. 31 (July 29, 1962). The course of events is described there as follows:*

> *And now the participants sat, expectantly clearing their throats, in the dining room of the Park Hotel, the measurements of which matched a train station. In one corner the protagonist was seated at a little table, slightly raised, as if he were to be served a different menu in front of everyone. Yet it was he who played the waiter and who served the answers to five cringe-inducing questions posed to him elegantly and appetizingly, like the courses of a meal. Since there was no sound system in the huge hall, the auditors had to leave the tables behind and move in quite close to the professor so that the dining stadium was suddenly transformed into Karl Barth's study. A reading lamp backlit him, creating a soft halo.*

Barth refers to this report in a letter to Helmut Gollwitzer dated July 31, 1962: "Are not other, new tongues needed to bring it to a halt [i.e., the whole "deluge" of the prevailing theological scene]. . . while I sit, as it is so exquisitely described in the Bayrische Gemeindeblatt *("Bericht über die Buchhändlertagung in Flims [Report on the Book Dealers' Convention in Flims]"), at a little table in the corner, pleasant, pert, smiling, in fact knowing everything better, respectfully listened to, but in the end not heard?" From K. Barth,* Briefe: 1961–1968, *edited by J. Fangmeier and H. Stoevesandt, (Zurich: Theologischer Verlag, 1975), 82.*

Barth had apparently not written down the key points for his answers to the five questions, which were addressed to him in writing (in a letter from E. Schwarzenbach, June 8, 1962, Karl Barth Archives, Basel), until he was in Flims, since they presuppose the lecture by F. Sigg on the previous day. His points are as follows:

Points for Barth's Answers

1. Baptism? Orientation on the baptism of J[esus] C[hrist] in the Jordan:
Act of obedience as the answer to God's call (*metanoia*)
Public statement of prayer, of readiness, of hope
Congregation confirms the confession of the baptized
To be received by the person being baptized in free responsibility
2. In the totalitarian state? = Bishop Sigg. Heard? Not better; only in [my] own words.
"Tot[alitarian] state" = Demands affirmation of its self-understanding
(*ideology*), of its *goals*, its *practice*
Goes for the *whole:* Thou shalt . . . Poses actually as a *deity.*
= *Comm*[unist] state. Yes, but . . . = Nat[ional] Soc[ialism]!
+ *every* state—in tendency [?] + occas[ional] practice (Switzerland, 1940–1962!)
+ totalit[arian] *society:* "they" ["*man*"]
+ totalitarian *world*: governed by principalities and powers:
ideas, fashion, sports, commerce, money—so *also* [the] state
Possibilities for the church: only *one*—to keep watch = wall!
To live [on the basis of] its faith more than ever!
by God's Word above all!
In freedom:
because God alone . . .—totalities are lies with short legs
because at the longer lever arm
because task remains, fear banned: "I have commanded you, . . .
[Be] strong and of good courage" [cf. Josh. 1:9].
People [?] in [?] view!
This their unique "possibility"—power
3. Agreement with Bultmann?
Agreed: *Task* = interpretation of the Bible
Historical-critical
Proclamation
NT truth [greater]!
Not agreed: presupposition of a kind of human understanding → to
understand the human from [the perspective of] God's Word
Reduction of NT statements to expressions of human self-understanding
→ statements about G[. . . ?]
Abstract interest in the faith of the individual → faith = answer to God's
universal Word [?]
4. Older theologians? Irenic? Mediating?
No, but interest in the *positive* rather than juvenile pleasure in the
negative

Polemic repressed: For the wrath of humans does not produce
In the confidence (Vengeance is mine . . .) that the wrong defeats itself
But is this not more powerful?
Or maybe still, unfortunately? Feldmann!?
5. *Protestant-Catholic?*
   Jesus *and* Mary, Jesus Christ *and* Church, revelation *and* reason, faith *and* works, Word *and* Sacrament
   But joy and respect in light of new developments
   True God *and* true human

1. Introduction

W. Weitbrecht: Dear friends, when we ask ourselves what the nicest part of our conference may have been—the mountain, the lake, the snow, yesterday, today—we cannot actually say. But at any rate, here comes the main attraction why so many of us decided to travel to Flims. And we thank you, esteemed Professor Barth, for having made this possible. And now we want to come to the point very quickly. Still, I would just like to tell you two book-dealer stories. They make such a nice introduction. We are used to speaking of the book dealers' wood from which we dealers are whittled. So there was this dealer in training, who was so excited about what he had read. At that time Anna Schieber's *Alle guten Geister* [All the good spirits],[1] Salzer Publishing, appeared and quickly became famous. And then Anna Schieber came to our store and said to my father, "So, Mr. Weitbrecht, your trainee has recommended my own book to me with such enthusiasm that I simply had to buy it." And do you know who this trainee was? Albert Lempp,[2] Karl Barth's publisher! And one more story. One time a book by a quite unknown Swiss pastor came out on the Epistle to the Romans. And a trainee read it. He was with Osiander in Tübingen, and he was so excited about the book that he came into the Stift, went from room to room, and said, "You students have to buy this. This is something marvelous. The book was Karl Barth's *Romans*.[3] And do you know who the trainee was? Hermann Leip, now at Rainer Wunderlich Publishing. Now, so much for the publishers' wood. May we do the same! But now let's begin and listen with bated breath.

Barth: Esteemed [?] friends, dear brothers and sisters, so now you want to enjoy another Swiss alphorn player or flag waver this evening, and it is my task to appear in this role—namely, in the form of trying to give answer to some questions that have been posed to me from your circle. It is therefore not a lecture that you will get from me, but a bit of a talk, a conversation with you, so to speak. And I would be glad if I were not the only one to speak here tonight, but after I have tried to say something about one of these questions, then please

---

1. A. Schieber, *Alle guten Geister* (Heilbronn: Salzer, 1907) [no known ET].
2. As owner of the Christian Kaiser-Verlag, Albert Lempp (1884–1943) accepted the distribution of the first edition of Karl Barth, *Der Römerbrief* (Bern: Bäschlin, 1919) in 1920 and afterward published the majority of Barth's writings until the Nazis prohibited Barth's collaboration with the publisher in 1937.
3. K. Barth, *Der Römerbrief*, 2nd ed. (Munich: Kaiser, 1922).

do join in occasionally, raise your hand, and say, "Professor, I don't understand that yet, or I have another opinion on that." You are allowed just to do that. I have become accustomed to objection and contradiction my whole life long. And I speak to you now as if I had my students in front of me, at the start of an exchange, a conversation, as I so often did as long as I had not reached the state in which I find myself now, so-called retirement. So without further preface, I want to start into the questions, in the same order as they were posed to me. I'll ask for a little help here if I don't answer precisely what that questioner asked, so that I can get it right. The first question posed to me is this:

2. The Understanding of Baptism

Question 1: Do you today still stand by your text on baptism?[4]

Barth: My text on baptism appeared during the war in the same remarkable year, 1943, as the much more famous text by Rudolf Bultmann on the New Testament and its demythologization, which created such a sensation.[5] My modest text on the church's doctrine of baptism was also something of a sensation. Apparently the person who posed the question has something to do with it. And I will now answer him.

If I am simply being asked, "Do you today still stand by your text on baptism?," I can answer in no other way than "Yes, I still stand by it." Nevertheless, nearly twenty years have passed since then. And during these twenty years I have read a great deal and reflected further about many things, including baptism. So, for that reason what I said then about baptism, I say a bit differently today. My views on the matter have become even more radical than before, and thus not somewhat weakened or softened, as one question puts it.[6] Rather, my views have become more precise and sharp. But I won't tire you with a comparison between my earlier views and my [current[7] . . .].

Let me keep it quite brief, for we could spend the whole evening talking just about baptism. Today I wish to understand baptism, even more strictly than I did twenty years ago, in relation to Jesus' own baptism at the Jordan, and therefore to understand it fundamentally as a person's response to God's call to the individual to repent: the word in the New Testament is μετάνοια [*metanoia*]. At the Jordan, Jesus placed himself among his own people and together with them took the path of acknowledging the divine judgment. As a sign of this, he took John's baptism upon himself, like all the other sinful people who had come there. His act [is to be understood] as a public announcement of his *prayer*—Luke's Gospel [3:21] speaks expressly of his prayer. It is a public announcement of his *readiness* to take upon himself the *commission* that is

---

4. K. Barth, *Die kirchliche Lehre von der Taufe*, ThSt 14 (Zollikon: Evangelischer Verlag, 1943).

5. R. Bultmann, *Neues Testament und Mythologie: Das Problem der Entmythologisierung der neutesta-mentlichen Verkündigung* (Munich: Kaiser, 1941); in Bultmann, *Offenbarung und Heilsgeschehen*, Beiträge zur evangelischen Theologie (BEvTh) 7 (Munich: Kaiser, 1941), 27–69; and in *Kerygma und Mythos: Ein theologisches Gespräch*, ed. H.-W. Bartsch (Hamburg: Reich, 1948), 15–53; reprint of first ed. of *Neues Testament und Mythologie*, ed. E. Jüngel, BEvTh 96 (Munich: Kaiser, 1988).

6. See below, Question 4, regarding "the irenic and therefore mediating attitude of older theologians."

7. Here a short interruption of the conversation occurs. Due to the lack of a microphone, people were having difficulty hearing.

his from God and to see it through to the end. It is a public announcement of his *hope* in God and in him alone, who called him and as whose servant, his vassal, he the Son of God there began to enter the path of fulfilling his office. In this context, I understand baptism [in general] as a public announcement of a person who has heard God's Word and is ready to respond in the act of repentance, obedience, prayer, and hope. Baptism is the confession of the one being baptized in response to what the baptizand has heard, to God's call to the confessor. The community that takes the one being baptized into its midst acknowledges this person as one who belongs to it, as one who together with the community waits for God's salvation, who together with it trusts in the name of God the Father, the Son, and the Holy Spirit, who together with it is resolved to serve this God.

From this understanding of baptism follows—and this is what in 1943 was perhaps most provocative—the necessity, in my opinion, of understanding and practicing baptism in relation to persons who *know what they are doing* when they make this confession, when they go public and confess the name of Jesus Christ and in their discipleship do what Jesus himself did, and now as members of the community intend to participate in its mission. These actions, which find their visible expression in baptism, are the actions of persons who know what they are doing. I don't mean that such a person is necessarily, as they say, a grown-up. There are also grown-up people who don't know at all what they are doing. But whether younger or older in this or that year of life, to baptism belongs a person, and baptism belongs to a person, who wishes to witness responsibly to their obedience. And even if the Christian church for centuries, indeed for millennia, has baptized little people who were not capable of [such] responsibility, that has been a disorder in its administration of baptism. And so I join with many others in the Christian church who say that things need to be different: We must again have a baptism like the one that Jesus himself received from John the Baptist—and that cannot be infant baptism.

That was the central thesis of my text.[8] And I must profess it today too. So let that be my answer to this first question. I don't wish to develop it further now. If the questioner or anyone else wishes to say anything, they should go ahead and not be afraid of me. I am not a professor whom one must fear.

Respondent: I am the questioner, and I am naturally very satisfied with this answer. I had imagined, however, that the answer would go in a different direction—because the move that this text made in 1943 in the direction of the baptism of believers did not find much of a response. Every student sometime or another has to encounter this text and then reads it and is immediately shocked, as when they first read it and find on page 29[9] what you just said in your concluding statements, and so one has to wonder that there hasn't been much of a response from the churches and the theologians. The response has been

---

8. K. Barth, *Die kirchliche Lehre von der Taufe*, 28–29: "Baptism without that willingness or readiness of the baptized person is true, real, and effectual, but it is *not correct* because it is not done in obedience, not properly ordered, and therefore is necessarily *obscured*. It must and may not be repeated. It is, however, a *wound* in the body of the church and a *sickness* in those who are baptized. This wound and sickness can be healed but are nevertheless so dangerous that a question poses itself to the church: How long will it make itself guilty of causing this wound and sickness because of a baptismal practice that is *arbitrary* in this regard?"

9. See n. 8 above.

limited, so far as I can see, essentially to going back into history. People have been contented with saying, If we can determine that entire "households" were baptized in the first two centuries—that is the famous thin thread about which you spoke and on which the justification of baptism of infants hangs,[10] and these are also the latest assertions about baptism that have appeared, for example, from Vandenhoeck[11]—if one can demonstrate historically that already with the first Christians, perhaps even in the first century, infants with the entire "household" were baptized, then we can be at peace, then Karl Barth's attack has been repulsed. For we then know that the early, young church practiced baptism of children, and therefore it is legitimate. And because we have the rite of confirmation as an equivalent means for the baptized person to answer the call received in baptism, everything can stay as it is. And I am surprised that up to now there has still been no response to you. That was really behind my question. Do you think that one should continue to try to provoke a response, or should one just wait until the time is finally ripe for these questions?

Barth: May I first pose a counterquestion? What were you expecting from me? You said that you were expecting an answer that would go in a different direction. Did you mean that I should pull my punches?

Respondent: Not that. We know you well enough, Professor Barth. You don't retreat even one step. But we had figured that perhaps on the basis of the controversy, on the basis of glancing back at history, you might have come to conclusion that the weight of history is so great and that the tradition has such considerable weight here, that dogmatics must take this into consideration.

Barth: I have not found the weight of history, of "the historical," to be so frightfully heavy. I don't share the opinion of our colleague Jeremias—you were alluding to him, weren't you?—but rather I believe that factually it was so that in the first two centuries the overwhelming majority of baptisms were of the kind that I have had in view here. Now, your question—what is it?

Question: The last question is What has priority: the weight of history, or dogmatic insight into the essence of baptism?

Barth: That is—if you don't mind my saying—not the right question. It can't be the case that one can say something in dogmatics that is in opposition to historical knowledge. For dogmatics has to do with the Bible but also with the tradition of the church. If I were convinced from Scripture and tradition (in this case, the first two centuries) [of the necessity of the baptism of infants], then I would probably have arrived at a different view all by myself. But for me there is no either-or. Rather, I see Scripture and tradition belonging to *one* trajectory, and that is what I believe I must assert. So there is for me no conflict here.

Well, would anyone else from the group still like to comment on this matter? It is a broad, broad field. A large section of the next volume of the *Dogmatics* will

---

10. See Acts 16:15 (cf. 16:33 and 18:8) and 1 Cor. 1:16, where it is stated that along with the one being baptized, "his household" was also baptized. K. Barth, *Die kirchliche Lehre von der Taufe*, 32, regards the reference to these passages to be the "thin thread on which one could possibly justify the baptism of infants from the New Testament (barely though!)," but indicates that also in these passages, the order is "Proclamation of the Word—Faith—Baptism."

11. J. Jeremias, *Die Kindertaufe in den ersten vier Jahrhunderten* (Gottingen: Vandenhoeck & Ruprecht, 1958) [ET: *Infant Baptism in the First Four Centuries*, trans. D. Cairns (Philadelphia: Westminster Press, 1960)]. The thesis of this work is historically debated by K. Aland, *Die Säuglingstaufe im Neuen Testament und in der alten Kirche*, ThExh NS 86 (Munich: Kaiser, 1961). [Trans.: Vandenhoeck & Ruprecht is a renowned German publishing house, from 1735 onward.]

be devoted to the question of baptism.[12] There I will bring together everything that I have just now only sketched, including the question of the baptism of children, which is only a final high point. What is decisive is this: Is baptism truly understood as a response that the one being baptized and the community jointly make to God's Word? Is that correct?

G. Ruprecht: Professor Barth, on the spur of the moment I just wish to add this: Those of us who hold to the baptism of infants understand it essentially as something in which God offers us a gift, though I don't wish to explicate that now in all of its different aspects. In what ritual of the church would you then locate that? For you too would probably say that all of God's goodness is for the benefit even of the infant. So, where in your view does the church express that, if it no longer finds its expression in baptism?

Barth: It goes without saying that Jesus Christ has also died for infants, and all of God's salvation is also promised to them. It is there, in this divine promise that is fulfilled in Christ, that I see the gift. And the church is to proclaim this gift: that is its commission. The church is a church with a mission, a church with a cause in the world. With regard to this gift arises just as certainly and necessarily the question of the human response: What will we humans say to the fact that God is so good to us and has done something so great for us? Here I see baptism [as just an expression of the human response], along with other elements to which I previously alluded: the church's confession of faith, the church's prayer, and, I could add, all in the church that belongs to the praise of God. I see that as including baptism. I see that as also including the Lord's Supper. You see, it is a reaction to the great action of God.

That is what I am drawing your attention to, and so I am very thankful for Mr. Ruprecht's contribution. That is what is truly offensive in my doctrine of baptism. Perhaps many people would still be willing to think some more about infant baptism. But people, not only Catholics and Lutherans but also among my Reformed brothers, don't like it that I think that I must treat baptism as part of this context. Just now I can't go into everything that is pertinent here. Perhaps you will read had my argument in its present and more fully developed form when I am able to bring it to publication. But that is the big question: Where does one look in the New Testament? Which place makes clear to us what baptism is? I believe that it has to be the place where *Jesus himself* is *the one being baptized.* There I see Jesus entirely in the posture of the servant of God who now begins his service in solidarity with sinners (that is so important!), takes baptism for the repentance of sins upon himself, and then—that is the business about the voice from heaven—is so recognized: "This is my beloved Son, with whom I am well pleased" [Matt. 3:17]. [He is] the one who comes, the one who does all that. And the church is to follow Jesus along this path, is to join in his response. So that is the function of baptism. Think about it! That at any rate is

12. Barth never completed this next volume of the *Church Dogmatics.* He allowed the chapter about baptism, which he had presented in the winter semester 1959–60 and in the summer semester 1960, to be published separately as *KD* IV/4, *Das christliche Leben (Fragment): Die Taufe als Begründung des christlichen Lebens* (Zurich: Evangelischer Verlag, 1967) [ET: *The Christian Life (Fragment): Baptism as the Foundation of the Christian Life, CD* IV.4, trans. G. W. Bromiley (Edinburgh: T&T Clark, 1969)]. The additional sections of vol. IV/4 that had already been prepared as class lectures were published posthumously: K. Barth, *Das christliche Leben: Die Kirchliche Dogmatik IV/4, Fragmente aus dem Nachlass; Vorlesungen, 1959–1961,* ed. H.-A. Drewes and E. Jüngel 2 (Zurich: Theologischer Verlag, 1976); 2nd ed. (1979); [ET: *The Christian Life: Lecture Fragments,* trans. G. W. Bromiley, *CD* IV/4 (Grand Rapids: Eerdmans, 1981)].

my proposal. I am not infallible. I have never asserted that I am, whether in the matter of baptism or in any other matter. But after having thought it through for decades, I have come to this conclusion, which I now leave to you for your kind consideration.

3. The Church in a Totalitarian State

Now I come to a difficult question, namely,

Question 2: What possibilities do you see for the existence of the church in a totalitarian state?

Barth: There are two points that make it difficult for me to answer this question. First, because it could all too easily happen that this evening we will get stuck in a discussion about the East-West problem, [about] Communism and anti-Communism, and that we will then suddenly stand in front of the Berlin Wall . . . ,[13] which, however, we do not want to have happen here. And then the other factor that makes the matter difficult is that we heard a rich and exhaustive answer to this question, factually and practically, yesterday afternoon from the mouth of Bishop Sigg.[14] Did we hear it? After I heard a few remarks yesterday evening, I asked myself, Was Bishop Sigg really understood correctly in this gathering? For if he had been understood, certain things could not have been said or could not have been said in such a way as they were said. (Since he is not here, I can praise him without embarrassment.) That was a magnificent address that he gave. What happened to me was something that actually rarely happens to me when I hear an address or even a sermon: I paid attention from sentence to sentence and didn't drift off into my own thoughts, but simply had to be entirely focused. I was also actually in agreement with Bishop Sigg from sentence to sentence and especially insofar as he gave, in my opinion, a profound and clear answer to just this question. I disagreed with only one sentence in the entire address. That was the sentence where he said, "I am no theologian."[15] If *he* is no theologian, then I want to know who is. And now my difficulty is this: dear friends, I cannot say it better than he said it yesterday. I can only say it a little bit differently, with my own words or in the context of my own thought. I also dare not promise that you, that everyone, will understand *me* correctly now, since apparently not everyone correctly understood Bishop Sigg yesterday. But I will now attempt to do my best even in regard to this difficult question.

So, at issue is "the totalitarian state" in which the church has to exist. And then the question is about "the possibilities of the church" in a totalitarian state.

---

13. On August 13, 1961, the German Democratic Republic began building the wall between West and East Berlin, thereby shutting off the last escape route still open from its territory to the West.

14. F. Sigg, "Der Christ in der Demokratie," in *Hauptversammlung 1962 in Flims-Waldhaus* (General Assembly 1962 in Flims-Waldhaus [Switzerland]), published by the Association of Evangelical Book Dealers and Publishers as a manuscript (1962), 1–16. For his part, Sigg on page 8 appeals gratefully to K. Barth, *Christengemeinde und Bürgergemeinde*, ThSt 20 (Zollikon-Zurich: Evangelischer Verlag, 1946) [ET: "The Christian Community and the Civil Community," in K. Barth, *Community, State, and Church: Three Essays* (Eugene, OR: Wipf & Stock, 2004), 149–89]. From 1954 onward, Ferdinand Sigg (1902–65) was Bishop of the Genevan Diocese of the Methodist Church, which extended from Belgium over North Africa, Switzerland, Austria, Yugoslavia, Czechoslovakia, Bulgaria, Hungary, and Poland.

15. F. Sigg, "Der Christ in der Demokratie," 7.

What is actually meant when one speaks of a totalitarian state? "Totalitarian"—
that somehow refers to something whole, comprehensive. And when one says
"totalitarian state," one apparently means a state that demands something *in its
entirety* from humans. It demands that it be affirmed, and indeed in the manner
in which it understands and presents itself—affirmed in its goals, affirmed in
its practice, in its actions—and that this affirmation take shape in the behavior
of those from whom it demands it; in other words, that they place themselves
without reservation at the disposal of its teaching and its will and its purposes.
The total state is a state that aims at the whole, a state that says, "You shall love
me with your whole heart, with your whole mind, from the entirety of your
soul, and from the entirety of your strength" [cf. Luke 10:27]. And there we
have the mystery: the total state, even when it poses as being atheistic, is a state
that arises[16] in the shape of a deity and wills to have from humans that which
only God can will to have from humans. That is the imposing thing about such
a totalitarian state: it is, so to say, a caricature of God. Even when it wishes to
be atheistic, it somehow has to represent God in a distorted form on earth. And
whenever humans attempt that, the result is always devil's play. It is nevertheless a curious contradiction: the godless atheistic state that presents itself,
reveals itself, and represents itself as divine.

The questioner was naturally thinking about the Communist state, right?
And I would say, yes, yes, one can and should also think about the Communist
state. And, I suspect, the questioner was probably thinking especially about the
East German state, the "Ulbricht state," as one says, with its Berlin Wall and all
that goes along with it. Yes, yes, that is also a total state, that also!

I would only have liked to ask the questioner whether it is clearly before his
eyes that this is not the first time there has been this kind of totalitarian state in
Germany. And if I wanted to be almost a little nasty, I would say, What stance
did the questioner take, when the other total state existed? Did he never cry out
"Heil Hitler!" at that time? Because whoever did that, affirmed the total state,
even if only in that way. And whoever had anything at all to do with that total
state at that time perhaps has to bite his tongue a bit, if he wishes to open his
mouth too wide against the total state of today. But let me leave the Hitler state
aside for the time being. I won't come back to it. All that should just be a little,
raised finger of warning against all too much eagerness in criticizing the Communist state now.

Is it clear to all of us that not only the Communist state and also not only in
its time the Hitler state, but rather every state has something of the totalitarian
state in it, that every state, even the finest and freest and most democratic, thus
resembles a large cat, which has fine paws to be sure, but whose paw has claws
stuck in it somewhere? And the claws in the cat's paw—that is the totalitarian element in *every* state: and one can never be entirely certain just when that
totalitarianism will appear. As I say, in every state! So I don't exclude Switzerland, for example.

Rather, I will illustrate the point [expressly?] with two examples [from] Switzerland. When the Second World War broke out, the Federal Council was given

---

16. Allusion to Th. Hobbes's thesis of the absolute state as an "earthly god." Hobbes, *Opera philo-
sophica quae Latine scripsit omnia*, ed. G. Molesworth, vol. 3 (London: Bohn, 1841), 131.

the so-called *Vollmachten* [writs of authorization].[17] And our Federal Council then ruled to a large extent in a totalitarian way. I personally experienced that. I had composed several writings, theological-political writings. My publisher at the time, Mr. Poyda, experienced what the Swiss totalitarian state did with these writings: they were formally forbidden, even though they were Christian writings.[18] And in Basel something even more curious happened along the lines of "totalitarianism." In 1940, as Hitler made his great charge through France, the honorable, loyal Basel church newspaper that is delivered to every house, printed without further commentary the chapter out of the prophet Habakkuk in which the grasshoppers are described. Nothing was added about present events. All that stood there was Habakkuk.[19] And then the police gave the church newspaper an official reprimand [*Verwarnung*]. I believe that copies were even confiscated. And so the prophet Habakkuk was censured after the fact by the Basel police authorities.[20] Yes, such things can happen in Switzerland.

And what we have experienced in the last half year in relation to the question of my successor—that was also a bit of the total state.[21] We had a candidate who was qualified in every respect and who would have been good, Helmut Gollwitzer from Berlin. [But] the political world in Switzerland and finally also the political authorities said: "Ah, yes, Gollwitzer. He has never expressed himself as sharply against Communism as we would have liked. And since his predecessor was the same way, we don't want to go through that again, such an unpredictable candidate." And Gollwitzer went down the drain. [That's a case in which] it had to do with systematic theology, mind you, and not politics! But he was not acceptable. That was the claw of the cat of the totalitarian Swiss

---

17. On August 30, 1939, with only two no votes, the [Swiss] Federal Assembly (upper and lower houses of parliament) authorized the Federal Council (the executive branch of government) to rule by direct decree. In this connection the Swiss ambassador in Berlin remarked that this action had also made Switzerland an "authoritarian state." Cf. J. Kimche, *General Guisans Zweifrontenkrieg: Die Schweiz zwischen 1939 und 1945* (Berlin et al.: Ullstein, 1962), 40.

18. Richard Poyda was the head of the publishing house of the Evangelical Society in St. Gallen [Switzerland]. Barth published his incriminating writings there, while his theological writings during this time appeared from the Zollikon Evangelical Publishing House. The censor forbid the following pieces: *Unsere Kirche und die Schweiz in der heutigen Zeit* [Our church and Switzerland in the present day] (1940); *Ein Brief aus der Schweiz nach Großbritannien* [A letter from Switzerland to Great Britain] (1941); *Im Namen des Allmächtigen! 1921–1941* [In the name of the Almighty] (1941); *Weihnachtsbotschaft an die Christen in Deutschland* [Christmas message to the Christians in Germany] (1941); all in K. Barth, *Eine Schweizer Stimme: 1938–1945* (Zollikon-Zurich: Evangelischer Verlag, 1945); 3rd ed. (Zurich: Theologischer Verlag, 1985).

19. Under the title "Ein Prophetenwort zur Lage," *Kirchenbote für die Glieder der evangelisch-reformierten Kirche Basel-Stadt*, ed. D. P. Burckhardt and the Reverends S. Dieterle, W. Lüthi, E. Thurneysen, vol. 6 (July 1940), printed on a full page the text Hab. 1:2–17; 2:1–14, 20, in the Zurich Bible translation. (A plague of grasshoppers [or locusts] is not in Habakkuk, but rather in Joel 1:4; 2:25; as well as Amos [4:9;] 7:1; [Nah. 3:15].)

20. In regard to the measures taken by the press censor [*Presseprüfungsstelle*] of the Basel police [*Platzkommando*], see E. Herkenrath, *Die Freiheit des Wortes: Auseinandersetzungen zwischen Vertretern des schweizerischen Protestantismus und den Zensurbehörden während des zweiten Weltkriegs*, diss. Phil. I (Zurich: Juris Dr. & Verlag, 1972), 185–86.

21. At the top of a list of three proposed by the theological faculty and as the only candidate of an expert commission and the trustees [*Kuratel*] of the University of Basel, Helmut Gollwitzer was nominated in 1961 for Barth's chair. Influential Swiss newspapers spoke out in opposition to the nomination: *Basler Nachrichten* (June 24/25, 1961; July 8/9, 1961; January 27/28, 1962; February 2, 1962), *Die Weltwoche* (June 16, 1961), *Badener Tageblatt* (June 7, 1961), *Appenzeller Zeitung* (July 1, 1961), *Neue Zürcher Zeitung* (July 3, 1961). Under the pressure of this press storm, Gollwitzer's nomination was withdrawn, and in April 1962 Heinrich Ott was elected to Barth's chair.

state. I don't intend to make any further references. Consider for yourselves what the situation in other countries may be!

You know, that's how it is with the totalitarian spirit: it doesn't begin with the state. Human *society*, if you will, is totalitarian as such. Society around us automatically demands certain things from us. It doesn't make much noise, as long as one goes along with it. But when one doesn't go along, when one swims against the stream, things get nasty. The philosopher Heidegger has a wonderful chapter about this notion of "they" [man] in his book *Being and Time*.[22] What "they" believe and think and do—this "they" governs "in the air" (cf. Eph. 2:2). Without police! No one lands in prison. But everyone has to do and has to approve what "they" do and approve. All of us know how it goes. So, things begin [with respect to totalitarianism] not with the state, but rather with society. Because society is always based on this "they," there is also occasionally a totalitarian state, [and then] its claws become more or less apparent, either so terribly as with the "Ulbricht" state or a bit less terribly, but still to be felt, as with the city of Basel.

Now, you see, something much larger stands behind the totalitarian society and then the totalitarian state. I would say [it is] a totalitarian *world*. Yes, what the Bible calls "the world" is a being full of totalitarian demands. When the apostle Paul spoke of it, he spoke of those powers and authorities that rule. Yes, that rule. He named them "thrones, principalities" and so on.[23] And that is not mythology. That is the truest reality.[24]

Reflect for a moment on what it means that all of us, no matter where we are—whether we are Africans or Asians or Europeans, or within Europe, English or German or Swiss—[that] all of us, as one says, stand under the power of certain ideas or ideologies that are simply there in our heads and govern us! And we can't think differently. Every day this ideology—with absolutely no need of the police, but simply through the newspaper—comes in drop by drop and governs us.

Or think about another of these powers and authorities: fashion! Yes, fashion is something mental, but to be sure also very physical. All of us are made "subservient" to fashion. I don't really see anyone in this room who has absolutely no concern for fashion, for example, among the women here. All of them go along with fashion, whether quietly or . . . Oh, you well know why—because today's fashion rules, is in force, right?

Or take something else. When you open the newspaper, especially on Monday, what governs the newspaper? What were people running after on Sunday? Sports! Soccer! Oh, those are events. And what has again taken place in Chile?[25] That is said to interest half of the world, and it does interest this half. Such a soccer player is a kind of secret king. And everyone, everyone somehow takes part,

---

22. M. Heidegger, *Sein und Zeit* (Halle: Niemeyer, 1927); 12th ed. (Tübingen: Niemeyer, 1972), 126–30.
23. Cf. Rom. 8:38; 1 Cor. 15:24; Eph. 1:21; 3:10; Col. 1:16; 2:10, 15.
24. In what follows, Barth draws from the lectures that he had given in summer semester 1961 under the title "*Die herrenlosen Gewalten* [The unruled powers]," which he planned for vol. IV/4 of the *Church Dogmatics* but then never published. Now in K. Barth, *Das christliche Leben*, 363–99, esp. 373–75. ET: *The Christian Life*, 213-33, esp. 219-20.
25. World soccer championships in the summer of 1962 in Chile.

and something goes off in us when we hear, "Three to nothing! We're ahead!" That is something totalitarian.

Or take something else, what we now call "traffic." Take a look at our streets with all these cars! I have just had this experience in America.[26] The Rev. Mr. Lüthi spoke about it this morning.[27] To have seen it and even to have been in America to see it—well, as he said, four cars next to each other in one direction and four in the other direction! And nonstop, day and night. You ask yourself, what's going on here? What are they all rushing to? Yes, they must rush. Things are in a hurry, yes, in a hurry. And so they hurry along. And then to realize that cars like this are rushing and racing all over the world! We wouldn't have it any other way. No, we wouldn't have it any other way. It must be so. But when something must be so, then it is something totalitarian. Modern people have mostly become car people, and to be sure, not in the sense that they govern cars, but rather that cars govern them.

What would naturally come next would be for me simply to say the word "money." You surely know, you dear Christian book dealers, what I mean. I will simply say, There, there! "Everything hangs on gold," as Goethe said.[28] I assume that applies widely to the Christian book trade as well. You [?] can't get around it. Money governs. . . . So now it should be evident to you that we live within an entire spiderweb of such powers and authorities, and you have before you what I call the totalitarian world.

But I have been asked about the possibilities of the *church* in a totalitarian state—and we could immediately add, in a totalitarian society, in a totalitarian world. I would like to say one thing above all: one should not speak of possibilities in the plural. For the church in a totalitarian world and in a totalitarian state, there is only *one* possibility—one alone, but it is a genuine possibility. And I would now like to describe it simply with the word in the third chapter of Mark's Gospel: "And looking around at those who sat about him" [Mark 3:34]. The Latin text of the New Testament puts it in a remarkable way: *circumspiciens ad eos, qui erant in circuitu* [sic]. I believe that this word *circuitus* is actually the proper word for "church." The church is those who are around Jesus and whom he looks at around him. And that the church be this *circuitus*, and so simply be *church* in the totalitarian world—that is its "possibility."

And now I could continue with another word of the Bible from the beginning of the book of Jeremiah, where it says: "I have made you a fortified wall" [Jer. 1:18; 15:20]. Did you notice? It's not that *others* have built a wall, and we now stand before the wall and make lament. Rather, the church *itself* is the wall that *God* has built. And that is its "possibility," namely, that it itself be the wall (and a completely different one from Mr. Ulbricht's)[29] and prove itself to be such. That the church [is that and] does that will simply consist in the church being the "circle" [around Jesus, and so the flock] of those who in a totalitarian world and also a totalitarian state simply nourish themselves from the Word

---

26. In April–May 1962 Barth visited the USA.
27. Sermon on the morning of June 24, 1962, in the church in Flims.
28. J. W. von Goethe, *Faust I*, 5.2802–4 (Evening):

Nach Golde drängt,	Everything presses toward gold,
Am Golde hängt	For everything hangs after all
Doch alles. Ach wir Armen!	on gold. Ah, we poor people!

29. See n. 13 above. [trans. note: Walter Ulbricht (1893–1973) was a leader of East Germany after World War II.]

of God and take joy in their faith in the Word of God and live in this faith. And the more totalitarian the world behaves, and the more it comes forward with its own claim to divinity, all the more joyful and all the freer they may believe and be obedient, because Jesus is there and the church is around Jesus. It is the circle around him, and he is the middle—that is its "possibility." When it does that, [namely, flocks around him], then its existence is possible (the word *möglich* [possible] actually is derived from the word *Macht* [power]), and then the church is [strong], no matter how powerless and even when it is oppressed and forbidden and when its children are taken away from it and when it is no longer permitted to print church newsletters and when the bookstores are harassed and whatever else! [But when it is that "circle" around him, then] the church is the safe place for freedom. And freedom means full of power. In that case [?] the church is powerful and perhaps the only powerful thing in a world that is powerless insofar as it has been overwhelmed and is ruled by powers. . . . [?] The church has the wonderful possibility, over and against the totalitarian state and the totalitarian world, to have the better leverage peaceably and joyfully—not always with a clenched fist. The church can wait. And it knows that it does not wait in vain.

The church knows that all the totalities of the world and society and also of the state are actually false gods and therefore lies. In the end you don't have to be afraid of lies. "Lies don't have any legs to stand on." And in the church one can know that. Whenever the church takes these lies seriously, then it is lost. With all calmness and in all peace, it must treat them as lies. And the more that the church lives in humility and knows that "we too are only human, and there are also many lies in us," then it will also know all the more surely that "God sits in governance"[30] over and against the lies that are in us and over and against the lies in the world and in the state and wherever else they may be. And in that case the church, regardless of the circumstances and no matter how entangled and difficult the situation, remains at its task and knows itself to be forbidden to fear for its future. Its future is the Lord. *He*, not the totalitarian state, is coming to the church.

But, of course, the church must *believe* that. The church must be in its place. The church must get serious about what it proclaims. If everything that the church has gotten out of the Bible for centuries [was] only a bunch of rubbish—things like, "What can man do to me?" (Pss. 56:11; 118:6), and "In everything God works for good with those who love him" (Rom. 8:28), and all the rest—if all of that was just empty chatter, then everything collapses when the totalities come. And it is better for it to collapse. It was nothing but a house of cards anyway. But does it really have to collapse? For we can remain calm and say with confidence: we know of something better; we look beyond this totalitarianism business to the first glow of the dawn (cf. Hos. 6:3) and to the coming of the bright "sun of righteousness" (Mal. 4:2). That is what we care about. And in the meantime it is our task to give witness to it to the people around us, whether with words or without, simply through our existence as a Christian fellowship. It will never be easy. It is not easy in Berlin. But I can assure you that it also is

---

30. From P. Gerhardt's song (1653) "Befiehl du deine Wege [Entrust your ways]" (*GERS* 275; *EKG* 294; *EG* 361), verse. 7: ". . . Gott sitzt im Regimente und führet alles wohl [God sits in governance and conducts all things well]."

not easy in Basel. The Berliners should not act as though they are the only ones where the situation is serious. The situation can be every bit as serious in any Swiss canton and in the Federal Republic [West Germany]. With regard to the question that really matters, we must stand by our confession [of faith]. Factually and practically, stand by it! Do we really *believe* what we confess—whether coming from Luther or from Calvin, whether Catholic or Protestant [*evangelisch*], do we *believe* it? Further, do we believe it with heart and deed? That is the question that stands before us wherever we are. And wherever we are, it is difficult to say "yes" to this question. But at the same time wherever we are, it is as easy as child's play.

So, I would counsel [those of] us in Germany not to make a big tragedy about East and West. I believe, so far as I can observe, that people behind the Iron Curtain[31] make much less of it than we do. I sometimes hear impressive words from behind the Iron Curtain, so that I say: They have understood it and have understood it better than the so-called free West, where the church can "live." Perhaps the church will only learn to *live* when it is subjected to a little pressure. We will not wish to come under pressure. But perhaps life is so ordered that only when things get serious do we also get serious about our faith and serious about the existence of the church.

So, I have not been able to keep my comments brief. But that is what I wanted to say about *the* possibility (not the possibili*ties*) of the church that is around Jesus: think once again about the *circuitus*—in a totalitarian state. We could probably keep discussing these till midnight tomorrow night. . . . [?] To be sure, I have focused only on this one question that was posed to me. There is a lot about which I have said nothing. Perhaps it would be good, in case anyone wants to say something, to stick to *this* question: the possibility of the church in a totalitarian state.

Response: Professor Barth, may I with all due respect make a comment? (Your presentation seems to me somewhat naive when I think about our congregations in Russia. A generation of leaders among the Baptists has disappeared. When you travel to Moscow, you are always very impressed by the congregation that gathers there.)[32] What you don't know is that there used to be fifteen Baptist churches in Moscow, and today there is only one. And in addition you probably don't know that of all the old leaders, not one is free anymore. To me it is immensely tragic that we do not know today: Are our brothers who are in leadership there really our brothers, or are they collaborators with the present state?

Barth: Dear friend, what you just said—was that out of faith, or haven't you just spoken in terms of a particular worldview [*Weltansicht*]?

The same respondent: May I go ahead and respond? I said those things out of deep concern. In 1957 I [?] participated in a [Baptist] World Council [?] Executive Committee Conference in Canada. We stayed in university housing. But the Russian brothers insisted on staying in a hotel so that they could report to Moscow every evening by telephone. They didn't say that to us: that was our

31. W. Churchill's designation of the border between Eastern and Western Europe, among other places mentioned in his Zurich speech of September 9, 1946, which Barth himself witnessed.

32. The text within parentheses is not present on the audiotape to which I had access, but is found on p. 13 of the published text edited by E. Schwarzenbach, mentioned in the introduction above.

educated guess. So I really ask out of deep concern. We have also published two books about the Stundites [*Stundismus*] in Russia and the situation up to the Second World War.

Barth: I wasn't present at the meeting in Canada. So I really can't say anything about this frightening news that you share with us. I also can't say anything about your suspicions about these brothers in Russia. They may be subject to great temptation. Things may be happening that should not be happening. But what would you say to them differently if you still want to talk to them now? Could you say anything different from what I have tried to say about the church in a totalitarian state? Whether they accept it, whether they can go along with it, whether they even want to go along with it—that's not in our hands. But when *we* are asked and ask ourselves, How do things stand with the church in a totalitarian state—and for that matter also in a totalitarian society and a totalitarian world—how else can we answer? Is there a better answer and really a more helpful one? What good is it if you hold the sins of these poor people up to them (*if* they are really such frightening sins as you suggest)? In relation to what is factually and practically true, I can only say, I have also heard other news out of Russia—not only from Stundite and Baptist circles, but even from circles of the Orthodox Church. It can be very difficult to see clearly through all of this. Human matters are always confusing. I don't doubt that there is also conformism there. But I also don't want there to be any doubt (just as Pastor Lüthi said this morning)[33] that there is also a church of Jesus Christ there, in weakness perhaps, in powerlessness, perhaps even in considerable unfaithfulness. But *we too* are able to be the church only in weakness, powerlessness, and unfaithfulness. And so it is better for us to admit that, than to throw stones at these people who have it so difficult there. I wish so terribly much that we could reflect on these matters with a different spirit from that with which— pardon me—you just gave your response. It was a little disturbing to me.

Respondent: I will attempt to formulate what lies behind this question or other questions that have not been posed here. When in a totalitarian state (I mean truly totalitarian states and not merely the totalitarian world)—when the souls of young people are drawn away from their parents, such that children in school are raised to lie and to act against their conscience, when they are examined about what their parents think about matters of faith (quite apart from the political stance that is also under examination), when that goes on for years and burdens the conscience of the parents who were raised as Christians and who remain in the church and now as before want to flock around Jesus—when all of that is so, which "possibility" does the Christian community have *here*, when it does not have influence on the school, does not have influence on public life, does not have influence on three-quarters of the young people's time? These are profound matters of conscience that we too experience as we learn of them from letters and personal encounters. And it weighs on us that the continuation of the Christian church appears to be secure for a while as regards the parents, but that the young people of the church are being inwardly estranged from the church, and the conscience of the older people constantly suffers.

33. See n. 27 above.

Barth: That weighs on me too. But would you conclude from what weighs on you in this regard, and on me together with you, that the question posed to me must be answered differently? Can we help these parents and children in any other way than by saying to them *there*—and insofar as they can hear *our* voice—what the Christian church is under in all circumstances? Do you really believe that the relationship of parents and children, let's say, in Rome or in Antioch at the time of the apostle Paul was happier than in the German Eastern Zone today? After all, life under Caesar wasn't great either. But the apostolic communities lived and suffered and made their witness *there*. Shouldn't we prefer to look at the matter from the inside rather than from the outside? Who among us will doubt that it is a difficult matter? And who will make light of the matter? I don't wish to make light of anything. But—the word "tragedy" was earlier used; the word "tragedy" is not a Christian word. It does not belong here; in view of all kinds of "tragedy," I do not wish suddenly to mistake and confuse the gospel with a message about a different, better world order. That would no longer be the gospel. Am I making myself clear? Or is what I am trying to say still entirely obscure?

Question: Professor Barth, I was still too young at that time, but I have just one question: Did you—I will not now say, make light of—but perhaps oversimplify your depiction of the existing German totalitarian state twenty-six years ago in the same way as you have depicted the Russian totalitarian state this evening?

Barth: Did any one hear me make light of the "totalitarian Russian state"? Have I said anything nice or good about it? I was asked about the *church*. And I said what the church even in a totalitarian state must be under all circumstances.

The situation in Germany at that time was not quite the same. There was after all a church then that was still able to speak but did not speak. And so, I did indeed say: speak!—exactly in the same sense in which I have spoken just now of the faith and its freedom. The situation behind the Iron Curtain is a bit different from what it was in Germany at that time. Without further consideration one can't demand from people there what one was permitted to demand, and was able and required to demand, from Germans at that time—and what Germans to a large extent never did, even though they still had everything: the schools and the parents and the children. Everything was fine. And despite that, the church made only a limited use of this freedom. It was a difficult time, for reasons different from what makes things difficult in the East today. But just because of that, one could ask if the more difficult situation that they are experiencing there externally isn't healthier for the church, because the church is then pushed down to the place where it has its only possibility.

Is that not at all comprehensible to you? I really don't believe that I said something different then—it has been almost thirty years—but rather just in a different situation and with different consequences. World history does not repeat itself. One can't throw everything into the same drawer. One can't draw the same lessons for all times. The lesson at that time was "You must resist!" And the lesson today goes perhaps more in the direction of the First Letter of Peter: Now has come the time for patience and suffering [1:6; 4:12–13; 5:10]. Both are forms of the one Christian possibility.

I don't believe that we are finished with this matter, but perhaps we must allow ourselves to be finished with this discussion. I repeat: If you didn't want to hear it from Bishop Sigg, I suspect that you don't want to hear it from me either. But to our dear guests from Germany: Please take with you this remembrance, that at least three people in Switzerland blew into the same alpenhorn. This remembrance has been given to you not in the form of a nice package (you did get a package, didn't you?), but rather in the form of a remembrance that by no means all but at least a couple of people in Switzerland think approximately as I have just tried to express.

Question: You just said that resistance on the basis of faith is also possible as a Christian stance. Would you also hold it to be possible for those in the Eastern Zone next to the other stance of patience?

Barth: I wouldn't even play with this thought unless I had first lived for three years in the Eastern Zone and personally experienced how things are. I would never presume to cry out from Switzerland: "You should maybe offer violent resistance!"

Questioner: I'm not thinking [about] violent resistance.

Barth: Speaking just in abstraction, I would not say: It is absolutely impossible. But *I* would not say it. And so far as I can see, there would be no sense in saying it now. That is the big difference between 1933 and 1962. One can't throw everything into the same drawer. One can't always say the same thing. Right now it may be time for something else. So for now let us be content that God will not abandon his church and that the right moment will come when he will show us new ways that will be his ways, not arbitrarily chosen ways.

Question: In relation to this answer that you have just given about resistance, may I still pose a question about basic assumptions? I fully agree with what you have said—in theory. But I wonder, Are we in the West really permitted and able to give an answer to this question about [the church] in a totalitarian state? Mustn't we leave the answer to the people over there, just as you said in relation to resistance? And along with that, another matter: A moment ago, you made a statement, the sense of which was that the church must believe it, and that it is just as difficult or just as easy to do so whether in Berlin or in Basel. That's right. But I think it makes a difference whether one must believe under the condition of going into the clinker or under the condition of a book being forbidden.

Barth: That is correct. That is a serious, a very serious difference. Having a book forbidden is perhaps not the greatest misfortune that can occur to a person. But then again, going into the clinker also need not be the greatest misfortune. So there is no great value in weighing them one against the other. This question has come to me from out of your midst, but I believe that what I have said here I would also repeat in East Berlin without hesitation. It applies to people there, and it applies to us here. And whether things are more difficult there or here probably can't be determined. In a particular case, something seemingly easy can be very difficult for a person, and something that seems terribly difficult can be relatively easy. Easy or difficult is no measure of things. Rather, we must measure things by [key questions]: What are we being directed to? What is commanded of us? What may we believe?—on this side and on the other side of the Curtain. And if we can somehow help those behind the Iron

Curtain, then [do so] by showing them: We believe together with you in the same Lord and in his power and in his truth. We do so where we are, in our way, under completely different circumstances. We don't demand anything of you. We don't advise you that you must do it this way or that. One can't give advice irrespective of the Wall to people over there. But we believe and we love and we hope together with you, not just as fellow humans but rather [also] as fellow Christians, and we pray together with you. That is what we are permitted to do in this situation without treading too closely (on the contrary!).

Respondent: But when you reminded us earlier about Bishop Sigg's presentation, we were advised to be every bit as thankful for the state over there in the East as for this state.[34] Isn't that advice? And I would argue that we cannot offer this advice because we live so far away.

Barth: Well, Bishop Sigg did say those things yesterday. And I agree. Perhaps I myself would not have said them without further qualification. But as I heard them, I immediately said, If you understand him rightly, he is right. After all, even the state behind the Iron Curtain is not a kingdom of the devil, rather [it] is a somewhat odd human kingdom. There too there is probably—not only probably, but certainly—something to be thankful for about the existence of the state, which maintains at least some order. Order is a gift of God. And there too the state maintains a bit of order. One should not exaggerate. Just as certainly as we here do not live in the kingdom of God, they behind the Iron Curtain do not live in the kingdom of the devil. Rather, the devil has a bit to do with us too, and God has not died behind the Iron Curtain.

All right, don't we perhaps want to go on? Now we come to something entirely different. I have been asked:

4. Understanding Bultmann's Theology

Question 3: Do you think that you and Bultmann have come to an understanding today?

Barth: "Today" is really good, because[35] [I have been concerned with this for a long time, not just for "today." To restate things, the two of us have come from a place of once having been very close to each other, but "today" have been led in different directions. I nevertheless still believe today that I am "in agreement" with him in at least four points. First, the "task" of theology consists decisively in the *"interpretation of the Bible."* We were in agreement on this matter from the beginning], and are to the present day.

I could go a bit further and say, We are also in agreement insofar as we believe to hear in the Bible of the Old and especially of the New Testament not

---

34. F. Sigg, "Der Christ in der Demokratie," 8: "Of the 10 countries for which I have oversight, five are behind the Iron Curtain. There too I find people who are thankful and wish to give thanks for the state." "As Christians and in praise of God," they receive "the given order . . . as something that makes it possible, after all, for them to live, to work, and to hope."

35. For the sake of the readability of the text, a hypothetical reconstruction of Barth's comments is provided within the brackets; his words are missing because at this place the recording tape had to be changed. The first two sentences attempt to indicate Barth's possible reflections on the key word "today." The next two sentences are a formulation based on the key words in Barth's outline for the conversation: "Agreed: task = interpretation of the Bible." The fifth sentence tries to make a link back to the original conversation.

only news from a distant time, but also a *message*, a *proclamation*. Bultmann, who is a great scholar, likes to use a foreign word and call it the "kerygma."[36] So in this point we are also in agreement: there is a kerygma in the Bible. And that is really a lot, that the Bible is for us not just another book, but one in which a voice resounds and calls us.

Further, though now on a somewhat secondary level, we are also in agreement, Bultmann and I, that one must read the Bible in a way that is—the technical term for it is "*historical-critical*." And "historical-critical" means that one must read the Bible, without prejudice to its character as message, also as a book full of documents of a particular time, along with all that that means. One must have this historical reality before one's eyes—that means "historical." And "critical" means that one makes differentiations because one sees: here it is so, and here it is so. So, we would also be in agreement in this respect.

I believe that we are also in agreement finally in a fourth and decisive sense: namely, we both are of the opinion that a truth and reality encounter us in the Bible, in the New Testament (for he is concerned chiefly with the New Testament), that is infinitely bigger than anything that we make of it, understand, and explicate—in other words, that we ever again stand there before a *mystery* to which one cannot devote enough attention ever anew.

I would say we are in agreement on these four points. But there are naturally a couple of things about which even to the present day we are not entirely in agreement. According to Bultmann, in order to read the Bible correctly, we first have to be in agreement about our understanding of man—to express it in a scholarly way, about a particular *anthropology*.[37] (Anthropology means "doctrine of man.") Bultmann would say that you first have to sit down and study anthropology. And you can do that best by studying Heidegger, for he has the right anthropology for our time. In his school of thought you can learn an existential ontology, and then you know who man is.[38] You put on these glasses when you open the New Testament, and with the help of this existential philosophy you can understand the New Testament, but otherwise not. To that, I say, no, no, not *that*! It's not a matter of first preparing a set of glasses with which to read the Bible! Rather, the Bible itself is written in such large letters that, even if you are half blind, you can roughly see what is going on. And so I let the Bible tell me not only who God is but also who man is. I don't have to bring something to the Bible, but rather I let something from the Bible come to me. That is the principal difference. Nothing else is as important as that. You could also say that [it has to do with] the relationship of philosophy and theology. I would like to have a theology that stands entirely on its own feet, although I also have a little bit of philosophy somewhere in my head. [I would like] philosophy to be subordinate to theology, and theology to be subordinate to the voice of God from Holy Scripture. In this matter we are not in agreement.

36. See, e.g., R. Bultmann, *Glauben und Verstehen: Gesammelte Aufsätze*, vol. 1 (Tübingen: Mohr, 1933), 4th ed. (1993), 172–87 [ET: *Faith and Understanding*, ed. R. W. Funk, trans. L. P. Smith (New York: Harper & Row, 1969), 204–19].

37. See R. Bultmann, *Jesus Christus und die Mythologie: Das Neue Testament im Licht der Bibelkritik* (Hamburg: Furche-Verlag, 1964), 50–67.

38. See, e.g., K. Barth and R. Bultmann, *Briefwechsel: 1922–1966*, ed. B. Jaspert (Zurich: Theologischer Verlag, 1971), 320; 2nd rev. ed. as *Briefwechsel: 1911–1966* (Zurich: Theologischer Verlag, 1994), 309.

That has several consequences. When Bultmann reads the New Testament—and I read it too—then, because he has this doctrine of man, this anthropology, in his glasses, he sees [man above all, and therefore] he has to reduce everything that he finds to statements that certain people make there about themselves or their situation: Paul, John, the Synoptic writers, and Jesus himself, as far as we can know something about him—all of them humans who lived on earth and left us their *"self-understanding."*[39] The New Testament witness is then the expression of their self-understanding, their self-explanation, their self-explication. To that, I clearly say again, No! What we find in the New Testament are not explications of man about himself but rather—and here this concept appears again[40]—*answers* that man gives to what has been *addressed* to him from God. What is decisive is that [the words of] Paul and John and, earlier, the prophets are like mirrors in which God himself and his Word are reflected, or echoes that answer to God's Word. For *this* reason the Bible is important, and for *this* reason the Bible has authority for us, because there and only there *the* Word of God, spoken in Jesus Christ, is reflected or can be heard as an echo.

I could also name a third point: Bultmann's entire theology revolves, so to speak, around the concept of faith. That plays an immensely large role for him.[41] It is always a matter of faith, and especially the faith of this or that Christian individual (faith understood as that person's self-understanding). Everything becomes a teaching of faith, an expression of faith, a statement of faith. The individual Christian as such [is central]. And the rest of the world strangely steps into the shadows—somewhat as Bishop Sigg described it yesterday when he spoke about the Pietists.[42] Rudolf Bultmann is a secret Pietist. I can't help it—that's what he is. He shares this perspective. Naturally he doesn't say, What must I do to get to heaven? But he does say, What can I do in order to live "authentically," existentially authentically?[43] That is finally just a translation of the pietistic wish to get into heaven. What receives far too little attention is the *world*, the human beings around him. There are the Christians, they have their faith, and they understand themselves in such and such a way. The New Testament gives them their direction. We also have the message of the cross of Christ—wonderful that we have that! . . . ? But what about everything outside? There everything happens differently. In faith we can only look away or look beyond. Nothing there fundamentally affects us. In this regard, a word from 1 Corinthians is important to him [namely, Bultmann]: we can be in the world only "as if [we were] not."[44] You remember the place where it says, "buy, as though not buying, be married as though not married . . ." [see 1 Cor. 7:29–31].

---

39. Cf., e.g., R. Bultmann, *Geschichte und Eschatologie* (Tübingen: Mohr, 1958), 50, 181.

40. See Barth's answer to Question 1, above.

41. Cf., e.g., R. Bultmann, *Glauben und Verstehen*, 1:37 [ET: *Faith and Understanding*, 64]: "Could faith then be the Archimedean point from which the world is moved off its axis and is transformed from the world of sin into the world of God? Yes! That is the message of faith."

42. F. Sigg, "Der Christ in der Demokratie," 3: "Why then is Pietism a false way? . . . The accent lies on the 'I.' As a consequence, this individual and this pietistic community sing in their song that you have to let everyone else simply wander along in their wide, open streets."

43. See R. Bultmann, *Glauben und Verstehen*, 145 [ET: *Faith and Understanding*, 176]; and *Geschichte und Eschatologie*, 50, 168.

44. See R. Bultmann, *Glauben und Verstehen*, 312 [the unpublished essay titled "The Significance of the Old Testament for the Christian Faith" is not included in the ET]; and *Neues Testament und Mythologie*, 31. See below, n. 19 in chap. 35.

Paul does say this. And for Bultmann, this is the great prescription for Christians: to live "as though not." But I would say to this: hold it, no, that's not right! When we truly believe, then it is as we heard yesterday and this morning:[45] we live on this earth, and we live in the flesh. Then the answer that we must offer is the answer to God's universal Word, namely, that "God so loved the *world* . . ." [John 3:16], not just a couple of existentially "authentic" people. Jesus Christ died "not only for our sins, but for those of the *entire world*" [1 John 2:2], and so on. Look again at what the Johannine writings have to say about the "world"! It seems to me that Bultmann pays too little attention to that. So we are also not in agreement in this third point.

That has several consequences. You will have noticed that I have said nothing about "*demythologization*," have I? If we have to, we can talk about that later. But that was never for me the burning question with Bultmann. It is just something that follows. Naturally if you place so much weight on *man*, then as a consequence you must read the New Testament as a person of *today*. That means for him [namely, Bultmann], I must accept what the average person accepts as science and as technologically possible. And that becomes the standard by which I measure the New Testament. What doesn't fit is shoved aside as myth, and what remains is only the self-statement of faith, which is preserved there in mythological form. Naturally, I don't join in that game. But I say that only in passing.

So, that's how things stand between me and Bultmann. Whereby in conclusion I can only say that I really like Bultmann simply as a person. To be sure, I haven't seen him for a long time. But we have always enjoyed being together as friends, and I hope that it will continue to be so. If someone were now to ask me, What do you think of Paul Tillich?, I would give a similar answer. My personal relations with Tillich—eye to eye, heart to heart—are splendid. When it is a matter of theology, ha!—we are far apart! But I have no desire to quarrel with Bultmann or Tillich. With that, by the way, we come to the fourth question[46]—but rather, I have only shown to you: "This is where I stand, God help me, I can do no other."[47] I see them saying the strangest things, which I, now as then, cannot say. I believe I must say something else. Does that suffice for the questioner or not?

Question: Actually, that wasn't my question. And for me your response is not sufficient. I would have liked an answer from you about a question that greatly concerns me in Bultmann's theology and in the theology of his disciples. Bultmann says, and I'll say it somewhat coarsely right now: "You Bible-readers who think that you can take the Bible at face value, who think that you can believe everything about the wondrous and unbelievable things there, who say so simply that Jesus is the Son of God, and who await his return in three-dimensional space, just as in the description of his ascension—you're going down the wrong road. And when you preachers preach such things and expect people to believe these unbelievable things, you put them under a law. But you should be a preacher of the gospel." What he thinks—and his disciples,

45. See nn. 14 and 27 above.
46. See n. 6 above.
47. See the words of Martin Luther before the Reichstag in Worms on April 18, 1521 (handed down in a different wording), in WA 7:838–39.

Ebeling, and others, think it all the more[48]—is that faith does not mean to regard difficult things as true and to affirm them, but rather that faith is something beautiful and light, fundamentally a state of floating along, just as we floated along earlier today.[49] You don't have to affirm anything difficult. Don't turn the Bible message into a law that requires people to believe all that, but rather let it be gospel! So, that is my question to you: does someone who expects others to believe that Jesus is the Son of God put them under a law?

Barth: Well, I'm in a curious situation here. I have the feeling that you have caricatured a bit, "somewhat coarsely." On the other hand, I have to say what he got right, for what he says, I also say in part. He is certainly correct when he says that we must preach the gospel and not the law. Now what he means by law is You *must* believe these things. I would rather say You *may* believe that Christ is God's Son. You *may* believe that he has risen. You *may* believe that he will come again. That sounds different, doesn't it? Well, he would probably say to me, I don't like that at all. And I would answer, Come on, but we have the *freedom*; we *may* believe those things! Yet I do agree when he says, Don't make a law here. You know, [the way you say it is just as they used to say it in the old Protestant Orthodoxy],[50] and that wasn't such a nice thing, when they simply said, you must hold such and such to be true.[51] You must? Faith is a great *freedom.* Everything depends on *so* proclaiming the Word of God and all of its content that it appears as a freedom that has been given to us humans.

Now I have to say that I find, unfortunately, a bit too little of this freedom in Bultmann and the Bultmannians. Instead, they all make such ominous faces—have you noticed that? By the way, that's a place where I can't go along with Bultmann [and his followers], when they are so abrasive and [set forth] their negations so almost fanatically. [That creates an atmosphere of dissension. If only it were a cable car that is floating along here! But][52] no, when I hear a Bultmannian speak and write, I hear a wagon that slowly creaks and rattles down the street. Unpleasant, and not at all floating along—not at all! It's not easy to deal with. You aren't elevated, let alone edified. On the contrary, you're put into an aggressive mood, [e.g.,] against those orthodox.

We don't want to be those orthodox, those scarecrows, whom they have in mind. And we need not be. [Rather, I would say]: Oh, my goodness, it is not that I *must* believe, not that I must, but rather that I *may!* Or one can also say: I am commanded, truly commanded, but I respond as one who obeys the command of God: in great joy and in great freedom. And they, the Bultmannians and Bultmann himself, don't quite understand that. That's my problem with them. But I found it important first to tell you where I am in agreement with

48. Cf. R. Bultmann, *Glauben und Verstehen,* 86, 259, 291 [ET: *Faith and Understanding,* 117, 276–77, 309–10]. G. Ebeling, *Das Wesen des christlichen Glaubens,* 15–30.
49. Allusion to the conference outing on the same day in an alpine chairlift, a "Sesselilift."
50. At this point, the sound on the tape was not clear.
51. Here Barth's understanding of the orthodox concept of faith follows that of his teacher W. Herrmann. See, e.g., W. Herrmann, *Christlich-protestantische Dogmatik* (Berlin: Teubner, 1906–9), in Herrmann, *Schriften zur Grundlegung der Theologie,* ed. P. Fischer-Appelt, ThB 36 (Munich: Kaiser, 1966), 298–361. In fact, the old Protestant Orthodox concept of faith was more nuanced. The kind of faith described here was designated only as *fides historica,* as distinguished from *fides salvifica.* See HpB 409–11 [ET: RD 518–21].
52. At this point, the sound on the tape was not clear. The text in brackets is reconstructed from the conference protocol written by E. Schwarzenbach, 23 (mentioned above, in the introduction to this chapter).

him, not where I disagree with him. That is, I believe, more instructive. Then you can maintain more distance in your comments the second time around, just as I have done. [You must] not immediately jump in.

Our dear Pietists in Germany shouldn't be so anxious. If I may say so—perhaps it is good, if I so express myself: you must guard against making martyrs out of Bultmann and the Bultmannians. There are some among them, especially younger ones, who are just waiting for the Pietists to be suspicious and accusatory toward them. Then they can once again say, "Yes, that's how it is. *That's* how you get treated in the church when you speak freely. Then these people come out against you with condemnations," and so on. I wouldn't do that [?]. Let things run their course for the time being. They won't prevail. You can remain calm. And be concerned for your part—or, I would like to say, for our part—that the gospel really sounds forth as the gospel: that is, good news! Then this whole existentialist thing will perhaps disappear like a ghost, and the gospel of Jesus Christ will have its day. So, have as little anxiety about this as about the Communists!

Comment: Professor Barth, it seems to me that the chief problem with Bultmann's teaching hasn't been mentioned yet. He teaches that the miracles are myths—and not only the miracles, but also Jesus' death on the cross is a kind of myth. [. . .][53] That doesn't leave much.

Barth: Yes, yes. But I have tried to show you how Bultmann comes to make such assertions. I fight him, to the extent that I fight him, at the roots. The fruit, as you have indicated, is bitter. But I would not say that it is the chief problem. Rather, the chief problem with Bultmann, what is messed up, if one may say so, is that he won't give the Word of God its freedom, but rather believes that he must help out the Word of God with a philosophy. And if you do that, then you end up with such things. That to me is what is important and the chief problem: this flaw at the bottom, not the foliage of the tree, which to be sure is not a pretty thing.

Question: Professor Barth, may I perhaps get you to answer? If I were able to question Professor Bultmann—I don't know if I could ask such a thing or if it would be inappropriate: "Professor Bultmann, do you have the Holy Spirit?" Because without the Holy Spirit, no one can call Jesus Lord [1 Cor. 12:3]; and faith too is a gift of the Holy Spirit. Perhaps he would say to me, "Yes, you have your assurance, so there is nothing more to discuss." But because he lets so many things [fall away], such as this Pauline teaching, I think about the words, "Cursed be all who proclaim a gospel different from the one that I have proclaimed" [cf. Gal. 1:8]. If I may ask you, Professor Barth: If Bultmann were to draw out the implications of his position, would not God himself have to be a mythical figure? There would have to be this further implication.

Barth: To your first question, would you really want to press this question on him? "Do you have the Holy Spirit or not?"

Questioner: This is a New Testament question.

Barth: Yes, good, but he could immediately turn it around [and ask you], "Do *you* have the Holy Spirit or not?" And then could you comfortably say, "Yes, I do, but you don't"?

Questioner: Comfortably, no.

---

53. Part of the response is unintelligible on the tape.

Barth: Well, there you have it.

Questioner: But we do know "that we have come out of death to life" [1 John 3:14].

Barth: Good, so let us *show* that it is so. It is not good to argue about who has the Holy Spirit and who doesn't. That doesn't work. The Holy Spirit, as we know, is recognized by [the Spirit's] *fruits*. And so it depends on what kind of fruits are there. You can't exclude the possibility that Bultmann, who has worked for his whole life on the New Testament, also knows something of the reality of the Holy Spirit in his life.

He does say things that you don't like to hear, and that I don't like to hear, where perhaps most of us would say that we can't go along with him. But perhaps there are also some who say, "But there is something to it." Well, that's how it goes. So it is in the whole church and in theology: all of us, you and I and Rudolf Bultmann, live in a battle of the Spirit against the flesh [cf. Gal. 5:17]. We're in this together. You must not speak about Bultmann with so little solidarity as though you were standing in your little pulpit being able to pass judgment on him from on high. That does not instruct him. It only makes him mad. Then he will make his Oldenburg face.[54] He will make big, round eyes and be unresponsive. That only scares people off. You must not approach him like that.

Question: Professor Barth, the question that I posed at the end: Is Bultmann consistent in his arguments and in his whole way of thinking?

Barth: Who of us is entirely "consistent in his way of thinking"? My goodness! Even those of us who say, "I want to go a different way than Bultmann does," are not entirely consistent. We're in this together. Don't you want [to let him go his own way] for a bit? Go in confidence your way! Live out your faith! And make a good witness to the gospel with your life or your publishing house, if you have one, or your bookstore! Don't try to rack Bultmann's brain, but rather rack your own!

Questioner: But if I may say one thing: the book [. . .][55] by Professor Barth about the Word of God was decisive for me.[56]

Barth: Ha, that's great. And now you aren't able to read Bultmann with the same joy. You don't need to read him if it bothers you so much. I do have to read him a little bit. You don't have to. If I [were in your place], I wouldn't lose time and energy with it—if Bultmann constantly annoys you. And as a matter of fact, I would like several friends here to [consider] this a bit: we have better things to be doing . . .[57]

But now we are coming very close to the fourth question. As I read the question, I laughed. It goes like this:

---

54. R. Bultmann was born on August 20, 1884, in Wiefelstede, in what was then the Grand Duchy of Oldenburg.

55. The words on the tape are partially unintelligible.

56. The reference is either to K. Barth, *Das Wort Gottes und die Theologie*, vol. 1 of *Gesammelte Vorträge* (Munich: Kaiser, 1924) [ET: *The Word of God and the Word of Man*, trans. D. Horton (New York: Harper & Row, 1928); reissued as *The Word of God and Theology*, trans. A. Marga, 2nd ed. (New York: T&T Clark, 2011)]; or to K. Barth, *Die Lehre vom Worte Gottes: Prolegomena zur christlichen Dogmatik*, vol. 1 of *Christliche Dogmatik im Entwurf* [Munich: Kaiser, 1927]); ed. G. Sauter 2 (Zurich: Theologischer Verlag, 1982).

57. Barth was interrupted here by a response that is nearly unintelligible. It apparently had to do with pressing him to answer the following two questions.

5. Of the Theological Existence of an Elderly Person

Question 4: Does the irenic and therefore mediating attitude of older theologians . . .
Barth: Oh yes, listen to this!
Question 4: . . . spring forth from the insight, which grows all the stronger in the course of a lifetime, that all human ability to know and to explain things is precarious, or is it to be explained more out of a diminished readiness to go into battle? (The dear questioner mentions a German theologian who seems to exhibit this irenic attitude, but he poses the question apparently because he wants to hear about this matter from you.)[58]
Barth: I understand that to be a personal question directed entirely to me. You see, I am an "older theologian." There's nothing more to do about it.

Two years ago Karl Kupisch in Berlin published a collection of my essays under the odd title *"The Idol Totters."*[59] When he told me that he wanted to give the book this title, I sat up a little shocked and said: "Everyone will surely apply that to me. He has turned seventy-five years old now—'*the* idol totters'!" But then he explained that he didn't mean it in that way, and so I let him go ahead. The book is now available under that title.

And now this question comes up: Is[n't] the "old theologian" getting a little soft, a little yielding, almost a little neutral? And is that to be explained by the fact that he is becoming so wise as he gets old? Or is it to be explained by the fact that his teeth are beginning to fall out and that he is no longer so stable on his feet and that all kinds of discomforts are announcing themselves, and so forth? Yes indeed, quite a question to pose! I acknowledge the real seriousness of this question. But I also laughed when I read it.

Let me just explain things to the extent that the question might touch upon me. I know what the questioner means when he places this question before *me*. He no longer hears me so often butt in, no [longer] say "no" so strongly, so sharply criticize, so clearly reject—for example, as you would have liked, if I had let loose a real anathema [against] Bultmann.[60] No, the old theologian doesn't do it. Is that "irenic"? Is that "mediating"? Or what really is going on? You see, I know exactly what you mean by my "attitude."

As far as I am concerned, it is simply that from a certain point on—perhaps, let's say, approximately from the end of the Second World War onward, and in part already long before that— . . . that I directed all my zeal into saying something *positive*: simply, *"so* it is, *there* we have it, *that's* what we need, *that* is true, *that* is real, *that* is good, *that* is helpful," and the like. That's what I mean by positive. [In contrast], earlier, as I now look back, I must say that I took an adolescent delight in saying no. "To the right as to the left one sees a Turk split in

---

58. The sentence in parentheses is an addition by E. Schwarzenbach to the question that someone else had posed to Barth. Schwarzenbach communicated this question, along with the others, to Barth in a letter of June 8, 1962 (original in the Karl Barth Archives, Basel).

59. K. Barth, *"Der Götze wackelt": Zeitkritische Aufsätze, Reden und Briefe von 1930 bis 1960,* ed. K. Kupisch (Berlin: K. Vogt, 1961). The title picks up on a phrase that Barth, alluding to Isa. 41:7, used on April 20, 1920, to characterize the current condition of liberal theology: "It is apparent that the idols are tottering." Bw.Th. 1:380.

60. See Barth's answer to question 3, above.

half, falling to the ground."[61] That's how it was, for example, in the *Letter to the Romans*.[62] And that's what made the *Letter to the Romans* so interesting to people, because so much blood was spilled. No one escaped: not the rationalists or the idealists, not the Pietists or the orthodox either, and [not] the religious and the unreligious. It was a battlefield. That made quite an impression on people, how everything got cleared out of the way. And I was of the same opinion that precisely those things had to be said now [?], that a clean sweep of everything had to be made. My last great atrocity of this kind was my piece against Brunner, which was simply called "No!," with an exclamation mark.[63] I wrote most of this piece in Rome. And that's where I also came up with the title "No!" When I saw St. Peter's and the pope,[64] I connected it to Brunner: the same thing is going on there. So: No! Then I heard a multitude of voices protest: But that's unkind. People said that to me in English and every other language: "How unkind" of you simply to say No! and to be so unchristian. I replied: Enough! Law! No! [The No] was uttered. [?]

Now, since I began speaking positively rather than in this way, I have lost some of my delight in cutting people off and putting them down. That doesn't mean that I have become any less decisive. But it does mean that I slowly got to thinking—I had to learn a lot!—about what Scripture says: "For the anger of man does not work the righteousness of God" [Jas. 1:20]. [Not] even a justified anger! I must say that there is even now perhaps more anger in me than people notice. I am now letting go of that anger a little. I keep quiet about it. I don't say as much. But I did have, for example, a hefty anger in me over the course of this spring about the things that transpired in Basel.[65] I didn't say anything, at least [not] publicly (sometimes a little in private, but I didn't make any noises in any newspaper), but rather let things take their own course, as they now have, and said to myself: I won't make things any better if I [intervene]. I will do better to remain confident that whatever is false and wrong, the lie (as I said earlier),[66] will come up short. "Vengeance is mine, I will avenge myself, says the Lord" [Deut. 32:35; Rom. 12:19]. What is false defeats itself whenever what is right is clearly set forth.

(I am depicting things from my own point of view, as they appear to me, as I understand them to be.) [From this perspective, the question pressed itself upon me] as to whether critique and also renunciation of a position don't emerge much more strongly in this way. If you say Yes quite forcefully, then it is almost obvious that the No is also present. I remember well what I experienced at the beginning, in the 1920s, long before my present "period of wisdom," and how the liberals were terribly irritated with me. Not because I attacked them, but rather because I, for example, once said, The statement in the Creed, "conceived by the Holy Ghost, born of the Virgin Mary," is a good statement,

---

61. From the ballad "Schwäbische Kunde [Swabian Tale]," by Ludwig Uhland. [Trans.: The ballad speaks of a battle in which a Schwabian's sword slices his enemy apart, so that his body falls down to the earth in halves.]
62. See n. 3 above.
63. K. Barth, *Nein! Antwort an Emil Brunner*, ThExh 14 (Munich: Kaiser, 1934).
64. Ibid., 32.
65. See n. 21 above.
66. See section 3 above, "The Church in a Totalitarian State."

and I hold it to be right.[67] [I] said nothing more than that, and people were crying out: "Watch out, here comes that orthodoxy again! Oh, he is going to be repressive!" They even spoke about Servetus.[68] "[So, now] he is going to torch his enemies," and I don't know what all.[69] I had very peaceably said only this: That's what it says, and I hold it to be right. A faith statement! And that is what I have generally experienced whenever I have in all calmness said something positive. It's precisely then that people have noticed that a renunciation is also included, even if perhaps a very quiet one. It doesn't have to be loud, but whenever someone *says* something definite, then of course one is *not* saying something else. At any rate, so it seems to me.

But I am not quite finished with my answer to this question. For when you look honestly at the human dimension of it, it is probably the case that when you are an "older theologian," such as I now am, this wisdom or patience or this confidence that truth takes care of itself, gets strangely mixed up a bit with the weakness of old age. You see, there you have again "spirit and flesh," which interpenetrate each other in such a peculiar way. I don't wish to raise my hand and swear an oath and say, "Oh, it's just wisdom that accounts for why I'm not so [abrasive] anymore." No, it also has to do with the fact that I no longer see so well—and everything else that happens when you get old. Your thinking is a little slower, and you forget a lot. So, becoming tame and peaceful can also be part of this development. Seen in this way, it's not [something] so terribly pretty, is it? But I hope that it is not simply [grounded in the fact] that I am losing my teeth, but rather that a little wisdom and patience may really be present in me.

Once before—it's more than ten years ago now—I also had difficulty in understanding and explaining myself. It was so: I was horribly attacked right here in Switzerland. That had already happened to me a couple of times. A statesman—later the man even became a *Bundesrat* [Federal Counselor]— attacked me something awful in public.[70] It had to do with different things. He said that I was one of the [theologically] orthodox; at the same time he said that I flirted with Communism; and then that I was just so abrasive, and then again so lenient. . . . Ah, he leveled a whole row of accusations at me. And that was

---

67. K. Barth, *Die Christliche Dogmatik*, 365–79; also, *CD* I/2:172–202, esp. 185–202 [*KD* 187–221, esp. 202–21].

68. The Spanish doctor Michael Servetus was put on trial in Geneva on account of his criticism of Calvin's doctrine of the Trinity and then condemned by the town council to be burned at the stake on October 27, 1553.

69. O. Pfister, in *Calvins Eingreifen in die Hexer- und Hexenprozesse von Peney 1545 nach seiner Bedeutung für Geschichte und Gegenwart* (Zurich: Artemis-Verlag, 1947), takes on Barth and Thurneysen, arguing that in the development of dogma and arguments about doctrine, he finds only "suppression" and "replacement" (193) of "the original heroic love of Jesus Christ as the salvation of humankind." For the references to Barth, see 133, 188, and 192–93.

70. In 1949–51, Markus Feldmann (1887–1958), at that time a member of the *Regierungsrat* [Governing Council] of the Canton of Bern (with responsibility for education and the churches), accused Barth of endangering the very foundation of the existence of Switzerland through his ecclesiastical "power demands" and his supposed friendliness with Communism. He published his critique in July 1951 in a pamphlet, printed at state cost, *Kirche und Staat im Kanton Bern: Dokumente zur Orientierung des Grossen Rates als Beitrag zur Diskussion* [Church and state in the canton of Bern: Documents for orienting the Great Council, a contribution to the discussion], edited by the Staatskanzlei of Bern. At the end of 1951, Feldmann was elected to the seven-member *Bundesrat* [Federal Council], the Swiss government. See *O.Br. 1945–1968*, 214–31, esp. 214–17.

picked up by all the Swiss press.[71] And I did not respond. I did not answer. At that time, I was over sixty and said to myself: Hey, he should have come at me when I was thirty! Then he would have gotten it. Then I would have shown him how a Basler can laugh and beat you up and knife you. Perhaps I could have given an answer that would have resulted in him not becoming a *Bundesrat*. I could have made a joke out of him. But I didn't do it.

But now—the story isn't over—I asked myself, Why didn't I do it? You see, good friends had said to me, You should answer him! You shouldn't just take that lying down! [So] I asked myself, Why then don't I answer? Why don't I destroy him [?], as I easily could have done? There were two possibilities: Either—and that would be the nice solution—I don't do it because I have read so deeply in the First Letter of Peter, a book that I especially like, where it is written, "Remain calm! Be patient! Be forbearing! Christ also bore his cross. Don't let the world make you so crazy that you return evil for evil, rather . . ." [cf. 1 Pet. 2:18–24; 3:9–10]. So! Was it that? I hope that it was something like that. But if I am honest with myself, I have to say [that] something else was also going on—not fear or something like that, but in truth a bit of human contempt. The guy seemed to me simply . . . *höö, hoh* [exclamation of despairing astonishment]! What in the world is that? A person behaving like that! . . . But that kind of response would be unchristian. You should not be contemptuous of your neighbor. That's unacceptable. And to this day I cannot say whether it was more the one or the other, or in which combination it was the one and the other. I can talk about these things freely now. [The man] is long since deceased and surely knows the answer better himself.

There is only one question left. The last question follows:

6. Protestant and Catholic

Question 5: What do you regard as the difference between Protestant and Catholic?

Barth: When I reflect on this matter—and I have already reflected on it a great deal—what always comes strongly to the fore for me is this: the difference lies in the little word "and." Roman Catholics add that word to what we take to be right according to Protestant understanding. We Protestants think we must confess that we believe in *Jesus*, the *Lord*. Period! Everything is contained in it: I believe in God, the Father, I believe in the Holy Spirit, in Jesus. Catholics say, yes, in Jesus—*and* in Mary. So this Mary comes along right next to Jesus—in a very important role for Catholics that I cannot explicate here. And we simply

71. See Barth's letter of August 25, 1951, to Christoph Barth (in the Karl Barth Archives, Basel), in which he says that Feldmann's pamphlet had thrown him "into the middle of a genuine Helvetic press storm . . . , which has gone on with almost no letup for close to four weeks. . . . Now the lake is raging and demands a victim. Nothing but old, stupid stories. . . . One newspaper after another between the Alps and the Canton of Jura [trans.: near the French border], repeats this stuff based on that pamphlet along with the corresponding commentaries, 'unable either to exhaust or empty itself [Schiller, *Der Taucher*].' . . . The Social Democrats have gone at me the hardest; the 'Volksfreund' of Spiez has let me off the easiest." Among other things, the *Schweizerische Politische Korrespondenz*, January 17, 1952, demanded that Barth be brought before the criminal court on charges of treason. See *O.Br. 1945–1968*, 306–7, esp. 307n13.

can't go along with this, at least if we are not just half Protestants who still accept a little bit of Mariology. Where we find this "and," Catholicism begins, as with Jesus *and* Mary. Honor to Mary! There is much good to say about Mary. But in no way should she be placed next to Jesus. It's the same with Jesus Christ *and* the church: the church as governed by the bishops and especially the pope as the highest authority. And it's the same in regard to the area of how we know God. Revelation—yes, Catholics agree, but then—*and* reason! Reason thus becomes a second principle: reason is not only in service of, reason is not only an instrument, but rather reason is a second source [of Christian knowledge] along with revelation. Faith—yes, say Catholics, but then they add: faith *and* works. So, not faith as expressed in works or something similar, but rather faith *and* works! The Word—*and* the Sacrament, say Catholics. Thus the sacrament becomes a second [principle]. As far as I can see, this "and" is a thread that runs through all of Catholic thinking. That's where I see the "difference."

But I would not want that to be now the last thing that I say about Catholicism. I wish to add—and not just because I am now elderly and at peace—that I track certain developments in today's Roman Catholic Church with joy and with respect. These developments are all pushing toward the disappearance of this "and." They are seeking to explain and proclaim even the strangest matters such as Mariology and the doctrine about the pope without such a duality, such a separation, such a distinction of two [principles]. I am happy that I have Roman Catholic *friends*—including some with whom I get along better than with many Protestants. As one of them, still a young man, stepped into my study last winter, I said to him, "O, Mr. So-and-so, what a shame that you are Catholic. Otherwise, you could be my successor!"[72]

But to end once again on a positive note, where we are united with Catholics is simply in our confession of Jesus Christ, which, to be sure, does include an "and": "true God *and* true man."[73] When we are dealing with *this* "and" and when both sides learn better to say this "and" together—well, I don't know that there will be a reunification before the return of Christ, and I also don't know about the council and what will happen there,[74] but in any case, we will still be *separated* brethren but nevertheless *brethren, separated* in faith, yet separated in the *same* faith.[75]

So much to this point five, then, with the necessary brevity. With that, I'm at the end.

---

72. A reference to Prof. Hans Küng.

73. See the formula of the Council of Chalcedon (451) about the two natures of Christ.

74. On January 25, 1959, Pope John XXIII called for what would later be named the Second Vatican Council. On December 25, 1961, he announced in the [Apostolic] Constitution *Humanae salutis* that he would call it into session in 1962, and on February 2, 1962, in the *Motupropio Consilium*, he set the opening of the council for October 11, 1962.

75. The term "separated brethren" (*fratres seiuncti*) as a designation for non-Catholic Christians came into official use in the Catholic Church through the Second Vatican Council. The term was already frequently used in the years before the council. So for example, on June 14, 1959, during an audience for teachers and students of the Greek Collegium in Rome, Pope John XXIII said, "Only when the Church presents itself as modernized and renewed in healthy measure can it say to the separated brethren: 'Come to us'" (as quoted in *Herder-Korrespondenz* 13 [1958/59]: 515). See also the *Prooemium* of the Decree on Ecumenism, *Unitatis redintegratio*, one of the conciliar documents: "Everywhere large numbers have felt the impulse of this grace, and among our separated brethren also there increases from day to day the movement, fostered by the grace of the Holy Spirit, for the restoration of unity among all Christians." See also chap. 1, art. 3; chap. 2, art. 7; and passim.

Herr X: Our dear honored Herr Professor, I would like to take just a minute to add a word. The applause of the assembly has just demonstrated how thankful we are to you for your visit. Now with a small example I would like to challenge all of us to take home with us—in the right way, thankfully—what we have heard here. We have spent the last three days in these glorious surroundings. The relaxation, the sense of well-being, and the peacefulness that here radiate everywhere remind us almost of a protected nature park. Just as we may have taken along a small memento from our excursion today or from yesterday, when we went swimming or from somewhere else, so too we should take along a memento from our days with you. We should pluck out something like a tiny bud, or perhaps even several, from what you, Herr Professor, have told us and plant it in our own little protected nature park. And we will want to do whatever we can to allow this bud to blossom and flourish after we have brought it safely home.

Barth: Thank you.

35. Conversation with the Schaffhausen Company of Pastors
1962

On the afternoon of August 30, 1962, Karl Barth had a conversation of around two and a half hours with the company of the Reformed pastors of the canton of Schaffhausen at the Restaurant Bruderholz in Basel. The regular meetings of this company of pastors, the Bartholomaeikonvent, were chaired by Dean Dr. Willy Meyer. The following documents survive from the discussion: (1) three typescript pages with the fourteen questions submitted by the pastors, in the margins of which Barth had written brief headings for his answers (present in the Barth Archive in Basel); (2) one handwritten record of the proceedings, about five pages long, written by Pastor A. Buchmann, who was then the secretary of the company. This document can be found in the large volume of "Konventsprotokolle 1947–1962," 366–71, in the State Archive of Schaffhausen. The following text reproduces this record of the proceedings. This version has not been changed in any way by the frequent insertions in square brackets, but has been supplemented in this way for better intelligibility: this seemed necessary because the record of proceedings skips over statements that are grammatically and, even more often, materially to be presumed. In the following, Barth's written headings are cited in a footnote at the start of each of his responses. The "questions" of the participants given in the record of proceedings have occasionally been supplemented from the typescript version.

Following the meeting, on November 3, 1962, one of the participants, Ernst Rippmann, sent Barth a letter, which is preserved in the Barth Archive in Basel. He wrote: "You did more good than you may think, and broke off the little barbs of the questioners in such a way that they themselves were astonished—and this by the power of the cheerfulness of your heart! [. . .] You no doubt noticed that every question concluded with a redeeming, approving laugh. Once or twice it was a little hesitant."

Question 1: You said in a lecture in Aarau, looking back on your earlier work, that you had only seen "half the truth" in that early period.[1] Is the radical denial of human religiosity, as you represented it in the *Epistle to the Romans*,[2] to be understood as that "half the truth"?

---

1. Karl Barth, *Die Menschlichkeit Gottes*, ThSt 48 (Zollikon–Zurich: Evangelischer Verlag, 1956) [ET: "The Humanity of God," in *The Humanity of God*, trans. J. N. Thomas and T. Wieser (London: Collins, 1961)], (a lecture given at the Conference of the Swiss Reformed Pastors Association [*Schweizerischer Reformierter Pfarrverein*] in Aarau on September 25, 1956), esp. 7 [ET: "partially in the right" (42)].

2. Karl Barth, *Der Römerbrief*, 2nd ed. (Munich: Kaiser, 1922); 3rd ed. (1923) [ET: *The Epistle to the Romans*, trans. E. C. Hoskyns (London: Oxford University Press, 1933)]; cf. there particularly the exposition of chap. 7 of the Epistle to the Romans on 211–53 [ET: 229–270], under the titles "The Frontier of Religion," "The Meaning of Religion," and "The Reality of Religion."

Barth:[3] Companions on my way have detected a change [in me].[4] However, this is not a matter of a new discovery, as Tillich and others thought.[5] The definition [of the insight of the *Epistle to the Romans*] as the "radical denial of human religiosity" is not correct. At issue there is something more fundamental. It is a question of a new discovery of God, of a resolute orientation toward his existence, his activity, his work for humanity. The accusation of Balthasar, that in my theology Schleiermacher has just been turned on his head when I speak of the absolutely sovereign God,[6] is wrong as well. It is not a question of idealist speculation. It is also not a question of advancing to a better anthropology: it is a question of theology.

But I could not rest there. Through my study of the history of theology, it dawned on me that, if there were not to be a new "halving of the truth," then the human being had to come into play. The doctrine of the two natures establishes that Jesus Christ is true human and true God. In the Old Testament we have the covenant of Yahweh with his people. God is always *first*, but God says *Yes* to the *human being*. That is the theme of the Bible: a Yes, in which admittedly a No is also included; but the human being even as a sinner is seen as God's covenant partner (Athanasius).[7] This was really the issue already in the *Epistle to the Romans* as well. But in the *Epistle to the Romans*, at that time, the right thing was said angrily. Mindful of the fact that one is supposed to "speak tenderly to Jerusalem" [Isa. 40:2], I have now emphasized more the goodness and grace of God, in which even according to my understanding today lies the most severe judgment, but precisely the goodness and grace in which the judgment is included, by which it is enclosed. "The healing grace of God disciplines us" [Titus 2:11–12]. When we speak of Christ, of the covenant, we will also inexorably come to speak of the grace of God understood in this way.

After the responses of colleagues Stamm, Koestler, and Urner, Professor Barth set forth further how Christianity at all times stands in danger of becoming a religion. Our duty is not the denial [of religion], but the critique of religion and, in contrast to an attempt to synthesize "Faith and Religion," the call to

---

3. Barth's headings for Question 1: "Not first in Aarau! Being, work, and Word *of God* > relates to humanity. Balthasar: inverted Schleiermacher! Bultmann: the *human being* confronted by this God. God's *covenant* with humanity. Judgment is *grace.*"
4. Cf., e.g., E. Brunner, "Der neue Barth," in *ZTK* 48 (1951): 89–100. [ET: "The New Barth," trans. J. C. Campbell, in *Scottish Journal of Theology* 4 (1951): 123–35].
5. It is possible that either Barth or the secretary of the company is here confusing Tillich with Brunner: cf. n. 4 above.
6. H. U. von Balthasar, *Karl Barth: Darstellung und Deutung seiner Theologie* (Cologne: Hegner, 1951); 2nd ed. (1962) [ET: *The Theology of Karl Barth: Exposition and Interpretation*, trans. E. Oakes (San Francisco: Ignatius Press, 1992). The point of this idea of Balthasar's is that Barth, in his critique of Schleiermacher, has taken over Schleiermacher's categories and that "the (certainly critical) style of the deployment of the categories . . . presupposes certain inclinations and tendencies of Barth, which as such manifest a questionable and partial conception of revelation" 253 [ET: 241]. "How should the accusation be suppressed here—the same one, which Barth so insistently raised . . . against Schleiermacher?" 256 [ET: 244].
7. At this point Barth presumably quoted a particular text of Athanasius. However, the abbreviated account of his answer in the record allows at most conjectures as to the exact citation. It is conceivable that the Athanasius text was something along the lines of *De incarnatione Verbi* 4 (SC 199:274–78; particularly 276, lines 4–10), according to which human guilt was straightforwardly the cause of the incarnation of the Logos. It is also conceivable that Barth, anticipating Question 3 and his answer to it, quoted a text that is attributed to Athanasius and that is quoted by Barth in CD IV/1:211 [KD 231]: *ho tōn holōn kritēs ekrithē dia se, hina sy hypsōthēs* = "The Judge of all people [or: of the universe] was judged for your sake, so that you might be exalted."

faith. There has to be historical-critical work. We should neither look down on the nineteenth century in theology, nor should we return to it.

Question 2: In your theology, is the reality of evil sufficiently seen, and is the judgment of God given sufficient weight? How does our speaking of sin preserve us from sin becoming simply a "negation," a *privatio boni* [deprivation of good]?

Barth:[8] The question is interesting in relation to question 1! [There was criticism of the *Epistle to the Romans* because, beyond the emphasis on the judgment of God there, grace was said to be missing. Now, because of the emphasis on grace, the judgment of God is said to be missing in my work.] We could describe our relation to God with the phrase "distance in community." Then the question posed to me would now be whether this distance is still sufficiently seen by me. But now I would like to ask you to what extent it is not sufficiently seen, when I actually write, Sin is a negation,[9] or if you want, a *privatio boni*, but that means really a *robbery* of the good! It is the epitome of the negation desired and enacted by the human being. By the grace of God we know not only the Creator but also the Reconciler [and the Redeemer]. Sin, however, is the negation of creation[, reconciliation], and redemption. We cannot therefore say that it is *only* a negation. It is the darkness right in the midst of the light of God; it is the realization of nothingness, of that which God has rejected. The human being draws chaos once again into the world that was created good by God. Sin is the impossible possibility. There is no freedom for sin, only [in reality] the act of sin. We only have freedom for obedience. Sin is imprisonment. The question in Deuteronomy [11:26–28; 30:1–3, 15–18], the decision between "blessing and curse," shows the possible and the impossible way.

To the question of the dean, whether according to Genesis 3 the human being had the freedom to sin or not, Professor Barth responded that sin was something so abominable that we should not trace it back to the performance of an act of true freedom. As the serpent approached the human being, it acted directly against the grace of God. In Genesis 3, the horror at this action becomes clear. Between Genesis 1–2 and Genesis 3 there is the greatest conceivable contrast.

M. Koestler pointed to the judgment parables of Jesus [e.g., Matt. 25]. *H. Urner* commented that in the decision for "No," freedom was still necessary.

Professor Barth stated: Even in the named parables, it is a matter of the proclamation of grace, not of a mere offer. The decision, which confronts us in this proclamation, is to be understood in the sense of "crisis." Americans distinguish between "liberty" and "freedom"; the second term expresses what is meant in Jesus' saying, "If the Son makes you free, then you are free indeed" [John 8:36]. It is so difficult to say what this freedom is that we have to ask for imagination in order to say it rightly. For this true freedom, which is not a freedom for sin, is disclosed to us by the grace of God. It is a matter here of the right proclamation of grace, grace that is *really* grace, and yet not *cheap* grace. We have to say both that grace is liberation and that grace itself is discipline.

---

8. Barth's headings for Question 2: "Interesting in relation to Question 1!! Facts in *CD*!? S[in] = negation of grace, of creation, reconciliation, redemption—only that? Act of darkness, cf. [*CD*] III/1. J[esus] C[hrist] died *propter nos* [for us]."

9. Cf. *CD* III/3:302 [*KD* 342]: Sin, evil, is "the *true Nothingness*, the *enemy*, with which there must be no peace, the *negative*, which is not simply the complement to a positive that confronts it" [rev.].

Paul Keller was of the opinion that we ourselves recognize grace as we proclaim it.

Professor Barth cited Romans 6[:4, 8] (died and buried with Christ). While praying and working, we should learn to speak of grace.

Question 3: Is not the actual center of the doctrine of reconciliation ("The Judge Judged in Our Place")[10] particularly alien to our congregations in the established churches [*volkskirchlichen Gemeinden*] today? (Seldom the object of proclamation, because the contemporary person has no feel for it.) Do you accept the claim that the gospel does not have the same center for every age (today, instead of reconciliation, [we speak of] liberation from threatening psychic and cosmic powers)?

Barth:[11] The center of the gospel can only be Jesus Christ. We should recognize him in his judicial, royal, and prophetic office (as "the light of the world" [John 8:12]). Christ must be proclaimed in his totality. If today the doctrine of reconciliation or something else is alien to the people, then the full proclamation has been lacking. The church does not yet have the fullness of the confession of Christ behind it as if it had been grasped already, but still before it.

W. Kuster emphasized that the full proclamation of Christ appeals to people more. There is also a pedagogy of grace. Gospel is to be proclaimed as εὐαγγέλιον [*euangelion*]. In answer to the question of Dean Meyer, whether the gospel does not have the same center in every age, Professor Barth suggested that shifts in accent in recognizing this center are possible and necessary, but the center always remains the same. We must always be open to such shifts in accent imposing themselves, but we must not then stand still in any one position.

Question 4: In your *Church Dogmatics* (IV/2) there is the beautiful sentence: "Love has, cultivates, and tolerates no anti-complexes. That is one of the secrets of its superiority, of its victory."[12] What is the difference between an anti-complex and a continually hostile attitude, for example, against the papal church, sectarians, a different theology, the state of mind of German nationalists, the *NZZ*,[13] the MRA,[14] and so on?

Barth:[15] Wherever a Yes is spoken in faith, it also implies a No. Faith says No to unbelief and to the works of unbelief. Is that a "hostile attitude"? As human beings who are on the way, we will indeed always experience the opposition of spirit and flesh and the like. That is to say, faith always has a certain direction and thereby excludes other directions. In the life history of the individual and in the history of the church, however, the concrete form of Yes and No is in principle always changeable. The concrete form of Yes and No must therefore

---

10. Heading of *CD* IV/1:211, §59.2 [*KD* 231, §59.2].

11. Barth's headings for Question 3: "'Center' is J[esus] C[hrist]: t[he] Judged = justif[ication]—t[he] roy[al] human being = sancti[fication]—t[he] Light of t[he] w[orld] = voc[ation].—[That this material is 'alien' to congregations today is one more reason to proclaim not this 'aspect,' but the work a[nd] Word of J[esus] C[hrist] in its totality.—Shifts in *accent* are possible, can be imperative. But *no abstractions!* Liberation presupposes J[esus] C[hrist] in his totality."

12. *CD* IV/2:834 rev. [*KD* 946].

13. The *Neue Zürcher Zeitung* [a major Swiss daily newspaper].

14. The Moral Re-Armament movement [*Moralische Aufrüstung*, founded by Frank Buchman and now known as Initiatives of Change].

15. Barth's headings for Question 4: "*Yes* of faith always implies a *No* to unbelief. The concrete form of the latter can and must change. If it becomes fixed (as a principle!), then the anti-complex arises. Conversation must continue—in *hope* in view of the opponent—in *readiness to learn*."

never become a matter of principle. There is only one *principium*: Christ. On that basis, changes in our concrete statements are certainly possible, because in certain cases a No can be less important than in others. However, even when a categorical "No" is expressed, it is only ever a matter of de facto opposites. We have to leave the opposites that exist de jure to the Judge of the world. In this world, everything remains in flux.[16] We must therefore endure one another as cocreatures, even when we express a Yes and a No. The danger is always that we create principles.

To Heinz Waser, who recalled that, in St. Gallen, Barth had once refused to call the liberals "brothers":[17] The differentiation between the hand of friendship and the hand of brotherhood was not meant nastily. The liberals at that time emphatically called themselves not "brothers," but "friends."

Question 5: How do you evaluate the most recent development in Old and New Testament theology in terms of its fruitfulness for systematic theology and for the life of the church?

Barth:[18] The Old Testament scholars have not become involved with existentialism, in contrast to many New Testament scholars. The effect of the Bultmannian and post-Bultmannian theology is that there are theologians who declare, "I cannot preach against this background." (Theology of the ὡς μή [*hōs mē*].)[19]

After responses by Stamm, Koestler, and Kuster, Professor Barth explained: Even if we want to credit New Testament exegesis today for taking more seriously the historical [*das Geschichtliche*] than was the case in the nineteenth century, we still have to ask what is understood by the term "historical [*geschichtlich*]." For the sake of the "historical [*das Geschichtliche*]," they want initially to disregard the historic [*historisch*] Jesus. However, this, as it is done there, leads eventually to the dissolution of the Synoptic Gospel tradition. Of late, at last, via many detours, the disciples of Bultmann have nevertheless returned to the "historic" [*das Historische*]."[20] However, the hunt for the historic [*Historischen*] has never yet been productive.

Question 6: How do you assess the American theologian R[einhold] Niebuhr?

Barth:[21] Niebuhr originally advocated a type of religious socialism. In the nineteenth century, Americans lived in great optimism. In contrast, Niebuhr in his anthropology contributed to a disillusionment and elaborated the concept

---

16. In the official record: "fluid [*flüssig*]."

17. Barth had given a lecture on September 24, 1935, at a gathering of the *Schweizerischer Reformierter Pfarrverein* [Swiss Reformed Pastors Association] in St. Gallen, on the general theme of the conference: "The confession of the Reformation and our confessing." In his final summation, after the discussion following the lecture, the following passage had caused a scandal and had also been exploited in the German National Socialist press: "And now—may I?—three pieces of advice or requests also addressed to . . . our liberal friends. (I will happily name them friends, but brothers in Christ—no, that is something which we are not at present, so long as we do not understand ourselves to be *in Christ* in the same way as all!)" K. Barth, *Das Bekenntnis der Reformation und unser Bekennen*, ThExh 29 (Munich: Kaiser, 1935), 36.

18. Barth's headings for Question 5: "OT: + NT: —."

19. Barth means the specific use of 1 Cor. 7:29–31 under the heading "detachment from the world" [*Entweltlichung*] as a structural element in R. Bultmann's theology. See above, chap. 34, sect. 4, "Understanding Bultmann's Theology," esp. the sources cited in n. 44; see also: R. Bultmann, "Jesus Christus und die Mythologie," in Bultmann, *Glauben und Verstehen*, vol. 4 (Tübingen: Mohr, 1965), 5th ed. (1993), 188–89 [ET: *Jesus Christ and Mythology* (Englewood Cliffs, NJ: Prentice Hall, 1958)].

20. Cf. J. M. Robinson, *A New Quest of the Historical Jesus* (London: SCM, 1959).

21. Barth's headings for Question 6: "(opponent—today). Social gospel—disillusionment, but Christology drops out—switch to autonomy."

of sin.[22] [However, he then] distinguished [all at once] between Christianity for the personal life (love) and an external Christianity (justice).[23] In practice, therefore, he took up the doctrine of the two kingdoms as Luther advocated it. We cannot accede to that. The decisive center, Christology, is missing in it all.

Question 7: How does one guard oneself against being a preacher of cheap grace?

[*Barth:*] The concern to avoid the proclamation of cheap grace and the emphasis on the discipline of grace has already been explored.[24]

Question 8: What value do you ascribe to study, and what to prayer and meditation in the life of a pastor?

Barth[25] referred to his book *Evangelical Theology: An Introduction*, with its sections on "Prayer," "Study," and "Service."[26]

Question 9: In your opinion, how does theological insight relate to its realization in the life of the church? For example, if one were to share your insight that the baptism of infants is not a New Testament fact, would that lead to personal disobedience against a church that was based on infant baptism?

Question 10: Why do you not fight concretely for adult baptism to replace paedobaptism in our church, since you have, after all, recently demonstrated again[27] that the baptism of infants is unbiblical according to your view?

Barth:[28] In the execution of correct theological confession, one lives in relation to the church in impatient patience or patient impatience. We must bear the weaknesses of the church, if we have seriously discovered any. When we see such weaknesses and simultaneously know what has to change there, we live in an interim: we have to realize that calmly. Nevertheless, "the interim has the joker behind it,"[29] in order to keep things always in suspense. Naturally, we cannot remain there! We are set in motion. And now it is just as Blumhardt said: we should wait and hasten.[30] The spiritual life of the church is

22. Reinhold Niebuhr, *Beyond Tragedy* (London: Nisbet, 1938), e.g., 12: "The consciousness of sin and the consciousness of God are inextricably involved with each other"; 18: "Modern man does not recognize the simple but profound truth that man's life remains self-contradictory in its sin . . ."; 20: "Without the cross, men are beguiled by what is good in human existence into a false optimism and by what is tragic into despair."

23. Cf., e.g., Reinhold Niebuhr, *The Nature and Destiny of Man: A Christian Interpretation*, Gifford Lectures: 1939 (London: Nisbet, 1943), 2:244–286.

24. See above, Question 2.

25. Barth's headings for Question 8: "Prayer--Study—Service."

26. K. Barth, *Einführung inm die evangelische Theologie* (Zurich: Evangelischer Verlag, 1962), 175–212 [ET: *Evangelical Theology: An Introduction*, trans. G. Foley (London: Collins, 1965), 148–82].

27. The question relates to Barth's dogmatics lectures in the winter semester 1959–60 and the summer semester 1960 on the doctrine of baptism: an excerpt of a record of these lectures, produced by Dorothee Hoch, was quite widespread in duplicate form. The text was later published: K. Barth, *Das christliche Leben (Fragment): Die Taufe als Begründung des christlichen Lebens*, KD IV/4, *Fragment* (Zurich: Theologischer Verlag, 1967) [ET: *CD* IV/4, *The Christian Life (Fragment): Baptism as the Foundation of the Christian Life*, trans. G. W. Bromiley (Edinburgh: T&T Clark, 1969)].

28. Barth's headings for Question 9: "Impatient *patience*—patient *impatience*. Dismantling through new understanding of the church, baptism, confession. Practical initiatives not without the congregation, but in it."

29. From the section "Sprichwörtlich" in the poems of J. W. von Goethe:

Das Interim	(The interim
Hat den Schalk hinter ihm.	Has the joker behind it.
Wie viel Schälke muß es geben,	How many jokers must there be,
Da wir alle ad interim leben.	Since we all live in the interim.)

30. Cf., e.g., Chr. Blumhardt, *Hausandachten für alle Tage des Jahres* (Stuttgart: Holland & Josenhans, 1916), new ed. (Berlin: Furche, 1932), 19: "With joyfulness wait for and hasten unto the future of your Lord" (following 2 Pet. 3:12).

needed, so that necessary changes come about in it. And that requires humility and a good dash of courage. We must have the courage to take stock of what the situation is systematically and exegetically, and to draw the consequences. And precisely the question of baptism has consequences. With this question, a new understanding of what the church actually is becomes burning. To the present day we have retained the established church [*Volkskirche*] of the Constantinian era. In that church, the doctrine of the Trinity or the doctrine of the two natures was to some extent sacrificed, but not the cantonal church [*Landeskirche*] which is based on the baptism of infants. In baptism, as I think I have to understand it according to the New Testament, an act of confession is supposed to be performed. If in the church the issue is believing in Jesus Christ, then clearly one cannot come into it as a minor. But I do not believe that another form of baptism already makes a new church, rather a new proclamation of the essence of the church will result in the right understanding of baptism. You pastors at the grassroots level must yourselves find the way [in which the particular changes can come about]. I have said my little piece.[31] —With this, question 10, which asked about concrete action in favor of adult baptism, has also been answered.

Question 11:[32] It is said that one of the hopes of the Second Vatican Council[33] is for a fundamental strengthening, an "upward revaluation," of the office of bishop.[34] Should this hope be fulfilled, would that actually be a welcome thing, or not? Would an "advancement" in the direction of an episcopal constitution not also be desirable for our Reformed cantonal churches? Is it not the case, however, that "episcopal figures" are paralyzed by our congregationalism?

Barth:[35] The battle between episcopalism and papalism, between curialism and conciliarism, has already existed in the Catholic Church for a long time. If you now desire a bishop for our churches as well, then my view is this: what a bishop should be, that can never so simply be explained dogmatically and established from the outset. Leuba explained that in any case the office of bishop could only ever exist as "event," not as "institution."[36] Certainly, even in other areas some Christians would be glad and thankful if a leading personality were there. It would be great if such persons were appointed from heaven, but it is something else if they are anchored in the constitution of the church. The contact with the ecumenical movement strengthens this opinion among some people, that such a leading personality is desirable.

J. Staehelin mentioned Vischer's booklet about the transformation of the Swiss churches.[37] The office of bishop belongs to the *bene esse*, not to the *esse* of the church.[38] G. Meyer mentioned the unpleasant circumstances that accom-

31. Cf. n. 27, and also K. Barth, *Die kirchliche Lehre von der Taufe*, ThSt 14 (Zollikon: Evangelischer Verlag, 1943); also ThExh NS 4 (Munich: Kaiser, 1947) [ET: *The Teaching of the Church regarding Baptism* (London: SCM, 1948)].

32. The incorrect numbering in the record of proceedings from this point on has been corrected.

33. The [Second Vatican] Council did not begin until October 11, 1962.

34. That is to say, relative to the papacy.

35. Barth's headings for Question 11: "Against 'Rome'—event, not institution."

36. J.-L. Leuba, *L'institution et l'événement: Les deux modes de l'œuvre de Dieu selon le Nouveau Testament; Leur différence, leur unité* (Neuchâtel and Paris: Delachaux & Niestle, 1950); German ed., *Institution und Ereignis* (Göttingen: Vandenhoeck & Ruprecht, 1957).

37. L. Vischer, *Der Schweizerische Evangelische Kirchenbund: Bund oder Kirche?*, Polis 13 (Zurich: Evangelischer Verlag, 1962).

38. Cf. G. Gaßmann, s.v. "Bischof. II. Das historische Bischofsamt," in *TRE* (1980), 6:686.

pany the search for a pastor. The congregations can certainly turn to a synodical council, but the authorities do not want to help.

Professor Barth answered in view of the desire for a bishop in distinction from the congregationalism, for which he had a preference:[39] this demonstrates a false understanding of congregationalism, which in substance is correct. In Italy, for example, the Waldensians have a moderator. Nevertheless, that does not cancel the fact that every congregation takes responsibility for itself, albeit in connection with all other congregations.

Question 12: In your view, what can the Swiss churches learn from the American churches, and what should they not learn?

Barth[40] reported something of what he had seen during his stay in the United States in the spring of the current year. The life of the congregations impressed him. Personal relations exist among the members of a church, which is something like a happy club [*ein fröhlicher Verein*]. The preachers are far more willing to call a spade a spade. The evidence of faith in love is stressed. They have many more offices. A shot of the American way might not be bad for us.

G. Amman [?] emphasized that at issue there are free churches.

Question 13: In your opinion, does the State of Israel have theological importance, and what would that be?

Barth:[41] Yes, the existence of this state as such is of theological importance. Israel was not only there in the Old Testament, but is also here in the present. It has already been said that the existence of the Jews is the only proof for the existence of God.[42] At the present time the Old Testament is stirring again in a curious way, as in a new "seizure of the land" and so forth. The life of this people is indeed part of the self-demonstration of the God of the Bible.

Question 14: Why do you judge Communism more leniently than National Socialism, given that both systems are equally brutal and hostile to humanity and rest on godless foundations?

Barth posed the counterquestion, whether anyone had ever heard him speak "leniently" about Communism? At the moment, Communism is not interesting enough to make a fuss about it. If it ever pressures us as temptingly as National Socialism did (Synod of Barmen,[43] *Frontenfrühling*,[44] etc.), then protest will be necessary. Then again, would one single person behind the Iron Curtain be helped by a special theological declaration against Communism? Among us here it would require no courage now to say something against it. Many people who speak against it anyway are really infected by the "anti-complex." Think

---

39. Cf. K. Barth, *Die Schrift und die Kirche*, ThSt 22 (Zollikon-Zurich: Theologischer Verlag, 1947), 44.
40. Barth's headings for Question 12: "Strengths and weaknesses: lively congregations—contact—practical interest."
41. Barth's headings for Question 13: "Emphasis on the existence of Israel—Jesus Christ—our guilt."
42. See above, chap. 25, n. 14.
43. The first confessional synod of the German Protestant Church, which took place on May 29–31, 1934, in Wuppertal-Barmen and whose "Theological Declaration" was directed in the first instance against the inner "alignment" of the church with the National Socialist worldview, an alignment that was propagated by the "German Christians [*Deutsche Christen*]."
44. National Socialist currents and movements in Switzerland in the 1930s, gathered together in the "National Front," whose mouthpiece had the title "The Front: Central Fighting Paper of the National Front [Die Front: Zentrales Kampfblatt der Nationalen Front]." Cf. M. Schmid, "Der Frontenfrühling (1930–1939)," in *Schalom! Wir werden euch töten: Texte und Documente zum Antisemitismus in der Schweiz, 1930–1980* (Zurich: Eco-Verlag, 1979), chap. 3.

of the case of Oistrakh,[45] or of Gollwitzer, who was not suitable for the chair in Basel![46]

Pastor Waser asked whether the silence of Barth on these problems behind the Iron Curtain was not being perceived differently than how he was presenting it here. He mentioned Professor Hromádka.

Professor Barth explained that Professor Hromádka advocated a particular type of philosophy of history.[47] With the October Revolution of 1917, according to Hromádka, an objective turning point in world history had occurred. In the long run, one could not keep living on the other side of this turning point, not even in the West. Christians should say to themselves: "That is God's way." Similar things were also said in Germany in 1933.[48]

W. Sonderegger pointed additionally to the dreadful consequences of Communism in the Soviet Union and at the "Wall of Shame."[49]

Professor Barth emphasized that we should not forget to remember those who had to live under this system. It is hard to be brave there. Our protest does not help those people at all. If we were there, we would not be so inclined to cause a commotion. One has to be in it. That is somewhat different than speaking out from a secure place here.

At the end the dean thanked Professor Barth for the service he had rendered us in focusing the telescope through which we had been looking from Athanasius to Hromádka. That the Schaffhausen company of pastors had met outside of Schaffhausen was unparalleled in its history.

---

45. The Russian violinist David Oistrakh, forbidden to appear at a concert in Zurich.

46. The election of Helmut Gollwitzer as Barth's successor to the chair of systematic theology in Basel was thwarted by a storm of publicity in the Swiss press, in which Gollwitzer was denounced as being politically intolerable for Switzerland. For more details, see above, chap. 34, n. 21].

47. Cf. Barth's letters to the Prague professor of theology Josef L. Hromádka, in K. Barth, *Briefe: 1961–1968*, edited by J. Fangmeier and H. Stoevesandt (Zurich: Theologischer Verlag, 1975), 2nd ed. (1979), 113–17, 132–34, 149–54, 256–57, and a letter in response from Hromádka in the same volume, 552–55.

48. Cf., e.g., the constitution of the German Protestant Church, confirmed in the *National Law Gazette* [*Reichsgesetzblatt*] on July 14, 1933, whose preamble begins with the words "In this hour, in which God allows our German people to experience a great historical turning point . . ." (quoted from W. Niemöller, *Kampf und Zeugnis der Bekennenden Kirche* [Bielefeld: Bechauf, 1948], 53).

49. Meaning the wall [that began to be] erected between East and West Berlin, on August 13, 1961, at the instigation of the government of the German Democratic Republic.

36. Conversation with the Editors of [the Journal] Evangelical Theology 1962

From September 30 to October 3, 1962, at the invitation of the publisher Christian Kaiser Munich, a theological conference concerning the issue "Christology Today between Barth and Gogarten" took place at the study center for evangelical youth workers in Josefstal, near Schliersee. Barth himself took part in the conference, for a discussion with him, "for several hours" although "he was heavily bandaged" (K. Barth, Briefe [Letters]: 1961–1968 [Zurich: Theologischer Verlag, 1975], 94). On September 16, while a guest at Ernst Wolf's vacation house on the Walchensee (Upper Bavaria), he had broken his arm. Until October 1, 1962, he stayed at the community hospital in Bad Tölz. The summary of the discussion with him is taken from the conference report by E. Wolf: "Josefstal 1962," in Evangelische Theologie 23 (1963): 216–18.

The second workday was devoted to *Karl Barth*. Professor *Diem* opened it with his lecture on Christology and justification according to Karl Barth.[1] His presentation was followed by a supplementary paper by *E. Wolf*. Wolf's paper was controlled by the question of whether and to what extent Karl Barth's doctrine of justification presented a necessary continuation of the Reformation conception in connection, at the same time, with Barth's liberation of traditional Christology from its static shape[2] in such a way that the doctrine of justification would thereby finally be brought to the theological place where it belonged, in terms of the approach of the Reformation period. . . .

The participants in the discussion were aware of certain difficulties of critical inquiries directed to Karl Barth, inasmuch as one finds time and time again that Barth himself had already taken up these questions in other places. Nonetheless, at least a few questions were outlined, such as the question of the extent to which here the third article of faith remains safeguarded in its relative independence; furthermore, the question of Barth's concept of "inclusive history";[3] and finally the question regarding the role of the concept of covenant in the theological thinking of Barth. "Covenant" is apparently the connection between the vertical and the horizontal, the linking of the element of God's faithfulness

---

1. H. Diem, "Christologie und Rechtfertigung bei Karl Barth," in *EvTh* 23 (1963): 197–213. The lecture as well as the discussion, which is reported in what follows, refers especially to Barth's doctrine of justification in *CD* IV/1:514–642, §61 [*KD* 573–718].

2. In the first draft, by mistake, "Statistik."

3. Cf. *CD* IV/1:16 [*KD* 16]: The Christian message bespeaks in its center "an inclusive history, i.e., it is one that includes in itself the whole event of the 'God with us' and to that extent the history of all of those to whom the 'God with us' applies. But it recounts this history and speaks of its inclusive power and significance in such a way that it declares a *name* . . . [trans. rev.]."

with the freedom of the human. The presenter[4] pointed out that precisely the close connection between the event of justification and election grounded in the freedom and faithfulness of God is a safeguard against turning the event of justification into an episode, an isolatable element, of arriving at a monism of justification in the manner of Holl or also Bultmann, in his own way.[5] For the time being, these are questions that should be posed to Barth himself in the afternoon.

Karl Barth was presented with a few questions from the preceding discussion. *First question:* If it is the case that an "ontological connection" exists between Christ and the justified, and if the history of God in Christ with humanity is an "inclusive history" that includes all people, whether they regard it as true or not, then is there not the impending danger that proclamation turns into mere information, into a mere narrative?

Barth said no. The history of God with humanity in Jesus Christ is, as a comprehensive history, of the sort that the proclamation of the message of this action[6] of God—which happens without the[7] human, for humanity, and from humanity—includes the humanity whom it addresses. To this extent it is always at the same time a history that happens. Here the whole dogmatic problem manifests itself: dogmatics concerns an analysis of the address of God to humanity.

The *second question* dealt with a matter of apostasy. The question as posed leads again and again to abstraction. The answer can only be given inasmuch as we must recognize ourselves as apostles and understand the life of faith as a movement between election and rejection. Election is, however, the first word. And the decision has taken place in Christ: it takes place in Christ and will take place in Christ, in the eschaton. Here again it becomes clear that the concept of the inclusive and including history is different from the one that is obtained here on the basis of history existentially interpreted.

Another question discussed in great detail was whether what Karl Barth has attempted dogmatically from the second article could also be undertaken on the basis of the third. Answer: of course the last word is not said with a christocentric structure, which is necessary against an overemphasis on the first article. It is certainly conceivable to develop the whole of dogmatics on the basis of the third article, into which the second article would have to be integrated. Even so, previous attempts in this direction regularly failed because of the seduction of developing a theology of the life of faith's experience. The intention of Schleiermacher is apparently still a theology of the Holy Spirit. Evidently, the first and third articles are much more easily isolated than the second. From there, the ever-present danger on the one hand consists in arriving at a theology and

---

4. Ernst Wolf.

5. Cf. K. Holl, *Die Rechtfertigungslehre im Licht der Geschichte des Protestantismus*, 2nd ed. (Tübingen: Mohr, 1922). Further, R. Bultmann, *Die Christologie des Neuen Testaments*, in Bultmann, *Glauben und Verstehen*, 9th ed., vol. 1 of *Gesammelte Aufsätze* (Tübingen: Mohr, 1993), 261–62 [ET: "The Christology of the New Testament," in R. Bultmann, *Faith and Understanding*, ed. R. W. Funk, trans. L. P. Smith, vol. 1 (Philadelphia: Fortress, 1966), 278–79]; Bultmann, *Geschichte und Eschatologie*, 3rd ed. (Tübingen: Mohr, 1979), 178–84.

6. In the first draft, ". . . happening, of action . . ."

7. It probably should read "*with* humanity . . ."

ontology of creation, and on the other consists in ending up with a dogmatics of the self-examination of the redeemed.

Barth had a counterquestion for von Rad: How do you explain the fact that Old Testament theologians[8] have not been infected with existentialism? Answer: That must have to do with Israel's experience of history. What is confusing is that Israel has started in so many drafts and has attempted in different ways to define the history of God. This cannot be subsumed under one common denominator.

Another question was whether a systematic entry point into church history might be obtained on the basis of the third article, of a theological explication of the communion of the saints. Barth answered in the affirmative with a reference to how the whole of the history of the church would look if one placed it under the key word: faith, forgiveness of sins.

At the end, the problem of the unity of the witness in the Old and New Testaments was raised and the question of the ultimate ground of the extremely rich differentiation in the biblical writings. For the New Testament that ground is not to be sought merely in the situation of the individual witnesses, in the diversity of christological statements to be explained on that basis. Rather, it must be expected in the object itself: in the richness of Christ. All the different statements really refer to him, whereas one cannot so clearly say the same thing for the Old Testament, that this Jesus Christ is always in sight. For this reason the concept of a theology of the Old Testament is still considerably more problematic. The question is raised for the New Testament whether the retreat to the kerygmatic formulations in the whole New Testament is not a retreat to "the minimal ration of a Christian in an apologetic key: What can still be held on to? What can still be asserted?" This retreat to a "minimal dogma" prevents, however, a really theological apprehension of the historically conditioned character of the individual witnesses.

---

8. In the first draft, "theologians"; corrected by Barth in his copy as "theologies."

37. Conversation with Zurich Doctoral Students 1962

On November 19, 1962, Barth met with six doctoral students from Zurich for a conversation in Basel's Restaurant Bruderholz: Christof Gestrich (later, Berlin), Friedrich Hertel (later, Stuttgart), Ulrich Luz (later, Bern), Walter Mostert (later, Zurich), Karl-Heinz zur Mühlen (later, Bonn), and Alfred Schindler (later, Zurich). "The current situation of theology" was generally agreed upon to be the topic of conversation. The ensuing conversation is reproduced here according to an abbreviated transcript of keywords taken at the time by Christof Gestrich.

1. The Theological Handling of the Concept of "Reality"

Barth: In Bultmann, Fuchs, and Ebeling a law by which everything else is measured is set up. Their books always begin by fixing a particular position, namely, where the modern person is now. As if they knew who the modern person was! Beyond that, I ask, Is there a universally valid concept of reality anyway?

Schindler and Mostert: These theologians certainly do use a concept of reality that is theologically qualified in a certain way: According to their view, it is precisely a consequence of the gospel that one can talk about reality at all. In this way, reality is not a static, fixed criterion for them. The issue is how, from the standpoint of the gospel, to determine what the human reality is.

Barth: That I can follow, as long as the gospel is master. However, I see more in Ebeling and Bultmann. There I find a prior knowledge concerning the reality of humanity. Also, the concept of the law in Ebeling's book *Theology and Proclamation*[1] is enigmatic to me. Of course, I say, gospel and law.[2] But there, quite Lutheran, I find the sequence *law* and *gospel*.[3] Isn't the message of the gospel "You are loved by God"?[4] And only then comes the law, the law of the promise,

1. G. Ebeling, *Theologie und Verkündigung: Ein Gespräch mit Rudolf Bultmann*, 2nd ed. (Tübingen: Mohr, 1963) [ET: *Theology and Proclamation: A Discussion with Rudolf Bultmann*, trans. John Riches (London: Collins, 1966)].

2. Set forth in Barth's programmatic essay *Evangelium und Gesetz*, ThExh 32 (Munich: Kaiser, 1935) [ET: "Gospel and Law," in *God, Grace and the Gospel*, trans. J. S. McNab (Edinburgh: Oliver & Boyd, 1959)]. Barth explains this view of "Gospel and Law" in *CD* IV/3:370 [*KD* 427] as "belonging to the basic substance of my dogmatics as hitherto presented." See further, *CD* II/2:509–12 [*KD* 564–67].

3. E.g., G. Ebeling, *Theologie und Verkündigung*, 81–82 [ET: 79–81].

4. Here Barth modifies a verse from Paul Gerhardt's hymn "Ist Gott für mich, so trete . . . ," *EKG* 250; *GERS* 259; *EG* 351, stanza 1, although its significance in this context is completely lost in the ET of the hymn; cf. chap. 16, n. 21.

of faith, of love—however one wants to say it. How is it with Ebeling? Indeed, Christ is really just an example there, the bearer of a new law.[5]

Luz: For Ebeling, the gospel in its miraculous power of liberation can only be understood against the backdrop of the fact that humans stand under the law. The distinction of law and gospel is already itself in a certain sense gospel. In any case, the gospel first makes clear to me what the law is. You, Professor Barth, only have Calvin's third use of the law in view: the law is what one believing in the gospel should do.[6]

Hertel: It's from the gospel I first realize that I am standing under the law. It's for that reason Ebeling asks, How do I understand the meaning of my being under the law?

Barth: The question is only, is there a canon of right understanding? Must it not arise in each case *in actu* [in the very act]? Naturally, I too want to be understood and to understand. The hermeneutical problem exists for me as well, yet not as a canon.

2. The Work of Theology and Theological Tradition

The doctoral students from Zurich explained Ebeling's endeavors to Barth concerning a responsible perception of how the work of theology is related to the theological tradition.

Barth: Good, but with Ebeling it is about cooking for an eternity instead of ever eating a happy feast. And I would suggest, not only Ebeling, but also one such as Biedermann has very conscientiously taken up the entire tradition and, just like Ebeling, attempted to transform the tradition [*traditum*] into the act of handing down [*actus tradendi*].[7] On that point Biedermann appeals to Hegel, and Ebeling even to . . .[8] I see affinity among them!

---

5. G. Ebeling, *Theologie und Verkündigung*, 88 [ET: 89]: "Christian faith can be seriously accepted as faith in *Jesus* only where we properly accept Jesus himself as example."

6. On the "third use of the law," Calvin writes in *Inst.* 2.7.12: "The third and principal use, which pertains more closely to the proper purpose of the law, finds its place among believers in whose hearts the Spirit of God already lives and reigns." See J. Calvin, *Institutes of the Christian Religion*, ed. J. T. McNeill, trans. F. L. Battles (Philadelphia: Westminster Press, 1960), 360. On Barth, see E. Jüngel, *Evangelium und Gesetz: Zugleich zum Verhältnis von Dogmatik und Ethik*, in *Barth-Studien* (Zurich et al.: Benziger, 1982), 199–202 [ET: "Gospel and Law: The Relationship of Dogmatics to Ethics" in *Karl Barth, A Theological Legacy*, trans. G. E. Paul (Philadelphia: Westminster Press, 1986), esp. 118–21]. Jüngel called it a "grotesque misunderstanding" to conceive of Barth's doctrine of the original interrelation of gospel and law in the sense of the doctrine of the "third use of the law," which grew on the soil of Melanchthon's theology, both in the sense that the gospel is a "new law," and in the sense that God's command is one that "is limited to the regenerate alone."

7. A. E. Biedermann, *Christliche Dogmatik* (Zurich: Crell & Füssli, 1869). In Biedermann's work, the presentation of the historical part (§§148–561) is followed with a "critical-speculative" part (§§562–1000), in which the author questions the tradition critically from the basis of the section containing "principles" placed at the beginning of his text (§§8–47). In the two-volume 2nd ed. of the work (Berlin: Reimer, 1884–85), the part containing principles (= vol. 1) has grown to 202 paragraphs (§§7–208); §§2–3 of the 1st ed. together now form the second "positive" part (= vol. 2), which is subdivided into: "I. Historical Dogma" (§§209–584) and "II. The Rational Core of the Christian Faith" (§§585–1000).

8. Here, Barth is likely thinking about Schleiermacher.

3. In the New Discussion of the "Historical Jesus"

Barth: What does Ebeling say? Jesus is the Word of God. And we can learn who Jesus is from the Gospels. If that were the case, we would quickly be of one mind. However, in the sixteen theses on Christology in Ebeling's book, *Theology and Proclamation*, Christ does not even appear in fifteen of the theses, but only anthropological considerations arise.[9]

In my theological life I have learned that the kerygma (I do not like using the word) is a matter of the news of the *encounter* and the fellowship between God and humanity. For that reason one can say, Jesus Christ himself is the gospel. For that reason the whole of theology has to reflect on this fact above all else. In Bultmann I always miss the concept of encounter. "Encounter" [*Begegnung*] suggests an "object" [*Gegenstand*]. To what extent does the kerygma in Ebeling have an object, concretely: *vere Deus, vere homo* [true God, true man]? In Ebeling everything is pressed anthropologically into the concept of faith.[10] Everything that is an "object" is already contained in faith. By the way, what is it with the "certainty of Jesus" in this book?[11] For me, in any case, it does not clearly enough involve the *two*: God and the human.

Of course I can see that Ebeling wants to take the concept of grace seriously. But then again, the *extra nos* [outside us] should also retain its dignity. Perhaps Ebeling also means that with the "historical Jesus"? In any case I place great weight on the *extra nos* because it is only from that point the *pro nobis* [for us] and the *in nobis* [in us] receive their dignity.[12] In Ebeling, Schleiermacher and Wilhelm Herrmann are pulled back out again. What I had overcome is repristinated. Ebeling is in a bottleneck. Perhaps he can still come out from it.

Zur Mühlen: With Ebeling it's the case that the *vere Deus* can only be taken seriously if the *vere homo* is also taken seriously. By the way, one cannot accuse Ebeling of a kind of "faith-monisn."[13] With him it is really a matter of Word *and* faith.[14]

Barth: I can only see in Ebeling a repristination of the circle of questions from the eighteenth and nineteenth centuries. Ebeling is a "hyper-Schleiermacher." He skips over the efforts I have made. All that is now wiped away, the old ways

---

9. G. Ebeling, *Theologie und Verkündigung*, 83–92 [ET: 82–93].

10. Pointing in the same direction, cf. Barth's critique of G. Ebeling's book *Das Wesen des christlichen Glaubens* (Tübingen: Mohr, 1959) [ET: *The Nature of Faith* (London: Collins, 1961)], in K. Barth, *Das christliche Leben: Die Kirchliche Dogmatik IV/4, Fragmente aus dem Nachlaß; Vorlesungen, 1959–1961*, ed. H.-A . Drewes and E. Jüngel, 2nd ed. (Zurich: Theologischer Verlag, 1979), 59n20 [ET: *The Christian Life: Church Dogmatics IV/4; Lecture Fragments*, trans. G. W. Bromiley (London: T&T Clark, 2004)]. [The ET, 39, does not include the footnote]: "Here too the *object* of something personal standing over against it *is absent* to faith as well. The fact that it cannot have such a thing is asserted, but not substantiated. Further, the polemic against the notion of 'objects' of faith has its power alone in the fact that the 'God' of this faith is apparently not a rich God, but a poor one" (trans.)]. See also *Gespräche 1963*, no. 11, footnote 84.

11. G. Ebeling, *Theologie und Verkündigung*, 89 [ET: 89]: "The certainty of Jesus is neither a partial aspect of his appearance, nor is it merely related to a part of reality; it is of the very nature of his person."

12. Cf. *CD* IV/4, *Fragment*, 17–23 [*KD* 19–25]; cf. further *CD* IV/1:212 [*KD* 232].

13. In *Das christliche Leben*, 59 [ET: 38], Barth speaks of "a new fideism, or fideimonism," in Ebeling's theology "that is threatening today."

14. Hence the title of the collection of essays: G. Ebeling, *Wort und Glaube* (Tübingen: Mohr, 1960) [ET: *Word and Faith* (London: SCM, 1963)].

are being repristinated. I thought I had gotten beyond the polarities: Ortho-doxy—Pietism, Orthodoxy—Schleiermacher, and so forth. I have indeed kept Schleiermacher "since my youth" [Mark 10:20], but then I couldn't breathe there any longer.

I'll come back to Ebeling once again: In the last instance he is concerned with the relationship of Christology to soteriology. However, the latter must—as indeed even Ebeling admits—be grounded clearly in Christology, so that it does not come down to an abstract dogma. But now, when I think about the "historical," then I think of Troeltsch and his great definitive work on his-toricism. I think of the keywords "immanence," "analogy," and so forth.[15] Even Bultmann still has these concepts of the "historical" held over from Troeltsch.[16] That's surely the reason he also defends himself so vehemently against Ebeling, that is, against the relevance of the historical Jesus in Ebeling. I would really like to know for Ebeling what the method of procedure [*modus procedendi*] is, the path by which he arrives at the historical Jesus?[17] Are there still remnants of Troeltsch to be found here? How does one actually come historically and criti-cally to "Jesus, in whom faith has come to expression."[18]

Schindler: In Ebeling, the traditional sense of the "historical" is certainly still present. He is attempting to keep this framework in its relativity and yet to open up new things within this framework.

Hertel: Troeltsch only wants to ascertain, "What has occurred?" Ebeling and Fuchs have learned from Karl Barth that in every case a text with its historical contents already stands in a specific relation to the exegete, just as in physics the experimenter is eo ipso included in the experiment.

Barth: I will come back one more time to the *pro nobis* [for us] of God. It has its power in an *esse dei in se*! [intrinsic being of God].[19] In order to arrive at the soteriological *pro nobis*, I will first refer to its grounding in the doctrine of God. And I ask, May there be no doctrine of God? In that case, is *CD* II/1 with the "attributes of God," and so forth,[20] all nonsense? Nothing but false objectifica-

---

15. E. Troeltsch, "Historische und Dogmatische Methode in der Theologie," in vol. 11 of *Gesam-melte Schriften* (Tübingen: Mohr, 1913), 729–53 [ET: "Historical and Dogmatic Method in Theology," in *Religion in History*, trans. J. L. Adams and W. F. Bense (Minneapolis: Fortress, 1991), 11–33]; Troeltsch, *Der Historismus und seine Probleme: Erste und Zweite Hälfte*, vol. 3 of *Gesammelte Schriften* (Tübingen: Mohr, 1922).

16. It is precisely because he follows Troeltsch on this point that Bultmann declares the person of the *historical* Jesus to be irrelevant for faith. See, e.g., R. Bultmann, *Theologie des Neuen Testaments*, 9th ed. (Tübingen: Mohr, 1984), 1 [ET: *Theology of the New Testament*, trans. K. Grobel, vol. 1 (London: SCM, 1952), 3]: "*The message of Jesus* is a presupposition for the theology of the New Testament, rather than a part of that theology itself." This message is a matter of the "kerygma proclaiming Jesus Christ—specifically the Crucified and Risen One—to be God's eschatological act of salvation. He was first so proclaimed in the kerygma of the earliest Church, not in the message of the historical Jesus. . . ."

17. R. Bultmann, *Das Verhältnis der urchristlichen Christusbotschaft zum historischen Jesus*, Sitzungs-berichte der Heidelberger Akademie der Wissenschaften, Phil.-hist. Klasse, Jg. 1960, 3. Abhandlung (Heidelberg: Winter, 1960), 8 [ET: "The Primitive Christian Kerygma and the Historical Jesus," in *The Historical Jesus and the Kerygmatic Christ*, ed. C. Braaten and R. Harrisville (Nashville: Abingdon Press, 1964), 18]: "The Christ of the kerygma is not a historical figure which could enjoy continuity with the historical Jesus. The kerygma which proclaims him is a historical phenomenon, however. Therefore it is only the continuity between the kerygma and the historical Jesus which is involved."

18. G. Ebeling, *Theologie und Verkündigung*, 119–20, 124 [ET: *Theology and Proclamation*, 124–25, 129–30.]

19. Cf. *CD* II/1:302–10 [*KD* 340–48].

20. On "The Doctrine of God" in *CD* II/1:322–677 [*KD* 362–764], Barth develops his doctrine of the attributes of God (although for Barth "Perfections" is the better term).

tion? Is there only soteriology and pisteology? If the answer is yes, then we are back in the eighteenth and nineteenth centuries. I don't read Ebeling without hope, but I don't see the end result just yet.

4. Conclusion

Barth: Gentlemen, I had expected that you would come from Zurich and launch a forceful attack against an old man like me. Strangely enough, I have to state that the conversation amounted solely to an apology for Ebeling.

Luz: Professor Barth, you are actually the one guilty of this by the way you directed the conversation and asked the questions.

38. Interview by Tanneguy de Quénétain
1962

On November 20, 1962, at Barth's house in Basel, Tanneguy de Quénétain of Paris conducted an interview with Barth about questions of ecumenism, in the French language. It was published under the title "Ce qu'un grand théologien protestant pense du rapprochement de Églises [What a Great Protestant Theologian Thinks about the Rapprochement of the Churches]," in Réalités: Fémina, Paris/London/New York, no. 205 (February 1963): 25–27. An English translation, "What Are the Hopes for Christian Unity? Réalités Interviews Karl Barth on the Ecumenical Movement," appeared in the English edition of Réalités, no. 150 (May 1963): 42–45, *and was reprinted under the title, "Prospects for Christian Unity,"* in Steps to Christian Unity: The Crucial Issues of Christian Unity Discussed by 24 Outstanding Ecumenical Leaders, *edited by J. A. O'Brien (London: Collins, 1965), 85–94. A German translation, "Über die Annäherung der Kirchen: Ein Gespräch zwischen Karl Barth und Tanneguy de Quénétain," appeared in* Junge Kirche: Protestantische Monatshefte 24 (1963): 304–9.*

De Quénétain: In your opinion, is the problem of the rapprochement of the churches the crucial problem for Christians today?

Barth: It is indeed one of the great problems we must face, and it is also a scandal. The division of the church is part of those scandals that a Christian cannot accept—like war, for example. We cannot resign ourselves to accept war, even if we know that there have always been wars and that perhaps there will be wars again. This being said, the unity of the church does exist already now, but on an invisible, spiritual plane. All those who have faith in Christ, who hear the Word of God as it has been communicated to us in the Scriptures, are members of this invisible church. A Christian theologian owes it to himself to affirm this invisible unity of the church. And my intention has always been to teach an ecumenical theology, which does not allow itself to be confined in the all-too-narrow framework of a given confession.[1]

---

* The present ET is based on the French text of the interview as found in Gesamtausgabe 25:528–36. The previous English translation was not consulted initially. The notes are those of the German translation in Gesamtausgabe 25:405–18, authored by the editor, Eberhard Busch.

1. Cf. CD 1/2:823 [KD 920]: Dogmatics "remembers that the only existence of the Church is in its one Lord and Head Jesus Christ. Necessarily, therefore, it is strictly ecclesiastical. It is so in a universal sense. It is, therefore, ecumenical. . . . Properly speaking, there is no such thing as dogmatic tolerance. Nor, properly speaking, is there a Catholic, Lutheran or Reformed dogmatics in undisputed and even deliberate independence and co-ordination. Where dogmatics exists at all, it exists only with the will to be a Church dogmatics, a dogmatics of the ecumenical Church."

True enough, I come from the Reformed tradition, but I think, like Calvin, that there is only one master of the church and the world.[2] As a result, it is not Calvin that I endeavor to obey: it is Christ. Still the fact remains that this invisible unity of the church should not be contradicted by visible divisions. All our efforts, therefore, must strain to allow for the realization of a visible unity. I do not know when this unity will be realized, but I know that it will surely happen since at the end of time Christ will return, and in him the church will find its visible unity.

De Quénétain: In the present circumstances, while the world develops an atheistic civilization, don't you believe that a decline in the ecumenical movement could deal a terrible, perhaps even fatal, blow to the cause of Christianity?

Barth: Of course not! Each era believed itself to be of utmost importance in the destinies of humanity. As for atheism, I am not at all convinced that our era is worse than the periods of civilization that were officially Christian. In the Middle Ages, for example, it was especially the external aspect of medieval civilization that was impressive through its Christianity. Christianity was an official institution. But behind these favorable appearances, one needs to look only at the way the kings, the lords, the priests lived and at the vulgar superstitions that the people embraced in order to recognize that the essence of the gospel message was not understood and lived except by a very small number. There are two types of atheism: practical atheism and doctrinal atheism (that of Nietzsche[3] or Sartre).[4]

All things considered, I find the first type much more pernicious than the second, to the extent that it is perhaps masked by an official Christianity. Look at the Christian Democratic Party in Germany. What relation actually exists between the politics of Adenauer and Christianity? Here we are smack back in the Middle Ages. At least doctrinal atheism has the advantage of being the sincere expression of the practical atheism of many so-called Christians. It is even superior to it insofar as it testifies to an authentic metaphysical anguish and obliges us, we others who are Christians, to take more seriously the Word of God.

De Quénétain: People have said that Protestantism was more in tune with the modern world than Catholicism. Calvin appears more indulgent than St. Thomas Aquinas toward the charging of interest and the possession of worldly goods. And so, he would have encouraged the development of capitalism and the industrial civilization.[5] What do you think of this?

Barth: This is certainly not what I prefer in Calvin, because from there people come very quickly to confuse the banker's interests with those of the Christian and to place their soul in his vault. In the same way, people have often drawn a

2. Cf. Calvin, *Inst.* 2.16.14.
3. Cf. *CD* III/2:231–42 [*KD* 276–90].
4. Cf. *CD* III/2:322–34 [*KD* 389–402]; Jean-Paul Sartre, *L'existentialisme est un humanisme* (Paris: Nagel, 1946) [ET: *Existentialism Is a Humanism*, trans. Carol Macomber (New Haven: Yale University Press, 2007).
5. This is the thesis of Max Weber, *Die protestantische Ethik und der Geist des Kapitalismus* (Tübingen: Mohr, 1904–5), in *Gesammelte Aufsätze zur Religionsphilosophie*, 2nd ed., vol. 1 (Tübingen: Mohr, 1922), 17–206 [ET: *The Protestant Ethic and the Spirit of Capitalism: With Other Writings on the Rise of the West*, trans. S. Kahlberg, 4th ed. (Oxford: Oxford University Press, 2008)]; also in Weber, *Die protestantische Ethik*, vol. 1, ed. J. Winkelmann, Taschenbuch 53 (Munich and Hamburg: Siebenstern, 1969), 27–190.

parallel between Protestantism and democracy because of the greater freedom of thought that may reign among us (in comparison to the Roman Church), and of the much more democratic appearance of the organization of our churches. This parallel is legitimate but only up to a certain point, and that is a crucial point. Western democracy, in fact, is much less a daughter of the gospel than the daughter of Jean-Jacques Rousseau.[6] It rests on a natural philosophy according to which it is nature that has created humans equal among themselves; and it is in order to respect nature that this equality must be respected in the Social Contract.[7] But, from the Christian point of view, the dignity of humans does not derive from nature: it is a free gift from God—a grace that permits his children to feel equal and to treat each other as equals in Jesus Christ. The point of view is not the same at all.

De Quénétain: In your opinion, what is the greatest obstacle to rapprochement between the Reformed Church and the Catholic Church?

Barth: The greatest obstacle? Oh well, one could say that it is one tiny word that the Roman Church adds on after each of our propositions. It is the word "and." When we say "Jesus," the Catholics say "Jesus *and* Mary." We seek to obey only our Lord the Christ; Catholics obey Christ *and* his vicar on earth, the pope. We believe that the Christian is saved by the merits of Jesus Christ; the Catholics add "*and* by one's own merits," which is to say, by his own works. We think that the only source of revelation is Scripture; the Catholics add, "*and* Tradition." We say that the knowledge of God is obtained by faith in his Word as it expresses itself in Scripture; the Catholics add, "*and* by reason." In fact, here one hits upon the fundamental problem of the relation between grace and freedom in the salvation of humans. It seems to us that the Roman Church lays far too much emphasis on the capability of the sinful human, in comparison with the omnipotence of God. There is something in the Catholic conception of free will that seems to us to detract from the majesty of God and his free gift of grace, which he has given us so as to accomplish our salvation. Obviously, this great problem is at the heart of our theological concerns. But, from the viewpoint of all the faithful, that which appears like the more visible line of demarcation between the two churches is certainly the cult of the Virgin Mary. If a little Catholic child were to enter a Protestant church, the first thing that would hit the youngster, without a doubt, would be the absence of a statue of the Madonna. We have been very much sensitized to this issue. We find that the exaltation of the Virgin—that is to say, of a creature—has been pushed much too far by Rome. We are very fearful that the Catholic Church one day might proceed to establishing its conception of Mary being *corredemptrix* [co-redeemer] as a dogma.

And then, equally problematic are the forms of the worship service that are very different. When I am present at a Catholic High Mass, I say to myself: "For

6. Cf. on this Karl Barth, *Die protestantische Theologie im 19. Jahrhundert: Ihre Vorgeschichte und ihre Geschichte* (Zollikon-Zurich: Evangelischer Verlag, 1947), 6th ed. (1994), 153–207 (about Rousseau) [ET: *Protestant Theology in the Nineteenth Century: Its Background and History*, trans. B. Cozens and J. Bowden (Grand Rapids: Eerdmans, 2002), 160–219 (the chapter on Rousseau)].

7. This is an allusion to the writing of J.-J. Rousseau, *Du contrat social ou Principes du droit politique* (Amsterdam: Rey, 1762) [ET: *The Social Contract and Other Later Political Writings*, trans. and ed. V. Gourevitch (Cambridge and New York: Cambridge University Press, 1997)].

whom is all this pomp and circumstance?" Can you imagine St. Paul returning among us and attending a pontifical ceremony in St. Peter's in Rome? What would he think of it? I prefer a simpler service, more concentrated. A Catholic Mass leaves me a little with the impression of a theater performance acted out in a foreign language. Certainly, all of this involves a question of personal taste. I have heard some Catholic preachers who offered excellent sermons. On the other hand, I have heard others who limit themselves to questions of the code of morality, virtue, and marriage. It is true that this is also all too frequent among us [Protestants]. And when a Protestant pastor's sermon is bad, then the result is even more disastrous since it is the preaching of the Word of God that constitutes for us the center of the worship service, while for the Catholics it is the sacrament of the Eucharist.

De Quénétain: In your estimation, which of these two forms of worship comes closer to the worship service of the early church?

Barth: Neither the one nor the other. The Catholic form of worship is too flowery, too overloaded. Our Protestant worship service, in the attempt to achieve greater purity, calls to mind the synagogue a little too much. One could say that the great temptation for Protestantism is Judaism, while that of the Catholic Church would be paganism.[8]

Recently in Bavaria I saw a Catholic priest[9] who had rebuilt his church according to new, totally interesting ideas (with the approval of his bishop, of course!). Naturally, the altar is in the middle, but it has the shape of a large table. It does not carry the tabernacle, which is placed on a small altar to the right of the main altar, facing the pulpit. The pulpit is placed in the same fashion on the other side of the main altar. On this pulpit there is an inscription drawn from the great Epistle to the Corinthians, reminding the faithful that "no one is able to lay another foundation than the one which has been laid, namely, Jesus Christ" [1 Cor. 3:11]. There is therefore a new equilibrium, which is established visually between the role of preaching and that of the sacrament. Moreover, the faithful commune at the same table as the priest. The communal aspect of the worship service is thereby considerably reinforced. Naturally, the priest says his Mass while facing the faithful. I would be happy if the Council would encourage the generalization of this formula.[10] In the traditional Mass, where the priest turns his back to the faithful, one has a little too much the impression that he is a kind of privileged representative, who is charged with

---

8. Cf. Karl Barth, *Die protestantische Theologie*, 520 [ET: *Protestant Theology*, 559]. For A. Schweizer, "the struggle against paganism is the special gift [*charisma*] of Reformed Protestantism, and the struggle against Judaism is the special gift of Lutheran Protestantism" (rev.). Cf. also Alexander Schweizer, *Die christliche Glaubenslehre nach protestantischen Grundsätzen*, vol. 1 (Leipzig: Hirzel, 1863), 8: "The anti-judaistic as well as anti-paganistic protest is common everywhere but has changed in its relationship, so that we see the Lutheran stance as presenting itself predominantly as anti-judaistic and the Reformed as anti-paganistic."

9. The encounter with Pastor Dr. Mogg had taken place while Barth stayed with Ernst Wolf on vacation in Walchensee (Upper Bavaria) in September–October 1962.

10. The deliberations about the schema on the liturgy, with which the Second Vatican Council as such opened, began on October 22, 1962, and were concluded on December 4, 1963, with the solemn proclamation of the constitution. The text *Constitutio de Sacra Liturgia* is in *LTK*, 2nd ed., Ergänzungsband 1 (Freiburg: Herder, 1966), 14–109 [ET: *The Constitution on the Sacred Liturgy (Sacrosanctum Concilium, 4 December 1963)*, in *Vatican Council II: The Conciliar and Post Conciliar Documents*, ed. A. Flannery (Collegeville, MN: Liturgical Press, 1975), 1–282].

praying to God in the name of the congregation, all the while he should be praying to God *with* the congregation. I do not know what the decisions of the [Vatican] Council fathers will be regarding liturgical matters, but I hope they will decide for a much greater use of the vernacular during the Mass in order to rid it of precisely this aspect of a "theater performance in a foreign language." Finally, it would be good for them to restore communion under both species for everyone instead of reserving [the wine] for the priest. Why this difference? Why should only the priest have the right to commune with both the body and blood of Christ? This is a kind of ecclesiastical privilege that I find disagreeable.

De Quénétain: People have often branded "the Roman intolerance" in a condemning way. Do you find that this charge is still justified?

Barth: The situation certainly has changed a lot since the sixteenth century. One should recognize, nevertheless, that there is still something like a natural inclination toward intolerance in the Roman Church. When it has an inferior status or is in the minority, it demands tolerance. But as soon as it is in the majority, it rapidly changes its opinion. In Spain, there is a small Protestant community that is subject to all sorts of harassing vexations.[11] It does not have the right to have steeples on its churches. If a Spanish Protestant does his military service, he is obligated to go to Mass every Sunday in lockstep with his Catholic comrades. And if he does not genuflect at the same time as the others, he is penalized. This is intolerance in its purest form. Even if one admits that we are heretics and that the Roman Church has to fight error, it is not by employing police methods that one must go to war against the devil. It is by appealing to the Holy Spirit.

De Quénétain: Which pathways do you think should be followed in order to achieve the rapprochement of the churches? After four centuries of theological discussions, one often has the impression, when viewing things from the outside, of an immense yet futile quarrel of words that is taking place on the margin of the modern world.

Barth: It is a quarrel of words, but these words are important because they define fundamental options in our conception of Christianity. I do not see how one can avoid the theological questions. We cannot shout, "Let's go! Let's walk on together!," if we do not know where we are going nor how we are to walk. The whole problem is to know to what extent we can come to an understanding among ourselves of the sense to be accorded to that little word "*and*" of which I was just speaking to you. For the moment, we do not agree with each other, but I do not deny that it may be possible to come to an agreement. For when the Reformed churches place Scripture above tradition, they do not deny the importance of the tradition for the interpretation of Scripture. They do not deny the responsibility of humans in the accomplishment of their salvation. They do not deny the benefits of the sacraments as signs of grace. But they do not give to these things the same emphasis as the Catholic Church. A lot of things can change, however. The Catholic Church itself admits change, not only in terms of the form of the worship service, which has seen considerable transformation

---

11. Cf. R. Hardmeier, *Die Lage der Protestanten in katholischen Ländern* (Zollikon-Zurich: Evangelischer Verlag, 1953), 85ff. Further, see Oficina de Información de Diplomática, ed., *La situación del protestantismo en España* (Madrid: Oficina de Información de Diplomática, 1950).

over the course of the ages, but also on the theological level. However, a Catholic theologian is not able to admit that all the forms may be changeable. For what comes into play for him is the magisterium [teaching office] of the church, which is able to promulgate a new dogma that becomes irreformable. This conception of the teaching office of the church culminates in the dogma of papal infallibility, which—in its present form—is unacceptable for Protestants.[12] But happily, the Catholic Church, even if it is unable to go back behind a dogma, can modify the interpretation of that dogma. And on this subject, Catholic theologians are extremely clever. Here is an example: only ten years ago I thought that an impassible wall separated the Protestant and the Catholic conception of justification by faith (and by works, for Catholics). Now one of my Catholic friends—an eminent theologian, Hans Küng—has written a book in which he asserts that there is no contradiction between the theories of the Protestant Karl Barth and the decisions of the Council of Trent on the problem of justification.[13] Certainly, in my conception of faith, I insist on the necessity of an active faith, which leads directly into works. But I believe that I have remained faithful to the true conception of the Reformed church, against which, in my eyes, the fathers of the Council of Trent formulated their views. Well, it appears that I have been wrong and that without realizing it we are really in agreement. Hans Küng has perfectly understood my own thesis, and I dare to think—but I am not very sure of it—that he has also perfectly understood that of the fathers of Trent. Besides, he is well regarded in Rome and has the support of three cardinals. Up to now, he has not been condemned. And if that which he proposes is really confirmed, then I am prepared to offer an expiatory prayer in honor of the Council of Trent and to say with a loud voice, "*Patres, peccavi* [Fathers, I have sinned]; . . . I have not understood you."[14]

De Quénétain: Do you think that Catholics and Protestants are closer to or farther away from one another than they were a century ago?

Barth: Infinitely closer—there is no comparison. And this despite the proclamation of the dogma of the Assumption [of Mary],[15] which has made such a poor impression among us Protestants. Now we are beginning to know each other, to consider each other on the same level, whereas previously we didn't know each other at all. At the beginning of the [twentieth] century, when I did my theological studies, reading a contemporary Catholic book was out of the question. For Protestants, such works were unreadable [*illisibles*]. In the same way, the Catholics who knew us mostly through books that only refuted us had a very strange idea of the Reformed church. Today the "iron curtain" is lifted, and I feel as though I am at home when I work with certain Catholic

---

12. *Constitutio dogmatica I "Pastor aeternus" de Ecclesia Christi* of the First Vatican Council, Session IV (July 18, 1870), chap. 4, "De Romani Pontificis infallibili magisterio," DS 3065–75.

13. Hans Küng, *Rechtfertigung: Die Lehre Karl Barths und eine katholische Besinnung*, Horizonte 2 (Einsiedeln: Johannes Verlag, 1957) [ET: *Justification: The Doctrine of Karl Barth and a Catholic Reflection*, trans. T. Collins, E. E. Tolk, and D. Granskou (Louisville: Westminster John Knox Press, 2004)].

14. Cf. Karl Barth's foreword "Ein Brief an den Verfasser" ("A Letter to the Author") in the aforementioned book by Hans Küng, 12 in the German ed.; also in *O.Br. 1945–1968*, 386. —"*Patres, peccavi* [Fathers, I have sinned]" is an allusion to Luke 15:18 Latin Vulgate.

15. *Constitutio Apostolica "Munificenntissimus Deus"* (November 1, 1950): Definitio assumptionis B. Mariae V., DS 3900–3904.

theologians. I have even written the foreword to Hans Küng's book,[16] and this book had the [official ecclesial authorization of the] imprimatur.* In fact, the rapprochement is essentially a question of knowledge. The more we learn to know each other, the better we understand that there is only one Christian faith, but several different ways to express this faith.

De Quénétain: In this rapprochement of the churches, what can be the most valuable contribution of Catholicism to Protestantism and, reciprocally, of Protestantism to Catholicism?

Barth: The great asset of the Roman Church is the impression of solidity and of continuity that it gives, even if this apparent continuity is problematic. As for us, there is an invisible continuity, but it is much less impressive because of the breaking up of the Reformation into different confessions; also because of the fact that with us the questions always remain open. Most Protestants who have converted to Catholicism were looking for rest, for intellectual and spiritual security that a church solidly organized and hierarchically structured can provide. On the other hand, the Reformation attracts those who thirst for movement and freedom. In fact, the two conceptions are necessary because they are complementary. There is no movement except in relation to stability, and vice versa. In general, I do not like conversions, the passing from one church to the other. First of all, the converts demonstrate an unbearable zeal: they grow into hyper-Catholics or hyper-Protestants. Look at the role that Mme. de Maintenon, that former Huguenot, played in the revocation of the Edict of Nantes.[17] Moreover, the conversions deny the invisible unity of the church, and this is deplorable. I find that everyone would do well to remain where they are and from there search to penetrate the gospel message more profoundly. This is the only way that a serious rapprochement will be accomplished.

De Quénétain: Do you believe that the decisions of the [Vatican] Council are bound to favor the rapprochement of the churches?

Barth: Naturally, one cannot give any definitive response. I am not the pope, and the pope has not asked my opinion. The organization and progress of this council are closely tied to the personality of Pope John XXIII, and he alone knows what he wants. Once this is said, I do not believe that Vatican II represents, as did Vatican I, one step further in the estrangement between Catholics and Protestants.[18] Without doubt, there will be no spectacular rapprochement, but at least there will be certain reforms of detail going in the direction of the rapprochement. Besides, the way Protestant observers are participating at this council is already very remarkable. They are present at all the sessions, not only the plenary ones, but also at the work of the commissions. And after each session, they are invited to give their opinion to the Secretariat for Promoting

16. Barth's foreword (see n. 14 above) in Hans Küng, 11–14 (German ed.); *O.Br. 1945–1968*, 383–89.*
* Trans. note: A previous ET adds here something that is not in the French ed. of this interview in *Gespräche: 1959–1962*, 25: "I embarked on that book rather as Noah embarked on the Ark, with a dove in my hand, and I awaited the deluge. But, so far, there has been none." See "Karl Barth: Prospects of Christian Unity," in *Steps to Christian Unity*, 95. The origin of these two sentences is unclear.
17. Françoise d'Aubigné, Marquise de Maintenon (1635–1719), secretly the spouse of Louis XIV, originally a Huguenot, converted to Catholicism in 1649. The Edict of Nantes (1598), which granted limited toleration to the Huguenots, was annulled by Louis XIV in 1685, in part at the initiative of the Marquise; the result was the expulsion and persecution of the Huguenots.
18. The First Vatican Council: 1869–70; the Second Vatican Council: 1962–65.

Christian Unity. Through this detour, they are engaged in some way in an indirect dialogue with the council fathers.

De Quénétain: The pope has added the name of Saint Joseph in the prayers of the Canon of the Mass.[19] Doesn't this decision risk agitating many Protestants?

Barth: Not me. Since Rome accepts the intercession of the saints, why should it keep Saint Joseph on the sidelines? Personally, I like Saint Joseph a lot. I have spoken about this recently with an American Jesuit.[20] As much as I am hostile to the development of "Mariology," just as much am I favorable to the development of "Josephology." The reason is that, in my eyes, with regard to Christ, Joseph has taken on the role that the church ought to play.[21] The Roman Church, I know, prefers to compare its role to the more glorious role of Mary. She [the church] brings to the world the gospel message in the same manner that Mary gave us Christ. But the comparison is fallacious. The church is not able to birth the Redeemer, but it can and must serve him with a humble and judicious zeal. Such was, precisely, the role of Joseph, who always kept in the background, leaving all the glory to Jesus. Such must also be the role of the church if we want the world to rediscover the splendor of the Word of God.

---

19. The insertion of Saint Joseph in the Canon of the Mass (first eucharistic high prayer) was ordered by the decree *De S. Joseph nomine Canoni Missae inserendo* of the Roman Congregation on Rites on November 13, 1962, *AAS* 54 (1962): 873.

20. Cf. Fr. L. Filas, SJ, *Joseph: The Man Closest to Jesus: The Complete Life, Theology and Devotional History of St. Joseph* (Boston: St. Paul Editions, 1962). See there esp. 462 with the reference to a conversation of the author with Barth about this subject. On April 27, 1962, Barth had met Filas, who was a professor in the department of theology at Loyola University, in Chicago.

21. Cf. Barth's letter of November 25, 1962, to his colleague Oscar Cullmann, who was in Rome as an observer at the [Vatican] Council: in Karl Barth, *Briefe: 1961–1968*, ed. von J. Fangmeier and H. Stoevesandt, 2nd ed. (Zurich: Theologischer Verlag, 1979), 103: "What has been decreed [at the Council] in the matter of Saint Joseph has pleased me greatly. I have waited a long time for something like this. Isn't the function of Joseph in relation to Jesus Christ ('foster father') the far more exact model for the church than that of Mary?"

39. Conversation with Agents of the Swiss Blue Cross
1962

On the afternoon of November 26, 1962, Barth was invited to a conference of the paid staff of the Swiss Blue Cross [Christian Organization helping those dealing with addiction] at the Hotel Blaues Kreuz in Basel, in order to answer submitted questions. The brief minutes of the conversation were written by Rudolf Kuhn. According to these minutes, Barth answered another, third question regarding the role of "destiny" (hereditary disposition) in the determination of human beings with just one sentence: "God stands above destiny." A recollection by Barth himself of the conversation can be found in his conversation with the Kirchliche Bruderschaft in Württemberg on July 15, 1963: Conversations 1963, number 11 (section 8).

Question 1: Does the Christian freedom that we have confessed in faith in Christ not also lead us as an obligation to Christian love and responsibility toward our neighbors, even to consistent abstinences in order to help them and provide guidance? Do we fall away from Christian freedom with these abstinences?

[Barth:] [It] was most of all the question of Christian freedom that concerned us [in the conversation]. Professor Barth first defined the term "Christian freedom" on the basis of the Scripture passages in 1 Corinthians 8 and Romans 14 and 15.[1] According to these, [Christian freedom] is the thinking and acting of the person in a Christian community, [which happens there] in a specific location, in a specific time and manner, [but always] in the responsibility before God and [in responsible relation] to one's fellow human beings.

Therefore, for us who are practicing abstinence from alcohol for the sake of our brothers and sisters, [abstinence] is a Christian freedom. [This is, however, only the case if it remains clear] that the work done with honest intent in the Blue Cross is a work within the Christian community. We as members of the Blue Cross must be aware that we never preach abstinence as a replacement for the gospel. [This is the danger for the members of the Blue Cross,] just as the theologian runs the risk of preaching only theory.

Question:[2] Sir, you are the general of theology students, aren't you? Why do you not send more of your soldiers to the heated front against alcoholism?

Barth: I am not a general but a servant of Jesus Christ. He, Jesus, sends his people to this front, not I.

Question 2: In practical life, we often meet "religiously unapproachable people," meaning those who do not want to hear about God, Christ, church,

1. Most likely esp. 1 Cor. 8:8–13; Rom. 14:1–6, 19–23; 15:1–7.
2. The following question and answer is inserted here according to a recollection by Hans Surer, Bern, communicated in a letter to the editor dated April 30, 1981.

Bible, and so forth. There are very different reasons that lead to such rejection, maybe even inner hardening. Now, as all human beings have come forth from God's creating hand, that is, they are originally linked to God, do we have to accept this standpoint as something complete and definitive? And how does our attitude toward them have to adapt itself? Are we allowed to let "stubborn people" simply stand out there and spend our time and energy on the "more approachable ones"?

Barth: We *all* often have difficulties to truly believe. We just do not say it. The "unbelievers" say it. However, it is exactly with these that we should engage. We are not allowed to simply give them the cold shoulder. Can we take credit for the fact that we are able to believe despite many problems? Is it not undeserved grace? Can this grace not also apply to the so-called unbeliever?

Index of Bible References

Index of Names

Descriptions of groups, e.g., Schaffhausen company of pastors, can be found in the index of subjects.

293

Index of Subjects

absolute/absolutes, 3–5, 26n110, 98, 162, 167, 169, 202, 239n16
abstract/abstraction, 3, 11, 31, 89, 92, 94–95, 101, 103, 112, 144, 163–64, 173, 184, 213, 220, 232, 247, 264n11, 271, 276. *See also* concrete
action, 213
  divine, 24, 48, 68, 87, 97, 174
  human, 126, 134n54, 156
  See also political action
Acts, book of, 15
Africa, 190, 238n14, 241
agnosticism, 186
aid, 32
America, United States of. *See* United States
American Civil War, 155, 224–26
Amsterdam, 104n94
analogia entis, 200–201
analogia relationis, 200–201
analogy/analogies, 41n12, 93, 107, 117, 162, 167, 200–202, 209–10, 215–16, 276
  to the covenant, 210
angels, 15, 108, 112–14, 117, 129
  fallen, 113
  guardian, 114
  Satan's, 84n14
anger (of man), 256
anknüpfungspunkt, 117n6. *See also* point of contact
anthropology, 47, 87, 102, 162, 169, 249–50, 262, 275
anthropomorphism, 89
antichrist, 33, 200
antinomianism, 91–92
anti-Semitism, 182
apocalypticism, 100n70
apokatastasis, 76, 178n24. *See also* universalism
apologetics, 176, 186, 223, 272
Apology (Plato), 152
apostasy, 271
Apostles' Creed, 81, 256
apostleship, 22
Asia, 190, 241

Assumption [of Mary], 283
atheism, 65–66, 96, 153, 159–60, 186, 190, 193, 239
  two types of, 279
atomic bomb. *See* nuclear weapons
atonement, 39–41, 45–53, 57–58, 95n49, 163, 177–78
  meaning and problem of, 48–53
authoritarianism, 240n17
authority, 26, 28, 94, 177, 181
  of the Bible, 250
  of Christ, 93, 132, 160
  civil, 188
  ecclesiastical, 187, 259
  penal, 41–42, 49, 56–57
  political, 240
  preaching/proclamation with, 96, 122–23, 142, 211
  ruling, 241–42
  temporal, 93–94
  of a theologian, 109
  See also specific topics/descriptions, e.g., police; pope
autocratism, 71

Bahnau Brotherhood [Bahnauer Bruderschaft], 8
baptism, 20–21, 59, 64, 107, 123, 126, 137–38, 202–3, 232, 234–38, 266–67
  Barth's doctrine of, 21n82, 237, 266n27
  of believers, 235
  function of, 237
  infant or adult, 133–35
Baptists, 134, 244–45
Barmen Declaration, 159n2, 268
Barth, Karl (subtopics, *e.g.*, Barth, Karl: as professor). *See under* Barth, Karl *in the index of subjects*
Basel, Switzerland, viii–ix, xi–xii, 29, 63–64, 66, 80–81, 84–86, 99, 104n93, 109n4, 136, 196, 241, 244, 247, 256, 269
  Barth's house in, 124n23, 145, 149, 192, 229, 278
  Brüdergemeine in, 105